W9-DAT-800

The Ordeal of Civility

THE ORDEAL OF CIVILITY

Freud, Marx, Lévi-Strauss, and the Jewish Struggle with Modernity

BY

JOHN MURRAY CUDDIHY

Basic Books, Inc., Publishers NEW YORK

FERNALD LIBRARY
COLBY-SAWYER COLLEGE
NEW LONDON, N.H. 03257

Excerpts from the *Collected Papers of Sigmund Freud,* edited by Ernest Jones, M.D., published by Basic Books, Inc. by arrangement with The Hogarth Press Ltd. and The Institute of Psycho-Analysis, London.

Excerpts from Ernest Jones, *The Life and Work of Sigmund Freud* (New York: Basic Books, 1953, 1955, 1957) reprinted by permission of Basic Books, Inc., Mrs. Katherine Jones, and The Hogarth Press, Ltd.

John Murray Cuddihy, "Jews, Blacks, and the Cold War at the Top," *Worldview* 15, no. 2 (February 1972): 30–40. Reprinted by permission of *Worldview.*

Excerpt from Walter Lippmann, "Public Opinion and the American Jew," *The American Hebrew* 110, no. 22 (April 14, 1922): 575. Reprinted by permission of *The Jewish Week.*

Excerpt from Howard Moss, "The Gift To Be Simple," *Selected Poems* (New York: Atheneum, 1971), © 1955 by Howard Moss. This poem originally appeared in *The New Yorker.*

DS
143
C75

67612

Copyright © 1974 by John Murray Cuddihy

Library of Congress Catalog Card Number: 73–90134

SBN: 465–05293–2

Printed in the United States of America

DESIGNED BY VINCENT TORRE

74 75 76 77 78 10 9 8 7 6 5 4 3 2 1

TO my grandfathers, Thomas E. Murray, an inventor, and Robert J. Cuddihy, a publisher, who were my first heroes, in gratitude for making the money which provided the leisure, allowing me the time to think about what was important to me (the money has now about run out);

TO my late father, H. Lester Cuddihy (1896–1953), and my mother, Julia Murray Cuddihy, in gratitude for their bringing me into the world and for their having brought me up a Catholic (although I am no longer a Catholic);

TO my wife, Heidi DeHaven, for marrying me, and for her love and constancy, and for constitutive help with this book; and

TO my three irrepressible children, Heidi, Johnny, and Julia, who have surrounded their father's life with life.

PREFACE

This study may be considered to be a long meditation on its own epigraphs. It unpacks them. It is their hermeneutic. It recurs to them throughout. It is a midrash.

EPIGRAPHS

The German Jews . . . were likely to be envied and resented by East European Jews for what would have been called their refinement.

Lionel Trilling, "Afterword" to *The Unpossessed* *

Ritual competence—perhaps the most fundamental socialization of all.

Erving Goffman, *Relations in Public*

"Are the Jews congenitally unsociable and rude, or are they this way as a result of having been segregated into ghettos?" Such was the form of the question over which argument raged in the Eighteenth Century, on the eve of Emancipation.

Léon Poliakov, "Anti-Semitism and Christian Teaching"

Or is it obvious to everyone what the Jews have learned from Christianity since it is obvious what the Jews have learned from modernity and it is obvious that modernity is secularized Christianity? But is modernity in fact secularized Christianity?

Leo Strauss, *Liberalism Ancient and Modern*

Freud deals directly with the whole range of feelings, thoughts and attitudes that fail to be successfully held back and hence, only less directly, with the rules regarding what is allowed expression. . . . For what will be later seen as a "symptom" first comes to attention because it is an infraction of a rule regarding affect restraint during daily encounters.

Erving Goffman, *Encounters*

No anti-Semite can begin to comprehend the malicious analysis of his soul which every Jew indulges every day.

Norman Mailer, "Responses and Reactions VI"

The prejudice against the Galileans [i.e., early Christians] was not due to their doctrine or their form of worship so much as to their bad manners. It was their attitude towards the non-elect that irritated people: not their faith.

Harold Nicolson, *Good Behaviour*

* Complete sources are listed in the Notes.

The gestures which we sometimes call empty are perhaps the fullest things of all.

Erving Goffman,
Interaction Ritual

I had to laugh at these *goyim* and their politeness. They aren't born smart, like Jews. . . . They're polite all the time, so they can be sure one won't screw the other.

Jerome Weidman,
I Can Get It for You Wholesale

When normals and stigmatized . . . enter one another's immediate presence . . . there occurs one of the primal scenes of sociology. . . . Thus, the "good" Jew or mental patient waits for "an appropriate time" in a conversation with strangers and calmly says: "Well, being Jewish has made me feel that . . ." or "Having had first-hand experience as a mental patient, I can. . . ."

Erving Goffman,
Stigma: Notes on the Management of Spoiled Identity

The Jews have always been students, and their greatest study is themselves.

Albert Goldman,
"The Real Lenny Bruce
Is Alive and Well in Brooklyn"

Socialism is not a science, a sociology in miniature—it is a cry of grief. . . . If it is not a scientific formulation of social facts, it is itself a social fact of the highest importance.

Émile Durkheim,
Socialism

The descriptions of the brute facts can be explained in terms of the institutional facts. But the institutional facts can only be explained in terms of the constitutive rules which underlie them.

John Searle,
Speech Acts

I seem to detect [in some few passages in Leslie Fiedler] the tone of an informer to the *goyim*, and the less said about that the better.

Philip Rahv, "Lettuce and Tomatoes"

And newcomer that I am, I am constantly brought up short by the split between the nobility of Jewish thought and the vulgarity and chaos of Jewish life.

Norma Rosen,
"Symposium: Living in Two Cultures"

One of the principal criteria of the pariah group is its separation by ritual barrier. This distinguishes it from a class in the ordinary sense. . . . I myself do not think that [Salo W.] Baron fully refuted Weber on this whole point. Very far from it! . . . Weber was quite right that the Jewish case was one to a very large extent of [ritual] self-exclusion rather than imposed exclusion by Gentile.

Talcott Parsons
at Max Weber Centennial, Heidelberg, 1964

It illustrates the tribal, rather than the civil, nature of Jewish culture. There is, and can be, no provision made whereby disaffected Jews might leave the fold with dignity and self-respect.

Anonymous,
"An Analysis of Jewish Culture"

By manners, I mean not here, decency of behaviour; as how one should salute another, or how a man should wash his mouth, or pick his teeth before company, and such other points of *small morals;* but those qualities of mankind, that concern their living together in peace, and unity.

Thomas Hobbes, *Leviathan*

Many of our ancestors, recognizing themselves as disgracefully backward, were overwhelmed by the contact with a superior civilization.

Michael Polanyi, "Jewish Problems"

Thoroughly naïve coarseness is the source of that absolutely complacent inability [of Professor Hans Delbrück] to understand the obligation to distinguish between personal considerations and the truthful analysis of facts.

Max Weber, *On Universities*

Humanity in the form of fraternity invariably appears historically among persecuted peoples and enslaved groups; and in eighteenth-century Europe it must have been quite natural to detect it among the Jews, who then were newcomers in literary circles. This kind of humanity is the great privilege of pariah peoples; . . . The privilege is dearly bought; it is often accompanied by so radical a loss of the world . . . that in extreme cases, in which pariahdom has persisted for centuries, we can speak of real worldlessness. And worldlessness, alas, is always a form of barbarism.

In this as it were organically evolved humanity it is as if under the pressure of persecution the persecuted have moved so closely together that the interspace which we have called world . . . has simply disappeared.

Hannah Arendt, "On Humanity in Dark Times"

CONTENTS

PART I

Sigmund Freud

PART II

Karl Marx and Claude Lévi-Strauss

PART III

The Demeaned Jewish Intellectuals: Ideologists of Delayed Modernization

PART IV

Children of the Founding Fathers of Diaspora Intellectuality: The Contemporary Scene

PART V

Conclusion

ACKNOWLEDGMENTS

I wish first to thank past teachers who, either in person or in their classrooms, have taught me important things: Mr. Root, Mr. Becker, and Mr. Kinney of the Lawrence Smith School in New York; William K. Wimsatt (now at Yale University), Frank E. Lally, John Howard Benson, W. G. Kelley, Leonard Sargent, O.S.B., Wilfred Bayne, O.S.B., Knute Ansgar Nelson, O.S.B. of Portsmouth Abbey School in Portsmouth, Rhode Island; Father Murphy, S.J., the late Father Toohey, S.J., and Philips Temple, librarian, of Georgetown University; William Gorman of St. John's College, Annapolis; Father Dore, C.S.B., Etienne Gilson, and Jacques Maritain of St. Michael's College, University of Toronto; E. A. Moody, P. O. Kristeller, John H. Randall, Jr., Lionel Trilling, Ernst Cassirer, Salo W. Baron, Arthur Hertzberg, and Ernst Kapp of Columbia University; Charles De Koninck and Aurèle Kolnai of Laval University, Quebec City; Benjamin Nelson, Bernard Rosenberg, and John O'Neill (on leave from York University, Toronto) of the New School for Social Research in New York; Professor Matilda White Riley and the late Bea Starr of Rutgers University. Also, Father William Fox, S.S.S., Father Pacifique Roy, and Father William Keller of Seton Hall; Professor Desmond Fitzgerald of the University of San Francisco; Paul Hilsdale; Donald Lawlor, M.P. of Toronto; Peter Maurin; Arthur Sheehan; Adé Bethune; Cary Peebles; Charleen and Herbert Schwartz; Mary Edwards Newell; Mary Gilsey; Audrey White; Judith Scheer Kasius; May Marks; Laura Davis; and William A. Anderson.

Photographs of the following persons—my intellectual heroes—are on my walls: Erich Auerbach, A. N. Whitehead, Jacques Maritain, Wallace Stevens, G. K. Chesterton, Talcott Parsons, Albert Schweitzer (*aet.* 30), Evelyn Waugh, Ernst Cassirer, Ludwig Wittgenstein, W. B. Yeats, and George Santayana. I hereby acknowledge idiosyncratic intellectual debts to all of them.

I owe more to two "underground" classics of the 1940s which deal with the problem of social modernization than is indicated in my book: Benjamin Nelson's *The Idea of Usury: From Tribal Brotherhood to Universal Otherhood* and Karl Polanyi's *The Great Transformation.* To these I must add *The Imperial Self* (1971) by Quentin Anderson and the pioneering study by Dr. Donald Clark Hodges, "Ethics and Manners" (an unpublished Ph.D. dissertation in the Department of Philosophy, Columbia University, 1954) which I put to work in Chapter 12.

Two psychiatrists, Edwin Kasin, M.D. and Valentine Zetlin, M.D., gave me understanding help in times of trouble. I want to thank them publicly here.

To Jeanne Wacker of Rutgers University, Professor George L. Kline of Bryn Mawr College, Professor Jeffrey Hart of Dartmouth College, and Rabbi Lloyd Tennenbaum of Huntington, Long Island, many thanks for much good talk over many years. For his timely assistance in statistics, I wish to thank Dr. Egon Mayer of Brooklyn College. Belle Sicourella of Rutgers proved unfailingly helpful. I wish also to acknowledge the kindness of Professor Walter Fairservis and of Helen Marcovics of Vassar College.

To the late Albert Salomon of the New School for Social Research and to Robert Merton of Columbia I owe my introduction to sociology as a discipline. In the fall of 1949, Salomon's "Balzac as Sociologist" course gave me a wholly new sense of the relation of the modern novel to modern society, of modernism to modernization. My Chapter 22, a "sociology of literature" of the more recent (1950–1970) American-Jewish writing, stems ultimately from that course. It was at the prompting, I believe, of Jay Schulman that I emigrated weekly from Philosophy Hall at Columbia to audit Merton in Fayerweather. Talcott Parsons's *The Social System* (1952) had just appeared and, week after exciting week, Merton's Talmudic *explication de texte*, especially of the chapter on the medical profession, opened my eyes to the full implications of differentiating the motivational and institutional levels of analysis. This crucial differentiation made clear, for example, why medically socialized male gynecologists do not break out with erection bulges as they examine their patients. (Ideology, as defined in my book, usually involves a confusion of the motivational and institutional levels of analysis.)

To Professor Harry Bredemeier of Rutgers University I owe much; his searching criticisms, his guidance, his patience, his brilliant teaching, and the unfailing generosity of his encouragement will never be forgotten.

From Professor Peter Berger of Rutgers, both as great teacher and as good friend, I learned the sweep and daring of sociology. Durkheim and Weber came alive in his teaching. In him, theory never lost its contact with everyday life. Without his encouragement and the prodding of his praise I would still today be seated among my five Glide-O-Matic, Goldsmith Bros. filing cabinets dreaming of a book. Thank you, Peter Berger. (Needless to say, any shortcomings anyone should find in this study are not to be blamed on Peter Berger or on any of the others mentioned.)

Lastly, I should like to thank the people at Basic Books, Inc.: my freelance copy editor, Bill Green, for a scrupulous and understanding reading of my manuscript; my project editor, Ruth Rozman, for her care and patience; Carol Vance, assistant to the President of Basic Books, for many acts of thoughtfulness, small and large; and lastly, Erwin Glikes, President and Publisher of Basic Books: he let me speak my mind as I saw fit to speak it. I have no greater praise than this.

The Ordeal of Civility

INTRODUCTION

Before becoming "privy to the true inwardness of Jewish modernity" * one must first break the stranglehold of paradigms—the pious paradigms that preempt the story of Jewish emancipation. The story of the exodus of Jews into Europe in the nineteenth century is a case study in culture shock. The hoped for "goodness of fit" between what Jews expected from emancipation and what Europe had promised its Jews became, instead, "the Jewish problem." The Jewish "great expectations" were utopian; the Gentile promises carried a caveat. An ethnocentric and family-oriented people—"one of the most familistic societies known," Eisenstadt tells us [1] —awoke "the morning after" emancipation to find itself in a world of strangers: the nonkinship, universalistic nation-societies of modern Europe. A slow disintoxication supervenes as Jewish emancipation fails to make good on its promises.

I give the problem of civility a thematic authority over this whole story because if, as Berger and Luckmann argue, "the most important experience of others takes place in the face-to-face situation, which is the prototypical case of social interaction," [2] this face-to-face encounter when it occurs between strangers in the West takes the form of a ritual exchange of gifts we call "civility." The encounter of Jew with Gentile was never able to remain near enough to the surface to achieve a genuine ritual consummation. Thus, the ratification of Jewish emancipation in social emancipation, in face-to-face social contact with the Gentile, never occurred. The failure of Jewish emancipation was a failure of ritual competence and of social encounter: no "ritually ratified face-to-face contact" [3] took place, no social rites of public behavior were reciprocally performed, nor were they performed for their own sakes. This failure of civility spread shock waves through nineteenth-century society. In arguing a larger alienation—since the norms of civility merely spell out and specify for face-to-face interaction the more general values of the culture—the failure of civility came to define "the Jewish problem" as this problem reconstituted itself in the era of social modernity. It is this ordeal, this problem of the ritually unconsummated social courtship of Gentile and Jew that is

* The phrase is Milton Himmelfarb's in *The Jews of Modernity* (New York: Basic Books, 1973), p. viii.

formative for the labors of the secular Jewish intelligentsia of the nineteenth and twentieth centuries. It is their hidden theme. This problem stems, ultimately, as we shall see, from a disabling inability of Judaism to legitimate culturally the differentiation of culture and society, or from what Philip Rieff calls "the disastrous Jewish attempt to maintain an identity of culture and society." [4]

Max Weber wrote about the Protestant Ethic. This book is about the Protestant Esthetic and the Protestant Etiquette, those expressive and situational norms ubiquitously if informally institutionalized in the social interaction ritual of our modern Western societies. More particularly, it is about the Protestant Etiquette ("etiquette" understood in the nontrivializing sense of public behavior and civility) and the spirit of Judaism, as Judaism took the form of *Yiddishkeit* when Jews, from the late eighteenth century up into our own time, entered the West from the ghettos and *shtetlach* of Central and Eastern Europe. The cultural collision, the *Kulturkampf*, between *Yiddishkeit* and the behavioral and expressive norms we call the Protestant Esthetic and Etiquette came to constitute the modern form of the ancient *Judenfrage:* the "Jewish question."

Thus, Jewish emancipation, assimilation, and modernization constitute a single, total phenomenon. The secularizing Jewish intellectual, as the avant-garde of his decolonized people, suffered in his own person the trauma of this culture shock. Unable to turn back, unable completely to acculturate, caught between "his own" whom he had left behind and the Gentile "host culture" where he felt ill at ease and alienated, intellectual Jews and Jewish intellectuals experienced cultural shame and awkwardness, guilt and the "guilt of shame." * The focus of his concern, often unacknowledged, was the public behavior of his fellow Jews, the *Ostjuden*.

The ideologies of the post-Emancipation era—Marxism, Freudianism, *Haskalah,* Reform Judaism—have a double audience: on the one hand, they have "designs" on their Jewish audience, which they wish to change, enlighten, or reform; but, on the other hand, they constitute an elaborate effort at apologetics, addressed to the "Gentile of good will" and designed to reinterpret, excuse, or explain to him the otherwise questionable public "look" of emancipating Jewry: secular Jewish intellectual ideologies are exercises in antidefamation, addresses in defense of Jewry to the cultured among its despisers.

In Marxism and Freudianism, the ideology is both a hermeneutic, a reinterpretation, and a praxis, an instrument of change. Beginning, in each case, with the public delict of Jewish behavior—the "scene" it was making in the public places of the Diaspora—it urges change (wholesale revolutionary change in the case of Marx, retail individual change in the case of Freud).

* See Chapter 5, "The Guilt of Shame."

Let us take the case of socialism. Universalist in its rhetoric and appeal, the socialist ideology that comes out of German Jewry, from Marx to the young Walter Lippmann, is rooted in the "Jewish question" which, for German Jewry generally, has always turned on the matter of the public misbehavior of the Jews of Eastern Europe (the proverbial "*Ostjuden*"). Marx in his 1843 essay "On the Jewish Question" views the problem—as we shall see—as one of eliminating "the *crudeness* of practical need" so conspicuously visible in Jewish economic behavior. (He equally indicts the *refinement* of Gentile economic behavior in which the civil nexus—civility—serves only as a hypocritical figleaf concealing the reality of the cash nexus.)

German-Jewish socialism, in other words, in its deep-lying motivation nexus is a sumptuary socialism. It is tailor-made for a recently decolonized "new nation" indigenous to the West whose now-dispersed "nationals" have had neither time nor opportunity to internalize that system of informal restraints we are calling the Protestant Etiquette. Protestant interiority and internalization—in the triple form of an ethic, an esthetic, and an etiquette—was the functional modernizing equivalent of what, for Catholics and Jews in the Middle Ages, had been a formally institutionalized set of legal restrictions on conspicuous consumption and behavior. (Jewry was in the nineteenth century exiting from its Middle Ages.) Feudal sumptuary laws—external constraints—took the modernizing form of internal restraints of moderation on consumption, trade, and commercial practices.

As we shall see, the ideology of the Jewish intellectual is frequently a projection onto the general, Gentile culture of a forbidden ethnic self-criticism. Shame for "one's own kind" is universalized into anger at the ancestral enemy. The intrapunitive theodicy of the *shtetl*—"We are in *Galut* as a punishment for our sins"—is secularized, after Emancipation, into either exteropunitive sociodicies—"You made us what we are today"—or into the great impunitive, ideological, "value-free" edifices of Freud and Marx—"Neither Jew nor Gentile is to be blamed for the *tsuris* of the Diaspora: it is but a *symptom* of capitalist exploitation [Marx] or a medical *symptom* of anxiety [Freud]." * The relation of the *secular* Jewish ideologists to the "Jewish problem" is frequently forgotten or obscured. The late George Lichtheim's essay "Socialism and the Jews," for example, obnubilates the "Jewish problem" matrix of Marxian as of other socialisms. Of this whole problem-complex, for example, he writes that, by a "stroke of bad luck, the problem has *somehow* become entangled with the issue of Jewish emancipation" [5] (my emphasis). Lichtheim exhibits a curious disinclination to explore this "somehow" entanglement. "Bad luck" rushes in where historians fear to tread.

* With Jewish secularization-modernization, the direction of punitiveness shifts, Judaism is psychologized into Jewishness, and the personal Messiah is depersonalized. These three axes define the direction of Judaism's secularization, its demedievalization into modernity.

Emancipating Jewry was thus making a "scene" in the Diaspora. Even if ordinary, *prost,* grass-roots Jewry did not realize this, the Jewish intelligentsia did. They knew how Jews "looked" to *goyim.* The Jewish intellectual placed himself between his people, "backward" and premodern, and their modern, Gentile status-audience. If Jews offended the *goyim,* the Jewish intellectual would perform the "remedial work" best suited to place that offense in a different light. In a brilliant essay, "Remedial Interchanges," Erving Goffman shows how in social interaction, when we violate a norm of civility, we resort to certain rites—accounts, apologies, and requests—thus "transforming what could be seen as offensive into what can be seen as acceptable . . . by striking in some way at the moral responsibility otherwise imputed to the offender." [6]

The intellectual elite of a modernizing, decolonized, or emancipated people performs, on the level of the culture system—through the creation of ideologies (socialism, liberalism, psychoanalysis, Zionism)—the functional equivalent of what are accounts, apologies, and excuses on the everyday level of social system behavior. This intelligentsia "explains," "excuses," and "accounts" for the otherwise offensive behavior of its people. All the "moves" made in the long public discussion of the Jewish Emancipation problematic constitute, in the case of the detraditionalized intellectuals, an apologetic strategy.

Attention must be paid to the deeply apologetic structure of Diaspora intellectuality. Why, for example, did psychoanalysis, as Martin Jay notes, prove to be "especially congenial to assimilated Jewish intellectuals"? [7] Because Freudianism, like Marxism, supplied the transformation formulas by which the "Jewish question"—that is, the *normative* "social conflicts" of emancipating Jewry (their "offensive behavior")—could be translated into *cognitive* "scientific problems." In this way, ritual social interaction offenses were "accounted for" as "depth" problems for which the offending parties were not responsible. Social conflict—i.e., the "Jewish problem"—was thus honorably buried in cognitive structures. Social delicts became mental symptoms. Relations in public became public relations. The apologists of Jewry—the Jewish intellectuals—thus made Jewry less disreputable.

This apologetic posture of Diaspora intellectuals toward their fellow Jews and toward the gentile host culture—the "virtual offender" and "virtual claimant," respectively, to use Goffman's phrases—is exactly analogous to that of second-century Christian apologists toward pagan thought. As the Christian fathers clothed their kerygma in Greek, the better to defend it, they ipso facto made it more acceptable and, ultimately, more respectable. The "offense" that Christ constituted in the Greco-Roman world—"folly to the Greeks, a scandal to the Jews," Saint Paul had said—underwent, in remedial interchange with the Hellenistic world and conducted in its language, a subtle sea change in the direction of intellectual respectability. In fact, pagan critics, Jaroslav Pelican tells us, often acknowledged the stubborn singularity of Jesus Christ in a manner "more trenchant than the theology of the Christian apologists," thus calling forth a more profound defense. Eventually, "as Christianity became more respectable socially, its apologetics became more respectable philosophically." [8]

In the era of the Jewish Emancipation, the nineteenth century, the prestige of science, not Greek logic, conferred intellectual respectability. Therefore, the "pariah capitalism" of emancipating Jewry and the social conflict it engendered, anti-Semitism—"the socialism of fools," Bebel said—were subsumed and "honorably buried" in "the socialism of the Jewish intellectuals," in Marxian or "*scientific* socialism." Later in the century, when social emancipation supervened on economic emancipation, giving rise to the bourgeois problem of "social anti-Semitism," Freud transformed various social offenses against the *goyim* into various psychological defenses against the id of the offending party (the ten Freudian "mechanisms of defense").

Public misconduct was, for each of these ideologies, symptomatic behavior. For the ordinary Gentile, these Jews were simply "troublemakers" who showed the wrong deference and improper demeanor. By treating this behavior of the ordinary Jew symptomatically—as a symptom of economic exploitation, or of regression, or of homelessness (Marxism, Freudianism, or Zionism)—the Jewish intellectual could rescue his fellow Jews from the demeaning implications of the normative "reality definitions" of their Gentile interactants. The result of Marx's argument, Richard Bernstein tells us, was to deemphasize the significance of anti-Semitism, "to see the 'Jewish Question' as only *a symptom* of the state of bourgeois society" [9] (my emphasis). Normative problems of behavior could be decorously buried in cognitive problems of understanding. Social issues became social science. When, during a didactic analysis with Freud, Joseph Wortis—thinking of the social behavior problem of Jews—challenges Freud's belief that they are "a superior people," Freud immediately moves to the cognitive: "I think nowadays they are," Freud replied. "When one thinks that 10 or 12 of the Nobel winners are Jews, and when one thinks of their other great achievements in the sciences and in the arts, one has every reason to think them superior." When Wortis, himself a Jew, cites Jewish "bad manners," Freud concedes the fact, attributes it to the fact that since Jewish Emancipation they have not always adapted to the social life of a "mixed society," and ends by translating the normative problem into a cognitive one: "They have had much to *learn*" [10] (my emphasis). In Freud's remedial work with Wortis on a face-to-face basis we see epitomized the apologetic thrust of psychoanalytic theory construction.

In Freud's "science," the social troubles of a modernizing Jewry receive a self-enhancing cognitive gloss: social malaise becomes a medical symptom, offenses become defenses, *kvetches* become hysterical complaints, *tsuris* becomes basic anxiety, social shame becomes moral guilt, deviance becomes incapacity, strangeness becomes alienation; to be badly behaved is to be mentally ill.

As Jewish intellectuals with cultural aspirations constructed putatively value-free social *sciences* with which to talk about the social encounter of Jew with Gentile in the West, rank-and-file Jews with social aspirations were seeking religiously neutral *places* in which to interact with bourgeois Gentiles. Sociologically, the quest of the Jewish intellectual for value-neutral social sciences and the quest of the Jewish bourgeois for value-neutral social places are one event.* The salon of Rahel Varnhagen, of the first generation of Emancipation, was to have been "a socially neutral place,"[11] cutting across class, religion, and ethnicity. Neutral social interaction meant interaction between secularized and modernized Jews and Christians. Thus when, at the prompting of Moses Mendelssohn, the marquis d'Argens wrote Frederick the Great, asking that Mendelssohn be given the needed special permission to live in Berlin, he couched his request as follows: "An intellectual [*philosophe*] who is a bad Catholic begs an intellectual who is a bad Protestant to grant the privilege [of residence in Berlin] to an intellectual who is a bad Jew."[12]

The lure that Masonry constituted for a socially aspirant Jewry lay in the fact that it offered a place—a piece of social space—the masonic "lodge," in which bad Christians and bad Jews could interact as social equals, and this at the very time when Jews were not "making it" socially in the larger society. (Later, in America, the "meetinghouses" of the Ethical Culture Society were to have become the analogously neutral places where socially and culturally aspiring Jews, for whom Reform Judaism had become an impossible option, could "meet" socially with their Christian counterparts.) "The novelty of Freemasonry," writes Jacob Katz, "was that it offered diverse sects and classes the opportunity to meet in neutral territory."[13] The "Enlightenment" stemming from Mendelssohn's circle in Berlin constituted a kind of prefiguration of the "neutral" society thought possible by both "enlightened" Jews and Gentiles of good will. All the ideologies constructed by secular Jewish intellectuals, from the *Haskalah* to Reform Judaism, from Marxism to Freudianism, from assimilationism to Zionism, form a continuing tradition which I call "Jewish Intellectual Culture." The "Jews of modernity" (as Milton Himmelfarb calls them) in each generation renew themselves, and sustain

* At the turn of the century in Germany, Martin Green notes, "Sociology was sometimes then called the Jewish science." *The von Richthofen Sisters* (New York: Basic Books, 1974), p. 24. In the 1920's, Milton Himmelfarb writes, "Friedrich Gundolf—born Gundelfinger—a friend of Stefan George's, was curious to know what sociology was all about, so he attended a sociological congress in Berlin. Afterward he said, 'Now I know what sociology is. Sociology is a Jewish sect.'" *The Jews of Modernity* (New York: Basic Books, 1933), p. 44.

their intellectual morale in *Galut*, by drawing on various strands of this tradition. Secular Jewish intellectuals speak out from the predicament bequeathed to them by Jewish Emancipation and modernization.

I have never found particularly convincing the patently self-serving theory that intellectuals construct about themselves—that they are "classless," or constitute an "interstitial" stratum (in Karl Mannheim's version), or are "unattached" (in Lewis Coser's version). Intellectuals I have known are "attached." To *their* productions, as to those of the truck driver, we must address the nervy, vulgar little sociology-of-knowledge question "Says who?" as Peter Berger puts it. There are many forms of "attachment": if we are not particularly class-bound, perhaps we are region-bound, or time-bound, or culture-bound, or subculture-bound.

The present volume, being an essay on the culture of secular Jewish intellectuals, is a study in subculture-boundedness. To make any kind of sense, it should be placed in the context of my interests and convictions, and a certain indulgence will be asked, allowing me simply to assert these convictions and interests, rather than to argue them: otherwise, my study will never get off the ground.

Edward Shils has remarked the curiously oppositional stance of the modern intelligentsia from the nineteenth century and earlier up to our own period. With perhaps unpardonable oversimplification, I should like to name the essential thrust of what they were opposing: they were opposing modernity. Hereby hangs a paradox: most of them were very "modern" men supposedly engaged in attacking the status quo, and the fact that their "traditional" opponents also considered them to be a dangerously modernist avant-garde only confirmed them in this, their cherished illusion.

What, then, is this "modernization" process? Its greatest theorist, in my conviction, is Talcott Parsons. His work culminates in a theory of the modernization process accurately described as the "differentiation model" of modernization. Modernization, in this conceptualization, is passing from the left to the right column of Parsons's famous pattern-variable scheme: from affectivity to affective neutrality, from particularism to universalism, from ascription to achievement, from diffuseness to specificity. Parsons, as an intellectual descendant of Calvin, has displayed, according to the conventional wisdom, an all but sovereign indifference to the high cost of this "passing of traditional society," as Daniel Lerner calls it, this "passage from home," as Isaac Rosenfeld calls it in his haunting novel by that name. Members of the Protestant core-culture, like Parsons, theorize from within the eye of the hurricane of modernization, where all is calm and intelligible. But for the underclass below, as for the ethnic outside, modernization is a trauma. Parsons views modernization—correctly, I contend—as a secularization of Protestant Christianity, much as Hegel, the secularizing Lutheran, viewed it in the nineteenth century.

Both of these theorists lived at what Shils calls the charismatic "center" of Western culture. What this center demands, as Parsons above all has seen, is differentiation: the differentiation of home from job; the differentiation of political economy (Marx) into politics and economy; differentiation of the culture system from the personality and social systems; differentiation of economy from society (Weber and Parsons and Smelser); differentiation of fact from value, of theory from praxis; differentiation of art from belief.

Differentiation is the cutting edge of the modernization process, sundering cruelly what tradition had joined. It splits ownership from control (Berle and Means); it separates church from state (the Catholic trauma *), ethnicity from religion (the Jewish trauma); it produces the "separated" or liberal state, a limited state that knows its "place," differentiated from society. Differentiation slices through ancient primordial ties and identities, leaving crisis and "wholeness-hunger" in its wake. Differentiation divorces ends from means (Weber's "rationalization"), nuclear from extended families. It frees poetry from painting, and painting from representation. Literary modernism differentiates the medium from the message.

Beneath the politics of the oppositional intelligentsia the antimodernist thrust is all too audible. Demodernization, from Marx to Mao, is dedifferentiation. In the Chinese Cultural Revolution, structural differentiation and the division of labor were denounced violently and explicitly and uprooted *as such.* This violent Maoist challenge to differentiation, Nettl and Robertson note, was "a much more open *prise de position* regarding differentiation than the uncomfortable and often contradictory *Stellungnahme* to the problem in the Soviet Union in recent times; even in the early days after the Bolshevik Revolution, differentiated modernity was hardly ever attacked as *specifically* as this. But then," they add, "the clearly expressed current notion of differentiated modernity did not exist [then] to this extent either" [14] (my emphasis).

Parsons is the sociologist par excellence of "differentiated modernity." He has seen it steadily and, like Hegel, he has seen it whole. Stemming from the Protestant Reformation, the Industrial Revolution, and the English, French, and American revolutions, modernization constitutes the infrastructure of what Gabriel Almond and Sidney Verba call "the civic culture." Introduction into this long and continuing revolution of differentiation is what we mean today by being "civilized." Inward assent to the disciplines of differentiation, and the practice of its rites, may be viewed as the *paideia* of the West. "Ideology" is the name we give to the

* The Boston Irish Catholic John F. Kennedy, for example, in the midst of campaigning for the presidency, made his way down to the *pays réel* of Houston, there to offer to the Protestant Ministerial Conference a separation of church and state wide beyond the wildest dreams of their theological avarice; shortly after, he left Canossa for Washington.

various resistance movements mounted to stem the onslaught of the differentiation process.* Essentially, these movements are demodernizing, dedifferentiating, rebarbarative. Winston White, in a neglected masterpiece, defines the oppositional intelligentsia as "resisting the emerging distinctions" and defines ideology as "the attempt to suppress differentiation." [15] And David Little notes that modern man, situated within the modernization process, socialized into "a differentiated social order containing the principles of voluntarism, consensualism, private initiative and toleration," finds himself, paradoxically, "compelled to be free." [16] The social change fostered by modern differentiations frees man from the old ascriptive cushions, and thus, White observes, it cannot—unlike previous changes—"be absorbed *for* the individual by the family, the church, a class, or an economic or political interest. It is one that the individual must confront by making choices without dependence on ascriptive guidance. He is, indeed," White concludes, "forced to be free" [17] (White's emphasis). Acculturation into modernity on the part of premodern and underdeveloped personalities and cultures is like the pleasure principle colliding with the social reality principle.† Strain and deprivation are undergone, together with intimations of freedom.

There is a further dimension to modernization that will lead us into this study of Jewish intellectuals. Once, in the office of Dr. Harry Bredemeier, apropos of my having used the word *modernization,* he popped a question (almost out of the blue): "What *is* modernization, Jack?" I was nonplussed; there was a long silent pause as I searched for a definition, and finally I came up with "refinement." Many things funded themselves into that answer. Differentiation on the level of the culture system is the power to make *distinctions* between previously fused—*confused*—ideas, values, variables, concepts. Almost all intellectual interchange boils down to pointing out "distinctions" or "aspects" of a topic that have been obscured or neglected. Intellectual distinction and originality are frequently a matter of making a new and important distinction or differentiation. Learning theory teaches us that wholes must be distinguished into their parts before wider relationships can be established. Parsons sees the rhythm of modernization itself as involving first differentiation, then extension, and finally upgrading. This too is the rhythm of the intellectual

* The differentiating scientific ethos does not "end" ideology, but it may deflate it. As Parsons and Platt write: "a major aspect of the ethos of science—i.e., all the intellectual disciplines—is organized scepticism. The *duty* of a scientist—a *Wissenschaftler* in Weber's sense—is to *question* the cognitive validity and/or significance of propositions. . . . The ideologist, on the other hand, always questions the level of his *commitment* to the ideology, including the cognitive belief component of it. Ideologies constitute forms of rhetoric which seek to mobilize *faith*" (emphasis in original). Talcott Parsons and Gerald M. Platt, *The American University* (Cambridge: Harvard University Press, 1973), p. 296, n. 43.

† I borrow the term *social reality principle* from Professor Benjamin Nelson, using it differently.

life on the plane of the culture system: crude, coarse, fused, undifferentiated wholes—roles, structures, functions, topics, personalities—are "distinguished" into their elements; they are refined (like crude oil in the cracking process).

This whole dimension of modernization can be put in a formula: in the West at least, the modernization process goes hand in hand with the civilizational process. They constitute one "package." The coarse feudal baron is refined into the gentleman. The emergence of cities, multiplying strangers, expelling us from our "tribal brotherhoods" into the "universal otherhood" of an urban "world of strangers," enables us to live with unknown others without transforming them into either brothers or enemies. Initiation into the social interaction rituals of civility equips us "to deal with strangers *routinely*" in urban public space (my emphasis).* [18] In the nineteenth century, the peasant or the "young man from the provinces" comes to Paris or London or Dublin: his "urbanization process" requires urbanity, his entry into civil society civility. For the first time, perhaps, he must differentiate relations in private from relations in public, behavior and intimate affect in private places from decorum in public places. Acquiring this private-public differentiation is a "great transition," neglected in sociology. "It is significant," Kenneth Boulding writes,

> that the word civility and the word civil derive from the same root as the word civilization. The age of civilization is characterized not only by conquest, military ruthlessness, and the predominance of the threat as organizer. It is also characterized by the elaborate integrative systems of religion, politeness, morals, and manners. The dynamics of this process whereby the rough feudal baron was turned into a "gentlemen"—again the literal meaning of the word is highly significant—is a process that has never been adequately studied, yet it may well be the most important single process in the whole dynamics of the age of civilization, for it is the process which permitted the rise of civil society, without which science would have been impossible.[19]

And it was into this "civil society" that Jewry was emancipated in the nineteenth century.

Because of "the tribal, rather than the civil, nature of Jewish culture," [20] Jewish Emancipation involved Jews in collisions with the differentiations of Western society. The differentiations most foreign to the *shtetl* subculture of *Yiddishkeit* were those of public from private behavior

* Themes of Benjamin Nelson and Lofland are combined here to illustrate how the differentiation of the stranger from both brother and enemy is at once a modernizing and a civilizing process.

and of manners from morals. Jews were being asked, in effect, to become bourgeois, and to become bourgeois quickly. The problem of behavior, then, became strategic to the whole problematic of "assimilation." The modernization process, the civilizational process, and the assimilation process were experienced as one—as the "price of admission" to the bourgeois civil societies of the West at the end of the nineteenth century.

It is in the light of this sociology-of-knowledge context of Jewish Emancipation that I shall examine Freud, Marx, Lévi-Strauss, and other figures. As the nineteenth century drew to a close, and as the problems of political and economic integration were put behind them, the advanced guard of emancipating Jewry encountered head-on the *specific* problem of social integration with the Gentile West. The emancipated Jew of this period, Max Nordau told the First Zionist Congress in 1897, was "allowed to vote for members of Parliament, but he saw himself excluded, with varying degrees of politeness, from the clubs and gatherings of his Christian fellow countrymen." It was precisely the relatively rapid "promotion rates" enjoyed by this Jewry in the political, economic, and cultural spheres that brought home to it the realization of that special misery of "relative deprivation" that was long to be its lot in the social sphere. "This is the Jewish special misery," Nordau continues, "which is more painful than the physical because it affects men of higher station, who are prouder and more sensitive. . . . All the better Jews of Western Europe," he concludes, "groan under this misery and seek for salvation and alleviation." [21] Freud heard their groans. Many of them were his patients and adherents.*

At least some of these groans derived from what I call "the ordeal of civility." Civility requires, at a minimum, the bifurcation of private affect from public demeanor. Many eighteenth- and nineteenth-century Dutch and French paintings take us inside the homes of the bourgeoisie. We speak of "bourgeois interiors." The faces and public behavior of these same people were a kind of "bourgeois exterior." In France, for example, the emergence of the civil *persona* took the form of the *honnête homme* —what Erich Auerbach calls the "adaptation of the individual's inner life to the socially appropriate, and the concealment of all unseemly depths." [22] In England it took the form of that tactful circumspection of surfaces we call "respectability." "Niceness" is as good a name as any for the informally yet pervasively institutionalized civility expected—indeed, required—of members (and of aspirant members) of that societal community called the civic culture. Intensity, fanaticism, inwardness—too much of *anything*, in fact—is unseemly and bids fair to destroy the

* As early as the nineteen-twenties Ludwig Lewisohn was to note that Freudianism functioned as a kind of Diaspora Zionism, that it was "first of all an effort on the part of the Jewish people to heal itself of the maladies of the soul contracted in the assimilatory process. . . ." *Mid-Channel: An American Chronicle* (New York and London: Harper & Brothers, 1929), p. 129.

fragile solidarity of the surface we call civility. The "great cultural triumph" of the middle class, writes Norman Podhoretz, "is precisely that it brought obsession into disrepute." [23]

Civility, as the very medium of Western social interaction, presupposes the differentiated structures of a modernizing "civil society." Civility is not merely regulative of social behavior; it is an order of "appearance" constitutive of that behavior. This medium is itself the message, and the message it beamed to the frontrunners of a socially emancipating Jewry came through loud and clear: "Be nice." "The Jews," writes Maurice Samuel looking back on the epoch of Emancipation, "are probably the only people in the world to whom it has ever been proposed that their historic destiny is—to be nice." [24]

This study, focusing on Freud, Marx, and Lévi-Strauss, explores a crucial dimension of this "historic destiny." It explores a dimension of the threat posed by modernization to a traditionary subculture. It explores the danger that the prospect of being "gentled" posed to an "underdeveloped" subculture indigenous to the West.[25] Ostensibly about Jewry and what Jews call "assimilation," the study is, in the end, only methodologically Judeocentric. Like Weber rummaging in India and China and ancient Israel, all the while on the prowl for his Calvinist and gleeful at *not* finding him—thus demonstrating once again the uniqueness of the West—my central interest also lies in the West and in the religious idea-and-value system secularized into its modernizing structures. We learn what this civilization is, in good part, from a study of the titans who, like Marx, hurled themselves against it or who, like Freud, grudgingly consented to its "discontents," just as Jews, from time immemorial, have resigned themselves to the *tsuris* of *Galut*. The perspective of this study involves the "synthetic assimilation of multiple generalizations," requiring "a flair for discerning hidden transformations as well as an eye for the more obvious continuities." [26] This study examines the "hidden transformations" of the everyday life problems of assimilating Jewry—the Jewish Emancipation problematic—into the very thought structures of Jewry's intellectual giants: Freud, Marx, and Lévi-Strauss. In a single sentence, Irving Howe catches the *Gemeinschaft*-affect of Eastern European *shtetl Yiddishkeit's* "life-is-with-people": "Having love," he writes, "they had no need for politeness." [27] But once he moved "beyond the pale" at the time of Emancipation and entered the "differentiating modernity" of the West, the *shtetl Ostjude* was to learn to his sorrow that in the larger society "love is not enough." Outer, "ecological" conflict with the *goyim* then became inner conflict with the self. Judaism became Jewishness. The advent of Freud's psychoanalysis is a registration of this continuing "hidden transformation," of this continuing ordeal.

PART I

Sigmund Freud

CHAPTER 1

THE MATRIX OF FREUD'S THEORY: THE JEWISH EMANCIPATION PROBLEMATIC

Sigmund Freud's lifework, and especially his masterpiece, *The Interpretation of Dreams* (1900), concluded one phase in the great nineteenth-century debate on "Jewish Emancipation": as the unruly wish can fulfill itself only in the form of a disguised dream, so the *Ostjude* is not admissible into the civil society of the Gentile unless he submits to social censorship, disguising his unruly importunity in socially acceptable ways. Just as we may find the clue to Marx's outlook in his first published article, his "Comments on the Latest Prussian Censorship Instruction" (1842),[1] so also in Freud's early work it is censorship that blocks the primary process—the primary or Jewish socialization—and produces the compromise which is the assimilating Jew.

Though some dreams are undisguised wish-fulfillments, it was the dream that dissimulates a wish which intrigued Freud, and that leads to the core of his interpretation of dreams:

> In cases where the wish-fulfilment is unrecognizable, where it has been disguised, there must have existed some inclination to put up a defense against the wish; and owing to this defense the wish was unable to express itself except in a distorted shape. I will try to seek a social parallel to this internal event in the mind. Where can we find a similar distortion of a psychical act in social life? Only where two persons are concerned, one of whom possesses a certain degree of power which the second person is obliged to take into account. In such a case the second person will distort his psychical acts or, as we might put it, will dissimulate.[2]

Then, at last, Freud gives us the social parallel he has been leading up to all along: "The politeness which I practise every day," he confesses, "is to a large extent dissimulation *of this kind;* and when I interpret my dreams for my readers I am obliged to adopt similar distortions" [3] (my emphasis).

It is my contention that Freud in fact began with his everyday social life, and then found a "dream parallel." Freud moves quickly from social censorship—politeness—to the effects of political censorship, and he writes of it in a way astonishingly similar to what the young Karl Marx had written fifty-eight years earlier. Freud continues:

> A similar difficulty confronts the political writer who has disagreeable truths to tell those in authority. If he presents them undisguised, the authorities will suppress his words—after they have been spoken, if his pronouncement was an oral one, but beforehand, if he had intended to make it in print. A writer must beware of the censorship, and on its account *he must soften* and distort *the expression* of his opinion . . . or . . . speak in allusions in place of direct references, or he must conceal his objectionable pronouncement beneath some apparently innocent disguise. . . . The stricter the censorship, the more far-reaching will be the disguise and the more ingenious too may be the means employed for putting the reader on the scent of the true meaning.* The fact that the phenomena of censorship and of dream-distortion correspond down to their smallest details justifies us in presuming that they are similarly determined.[4] [My emphasis]

In 1919, after World War I, Freud added a footnote to this passage using the analogy of postal censorship: "The postal censorship makes such passages unreadable by blacking them out; the dream censorship replaced them by an incomprehensible mumble." In the dream illustrating this—the dream of a cultivated and highly esteemed widow of fifty who wished for sexual intercourse—a staff surgeon "mumbles" some unintelligible proposal and is soon ushering her "most politely and respectfully," Freud notes, up a "spiral staircase." [5]

Thus, if there is one agency in the dreamer that constructs the dream-wish, there is another that softens or distorts "the expression of the wish." [6] This agent is the "censor," which stands at the borders of consciousness and says: "Thou shall not pass." All through the nineteenth century, the Eastern European Jew had sought admission to bourgeois Western civil society. At first he experienced economic and political exclusion; by Freud's time he was seeking social acceptance and experiencing social rejection. This importunate "Yid," released from ghetto and *shtetl*, is the model, I contend, for Freud's coarse, importunate "id." Both are saddled with the problem of "passing" from a latent existence "beyond the pale" of Western respectability into an open and manifest relation to

* Professor Leo Strauss in his *Persecution and the Art of Writing* (1952) takes up once more this obsessive theme of Diaspora Jewish intellectuals. Freud's subject was dreamwork—or persecution and the art of dreaming.—J.M.C.

Gentile society *within* Gentile society, from a state of unconsciousness to a state of consciousness. Freud's internal censor represents bourgeois-Christian nineteenth-century culture: "Not only moral standards, but *all the components of the common culture* are internalized as part of the personality structure," writes Talcott Parsons in crediting Freud with the discovery of the phenomenon of "internalization" [7] (Parsons's emphasis). The internal censor, writes Freud, "allows nothing to pass without exercising its rights and making such modifications as it sees fit in the thought which is seeking admission to consciousness." [8] It is the phenomenon of Jewish "passing" and its cognate, the "Jewish joke," that lie behind Freud's discovery of "internalization." An examination of these allows one to glance "behind the scenes" of Freud's discovery.*

Freud began his study of the unconscious by examining the psychopathology of everyday life: slips of the tongue and pen, awkward "parapraxes" which violate the decorum of public places, and jokes—especially Jewish jokes—which he often exchanged in correspondence with his friend Fliess. Freud was fascinated with the phenomenon of "unsuitable affect," its expression, suppression, and repression, and of how it "passes" or fails to "pass" the censor. He was an expert on the status of the emancipated Jew in the late nineteenth century; he studied how he coped or failed to cope with the ambiguity involved in the terminal (and most difficult) social stage of Emancipation. Freud deals directly, Erving Goffman notes, with the whole range of feelings, thoughts, and attitudes "that *fail* to be successfully held back and hence, only less directly, with the rules regarding what is allowed expression" (my emphasis). A slip, a neurotic symptom, an incivility, Goffman continues, "first comes to attention because it is an infraction of a rule regarding affect-restraint during daily encounters." [9] Freud was interested in pariahs, especially in what could be called "pariah affect," the unruly, coarse "id" and the vicissitudes of its difficult domestication in the bourgeois-Christian West. His interest in the discontents of civility preceded his concern with *Civilization and Its Discontents* (1930). The "primary component" in the socialization and self-image of Jews, writes James A. Sleeper, "is the *pintele yid*, that ineradicable . . . Jewishness which surfaces at least occasionally to create havoc with carefully calculated loyalties and elaborately reasoned postures." [10]

For 150 years, in fact, a whole genre of post-Emancipation Jewish humor has been predicated on the "sudden havoc" that the involuntary eruption of *Ostjude* identity from beneath the skin of the "passing" exception-Jew can create in a public place. Freud's interest in "slips" can

* Similarly, Jacob Katz, the noted authority on Jewish Emancipation, explores the subject of the changing status of Jews in nineteenth-century Freemasonry as an index of their position in the general society. Katz's subject "allows one to glance behind the scenes." *Jews and Freemasons in Europe, 1723–1939*, trans. Leonard Oschry (Cambridge: Harvard University Press, 1970), p. 213.

be seen as deriving from interest in this archetypal "slip." A recent example of such humor goes as follows: "A *nouveau riche* Jewish couple moved to a non-Jewish neighborhood, changed their name from Cohen to Cowles, and sought admission to the country club that frowned on Jews. Finally admitted, they show up at the Sunday night club dinner, Mrs. Cowles, née Cohen, decked out in all her jewels and a brand new gown. The waiter serving soup slips and it lands in Mrs. Cowles's lap. She lets out a shriek: '*Oy Gevalt*, whatever that means.' "[11] A story such as this has different "functions" depending on the context in which it is told. If told by a member or representative of the Jewish community, as this one was, it is an "instrument of social control," a whimsical warning to Jews not to try to assimilate and leave the Jewish community because, in a pinch, it will fail.* (Like the function of gossip in life—or in a Balzac novel—such jokes both are enjoyable in themselves and serve to keep people in line by citing the informal sanctions of self-defeating behavior.) If told by an assimilating Jewish intellectual, however, such a joke serves as an objective correlative of his subjectively ambiguous situation. A revolutionary Jew like Marx refused with solemn "prophetic" anger the obliquity and gentle irony of the Jewish "joking-relation" to their post-Emancipation situation; for him, such humor was a compromise, a "copout," a substitute for direct, virile attacks on Western institutions.

I argue that a classical genre of Jewish joke, the inner structure of Freud's theory of dreams, and the public discussion in nineteenth-century Europe of the eligibility of the Eastern European *shtetl* Jew for admission to civil society—the so-called Jewish Emancipation problematic—all have the same structure: there is (*a*) the latent "dark" id or "Yid" pressing for admission to consciousness or civil society; (*b*) there is the social-moral authority—the censor (external or internalized)—insisting that to "pass" properly into Western awareness or Western society the coarse id-"Yid" should first disguise itself (assimilate) or refine itself (sublimate)—in a word, civilize itself, at whatever price in discontent; and finally, (*c*) there is the id-"Yid" in the very act of "passing," its public behavior in Western public places carefully impression-managed by an ego vigilant against the danger of "slips," in which the unseemly pariah will show through the parvenu. This isomorphism of structure (in joke, dream theory, and civil emancipation) reflects the fact that for the Jew—a latecomer to the modernization process—to leave the Middle Ages which were

* In Harold Garfinkel, "Passing and the Managed Achievement of Sex Status in an Intersexed Person, Part 1," in *Studies in Ethnomethodology* (Englewood Cliffs, N.J.: Prentice-Hall, 1967), which I consider a cryptoanalysis of ethnic passing, Garfinkel's subject says: "I have to be careful of the things I say, just natural things that could slip out. . . . I just never say anything at all about my past that in any way would make a person ask what my past life was like. I say general things. I don't say anything that could be misconstrued" (p. 148). Eternal vigilance is the price of passing.

his ghetto or *shtetl* and to enter modern Europe was to experience the modernization process and the civilizational process as one thing: he could not become a *citoyen* without becoming a *bourgeois*. In theory, these dimensions were analytically distinct (after all, the act of voting is not the act of speaking German or French, say); in practice, they were a "package" since, fortunately or unfortunately, Jewish Emancipation occurred in the bourgeois liberal era of the West. No one realized this more than Freud, born in culturally peripheral Freiberg, Moravia, in 1856, but soon to move to Pfeffergasse Street in the largely Jewish quarter of Vienna called Leopoldstadt. Sophisticated and cosmopolitan Vienna was to become Freud's reference group.

Freud records the following joke in *Jokes and Their Relation to the Unconscious* (1905): "A Galician Jew was travelling in a train. He had made himself really comfortable, had unbuttoned his coat and put his feet up on the seat. Just then a gentleman in modern dress entered the compartment. The Jew promptly pulled himself together and took up a proper pose. The stranger fingered through the pages of a notebook, made some calculations, reflected for a moment and then suddenly asked the Jew: 'Excuse me, when is Yom Kippur (the Day of Atonement)?' 'Oho!' said the Jew, and put his feet up on the seat again before answering." [12] All the elements are here: the public, social place (a train); the identification of the Jew as an *Ostjude* (Galician); the relaxed, "regressive" behavior (misbehavior) in a public place; the advent of the "gentleman" stranger as the modernizing West ("in modern dress"); the "pose" of good manners struck, and, finally, the polite intrusion: "Excuse me. . . ." The sudden disclosure of a shared ethnicity reconstitutes the premodern *Gemeinschaft* which knew no "public places" with their "situational proprieties," which encountered no strangers, which made no private-public cleavage.

Freud returns to this train joke later and, instead of the natural "feel" of its immanent meaning we get a lumberingly apologetic "interpretation" written with the Gentile reader in mind. This anecdote of a Jew in a railway train "promptly abandoning all decent behavior when he discovered that the newcomer into his compartment was a fellow-believer . . . is meant to portray," Freud hastens to assure us, "the democratic mode of thinking of Jews, which recognizes no distinction between lords and serfs." * [13]

And there, embalmed in its edifying, obviously apologetic interpretation, the train joke was to remain for nearly fifty years, until it was resurrected by one of Freud's surviving disciples, Theodor Reik, reinterpreted—one should say, restored—and placed at the center of his book *Jewish Wit*. Clearly, Freud had been uncomfortable remaining on the level at which the joke had been told, the social level. It is decisive for

* Freud even adds that this mode of thinking "also, alas, upsets discipline and cooperation (see note 13).

any understanding of Diaspora Jewry's encounter with the West in the era of social Emancipation that we recognize how difficult it is for us to get from them (except via an assimilator like Simmel) a view of the social category that is inward to the social—i.e., a member's—viewpoint. The social nature of society is either politicized, psychologized or economized (i.e., construed on the model of the market). (Hannah Arendt is but the latest in a long line of European Jewish thinkers to experience society as a "curious, somewhat hybrid realm between the political [*polis*] and the private [*oikos*]." [14])

Reik maintains that this Jewish train anecdote derives from Artur Schnitzler's novel *The Way to the Opera,* in which it is told by the Jewish writer Heinrich Berman to his aristocratic friend George von Werkenthin. Heinrich explains this "deep" joke to his friend as expressing "the eternal truth that no Jew has any real respect for his fellow Jew. . . . Envy, hate, yes, frequently admiration, even love . . . but never respect, for the play of all their emotional life takes place in an atmosphere of familiarity, so to speak, in which respect cannot help being stifled." [15] Reik later returns to the train story, and—in a section on "The Intimacy of Jewish Wit"—finds that the anecdote does indeed show "that once it is recognized that the other person is also Jewish, *one need not 'behave'* " [16] (my emphasis). But then, shifting his focus, Reik prefers to stress not the absence of respect but the presence of intimacy in intra-Jewish relations, in Jewish wit. Not a "democratic way of thought," as Freud contends, but a certain kind of familiar intimacy is the "distinguishing and decisive mark of Jewish jokes. The closeness, immediacy, and warmth that exists between priest and penitent, analyst and patient, teacher and student is different," for "the intimate relationship of parishioner and priest, of student and teacher includes a certain measure of respect." [17] Eastern European Jewish intimacy, stemming from the high moral density of "life-is-with-people" in the *shtetl,* excludes "respect."

Reik, to define this intimacy, then isolates an aggressive component in this genre of jokes, in which (for example) there is mocked a "too quick and artificial adjustment to the capital of Berlin and its manners." With the addition of this aggressiveness, he writes, "we are approaching the core of that intimacy whose character we tried to define. Yet we cannot grasp its peculiarity." The derisory aggression expresses, somehow, "not bitter hostility and estrangement, but confidence and intimacy. More than this . . . it is precisely that familiarity which results in the courage to criticize, to attack. But how about that? Intimacy as a premise of aggression? That is psychologically difficult to grasp." [18] In this genre of joke "aggression does not produce estrangement, but puts an end to it, cancels it. A pathos of distance will not be tolerated in this group of jokes." [19]

What Reik is saying here is that the famous Jewish social "impudence"—there is no faithful translation of the Yiddish heart-word, *chutzpah*—works at once to destroy aggressively the artificiality of Western "passing" and to restore the old familiarity of the pre-Emancipation *shtetl* Jew. The ambiguity of the European social distance-relation of "respect" is overcome and dissolves in the Polish Jew's "*Asoi!*" It is the Jewish conviction of the unreconstructed "Yid" beneath the civil appearance of Jews who are "passing" that Freud turns into a "science." In psychoanalysis, the "id" is the functional equivalent of the "Yid" in social intercourse: on the train, the discovery of a shared ethnicity legitimates abandoning the later-acquired, "higher," more "refined" forms of Gentile social intercourse. *Yiddishkeit* * is "old equalizer." For Freud, the "id" is "old equalizer." The whole business of courtship and the sexual courtesies deriving from the feudal court are confronted, by Freud, with the "reality" of an erect penis. (With Marx, the myth of another set of "brute facts" is used in an attempt to subvert the "hypocrisy" of "appearance.")

"A neurotic patient I treated was impotent with his wife," Reik relates, "except when he first addressed her in vulgar sexual terms. In this downgrading, an emotional mechanism similar to that in the Jewish jokes, is performed in order to bring the object closer to yourself. The significant difference is that in this case the aim is sexual in its nature, while in the Jewish joke social intercourse is facilitated or rather made possible by such levelling." [20] The person can be either *downgraded* to one's own level, or *degraded* beneath one's own level. The latter will express sadistic tendencies. What Freud does is to take the mechanisms at work in this genre of Jewish wit and "kick them upstairs," turning them into an "objective" science. Reik cites an old Eastern European joking question: "How grows man? From below to above—because below all people are alike, but above the one is taller and the other smaller." [21] It is irrelevant in this type of wit whether it "concerns a person from an alien culture [read: Gentile] or a Jew who seems to disavow his Jewishness [read: an assimilator]"; [22] the intention to dissolve aloofness, remoteness, gentility, and the distantiations of "respect" is the same.

Helene (Rosenbach) Deutsch (b. 1884), one of the Freudian pioneers, recalls an incident from her childhood in Przemysl, Galicia (Poland), before the turn of the century, when the Jewish wood dealer, the one-eyed Mr. Stein, barged into the upper-middle-class Rosenbach apartment without knocking, with nobody home but little "Hala" lying on the dining room couch reading, practically naked but for a light robe: "I jumped up and demanded angrily, 'Mr. Stein, couldn't you knock first?' The answer was: 'Why? Isn't this a Jewish house?' All the Jewish tradespeople we dealt with had this same feeling of solidarity with us despite the fact that we were members of the 'aristocracy.'" [23]

* I.e., the values, feelings, and beliefs of the premodern *shtetl* subculture: the "Jewish fundamentalism," as I like to call it.

Ernest Jones remarks that Freud "felt himself to be Jewish to the core, and evidently it meant a great deal to him,"[24] and notes his "fondness for relating Jewish jokes and anecdotes"—jokes, incidentally, that often turned on a punch line that revealed Jews to be Jewish only at the core, not to the core. Consider, for example, Freud's version of the famous joke about the Baroness Feilchenfeld's confinement: "The doctor, who had been asked to look after the Baroness at her confinement pronounced that the moment had not come, and suggested to the Baron that in the meantime they should have a game of cards in the next room. After a while a cry of pain from the Baroness struck the ears of the two men: *'Ah, mon Dieu, que je souffre!'* Her husband sprang up, but the doctor signaled to him to sit down: 'It's nothing. Let's go on with the game!' A little later there were again sounds from the pregnant woman: *"Mein Gott, mein Gott,* what terrible pains!'—'Aren't you going in, Doctor?' asked the Baron.—'No, no. It's not time yet.' At last there came from next door an unmistakable cry of *'Aa-ee, aa-ee, aa-ee!'* The doctor threw down his cards and exclaimed: *'Now* it's time.' " *[25]

While Freud's analysis makes no mention of the baroness's Jewishness, but merely speaks of the cries of pain uttered by "an aristocratic lady in child-birth,"[26] we note that it is her third and last cry that Freud calls the "unmistakable cry" that discloses her true identity. For Freud the joke "demonstrates" two things: it shows how pain causes "primitive nature to break through all the layers of education" and how an important decision can be properly made to depend "on an apparently trivial phenomenon."[27] It is my conviction that we have here the prototype of Freud's concepts of "sublimation" and "regression." If so, once again we see how Freud began with a social psychological phenomenon—better, a phenomenon of sociological psychology, namely, the phenomenon of "passing," and psychologized it. The French layer is peeled away, then the German layer, finally laying bare the *"mama-loshen"* † of primary socialization "underneath." Freud's "primitive nature" that breaks through the cultural restraints of a Westernized superego is the premodern Jew of the preemancipated *shtetl.* Freud turns it into a quasi-biological "id." He well knew that these "slips" were by no means trivial phenomena, but revelatory of primordial identities upon which cultural strata had been superimposed. In Reik's account of the same joke, the transition from French to German to Yiddish cries is of interest because the return to the mother tongue or to the jargon once spoken restores the emotional at-

* Once again, Freud's account, as against the story as told by Reik in *Jewish Wit* (see note 15), launders the Jewish-Yiddish component. In Reik's version, the baroness's final cry is "Ai-ai-ee-weh mir!" (p. 34)—a somewhat hysterical rendition of *"Oy vay iz mir!"* ("Oh! Woe is me": *vay* is from the German *Weh,* "woe"). Leo Rosten, *The Joys of Yiddish* (New York: McGraw-Hill, 1968), refers to the "protocol of affect" governing the intensity and duration of this cry of ancestral woe (p. 273).

† The "mother tongue"—i.e., Yiddish.

mosphere of childhood and "sweeps away all the superstructure." [28] Here we have the paradigm for Freud's concept of the "superego": that baggage of secondary socialization—morals, "education," language, taste, and affect-restraint—needed by *shtetl* Jewry to "make do" and "pass" socially into the modern West. Thus it is that there is a long history behind Freud's view, in the case of the pain of the baroness, that it causes "primitive nature" to break through "all the layers of education." [29] "Education" (*Bildung*) is the nineteenth-century German burgher's word for "rising," as it was the nineteenth-century German Jew's word for the mind-work of "passing."

Jacob Katz informs us that a famous Berlin actor, Albert Wurm, excelled in representing Jewish characters not only on the stage but in the houses of the Berlin burghers: "His favorite piece was his imitation of a Jewish woman who wished to entertain her guests by rendering one of the well-known poems from the German classics. The Jewess makes a tremendous effort to sustain the standard of High German in pronunciation and intonation. At the beginning she does indeed succeed. In the process of the performance, however, she gets carried away and reverts to the common Judendeutsch she has been trying so hard to avoid. The whole business becomes a farce." [30] Our conviction that with this Jewish variation of the social parvenu we are in the presence of the (Lockean) sociology-of-knowledge "original" of several of Freud's core concepts is confirmed by Freud's own account of his reaction to Austria's declaration of war in 1914. At first, he was elated. For the first time in thirty years—he was fifty-eight at the time—he felt himself to be an Austrian. But scarcely two weeks had passed before Freud, as Jones writes, "came to *himself*. Very characteristically he described this by means of a Jewish anecdote in which a Jew who had resided in Germany for many years and adopted German manners returns to his family where the old grandfather, by examining his underclothes, decides that the German part was only veneer" [31] (my emphasis).

Three years before Freud in Vienna used this primordial, "primitive" identity beneath the "superimposed" identity of the assimilating Jew to construct his ideology of psychoanalysis, Durkheim in Paris was using it to found sociology as a science. In his *Suicide* (1897) Durkheim's law of positive correlation of the frequency of "egoistic suicide" with increasing education and reflection collides with the conspicuously low suicide rate of Jews—lower than Catholics and Protestants. For Durkheim the premodern, "medieval" self of his fellow Jews was literally, as he called it, "privileged" in its "immunity" to the solvent of modernity. What for modernizing Catholics, even more for modernizing Protestants, had been an immanent, autotelic change was, for Jews, largely accommodative, allowing the "mechanical solidarity" of Jewish identity to continue relatively undisturbed "beneath" the modernization process (a kind of sociological "marranoism"). Far from being the norm, as it was to become in the form of Freud's normative id, this Jewish resistance to the suicidogenic forces of modernity was, for Durkheim, the anomalous exception. For Durkheim, the exception proves the rule. Unlike the modernizing Protestant or Catholic,

> the Jew . . . seeks to learn not in order to replace his collective prejudices by reflective thought, but merely to be better armed for the struggle. For him it is a means of offsetting the unfavorable position imposed on him by opinion and sometimes by law. And since knowledge by itself has no influence upon a tradition in full vigor, he *superimposes* * this intellectual life [*superpose cette vie intellectuelle*] upon his habitual routine with no effect of the former upon the latter. This is the reason for the complexity he presents [*la complexité de la physionomie*]. Primitive [*primitif*] in certain respects, in others he is an intellectual man of culture [*un cérébral et un raffiné*]. He thus combines the advantages of the severe discipline characteristic of small and ancient groups with the benefits of the intense culture enjoyed by our great societies.†
>
> He has all the intelligence of modern man without sharing his despair. Accordingly, if in this case, intellectual development bears no relation to the number of voluntary deaths, it is because its origin and significance are not the usual ones. So the exception is only apparent; it even confirms the law. Indeed, it proves that if the suicidal tendency is great in educated circles, this is due . . . to the weakening of traditional beliefs and to the state of moral individualism resulting from this.[32] [My emphasis]

The Jewish social parvenu, who "tried at a bound to bridge the gap between his aspiration and his real social status" became a permanent figure on the stage, "much laughed at by the Gentiles and resented by Jews."[33] It was these value-laden social slips and gaffs, betraying the pariah id-"Yid" beneath the awkward parvenu, that Freud was to transform into value-free medical symptoms. ‡ Social unease became mental dis-ease. Psychoanalysis was to be a forensic medicine for a difficult

* It would appear that the formulation of Berger, Berger, and Kellner, that modern structures of consciousness are "*superimposed* upon the human mind" is particularly relevant to groups outside the modernizing Protestant mainstream (my emphasis).—J.M.C. *The Homeless Mind: Modernization and Consciousness* (New York: Random House, 1973), p. 144.

† This is the phenomenon modernization theorists like Robert Bellah call "neotraditionalism."—J.M.C.

‡ This insight—regarding the transformation of the social delict into the mental symptom—I learned from Erving Goffman's works, cited throughout. My contribution is to note the powerful apologetic motive at work historically *behind* Freud's transformation.

time (the era of Jewish social Emancipation). Gaffes defined as symptoms invite neither Jewish shame nor Gentile laughter.

In Paris, in the same year as Freud's *Interpretation of Dreams* (1900) and one year before his *Psychopathology of Everyday Life* (1901), the Franco-Jewish philosopher Henri Bergson published his book on laughter, *Le Rire*. He was working with the same phenomenon: the problem of social maladaptation with its "slips" and "parapraxes." To Bergson, "the comic expresses, above all else, a special lack of adaptability to society." The comic is that element by which the person "unwittingly betrays himself—the involuntary gesture or the unconscious remark." [34] (The demonstration of the connection in Bergson between the ridiculous and the unsociable, and of both with the prolongation into the elastic "organic solidarity" of modernizing society of a premodern "mechanical solidarity"—i.e., Jewish *ethnic* identity—which is derived in turn from Durkheim's *Division of Labor in Society: A Study of the Organization of Superior Societies* (1893), awaits further examination.)

Hannah Arendt notes how closely the assimilation of Jews into society "followed the precepts Goethe had proposed for the education of his *Wilhelm Meister*, a novel that was to become the great model of middle-class education." [35] The young burgher is educated by noblemen and actors in the "presentation of self" (as we might say today) so that he may learn "to present and represent his individuality," since, for the middle classes and the Jews—i.e., those outside high aristocratic society—"everything depended upon 'personality' and the ability to express it. . . . The peculiar fact that in Germany the Jewish question was held to be a question of education . . . had its consequence in the educational philistinism of both the Jewish and non-Jewish middle classes, and also in the crowding of Jews into the liberal professions." * [36] This educational program of German idealism, in its effort to "spiritualize" the middle class, instructed the son of both burgher and Jew in two things: the stage taught him "to coordinate his body, practically forgotten in schoolrooms and offices, with his inner being and to make appearance and gesture express some meaning," while the noblemen set the example of a fuller development and use of his personal faculties together with greater "confidence and courage." [37]

Let us return to the passage in Freud's *Interpretation of Dreams* where he first broaches the idea of a psychic censor which defends the

* Arendt finds "amusing" the close resemblance between the devices by which Jews assimilated into gentile civil society and Goethe's precepts by which aspiring burgher sons advanced to nobleman status (*Origins of Totalitarianism,* p. 59—see note 37). Perhaps her point is that it is ironic how knowledge itself can be a "means" of "crashing" civil society. This is perhaps what Arendt intends by the term "educational philistinism," viz., the depressing vision of education being used to facilitate *social* assimilation. This European Jewish background is at the root of her otherwise "perverse" attack on the Supreme Court's "desegregation" decision of 1954 (see her "Reflections on Little Rock," cited in note 14).

self against contents entering consciousness by disguising them, just like "the politeness which I practise every day is to a large extent dissimulation"; [38] a form of "affect restraint" prevents the expression in behavior of uncivil ideas and affect, or affect expressed coarsely and directly. Freud's earliest reference to "the process of censorship" is in connection with "affects of shame, of reproach, of psychic pain, or the feeling of injury." [39] The next year, in a paper entitled "Further Remarks on the Defense Neuro-Psychoses" (1896), the concept moves a step closer to its meaning in *The Interpretation of Dreams*. In this paper, in consequence of "the censorship exercised by the repression," there is effected "a compromise between the resistance of the ego and the strength of the idea under repression" which results in "distortion." Freud writes of Frau P., a patient, that her words always had the character of "*diplomatic* indefiniteness; the distressing allusion was usually closely hidden, the connection between the particular sentences being disguised by a strange tone of voice, unusual forms of speech and the like . . . [a] compromise-distortion" (my emphasis). Whenever she would recount the threats from her husband's relatives, these threats "were always so mildly expressed" as to stand in remarkable contrast to the pain they had admittedly caused her.[40] Sometimes, especially in discussing neurotic symptom formation, Freud uses the language of compromise. This, too, of course, has social parallels: an interpersonal compromise to mend a quarrel, a political or parliamentary compromise in which each side must compromise with others in order to protect one's interests. Repressed material, too, must submit to "a compromise which alone makes its entry into consciousness possible." [41]

In a paper written four years later, "Screen Memories," in which he disguises his own memories, imputing them to "a man of university education, aged thirty-eight," Freud writes of the compromise "on the analogy of the resultant in a parallelogram of forces," [42] in which a later unconscious fantasy of lust is "toned down into" a synthetic childhood memory: "It is precisely the coarsely sensual element in the phantasy which explains why it does not develop into a *conscious* phantasy but must be content to find its way allusively and under a flowery disguise into a childhood scene." [43] The fantasy is "transformed," expressed "figuratively"; the "raw material" is "remodelled," [44] and "the raw material of memory-traces out of which [the screen memory] was forged remains unknown to us in its original form." [45]

Freud's theory, then, is a theory of the relation of the coarse to the refined, of the raw to the sublime. It aroused indignant opposition by asserting that all men have ids (that is, all men are Jews). His theory refused to the fine arts—that is, to the arts that refined—all autonomy. His theory of sublimation unmasked the autonomy of the fine. Freud knew that his theory offended not so much because it sinned against truth but because it sinned against good taste. "He had fallen in love," Philip Reiff writes, "with a coarse Galatea." [46]

In the Emancipation process in the nineteenth century, the Eastern European Jew had been "refined." Freud was very ambivalent about that "achievement." As the emancipated Jew moved *out* from ghetto and *shtetl* and "passed" into Gentile society, he moved *up* from ghetto and *shtetl* and "passed" into middle-class Gentile society. In Warsaw, Vienna, Berlin, and Paris, assimilation into *Gesellschaft* life had not been easy. Ambition, impulse, self-expression—all had to submit to the censorship of Western norms, to the tyranny of bourgeois-Christian decorum; affect-restraint, idea-restraint, in real life as in dream life, was the rule. In 1882, Freud writes his fiancée: "I have such unruly dreams." [47] A year later, he writes her—in a passage, Ernest Jones notes, "pregnant with ideas that came to fruition half a century later, particularly in *Civilization and Its Discontents*" [48]—that "the mob give vent to their impulses [*sich ausleben*], and we deprive ourselves. We do so in order to maintain our integrity, . . . we *save up for* something, not knowing ourselves for what. And this habit of constant suppression of natural instincts," he concludes, "gives us *the character of refinement*" [49] (my emphasis). Of all the connections Freud was later to establish—between sick and healthy, trivial and important, ordinary and extraordinary, "the wound and the bow"—none was so offensive as his linking of the coarse to the refined (or, if you will, finding the coarse in the refined: Freud's metaphor for finding the pariah Jew in the parvenu Jew, or the "Jew" in the Gentile gentleman). It was this particular unmasking operation of psychoanalysis that gave rise to what Rieff calls the "vulgar accusations of vulgarity." [50] Freud had encountered Weber's Protestant *Ethic;* but he had *experienced* it—like others from the subculture of the *shtetl* or its equivalent—as the Protestant *Etiquette.* It is a task of historical sociology to understand (*verstehen*) that particular inner experience for what it was, and still is.

Freud's lifework was to make sense of the Jewish Emancipation experience. His basic unspoken premise can be put in lapidary if vulgar form as follows: the id of the "Yid" is hid under the lid of Western decorum (the "superego"). Again, put crudely: Freud's "psychologism" systematically "translated" the problematic of Jewish social intercourse with Gentiles in the Diaspora into problems of sexual intercourse. The public misbehavior of emancipating Jewry, slips and parapraxes, lapses—*lapsus linguae* and *lapsus calami*—or public backslidings into *Yiddishkeit* (the "Jewish fundamentalism") revealing the "unseemly" premodern "Yid" were universalized into revelations of Everyman's "id." In the West, Hannah Arendt remarks, the pariah Jew "was masked, . . . he concealed his true nature wherever he went, and through every hole in his costume his old pariah existence could be detected." [51] Freud, a conscious pariah, was a connoisseur of these "holes" in Viennese parvenu Jewry. But his was not to be a "Jewish science"—one of his deepest forebodings—precisely because of his conviction that coiled beneath the highest refinements of the high-minded *goyim* lay this same uncivilized and essentially unreformable "id." The id, in other words, was a moral equalizer legitimating "scientifically" social equality between Jew and Gentile in late nineteenth-century Europe. The mind of a moralist had used science to construct a "scientific psychology" as Marx before him had constructed a "scientific socialism." Freud's theory was one more ideology of the Emancipation process, joining socialism, Zionism, Reform Judaism, assimilationism, and communism. Freud's theory, like Marx's, had its praxis or therapy. It was to be a liberal-stoic strategy for "living-the-Diaspora." We now turn to it.

CHAPTER 2

THE MATRIX OF THE METHOD

The method Freud discovered for reaching the unconscious id he called "free association." While it developed out of the "cathartic method" of his colleague Breuer, Ernest Jones finds its source in an essay of Ludwig Börne entitled "The Art of Becoming an Original Writer in Three Days." Write down for three days in succession, Börne prescribes, everything that comes into your head, "without any falsification or hypocrisy." This "seed" sprouted twenty years later in the prescription, the "primary rule" of the psychoanalytic situation, in which the patient was to give his thoughts and feelings absolutely free play, verbalizing everything. "Ludwig Börne (1786–1837)," writes Jones, "who had in 1818 adopted this name in place of his own (Baruch Löb), was an idealist, a fighter for freedom, honesty, justice, and sincerity, and always opposed to oppression. . . . The graves of Börne and Heine were the only two Freud looked for when he visited Père Lachaise" cemetery in Paris.[1]

What Freud does is to create a social situation—the "analytic situation"—which is the inversion of the "civil society" outside the door of his Viennese consulting room. Marx had stood Hegel on his head as a prelude to standing bourgeois society on its head. By the century's end, revolution had failed. The emancipated Jew had become further embourgeoised; his internalization of the norms of Western culture had proceeded, in Freud's view, to the point of no return. The censorship that was politeness had, as we have seen, entered his very dreams, disguising the wishes of the uncivilized id.

In an address of capital importance delivered by Freud in 1910 before the Second International Psycho-Analytic Congress at Nuremberg—"The Future Prospects of Psycho-Analytic Therapy"—he betrays the sociocultural "secret" of the origins of psychoanalytic therapy, its free-association method, and the social situation (the dyad of analyst and analysand) congruent with its praxis:

> Suppose that a number of ladies and gentlemen in good society had planned a picnic at an inn in the forest one day. The ladies make up their minds that if one of them wants to relieve a natural need she will say aloud that she is going to pick flowers; but a malicious fellow hears of this secret and has printed on the programme which

> is sent around to the whole party—"If the ladies wish to retire they are requested to say that they are going to pick flowers." Of course after this no lady will think of availing herself of this *flowery pretext,* and other freshly devised formulas of the same kind will be seriously compromised by it. What will be the result? The ladies will own up to their natural needs without shame and none of the men will take exception to it.[2] [My emphasis]

This "just suppose" story of Freud is, as Philip Rieff notes, "a parody of the reticent manners and morals of the cultivated classes of the nineteenth century. . . . Freud is that malicious person" [3] who "reversed, once again, the usual conception: man's chief moral deficiency appears to be not his indiscretions but his reticence." [4] Freud undertakes—at least within the modest limits of a fifty-minute hour—to deflower * the chaste reticence of bourgeois-Christian social life.

As one enters the analytic situation one must check one's manners and morals at the door. All rules—of syntax, of morality, of propriety—are to yield to the primary rule of saying whatever comes to mind. On the couch, the polite social conversation of the *Gesellschaft* with its forced associations is to yield to the indiscretions of the free associations of the impolite monologue of psychoanalysis. "Freudianism was to be indiscreet on principle. . . . The therapeutic hour . . . puts an end to decorum." [5]

By thus inventing a social situation of minimal inhibition Freud provided a legitimate setting in which Viennese Jewry—and other "honorary Jews"—could legitimately desublimate (de-Westernize) and regress to their premodern "ids." The analytic situation is a teleological suspension of the civil, an *epoché* of the civility and decorum "natural" to the West. The analytic situation is an oasis of temporary relief † for Jewry's "discomfort in the cultured state." ‡ The primordial identity supposed to emerge in the permissive format of the psychoanalytic situation is a function of abstaining from the social norms outside that situation. Whereas Durkheim in formulating his program for a science of sociology stipulated that "the first and most fundamental rule is: *Consider social facts as things*" [6] (Durkheim's emphasis), Freud's manifesto for a science of psychology might well have begun with, "Consider social facts as nothings."

* Apropos of the "flowery pretext" masking coarse "natural need," recall the 1899 paper on "Screen Memories" in which Freud's own later wish "for deflowering a girl" (p. 64) is projected backward and "toned down into the childhood [screen] memory" (p. 63) of snatching away her bunch of yellow flowers (p. 56).

† "An oasis in the desert of reticence," as Rieff calls it in *Freud,* p. 332.

‡ Konrad Kellen remarks that the title of Freud's book is badly translated as *Civilization and Its Discontents* and suggests this phrase as having the "feel" of the original. "Reflections on *Eichmann in Jerusalem,*" *Midstream* 9, no. 3 (September 1963): 26.

This deliberate abstention from the civilities is used as a therapeutic instrument promoting free association, regression, and transference. This rule of civil abstinence, Donald Kaplan writes, prevents the analytic dialogue from lapsing into "ordinary conversation." For example, at the end of an analytic session, "a cordial 'Good Afternoon,' or a variation of it, is exchanged as the patient leaves the consulting room." But if the session has been an especially upsetting one, the analyst may feel the impulse to add, 'I'll see you tomorrow.' . . . If the analyst withholds the impulse, he has 'abstained.' . . . The goal of analysis is to increase the abstinence until the basis of the relationship between analyst and patient is extinguished." [7] (If improperly "dosed," of course, this analytic "incivility" can turn the consulting room into an insulting room.) Psychoanalysis is, indeed, as Hannah Arendt says—justifying her nonuse of it—a "modern form of indiscretion." [8]

But it is also, in a deeper sense, a mirror inversion of the social world, a kind of heresy. C. S. Lewis, in *The Personal Heresy,* asks: "Is there, in social life, a grosser incivility than that of thinking about the man who addresses us instead of thinking about what he says?" [9] It is significant that just before Freud constructs his bourgeois picnic in the country, to show how "the indiscreet revelations of psycho-analysis," "our work of revelation," [10] can bar the flight into illness that is "secrecy" (i.e. politeness) and break the spell of the bourgeois civilities ("in fairy tales you hear of evil spirits whose power is broken when you can tell them their name which they have kept secret" [11]), he pits his own "revelations" against those of Bernadette of Lourdes:

> Think how common hallucinations of the Virgin Mary were in peasant-girls in former times. So long as such a phenomenon brought a flock of believers and resulted perhaps in a chapel being built on the sacred spot, the visionary state of these maidens was inaccessible to influence. Today even the priesthood has changed its attitude to such things; it allows police and medical men to visit the seer, and since then the Virgin appears very seldom. Or allow me to study *the same processes* . . . in an analogous situation which is on a smaller scale. . . . Suppose that a number of ladies and gentlemen in good society had planned a picnic. . . .[12] [My emphasis]

In Catholic peasant-girls, as in bourgeois ladies and gentlemen, a collective neurosis flourishes, and it is the "secondary gain" of this illness that keeps it in business, and it is secrecy that keeps this gain from analytic dissolution. The "indiscretions of physicians" alone can break the stranglehold of these hallucinations, from Mariolatry to civility. "Disclosure of the secret will have attacked, at its most sensitive point, the 'aetiological equation' from which the neuroses descend, will have made

FERNALD LIBRARY
COLBY-SAWYER COLLEGE
NEW LONDON, N. H. 03257
67612

the 'advantage through illness' illusory."[13] We may presume to know what Freud had in mind as the "secondary gain" of the hallucination of an appearance of the Virgin to a peasant girl; but what, precisely, the "secondary gain" is in that collective neurosis which is bourgeois respectability Freud does not explicitly tell us. It is one of his deepest "secrets." It is his animus against the sublimation called refinement. It is the grudge against the beauty of the West harbored by the emancipated intelligentsia of Jewry. Since Solomon Maimon it had been assaulting them, making them look ugly to themselves, in their own eyes, against their own wills. Of the "Mrs. K," the teacher in Brownsville who had inducted the young Norman Podhoretz into the "mysteries" of good taste, into the Western bourgeois-Christian culture system—of her the grown man asks, rhetorically, how could she have explained to me "that there was no *socially* neutral ground to be found in the United States of America, and that a distaste for the surroundings in which I was bred, and ultimately (God forgive me) even for many of the people I loved, and so a new taste for other kinds of people—how could she have explained that all this was inexorably entailed in the logic of a taste for the poetry of Keats and the painting of Cézanne and the music of Mozart?"[14] (my emphasis).

Freud's ideas, George Steiner notes, "are firmly bound to the expressive and suppressive idiom of the Central European, largely Jewish middle class of the late nineteenth century in which Freud himself came of age."[15] In one respect, at least, Freud's ideas are even more profoundly subculture-bound than Steiner realizes: in the Jewish subculture from which Freud and the majority of his patients had emerged, there was no privacy *as such*. "It is proverbial," Zborowski and Herzog write,

> that "there are no secrets" in the *shtetl*. . . . It is a joking point rather than a sore point, because basically the *shtetl* wants no secrets. . . . The great urge is to share and to communicate. There is no need to veil inquisitiveness behind a discreet pretense of "minding one's own business." . . . Isolation is intolerable. "Life is with people,"

they conclude, echoing the book's title.[16]

In the nineteenth century, Eastern European Jewry enters the West and commits a stupendous "category mistake": * systematically, it mistakes privacy for secrecy. Because, in the *Gemeinschaft* of their past, "privacy is neither known nor desired,"[17] the many ways in which European burgeois culture managed to institutionalize the need to be *private in public*—the "decencies," the decorum of public behavior in public places, yes, alas, "respectability"—all this is lost on the Jewish intelli-

* I take this phrase from Gilbert Ryle.

gentsia of the nineteenth century. To them, it appears as so much hypocrisy. Insistently, they moralize it. "What is for Freud 'repression,' psychologically understood, is 'secrecy' morally understood. Secrecy is the category moral illness, for it provides a hiding place for false motives." [18]

For Freud, civility and politeness were not a social reality sui generis. He interpreted them in a moralizing fashion, as hypocrisy, secrecy, "reaction-formation." The *Gemeinschaft* "space" of the psychoanalytic situation constituted a counter-*Gesellschaft,* in which direct expressions of affect were rewarded and civil exchanges penalized. "You act as if psychoanalysis stood high and perfect, and only our own faults keep us from accepting it," exclaimed Joseph Wortis, stung, as a "nice," bourgeois, Jewish-American medical student–patient, by Freud's unabashed dogmatism. "It does not seem to occur to you that it is simply polite to reckon with one's own prejudices, too." "An analysis is not a place for polite exchanges," replied Freud, according to Wortis's diary of his psychoanalysis (for October 26, 1934): "An analysis is not a chivalrous affair between two equals." [19] "A science cannot be bourgeois," he later informed Wortis, "since it is only concerned with facts that are true everywhere." [20] On December 13, Wortis asked Freud how was one to know if the interpretation of a dream is correct:

> "How does the patient react when it is wrong?" I asked.
>
> "He usually says nothing," said Freud, "because it doesn't concern him."
>
> "But I am accustomed to respond to things that are said to me; it is only polite," I said.
>
> "Politeness doesn't enter into analysis," Freud said.
>
> "It is a habit with me," I insisted. "Perhaps," I added, "I have the wrong idea of the unconscious."
>
> "To be sure," said Freud, "but what you have said has given you away." [21]

Freud knew, of course, at once, that he was in the presence of a hopeless case. Politeness out of expediency is one thing; politeness for pleasure is remediable; * but politeness out of *habit,* politeness as inner-worldly asceticism (Weber's *innerweltliche Askese*) and cathected for itself betrays the depth to which bourgeois "niceness" has insinuated (internalized) itself. Wortis, in effect, is habitually, *unconsciously* polite. This is not the "unconscious" Freud had in mind. Wortis's analyst then and there writes him off: the patient has "given himself away," betrayed himself as

* Unlike "these *goyim* and their politeness," Harry Bogen muses, "I didn't have to be polite, except for pleasure." (Jerome Weidman, *I Can Get It for You Wholesale* [New York: Modern Library, 1937], p. 236.)

"objectively" part of the bourgeois Gentile world. (Marx's "we-they" cleavage had been more crassly economic; Freud's cleavage is more nuanced, more sociocultural, as befits the central conflict in the era of *social* emancipation.) *

Wortis's entry in his diary for January 17, 1935 (already noted), is particularly important: he forces from Freud the admission of a differentiation between the moral and intellectual life, on the one hand, in which categories Freud has been making a case for the preeminence of the Jews, and the social life of mixed society, on the other. The entry reads:

> "Ruthless egotism is much more common among Gentiles than among Jews," said Freud, "and Jewish family life and intellectual life are on a higher plane."
>
> "You seem to think the Jews are a superior people, then," I said. "I think nowadays they are," said Freud. "When one thinks that 10 or 12 of the Nobel winners are Jews, and when one thinks of their other great achievements in the sciences and in the arts, one has every reason to think them superior."
>
> "Jews have bad manners," I said, "especially in New York."
>
> "That is true," said Freud, "they are not always adapted to social life. Before they enjoyed emancipation in 1818 † they were not a social problem, they kept to themselves—with a low standard of life, it is true—but they did not go out in *mixed society*. Since then they have had much to learn." [22] [My emphasis]

Not least among the things to be learned "beyond the pale" was the difficult knowledge that "civic betterment"—Dohm's *bürgerliche Verbesserung* [23]—was to involve more than the exercise of bourgeois rights (the franchise, careers *ouvertes aux talents,* etc.); it was to entail also the performance of bourgeois rites governing the exchange "in mixed society"—i.e., with strangers—of those gifts known in the West as civilities. The rights and duties of the *citoyen* integrated the Jew into a remote solidarity with the Gentile West. Political, economic, and legal entitlement involved, as such, no direct, face-to-face, social interaction with one's fellow citizens. It was a mediated, not a situated, solidarity, placing little or no strain on the personality system of emancipating Jewry. Its "collective representation" was the Enlightenment's declaration of the "Rights of Man." Membership in *that* community came for the asking. But, by

* This conflict was not to reach final formulation until 1950 when Maurice Samuel published *The Gentleman and the Jew.*

† It would appear that the date 1818 is an error. Prussian Jewry's Emancipation Edict was granted on March 11, 1812. See Salo W. Baron, "The Modern Age," in *Great Ages and Ideas of the Jewish People,* ed. Leo W. Schwarz (New York: Random House, 1956), p. 327.—J.M.C.

1830, and certainly by 1848, the French revolution was seen—notably by Marx—as a bourgeois revolution. Social solidarity with "respectable" bourgeois society was to be consummated in immediate, face-to-face encounters or not at all. The social skills for negotiating such solidarity must be learned, often, by mingling with members of bourgeois society itself. This was especially difficult for a "pariah people" closed out from social solidarity with respectable society because it was deemed wanting in respectability in the first place.

CHAPTER 3

"PASSING" INTO THE WEST: THE PASSAGE FROM HOME

What Howard Morley Sacher refers to as "the *unconsious* desire of Jews, as social pariahs, to unmask the respectability of the European society which closed them out" [1] (my emphasis) was, in Freud's case at least, the conscious desire of a conscious pariah. "There was no more effective way of doing this," Sacher continues, "than by dredging up from the human psyche the sordid and infantile sexual aberrations that were frequently the sources of human behavior, or misbehavior. Even Jews who were not psychiatrists must have taken pleasure in the fact of social equalization performed by Freud's 'new thinking.' The B'nai B'rith Lodge of Vienna, for example, delighted in listening to Freud air his theories." [2]

But the "shocking" content of Freud's theory and the "shocking" praxis of his therapy were far more than an occasion for Freud's *Schadenfreude*. The "shock" of Jewish Emancipation had come first. Lured by the promise of civil rights, Jews in the nineteenth century were disillusioned to find themselves not in the *pays légale* of a political society but in the *pays réel* of a civil society. Lured by the promise of becoming *citoyens,* they found that they had first to become *bourgeois*. The ticket of admission to European society was not civil rights but bourgeois rites. The price of admission was not baptism, as Heine thought, but *Bildung* and behavior. This "brutal bargain" of Jewish Emancipation is structurally built into the theory and praxis of Freud no less than into that of Marx before him. "The price to be paid for being cultured is, after all, a doctrinal point of major consequence to Freud," writes Philip Rieff.[3] Reiff never notes the connection with the continuing nineteenth-century debate on Jewish Emancipation. Only when we ask the vulgar sociology-of-knowledge question "*Says who*?" [4] (emphasis in original) of Freud's universalistic formulations—such as, "Ontogeny recapitulates phylogeny"—can we unpack them into (for example) "Each of my patients repeats the pattern and problems of nineteenth-century Jewish Emancipation."

The most cursory glance at Freud's works bears this out. For example, chapter 1 of *The Psychopathology of Everyday Life* (1904), "Forgetting of Proper Names," turns on "the journey with the Gentile stranger":

"I journeyed by carriage with a stranger from Ragusa, Dalmatia, to a station in Herzegovina. . . . We had been discussing the customs of the Turks. . . . I wished to relate [that] these Turks value the sexual pleasure above all else. . . . I refrained from imparting this characteristic feature because I did not wish to touch upon such a delicate [read: coarse] theme *in conversation with a stranger*" * [5] (my emphasis)—and, as a result, Freud couldn't bring to mind the name of the painter Signorelli. One is in danger of forgetting how widespread, up into our own time, "and not least among Jews, was the association of Jewishness with vulgarity and lack of cultivation," [6] Norman Podhoretz reminds us. Freud's chapter 2, "Forgetting of Foreign Words," opens by revealing again the Jewish milieu from which so much of his material derived: "Last summer, while journeying on my vacation, I renewed the acquaintance of a young man of academic education, who, as I soon noticed, was conversant with some of my works. In our conversation we drifted—I no longer remember how †—to the social position of the race to which we both belonged. He, being ambitious, bemoaned the fact that his generation, as he expressd it, was destined to grow crippled, that it was prevented from developing its talents and from gratifying its desires. He concluded his passionately felt speech with a familiar verse from Virgil about a new generation that would "take upon itself vengeance against the oppressors." [7]

The aggravation (*tsuris*) of Jewish Emancipation is the matrix of Freud's material, whether it be jokes, slips, dreams, or patients. He goes to considerable pains to reduce social gaffes and parapraxes to a nonsocial level. In the same book, he is his own case in point, as he recounts how he and a girl who had caught his fancy jumped up together to get a chair for the girl's elderly uncle when he entered the room. Freud ended up somehow embracing her from behind. It did not occur to anybody, he remarks, "how dexterously I had taken advantage of this awkward movement," and concludes: "An apparently clumsy movement may be utilized in a most *refined* way for sexual purposes" [8] (my emphasis). Even the classic stalemate of refined polite form, when two people attempting to pass on the sidewalk move simultaneously to right and left and end up as blocked as before, Freud reduces to a "coarse" sex drive. This "barring one's way" "repeats an ill-mannered, provoking conduct of earlier times and conceals erotic purposes under the mask of awkwardness. . . . The so-called naiveté of young people and children is frequently only such a mask," he concludes, "employed in order that the subject may *say or do* the indecent thing without restraint" [9] (my emphasis).

* One must be "delicate" about what is "coarse" with a Gentile stranger. See Freud's 1910 essay, "The Antithetical Sense of Primal Words," in *Collected Papers* (see note 15), 4: 184–91.

† A case of "forgetting improper subjects"?—J.M.C.

In 1908 Freud wrote "'Civilized' Sexual Morality and Modern Nervousness"—the quotation marks indicate his irony—which is a critique of bourgeois civil society and the renunciations it demands (sexual gratification postponed long past puberty, the institution of monogamous marriage, etc.). "Our civilization is, generally speaking, founded on the suppression of instincts. Each individual has contributed some renunciation—of his sense of dominating power, of the aggressive and vindictive tendencies of his personality." [10] Like Marx before him, Freud is convinced that this bourgeois era of "renunciation has been a progressive one in the evolution of civilization," with the single steps in it "sanctioned by religion." [11] But, unlike Marx, he has no hope another stage will inevitably succeed this one, ushered in by revolution. Freud takes a liberal-stoic stance, with "sublimation" his resigned equivalent for Marx's "revolution."

Freud's clientele was drawn from a new largely Jewish middle class of late nineteenth-century Europe, only recently entering the modernization process. Coming with "great expectations," they would remark to Freud: "We in our family have all become nervous because we wanted to be something better than what with our origin we were capable of being." [12] Freud's patients, by and large, had not internalized the Protestant-Ethical equipment that would enable them to ride the late nineteenth-century modernization process. Freud sees neurosis, Rieff notes, as "the penalty for ambition unprepared for sacrifice." [13] These patients were caught between the *shtetl* subculture of *Yiddishkeit* and the *Gesellschaft* norms of a modernizing Vienna. Hannah Arendt has drawn their portrait in "The Jews and Society: Between Parish and Parvenu." [14] Freud, in a sense, was their self-appointed intellectual elite, mediating them over into the promises and perils of modernity. Himself a *"Galitzianer,"* he understood their problems from the inside. He built his analytic situation as a resocializing station, as a moratorium for their "identity crisis." There they could recontact their "backward" past. There they could learn that they were "suffering from reminiscences" of the *shtetl*. There, "uneasy in their refinement," [15] they could hear from Freud the same message Kafka in 1912 told his audience of Prague Jews just before a Yiddish theater troupe began its performance: "Before the Polish Jews begin their lines, I want to tell you, ladies and gentlemen, how very much more Yiddish you understand than you think you do." [16] It is significant that it is in this very essay on "'Civilized' Sexual Morality" that Freud informs us that the psychoanalytic physician frequently observes "that neurosis attacks precisely those whose forefathers, after living in simple, healthy, country conditions, offshoots of rude but vigorous stocks, came to the great cities where they were successful and were able in a short space of time to raise their children to a high level of cultural attainment." [17] As Norman Mailer puts it: "Psychoanalysis came into being because a great many *arrivistes* arrived during the 19th century." [18]

If we turn now to the most celebrated of the psychoanalytical patients drawn from this "arriviste" German-Jewish milieu, "Anna O," we learn in privileged detail the remarkable congruence of situation and symptom in the developmental history of psychoanalysis. When, in 1895, in the pages of Josef Breuer and Sigmund Freud's *Studies in Hysteria*, literate, progressive Viennese puzzled over "The Case of Anna O," few realized that this hysterical analysand of Breuer was Fräulein Bertha Pappenheim, daughter of a newly rich Orthodox Jewish father, Siegmund, of Liechtensteinstrasse, cofounder of the Schiffschul Synagogue in Vienna. Never a patient of Freud's, her case was nevertheless to become the catalyst of Freud's psychoanalytic method. From her recorded case history, readers learned tantalizingly little of her social circumstances: "Anna" was twenty-one when her breakdown occurred; her parents were "nervous, but healthy"; she was bright and stubborn, her will relinquishing its aim "only out of kindness and for the sake of others"; she became ill while caring for her father through his last illness; she remained at home, in bed, where Dr. Breuer found her on his first call in Christmas week of 1880.[19]

The first and decisive therapeutic breakthrough occurred in the Pappenheim country home in the following summer in connection with her "hydrophobic" revulsion at drinking a glass of water despite a tormenting thirst. She had been living exclusively on fruits and melons for six weeks. Under hypnosis, Breuer reports, Anna disclosed the decisive conflict:

> She spoke about her English governess, whom she did not like and then related, with all signs of disgust, how she once entered [the governess's] room and saw her little dog, that disgusting animal, drink out of a glass. She said nothing *because she wanted to be polite*. After she gave energetic expression to her strangulated anger, she asked for a drink, and without any inhibition drank a great deal of water, awaking from the hypnosis with the glass at her lips. With this the disturbance disappeared forever." [20] [My emphasis]

Anna O's predicament may thus be summed up: anger strangulated, or censored,* by politeness. This, the first symptom ever to be dissolved by psychoanalysis—under hypnosis, by the "cathartic method" (what Anna O was to christen "the talking cure")—was itself a psychological expression of the socio-cultural "ordeal of civility," of that classically Freudian malaise: discontent in civil or bourgeois society (to be later metapsychologically elevated to "civilization and its discontents").

It behooves us to give a close reading to this bit of case history: it was the takeoff for the psychoanalytical movement. The affect Anna O

* The idea of censorship was already present in 1895. See Breuer and Freud, *Studies in Hysteria* (cited in full in note 17), p. 201.

had kept under wraps was neither lust nor disgust, but "anger." The desire to give vent to the anger was strangulated not by morality but by "politeness." More exactly: the desire to be angry collided not with politeness but with another desire—namely, "she said nothing because she *wanted to be* polite" (which is a far cry from *being* polite). All this occurred in the presence of the Gentile "nanny" her family had brought in from England and whom she disliked. Under hypnosis, she was able to give "energetic expression to" this anger; that is, in the absence of the original object of her anger—the Gentile governess—and in the presence of the permissive Viennese—the Jewish doctor—she was able, with impunity, to be impolite. With that, the symptom disappeared. It was from the inspection of this particular sequence of events that Freud was to arrive at his momentous claims. He concluded that his colleague Breuer had made, in the words of Anna O's biographer, "two fundamental discoveries out of which psychoanalysis developed: a neurotic symptom results from emotions *deprived of their normal outlets,* and the symptom disappears when its unconscious causes are made conscious"[21] (my emphasis).

From this account, it is abundantly clear that the origins of psychoanalytic therapy rest not on a *cognitive* discovery of fact but on a decision as to what is *normative,* what is a "normal" expression for a vehement feeling such as, in this case, anger. In the provincial hinterlands of the *shtetlach,* from which so many of Anna O's parental generation had emigrated into Vienna, the expressive norms of *Yiddishkeit* governing what was a "normal outlet" for anger were proverbially more relaxed and permissive than the rules regarding affect restraint that prevailed among the upper-middle-class Viennese whom the new arrivals had chosen as their reference group. Anna's disliked English governess, we may hazard, acted as the "carrier" of an affect-discipline considerably more severe than that which she had absorbed from her parents in the earliest stages of her primary socialization. In this sense, Anna undoubtedly did suffer emotional deprivation in the sense of emotions "deprived of their normal [that is, earlier] outlet." Her secondary socialization was an unsuccessful assimilation to out-group norms, which were experienced as a deprivation. Her parents, moreover, situated "between pariah and parvenu," were undoubtedly divided in their own minds as to what was a "normal" and "proper" expression of anger and what not. This, then, is the family setting which produced an Anna who "said nothing [to her governess] because she wanted to be polite," who restrained her anger rather than commit an infraction against politeness. But Anna O had never really internalized and made her own these rules of polite affect restraint. They were ever to be constraints, a matter of conforming externally to the rules of others by concealment and dissimulation, a politics rather than an ethics or an etiquette. "The politeness which I practice every day," Freud had confessed, "is to a large extent dissimulation." [22] It is in this sense that we can say that Anna O had tried and *failed* to be polite with her governess. She had "passed" as polite. "For what will be later seen as a 'symptom,'" Erving Goffman reminds us, "first comes to attention because it is an infraction of a rule regarding affect restraint during daily encounters." [23]

"Until 1890, I led the life of a daughter of a middle-class Orthodox Jewish family," Bertha Pappenheim ("Anna O") writes.[24] After 1890, she would become the first Jewish feminist and a social reformer of legendary integrity. This "first lady of psychoanalysis," whose identity as the "Anna O" of the *Studies in Hysteria* was not widely known until 1953, when Ernest Jones hailed her as "the real discoverer of the cathartic method," [25] broke her lifetime of silence on psychoanalysis only once. At a board meeting of her Frankfurt home for "wayward" Jewish girls a board member had suggested that Manya, a Jewish farmgirl from Poland who had been abandoned by a "white slave dealer" at the railroad station in Frankfurt when he fled the police, should see a psychoanalyst. "On hearing the suggestion," Bertha Pappenheim's biographer relates, she "abruptly stood up and said, her voice emphatic, 'Never! Not as long as I am alive.' A hush fell over the room. The other women did not understand her dramatic reaction but realized she spoke out of deep feeling. Then she said, 'Let's go on to other matters,' and sat down." [26] Bertha Pappenheim, as Ernest Jones writes, "deserves to be commemorated" [27]—but not, surely, as a doyenne of psychoanalysis.

It was as a pioneer Jewish feminist that Europe was to recall Bertha Pappenheim when, in 1954, the Bonn government, at the suggestion of Rabbi Leo Baeck, issued a stamp in her honor in its "Helpers of Humanity" series. But even as a feminist her implacable independence set her apart. "Abortion is murder," she announced to a panel on abortion, meeting at Bad Durkheim, Austria, in 1930, sponsored by her own Federation of Jewish Women.[28] Her reliability as a Jewess was also suspect; a lifetime of unselfish devotion to the welfare of Jewish orphans, illegitimates, and the *Agunah* * was never to erase the fact that she had had the "bad taste" freely—and, what was worse, publicly—to criticize the lay and rabbinical leadership of the Jewish community for concealing their "dirty linen" from the eyes of the *goyim*.

As we read her letters we witness a curious, hidden dimension of Jewish Emancipation. In her struggle against the Jewish community's practice of concealing its "dirty linen" from the *goyim,* which some Jews justified as required by their minority situation, she found herself dis-

* An *Agunah* is a Jewish wife who had been abandoned or lacked Jewish legal proof of her husband's death, and so could not remarry. As Rabbi Arnold Jacob Wolf writes: "Rabbi Gershom [of Mainz] a thousand years ago began to end Jewish polygamy and its evil effects; Bertha Pappenheim finished his work." Introduction to Edinger, *Bertha Pappenheim* (see note 22), p. 7.

advantaged by her own kind of concealment—namely, the incompletely internalized restraints of good manners and decorum. Their constraint seems a mocking echo of her restraint. She writes from Budapest in March 9, 1911, of a visit, with a leading feminist of Budapest, to the city's chief rabbi, "a tall decorative gentleman in Hungarian-clerical garb. He let us wait for a long time. Without a word, like a stone, he let me look at his not-noble profile, and talk. When I had finished and asked him to help [in the matter of prostitution] in the interests of individuals and of the entire Jewish community, he said, without a quiver of his eyelids: 'I'm not interested in this matter.' . . . *Well-mannered, quiet and restrained as I am, I tried to say: 'But. . . .'* The decorative pastor of the Jewish congregation of Budapest, raised his hand forbiddingly and said: 'I do not allow myself to be converted' "[29] (my emphasis). Irresistibly, we are carried back thirty years to that young patient of Breuer, Anna O, who had said nothing "because she wanted to be polite" and who could not give expression to her "strangulated anger."

In May of the following year, she writes from Saint Petersburg of the experience of having the fact of her own Jewishness, in the presence of Gentile patrician ladies, become an "unmentionable." "Of course," she writes,

> the unquestioning way with which the white slave dealers, procurers, and so on, are called "JEWS" is truly shocking. It would help very little if the Russian committee and some other people would get acquainted with me as with a Jewish woman who feels the shame and tries to work against it. The Jews are supposed to *suffer quietly this kind of concealing*. I want to vary the expression that everybody who is not against the meanness of our community is for it. One should not imagine that our enemies do not know what demoralization exists in the broad masses of the Jewish people. . . . The [Jewish] leaders do not want to look, and speak only about sham ethics and solidarity. I would have liked it if the noble members of our Jewish people had been at the tea table of the Russian Princess yesterday and have noticed *under the smooth, well-educated forms* what I was feeling.[30] [My emphasis]

Six days later she writes from Moscow of the Countess Barbara B., who takes her to see "Moscow's Whitechapel" and who turns out to be anti-Semitic. A fierce but fastidiously polite argument occurs between the two women. Our interest centers in Bertha Pappenheim's ceaseless, anomic monitoring of the gulf between her inner feelings and the social and logical forms, her "ordeal of civility." The letter goes as follows:

> "Jewish ethics and aesthetics were completely different [from Christian]." I tried to explain that Christian ethics were Jewish as well:

> "Ce n'a jamais été, jamais, jamais. (Never, never!)." I could not convince her about ethics, and about our [alleged] lack of idealism —I might have introduced myself as a Jewish woman living for an idea. As to aesthetics, the adaptability and crookedness of our race, I had to be silent, for Countess B. was right. She can only see the product of our difficult history. Both of us were deeply stirred. Our contact would have been different had we not been *restrained by education, and civilization,* had we met outside a speeding car [*sic*], a Christian and a Jewish woman, in a wilderness, a desert. Physically she would have been victorious, maybe also spiritually, for my enemy was right: they work for the "relèvement du peuple" (bettering the people) but we Jews watch the demoralization, and the annihilation and destruction of our people with a happy grin.[31] [My emphasis]

Shortly after, the Russian countess and the Viennese Jewess place around their substantive differences (it was 1911) the brackets of bourgeois civility: they perform the social rites, the offering of thanks, handshakes, and "goodbyes." The countess, Bertha Pappenhneim writes, "was kind enough to take me to my hotel" at 11:00 P.M. "I thanked her. I said that I owed her thanks, for she had given me most important experiences and impressions. She said she would be happy if she had been useful to me." To this, Anna O adds, with that implacable loneliness born in part of a Kantian moral rigorism that plagued the best of the children of the German-Jewish Diaspora: "My thanks were sincere, though I knew that, conventionally and politely, I shook hands with an enemy."[32] As a member of the new Viennese Jewish middle class Bertha Pappenheim, Lucy Freeman writes, had been "brought up to be polite to people"; she had been carefully taught to live secretly with certain feelings "she had not expressed because she felt them impolite."[33] The predicament of the attempt of this generation of emancipated Jews to integrate into a "societal community" founded neither on the revolutionary "idea of fraternity" nor on the ethnic idea of "tribal brotherhood" but on the impersonal liberal-bourgeois idea of "civility" was a circumstance not lost on someone of Freud's background.*

* Freud's patient, Dora, was drawn from the same new Viennese Jewish bourgeoisie as was Anna O. As in Anna O's case, Steven Marcus notes in his sensitive essay "Freud and Dora: Story, History, Case History," "normative" assumptions were central to Freud's analysis. These norms which informed his interpretations were "relatively crude and undifferentiated" and Dora "resisted" their application to herself (*Partisan Review* 41, no. 1 [1974]: 98, 99). Dora's family situation, as far as I have been able to ascertain, was not even remotely of the "classical Victorian" variety. Her Jewish grandfather emigrated from Prague to Vienna where he made money and converted to Catholicism. Her father, it would appear, was a socialist leader and physician who, after his marriage, converted to Christianity "to save his children from embarrassment," as the story goes. Her home was the scene of a *ménage à trois*. Her brother was a physicist and radicalized socialist who was to assassinate at a later date a leading Austrian political figure. As youths, her father and Freud, it seems,

Freud thus saw the pathos of his patients' predicament: Jews were undergoing emancipation, modernization (urbanization), and civilizational processes all at the same time—even as he himself was. Today, psychoanalysis looks less and less like a science "and more and more like an inspired construct of the historical and poetic imagination, like one of those dynamic fictions through which the master-builders of the nineteenth century—Hegel, Balzac, Auguste Comte—summarized and gave communicative force to their highly personal, dramatic readings of man and society." [34] As we look at the famous picture of the Psychoanalytic Committee in Berlin in 1922 [35]—Otto Rank, Karl Abraham, Max Eitingon, Ernest Jones, Freud, Sandor Ferenczi, Hanns Sachs—we must learn to see them on the colonial model, as a modernizing elite, constructing plausible ideologies for their decolonizing people, for themselves, and for the "imperial" power.

Helmut D. Schmidt tells us that in the great public debate on Jewish Emancipation in Germany (1781–1812) the collective names applied to the Jews as a community were "nation" and "colony" and sometimes also "Jewry" (*Judenschaft*).[36] The fact that Jews in the West are a decolonized and modernizing people, an "underdeveloped people" traumatized—like all underdeveloped countries—by contact with the more modernized and hence "higher" nations of the West goes unrecognized for several reasons. First, because they have been a colony *internal to* the West; second, because decolonization has been gradual and continuous; third, because of the democratic manners of the West (only Max Weber called them a pariah people, i.e., a ritually segregated guest people); and fourth, because the modernization collision has been politicized and theologized by the charge of "anti-Semitism" (as, in noncontiguous Western colonies,

---

had had a violent philosophical argument in which Freud "behaved very rudely to his philosophical opponent and obstinately refused to apologize; there was even for the moment some talk of a duel" (Ernest Jones, *The Life and Work of Sigmund Freud,* vol. 1, *The Formative Years and the Great Discoveries 1856–1900* [New York: Basic Books, 1953], p. 43). In his concern to assimilate Freud (in part) to literary modernism, and the case history genre to the nineteenth-century bourgeois novel, Marcus rediscovers Dora as "Victorian maiden" (p. 103) and finds her family constellation interpretable as "a classical Victorian domestic drama" (p. 15). This is preposterous. Dora, like Anna O, and like Freud himself, is as embedded in East European Jewish culture as James Joyce is in Irish Catholic culture. The new "new criticism" of the *Edelfreudianer,* in its impatience with the gross details of history, genesis, and ethnicity, is even more utterly *luftmentshish* than the old. It is a bizarre discovery, but one fact which we now know that Freud did share with the stereotype, at least, of Victorian family life is that, on his own admission, his marriage had petered into what was virtually a *mariage blanc.* (See the letter of November 6, 1911 of Emma Jung to Freud, in *The Freud/Jung Letters: The Correspondence between Sigmund Freud and C. G. Jung,* ed. William McGuire, trans. Ralph Manheim and R. F. C. Hull [Princeton, N.J.: Princeton University Press, 1974], p. 456.) This information has been available heretofore only in the shuffling version of Jones. (See Ernest Jones, *The Life and Work of Sigmund Freud,* vol. 2, *Years of Maturity 1901–1919* [New York: Basic Books, 1955], pp. 386, 482, n.6.

the charge of "imperialism" effectively obscures the real nature of the collision—namely, between modernizing and nonmodernized peoples).[37]

Let us return now, and get perfect pitch on what Freud was up to by a quotation from Erich Heller: he speaks of Freud's campaigns "against the decorous lies of a superficially civilized consciousness stubbornly refusing to acknowledge the teeming incivilities beneath the surface."[38] Freud's campaign, then, was not for truth and against lies; it was for shocking truth and against *"decorous* lies." An important feature of Freud's thought, Harold Lasswell writes, "was its shocking content. It violated the mores, especially by insisting on the sexuality of infants and children." William James, with whom Lasswell contrasts Freud, was a psychologist who also had many shocking things to say, but when James said them "he phrased the point with tact and glided smoothly past."[39] Why this difference? It goes deeper in Freud than *épatisme* (though Freud did have a romantic-"bohemian" streak that enjoyed "shocking the bourgeoisie" for its own sake). James, too, was deeply rebellious, but he was able to master this rebelliousness in ways that made it unnecessary for him to "adopt provocative language or to break the smooth surface of his urbane manner."[40] Lasswell contrasts James's "tactful modes of expression" and "balanced presentation of human nature" with Freud's "counter-mores modes of expression" and "'Hobbesian' presentation of human nature,"[41] and he seeks the source of the difference. He finds that Freud was "marked by scars from deprivations of *respect,* partly because of the cultural minority to which he belonged, and partly as a result of the stresses connected with an improving status in the social class system (the respect structure)."[42] This led to Freud's "acute sense of grievance."[43] This led in turn to Freud's including in his personality a "strong demand upon the self" to "tolerate no acts of contempt, or other unjustifiable deprivation, without strong counteraction." And the root of this "demand upon the self"? Lasswell finds at least one of its roots in "the humiliation that Freud felt as an eleven-year-old when his father acceded to a humiliating command by an anti-Semite. It has often been proposed that if Freud had not given in to his rebelliousness he might have *phrased* the discoveries regarding sexuality in less flagrantly provocative language"[44] (my emphasis). If we pursue this suggestion—Lasswell does not—and follow its lead, we will in the end discover, I believe, the heretofore undisclosed source of Freud's famous theory of the Oedipus complex.

CHAPTER 4

THE PRIMAL SCENE

Freud in *The Interpretation of Dreams*, in the course of analyzing the infantile matrial in his own dreams, speaks of Paris and Rome as goals of his early longings.[1] Many of his dreams took him to Rome. As a boy, when he studied the Punic Wars, he had identified with the Carthaginians against the Romans and, he writes, "to my youthful mind Hannibal and Rome symbolized the conflict between the tenacity of Jewry and the organization of the Catholic church," adding that "the increasing importance of the effects of the anti-semitic movement upon our emotional life helped to fix the thoughts and feelings of those early days." [2] The wish to go to Rome, like Hannibal's lifelong wish, had become in Freud's dream life "a cloak and symbol for a number of other passionate wishes," [3] one of which Freud immediately recounts as follows:

> At that point I was brought up against *the event in my youth* whose power was still being shown in all these emotions and dreams. I may have been ten or twelve years old, when my father began to take me with him on his walks and to reveal to me in his talk his views upon things in the world we live in. Thus it was, on one such occasion that he told me a story to show how much better things were now than they had been in his days. "When I was a young man," he said, "I went for a walk one Saturday in the streets of your birthplace [Freiberg, in Moravia]; I was well dressed, and had a new cap on my head. A Christian came up to me and with a single blow knocked off my cap into the mud and shouted: "Jew! get off the pavement!" "And what did you do?" I asked. "I went into the roadway and picked up my cap," was his quiet reply. This struck me as unheroic conduct on the part of the big, strong man who was holding the little boy by the hand. I contrasted this situation with another which fitted my feelings better: the scene in which Hannibal's father, Hamilcar Barca, made this boy swear before the household altar to take vengeance on the Romans. Ever since that time Hannibal had had a place in my phantasies.[4] [My emphasis]

The shout that Jacob Freud heard was probably the ancient command that a Jew frequently heard when he encountered one of the *goyim* in a narrow street or defile—"*Machmores Jud!*" ("Mind your manners, Jew!") —whereupon the Jew would obediently step into the gutter, allowing the Gentile to pass.* Did Jacob Freud use this ancient phrase when he told his son this story? We do not know. If he did, and it is not unlikely, the son by 1900 had "forgotten" it. But the meaning of the event was clear, and its sting rankled. A later talk Freud had with his half-brother "had the effect of softening the criticism of his father over the cap-in-the-gutter episode," Ernest Jones notes, but "his father never regained the place he had held in his esteem after the painful occasion. . . . The lack of heroism on the part of his model man shocked the youngster who at once contrasted it in his mind with the behavior of Hamilcar." [5] The young Freud was shocked, indignant and, far more important, ashamed—ashamed of his own father.

It was only a year after publishing *The Interpretation of Dreams* containing the aforementioned episode that Freud published *The Psychopathology of Everyday Life* (1901), in which we read the following: "Occasionally I have had to admit to myself that the annoying awkward stepping aside on the street, whereby for some seconds one steps here and there, yet always in the same direction as the other person, until finally both stop facing each other, that this 'barring one's way' *repeats an ill-mannered, provoking conduct of earlier times* and conceals erotic purposes under the mask of awkwardness" [6] (my emphasis). What does this cryptic allusion to "an ill-mannered, provoking conduct of earlier times" mean? Nowhere are we told. But we are told that manners conceal libido when they do not conceal aggression (the two "faces" of the repressed "id").

Later in the same work, he devotes part of the chapter on "Errors" to the motivated errors of his own *Interpretation of Dreams* of the previous year. We read:

> On page 165 [of the first edition of *Interpretation*] Hannibal's father is called Hasdrubal. This error was particularly annoying to me. . . . The error Hasdrubal in place of Hamilcar, the name of the brother instead of that of the father, originated from an association which dealt with the Hannibal fantasies of my college years and with the dissatisfaction of my father towards the "enemies of our people." I could have continued and recounted how my attitude toward my father was changed by a visit to England, where I made the acquaintance of my half-brother, by a previous marriage of my

* Although references are hard to locate, Professor Ben Halpern of Brandeis writes me that "it is so well known that perhaps it requires no citation" (personal communication, April 6, 1972).

> father.* My brother's oldest son was my age exactly. Thus the age relations were no hindrance to a fantasy which may be stated thus: how much pleasanter it would be had I been born the son of my brother instead of the son of my father! This suppressed fantasy then falsified the text of my book at the point where I broke off the analysis, by forcing me to put the name of the brother for that of the father,[7]

the father who had so meekly submitted to the insult from the "enemies of our people" he had encountered on the street in Freiberg long ago.†

Now let us turn to Freud's Oedipus complex. On June 16, 1873, the seventeen-year-old Freud, fresh from graduating *summa cum laude* from the Sperl Gymnasium, writes his friend Emil Fluss about his *Matura,* the final exam:

> In Latin we were given a passage from Virgil which I had read by chance on my account some time ago; this induced me to do the paper in half the allotted time and thus to forfeit an "exc." [i.e., "excellent]. So someone else got the "exc.," I myself coming second with "good." . . . The Greek paper, consisting of a thirty-three verse passage from *Oedipus Rex,* came off better: [I was] the only "good." This passage I had also read on my own account, and made no secret of it.[8]

Twelve years later, in 1885 in Paris, Freud goes to see *Oedipus Rex.* "*Oedipus Rex,* with Mounet-Sully in the title role, made a deep impression on him."[9] Why? We are not told. But twelve years after that (in 1897), in the midst of his self-analysis and the writing of *The Interpretation of Dreams,* he attempts to make sense of "the gripping power of *Oedipus Rex.*" He writes to his friend Wilhelm Fliess that only one idea of general value has so far occurred to him in the course of his attempt

* Freud made this visit to his half-brother Emanuel in 1875, when he was nineteen. "He never ceased to envy his half-brother for being able to live in England," Ernest Jones writes, "and bring up his children far from the daily persecutions Jews were subject to in Austria." Jones, *Life and Work* (see note 5), 1: 24. Freud's own eldest son, Martin, was to pay his eighty-year old "Uncle Emanuel" a visit in 1918 in Southport, whence he had retired from the textile business in Manchester. "Uncle Emanuel had become in every possible detail a dignified English gentleman," he writes, "and this applies to his dress, his manners and his hospitality." Martin Freud, *Sigmund Freud: Man and Father* (New York: Vanguard Press, 1958), pp. 12–13.—J.M.C.

† Freud had a long memory for such things. Three pages later he recounts how, on a trip from Munich to Rotterdam where he was to take a midnight steamer to England, he missed train connections for Rotterdam at Cologne. Exasperated, he stood on the railroad platform: "I pondered whether or not I should spend the night in Cologne. This was favored by a feeling of piety, for according to an old family tradition, my ancestors were once expelled from this city during a persecution of the Jews." *Psychopathology* (see note 6), p. 183.

at "being entirely honest with oneself": "I have found love of the mother and jealousy of the father in my own case too, and now believe it to be a general phenomenon of early childhood. . . . If that is the case, the gripping power of *Oedipus Rex* . . . becomes intelligible, and one can understand why later fate dramas were such failures."[10] It is of capital importance that we do not miss what is occurring in this letter, the very matrix of psychoanalytic theory construction. Freud is putting forth a theory. A theory is offered in explanation of some fact or set of facts, some experience. What does this nascent theory purport to explain? Freud offers to Fliess an explanation of why he, Freud, finds reading and viewing Sophocles' *Oedipus Rex* such a "gripping" experience. (If you will, Freud is resuming Aristotle's task, in the *Poetics*, of exploring why *Oedipus* is the exemplary tragedy in its power to evoke the audience's pity and terror.[11]) Freud's explanation is that the Greek myth which supplies the plot of the play—the logic of its episodes—"seizes on a compulsion which everyone recognizes because he has felt traces of it in himself. Every member of the audience was once a budding Oedipus in phantasy, and this dream-fulfilment played out in reality causes everyone to recoil in horror, with the full measure of repression which separates his infantile from his present state."[12] Almost a month passes. "You have said nothing about my interpretation of *Oedipus Rex*,"[13] he complains in a letter to Fliess. Once more we must note that Freud is not trying to explain infantile material, about his early relations to his father and mother, dredged up in the course of his self-analysis and dream analysis. He is offering an "interpretation of *Oedipus Rex*," a play, and proposes a theory to explain the play's power over him and to make "intelligible" why he should identify so deeply with its hero, Oedipus. It is in the course of that effort that the core of the theory of psychoanalysis is born.

Now let us examine the play itself. Using the Loeb Classical Library translation of F. Storr, let us turn straightway to the climactic soliloquy of Oedipus, where for the first time he reveals to his queen consort, Jocasta —and to the listening audience—the story of his past, the plot of the play. He relates how, having left Corinth for Delphi, where the oracle warns him that he will slay his father and marry his mother, and thus resolved not to return to Corinth and to his foster parents—whom he believes to be his real parents—he sets off with his staff down the road leading in the opposite direction:

> Then, lady,—thou shalt hear the very truth—
> As I drew near the triple-branching roads,*

* See how ingeniously Seth Benardete resolves the apparent contradiction between the "triple road" (τριπλὴ ὁδός) Oedipus speaks of here and the earlier reference by Jocasta (line 733) to the "split road" (σχιστὴ ὁδός). "Sophocles' *Oedipus Tyrannus*," in *Sophocles: A Collection of Critical Essays*, ed. Thomas Woodward (Englewood Cliffs, N.J.: Prentice-Hall, 1966), p. 117.—J.M.C.

A herald met me and a man who sat
In a carriage drawn by colts—as in thy tale—
The herald in front and the old man himself
Threatened to thrust me *rudely* from the path,
Then jostled by the driver in wrath
I struck him, and the old man, seeing this,
Watched till I passed and from his carriage brought down
Full on my head his two-pointed goad.
Yet was I quits with him and more; one stroke
Of my good staff sufficed to fling him clean
Out of his seat and laid him prone.
And so I slew them every one.[14] [My emphasis]

This passage is from the play the seventeen-year-old Freud busily boned up on to pass his *Matura,* and saw enacted in Paris in 1885, and read many times, and, avid to break the secret of its hold over him, returned to in the late nineties in the course of plumbing dreams and early memories. The story his father had told him at ten or twelve, I shall argue, bears an uncanny resemblance to the event that precipitated the Oedipus story: the chance meeting on the street, the incivility of the threat to "thrust [one] rudely from the path." This time the son doesn't "take it lying down" but, when "jostled," strikes back in anger at the driver. Then, just as with Freud's father years back, Oedipus is struck "full on the head" (*μέσον κάρα*), but this time, instead of the "unheroic conduct" of his father meekly fetching his cap out of the muddy gutter, Oedipus in his fury strikes back again and kills . . . his father.

Sir Richard Jebb in his note on this passage writes as follows:

> I understand the scene thus. Oedipus was coming down the steep narrow road when he met the herald (to be known for such by his stave, *κηρύκειον*) walking in front of the carriage (*ἡγεμών*). The herald *rudely* bade him stand aside; and Läius, from the carriage, gave a like command. . . . The driver (*τροχηλάτης*), who was walking at his horses' heads up the hill, then did his lord's bidding by actually jostling the wayfarer (*ἐκτρέποντα*). Oedipus, who had forborn to strike the sacred herald, now struck the *driver:* in another movement, while passing the carriage, he was himself struck on the head by Läius. Oedipus dashed Läius from the carriage; the herald, turning back, came to the rescue; and Oedipus slew Läius, herald, driver, and one of two servants who had been walking by or behind the carriage; the other servant (unperceived by Oedipus) escaped to Thebes with the news.[15] [My emphasis]

And it is the fateful arrival on the scene of this last surviving witness to the murder that is awaited as Oedipus offers his version of his past. This servant will tell Oedipus whether it was a stranger he slew or his father, Läius.

An important structural parallel should be noted: the insulting language and the murder on the road are not part of the spectacle of *Oedipus Rex:* the episode is not seen, but heard related. Strictly speaking, as Aristotle noted, these events lie "outside the tragedy" (ἔξω τῆς τραγῳδίας).[16] So also, the young boy Freud only heard the hat-in-the-gutter episode from his father's mouth, years after it happened; he did not witness it. When his young son asks him, "And what did you do?" Jacob Freud astounds him with his "quiet reply." Contrast with Oedipus's account of his retaliation—"and then some"—against his aggressor. C. M. Bowra notes how Oedipus tells of his "fatal encounter with Läius: 'But I / When one led the horses jostled me, / Struck him in anger,' and no doubt he slew Läius in the same spirit. Even in his account of the episode to Jocasta we can see the excitement with which a man of action feels in recounting his exploits, and the thrill of battle which the memory of them revives."[17]

It is the contention of my theory that Freud's fantasy of himself as a "conquistador," though early in his life identified with Hamilcar and Massena, later, when he came to read, see, and understand *Oedipus Rex,* identified with Oedipus. The superego and its ideal is formed, as Freud taught, to compensate for the loss of the parental "object-cathexis." Freud, on the day he heard from his father's lips the story—to him, ignominious—of his father's encounter with an "enemy of our people," at that moment in his shame and rage he "slew" his father, adopting the more heroic ego-ideal of Hamilcar Barca. To be ashamed of a father is a kind of "moral parricide." Freud presumably experienced not only this rage and shame, but guilt about the rage and shame.* He quickly "censored" these unacceptable feelings, unacceptable to a dutiful son ostensibly proud of his father; he "repressed" them. Years later he encounters Sophocles' tragedy and it lays a spell on him. As he ponders the strange grip it has on him, he comes to believe that its power lies in the secret correspondence between the play's manifest, overall plot design—the son unwillingly kills the father, marries the mother—and the repressed desire of every son to do just that, to kill his father because he desires his mother. But the *idée fixe* that Oedipus was to become for Freud, I maintain, hinges on a small detail (small, but structurally indispensable for the action of the story) that Freud never mentions in all the countless times he retells the "legend"; † the whole plot starts from a social insult, a discourtesy on the road, stemming from someone in a position of social superiority (King Läius to the unknown wayfarer, Oedipus, just as the Christian in Freiberg

* See Chapter 5, The Guilt of Shame, pp. 58–63.

† "I must read more about the Oedipus legend—I do not know what yet," he writes Fliess. *Origins of Psychoanalysis* (see note 10), p. 252.

who forced Jacob Freud into the gutter). In both cases the inferior person is "called on his manners" by those who have no manners themselves and who use manners as a mask for violence or lust. (Recall Freud's unmasking of the "stalemate of good form" in the street, with each party moving simultaneously from left to right—like Gaston and Alphonse—as, "in reality" concealing "erotic purposes." [18]) Behind decorum Freud finds violence. In both stories, the head is struck.

Clearly, Oedipus *does* what the young Freud *wished* his father had done. It is a forbidden wish, one that Freud cannot admit into consciousness except in "sublimated" form. He will unmask these *goyim*. Like Hamilcar's son Hannibal, he will storm Rome seeking vengeance. He will control his anger, as his father had done, but he will use it to probe relentlessly beneath the beautiful surface of the Diaspora to the murderous rage and lust coiled beneath its so-called civilities. Imagine Freud's fascination as he watches *Oedipus Rex:* "There is in Oedipus," notes C. M. Bowra, "a tendency to uncontrolled anger. . . . This appears in his pride of kingship, even in his relentless pursuit of what he believes to be the truth. . . . He is the man who retaliates with force and does not shrink from killing an aggressor." [19] Finally, Freud reaches Rome. He liked the first Rome, ancient Rome, which he contemplated undisturbed. Not so "the second Rome," medieval, Catholic Rome, superimposed on the first. "I was disturbed by its meaning," he writes Fliess on September 9, 1901, "and, being incapable of putting out of my mind my own misery and all the other misery which I know to exist, I found almost intolerable the lie of the salvation of mankind which rears its head so proudly to heaven." [20] As we shall see subsequently, for Freud this "lie of salvation" assumed protean forms.

In mid-December of 1883, on the train between Dresden and Riesa, an event occurred which duplicated all the essential elements—except the ending—of Freud's father on the street. Freud opened a window on the windy side of the train to get some fresh air. There were shouts to shut it. An argument ensued. A shout from the background was heard. "He's a dirty Jew!" And with this, Freud writes his fiancée from a Leipzig hotel, "the whole situation took on a different color. My first opponent also turned anti-Semitic and declared: 'We Christians consider other people, you'd better think less of your precious self,' etc." Freud held his ground, challenged one man to a fight. Soon "the anti-Semite, this time *with ironic politeness,* renewed his request [that I close the window]. No, I said, I'd do nothing of the kind" (my emphasis). The conductor refused to take sides. Finally, another railroad official "decided that in winter all windows had to be closed. Whereupon I closed it. After this defeat I seemed to be lost—a storm of jeers, abuses, and threats broke out." Freud turned and again yelled a challenge at the ringleader, who declined to take it up. Then all was quiet.[21] All the essential elements of the paternal encounter repeated themselves: the public place, the dispute about the propriety of certain behavior in a public place, the charge of incivility itself made incivilly (like shouting at a child to be quiet), the physical challenge, and the "ironic politeness" of the Gentile's renewed request—all with one important difference: Freud's calling their bluff by an open challenge to stand up and fight.

Years later, Freud will write his book on Moses, with whom he identifies. Bestowing on Moses all the indignation and fury conspicuously absent from his father's behavior and prominent in the behavior of the Greek *goy*, Oedipus, Freud writes: "The Biblical story itself lends Moses certain features in which one is inclined to believe. It describes him as choleric, hot-tempered—as when in his indignation he kills the brutal overseer who ill-treated a Jewish workman." * [22] The impact of such impassioned and indignant conduct—a far cry from the ignominious Diaspora passivity of Jacob Freud—which recalled the fury of Oedipus, was reason powerful enough for Freud to "offend the Jewish people" by declaring Moses a Gentile.

One further detail should be mentioned: the "narrow defile" † in which Oedipus slayed his father reappears in the life of another of Freud's heroes, Hannibal, son and avenger of Hamilcar Barca against the Romans in the Second Punic War (218–201 B.C.). Hannibal in the spring of 217 crossed the Apennines and advanced through the uplands of Etruria, provoking the main Roman army to a hasty pursuit: "Catching it in a defile on the shore of Lake Trasmenus [Hannibal] destroyed it in the waters or on the adjoining slopes." [23] In more detail: the Roman consul C. Flaminius following, Hannibal occupied the heights on the north, "commanding the road from Cortona to Perugia . . . so that when the Roman army had entered the valley . . . there was no escape except by forcing a passage." [24]

Only Karl Abraham among psychoanalysts, to my knowledge, ever developed a public interest in the actual Sophoclean scene of the parricide, and this was a by-product of exploring the ways the wish to murder the father is concealed in its opposite, the desire to rescue him. In his paper, "The Rescue and Murder of the Father in Neurotic Phantasy-formations" (1922), he notes that the murder of Läius by Oedipus does not occur in the royal palace "but in the road. This detail . . . cannot be without significance," he writes, and he goes on to suggest that what the road signifies is the female genitalia. In his search for elements in the Oedipus legend which "have hitherto passed unnoticed," the "road over which father

* The biblical passage reads: "In those days after Moses was grown up, he went out to his brethren: and saw their affliction, and an Egyptian striking one of the Hebrews his brethren. And when he had looked about this way and that way, and saw no one there, he slew the Egyptian and hid him in the sand." Exodus 2: 11–12.

† It is curious that the English word *defile* means "to pollute," "to violate the chastity of," and, as a noun, "a narrow passage."

and son quarrel hardly needs further commentary," he writes. All the concrete details which, to us, cry out for a sociocultural interpretation illuminating why Freud was so drawn to the play are subsumed under the rubric of universal Freudian symbolism. The king and the driver "attempt to push away the approaching Oedipus," Abraham writes, in the very area where the text invites the interpretation of *social* insult (common sense invites it: two people in one another's path, each refusing to move, trading insults, passions mounting). The king strikes Oedipus. "The symbolical language here is transparent," Abraham writes. "The blow on the head is a typical castration symbol. . . . [All such symbolism] is easily recognizable to the initiated." [25] But what did *Freud* originally *feel* when he read or heard the son speak of the blow on the head? When his father's new fur hat was knocked into the gutter by a blow on the head, his father was not castrated. He didn't react with courage, that's all. It wasn't the blow to the head that demeaned the father in the child's eyes, but his "unheroic response."

It so happens that Abraham, in August 1921, sent a copy of this paper to Freud (before publication) for his advice. In his reply Freud carefully refrains from any overall estimation of the paper, but draws Abraham's attention to

> an awkward feature of the Oedipus passage which has *already caused me a great deal of trouble*. You write of the "hollow way" as the place of meeting [between Läius and Oedipus], and that is just as suitable to us as a symbol of the genitals as it is suitable as a spot for giving way. . . . But the Greek text known to me [was this the same text the seventeen-year-old had used to pass his Greek exam at the Sperl Gymnasium?] talks of a σχιστὴ ὁδὸς, which means, not "hollow way," but cross-roads, at which one would suppose giving way would not be difficult. Would it not be as well to consult a scholar before you publish? [26] [My emphasis]

I like to think that Freud's scruple, here, for the actual Greek text of Sophocles represents, at a deeper level, his fidelity to those detailed elements in the encounter of Läius and Oedipus that repeated those of his father with the "kingly" *goyim* back in Freiberg and that, indeed, accounted for the play's grip on him, which is what, in the first place, the Oedipus "complex"—on my theory—was designed to explain: the congruence, namely, between the story his father (in life) told him about the past and the story Oedipus would tell him (on stage, in print) about an event in his (Oedipus') past. "If Freud had lived and carried on his inquiries in a country and language other than the German-Jewish milieu which supplied his patients," Hannah Arendt writes, "we might never have heard of an Oedipus complex." [27] If we recall that Freud's first patient was Freud, that psychoanalysis began with Freud's self-analysis, Arendt's statement becomes, I think, in an unsuspected way true.*

* Since writing the above, I have come across two other students of Freud who find significance in the anecdote about Freud's father, but neither makes any close analytic connections with the Greek tragedy. Vincent Brome asks: "Could it be that, when Viennese medical circles ordered him off the medical pavement because of his sexual theories, he refused to move with such indomitable will because the humiliating picture of his father remained an unconscious driving force within him? . . . because he was not going to repeat his father's weaknesses?" *Freud and His Early Circle* (London: Heinemann, 1967), p. 245. Henri F. Ellenberger writes that the young Freud "was indignant about what he felt was cowardice in his father. An anecdote of that kind illustrates the gulf between the young generation and its elders, and may help"—he adds cryptically—"to explain the genesis of the concept of the Oedipus Complex." This is picked up once more when, noting the lack of any positive references to his father in *The Interpretation of Dreams,* Ellenberger allows as how "this makes one wonder whether Freud had not more deep-reaching reasons for this attitude toward his father than just the early childhood rivalry for his mother." *The Discovery of the Unconscious: The History and Evolution of Dynamic Psychiatry* (New York: Basic Books, 1970), pp. 423, 452. In 1880, Jacob Bernays, the uncle of Freud's fiancée, wrote a book on the concept of catharsis in Aristotle's *Poetics,* a fact that reinforces my theory of the close tie between the details of the drama's plot and the details of Freud's father's story. Ibid., pp. 485; 561, n. 280.

CHAPTER 5

THE GUILT OF SHAME

A step in the analysis at this point ought to be spelled out more explicitly. In finding the origin of the Oedipus complex theory in an incident of Gentile insolence told to the young Freud years earlier, and in the son's embarrassment at his father's shameful response to this challenge, I am proposing not a "reflection" theory of the origin of the Oedipal theory—namely, that a *psychological* theory of Freud mechanically "reflects" a *sociological* incident of his life (and of his father's life)—but a dynamic theory: I propose that the psychoanalytic theory of the person *is* itself an active, unconscious suppression (by Freud) of sociobiographical fact, and that this suppressed *social shame* "returns" in the more legitimate and (for Freud) more tolerable admission of *moral guilt* spelled out in the Oedipal theory.

Peter L. Berger, in a brilliant account of sociological "conversions," speaks of "massive social mobility" itself as involving, on the part of the children, a kind of "moral parricide" of the father, a kind of symbolic murder of the parent in "a sacrificial ritual of the mind." If there is, as he writes, "an embarrassing former self, long left behind," there is perhaps an even more embarrassing "former" parent also left behind. "It is no wonder, incidentally," he adds, "that the Freudian mythology of parricide has found ready credence in American society and especially in those recently middle-class segments of it" in whose lives massive social mobility has been so conspicuous.[1] If it is understandable how the socially mobile would give ready credence to the "Freudian mythology of parricide"—allowing it, in the sociology-of-knowledge sense, to pass for knowledge—how much more understandable it is that the socially and *culturally* mobile Freud should have given credence to the Oedipus *mythos* of Sophocles, finding it so inwardly convincing that he was helpless to resist taking it for knowledge, thus transforming Sophocles' tragedy into a cognitive theory of psychosexual development and sending it out into the world as psychoanalytical "science." If moves up the social ladder can be experienced as parricidal betrayal, they will be doubly so experienced if they coincide—as they do in the Jewish case—with moves across the cultural divide.

It is my contention, based on the texts, that Freud was ashamed of his father's behavior. I further contend that he felt guilt for being thus ashamed—what I call the "guilt of shame." Guilt has been studied from every side, and shame has recently come in for its share of attention.[2] But nothing has been done, so far as I know, on the "guilt of shame." This is a highly specific experience, especially germane to the experience of members of acculturating and assimilating subcultures. It is an affect sui generis and phenomenologically irreducible to either guilt or shame. It is the "subjective" social psychological correlate of the "objective" sociological occurrences of social mobility, modernization, "alternation," and assimilation, especially as these forces are experienced by "ethnics."

We experience guilt, usually, when we violate some value that we hold, when we go (actively) against what our conscience "tells" us: we break a promise, tell a lie, "cheat" on an exam or on our wives, betray a friend. Shame, on the other hand, is involuntary: we "find" ourselves embarrassed and ashamed (of ourselves, or of people with whom we are ascriptively identified: parents, marital partners, our own children, fellow nationals or ethnics, etc.). Shame is a "condition" rather than an action. Shame may be about something specific (e.g., after the class period is over, the teacher suddenly discovers that his trouser fly had been unzipped all the time), but the affect itself is general, it "suffuses" one's whole being: one *is* embarrassed. (Nothing had been *done* intentionally; at best, something had been left undone—e.g., unzipped.) A specific, *guilty* deed is, in a sense, alterable, forgiveable, retractable. Shame echoes and reechoes long after the event. Shame is an exposure, not a deed.

The next step in this argument is: to be ashamed *of* another or *for* another—such as a parent—is an even more shattering experience than to be ashamed of or for yourself. "Because of the pervasive and specifically unalterable character of experiences of shame," Helen Lynd writes, "shame for one's parents can pierce deeper than shame for oneself. . . . No matter how disgusted I am with myself, in some respects I can perhaps change. But the fact that these are my parents . . . is unchangeable. 'Shame in a kindred cannot be avoided,' says a seventeenth century proverb." [3] I look on Freud's shame as an example of what Miss Lynd calls "the special character of shame felt by children for their parents." [4]

But filial shame takes a further dimension when it is the embarrassment of the child who has "passed beyond" the parent socially and, especially, culturally. Jewish Emancipation supplied an "ideal" matrix for such experiences: "For a child of immigrant parents there is often acute conflict between the desire to look up to his parents and the shame he experiences for the exposure of their different ways and their uncertainty and unseemliness in a strange land." [5] The ignominious obsequiousness of Freud's father was, for the son, just such an exposure experience. Helen Lynd speaks of "the widely felt, if not widely acknowledged, shame of children who become aware that their parents are not secure or at home in their social environment," giving as one of her examples of the object of this filial shame, "deference toward other persons on the part of parents, their not 'knowing what to do' in a situation that calls for competence, their smiling acquiescence in the place of strength"—their ignominious acquiescence, we might add, in place of the courage the child would have wished them to have displayed. Such shamefully submissive ineptitude "may arouse in their children pity or protectiveness when they want to give respect—a feeling hard to acknowledge and hard to bear." [6]

Why is this specific experience "not widely acknowledged . . . ," "hard to acknowledge" compared to confessions of guilt, and, even when acknowledged, "hard to bear"? (The whole thrust of Lynd's book is to urge "confrontation" with shame, rather than with guilt, as the uniquely necessary "spiritual exercise" for the achieving of modern identity. She opposes this Eriksonian "discipline" of shame to the Freudian "working through" of guilt.) The answer is, that for the son to own up to shame for the parent, rather than to his parent's guilt, is to admit to parental inferiority rather than to his own wrongdoing. The latter is an admission about his own person; to admit the former is to "consent" to parental inferiority in the eyes of others (in this case, the general Gentile culture).[7] The guilt of wrongdoing is easier to face than the shame of inferiority, especially when seen in a parent. Guilt, we all know, is remediable; meaningful change is possible through subsequent acts of the guilty party: repentance, restitution, or forgiveness in the moral order, apology in the social order. But the experience of "being ashamed" collides with the opaque facticity of "all those others" who cannot be changed in their appraisal of—in this case—the parental inferiority (except by revolution: Marx).

But—and this is the crucial step—precisely because the parent is blameless (morally), we feel ourselves guilty for feeling ashamed of him, since it is we who have freely chosen "these others" as the new reference group in terms of which the parent now appears vulgar to us. Our leaving the orbit of the parental subculture is experienced as a free act ("assimilation"). The distance we thereby put between our parents and ourselves is the very freely chosen condition without which we would not have winced in shame of them in the first place. So, paradoxically, it is *we* who are guilty for achieving those things—social mobility, refinement, assimilation—in virtue of which we experience our own parents as embarrassing and distasteful to us. To have remained within the primitive togetherness of the parental subculture of our origin would have immunized us against being ashamed of it. Alternatively, to experience shame of that subculture is to admit the guilt of having moved "beyond" it and so "betrayed" it. This is the "guilt of shame": secretly, we know that *we* are responsible for being ashamed, not the parents for being shameful (or shameless). Their appearing vulgar to us is the price we must pay for becoming refined. Cultural conversion changes a person's taste. There is an inexorable logic of taste involved in the modernization process not unlike the logic of fate inherent in Greek tragedy. A cultural convert will often rue his first, small, "blind" steps in a process that leads in the end, one of them writes,* to "a distaste for the surroundings in which I was bred, and ultimately (God forgive me) even for many of the people I loved, and so [to] a new taste for other kinds of people. . . . All this was inexorably entailed in the logic of a taste for the poetry of Keats and the painting of Cézanne and the music of Mozart." [8]

If all of this makes sense, it will be apparent why we are anxious to hurry the initial shame experience into an admission of guilt. We move from the initial affect of shame—which is intolerable, relatively—to the meta-affect of "guilt about our shame." Writing of George Eliot's character Dorothea in *Middlemarch,* Helen Lynd notes her "eagerness to exaggerate her own guilt rather than to admit [in shame] inadequacy in the possibilities of love or loss of faith in the people and the world she had trusted." [9] Shame—like envy—is a sociological affect par excellence.[10] It is deeply entwined with experiences of meaninglessness and anomie, with the brute *givenness* of social evil. Traditional theodicy can handle moral evil—guilt—relatively easily. But certain cultural evils, irreversible maldistributions of specifically sociocultural values—the relative superiority-inferiority of the deference and prestige dimensions of stratification and the irreversibility of history (e.g., "We got here first and set up the rules")—have only revolutionary "solutions" for the deep kind of woes they set going in people. Otherwise, only shame answers to their facticity. "Sin, guilt, punishment—each is, in one sense, an affirmation of order and significance. Shame questions the reality of any significance" [11] because it obscurely intuits the irreversible *arbitrariness* of the conditions that generate it. That is why political revolution achieves its deepest and most secret ambition in the rewriting of history itself.

With this as background, we can return to Freud. The "parricide" Freud committed was committed by Freud's shame of him. The opposite of shame is courage. In Sophocles' *Oedipus Rex* Freud sees passive shame reenacted as courage. "Courage," Lynd writes, "is the counterpart of shame." [12] *Oedipus Rex* enables Freud vicariously to convert passive shame into active courage, avenging himself and his father against both his father and the general culture. *Oedipus Rex,* in fantasy, "solves" many of Freud's "problems." But everything *begins* in the shame experience.

* The following passage by Norman Podhoretz, which I advert to more than once, concludes his chapter "The Brutal Bargain" of part I, "A Journey in Blindness," in the autobiographical *Making It* (see note 8). The sentence is put as a rhetorical question to certain others who have no way of understanding the "logic" it identifies.

The two traits of the sociocultural infrastructure of this shame—which structure constitutes its sociological sine qua non—are its arbitrariness and its (historicotemporal) irreversibility. So Freud mutates the shame into guilt, since it is more tolerable because more alterable to want to kill your father than to be ashamed of him. (And, besides, Freud in fact does experience guilt as part of the complex emotional "complex" he suffers, but it is the "guilt of shame," the guilt of having "deauthorized" the parent, not the guilt of having entertained the forbidden wish to kill him in order to possess the mother.) It is more permissible and tolerable to own up, to blame yourself for being a parricide (in fantasy), than to be ashamed of your father (in reality) for his, and consequently your, misfortune in having been born a Jew. So Freud converts the shame into guilt. He transforms the sociohistorical "givenness" of Judaism into the psychomoral "takenness" of Jewishness. From a misfortune it becomes a problem. From historical *tragedy* it becomes a solvable scientific *problem*. "After some experiences of shame," Helen Lynd writes, "we may welcome guilt as a friend." [13]

Finally, what about the "positive" component in the Oedipus complex theory, the sociocultural core of the lust for the mother which sets the whole thing going? Is this forbidden "lust-for-the-mother" aspect of Freud's Oedipus complex (its manifest content as *culturally* tabooed as the "guilt-at-desiring-the-death-of-the-father" aspect) nevertheless Freud's "scientific" veneer for a latent wish—desire for the Gentile girl (the *shiksa* *)—that, *sub*culturally, is perhaps even more forbidden? I undertake, briefly, in answer, the following socioanalysis. Leslie Fiedler in "The Jew in the American Novel" analyzes the "Zion as Eros" theme that surfaced in the American Jewish novel from Abraham Cahan's *Rise of David Levinsky* (1917) to Ludwig Lewisohn's *Don Juan* (1923) and Ben Hecht's *A Jew in Love* (1931). "It is in the role of passionate lover that the American-Jewish novelist sees himself," Fiedler writes, "at the moment of his entry into American literature"—as Heine had seen himself in the early second generation of Jewish Emancipation in Europe—"and the community with which he seeks to unite himself he sees as the *shiksa*." [14] By Freud's time, at the end of the century, all the strands in the importunate "wish" behind Jewish Emancipation had faltered or failed: Rahel Varnhagen's social emancipation, Marx's "species" emancipation, Heine's literary-erotic emancipation—all were seen as illusory utopias. Freud codified this failure in his theory of the problematics of social and sexual intercourse with the *shiksa* as Gentile community. But in Freud, Abraham Cahan's view (as Fiedler puts it with regard to *David Levinsky*) "of ghetto Judaism as a castrating force" [15] is internalized and psychologized as the castrating father. In Freud the deepest taboo of Judaism, the taboo against intermarriage, the forbidden lust of the Jew for the Gentile *shiksa*, for

* From the Hebrew *sheques:* "blemish."

the *shiksa* as "the promise of fulfillment,"[16] is rationalized, psychologized, and reinterpreted as the desire for the *mother,* which desire is held taboo by everyone, of course, not just by Jews. The particularist, ritual taboo of the *Jewish* subculture—intermarriage, *connubium*—is reconceptualized (and psychologized) as the universalist, "scientific," anthropological taboo on incest. Another of the tantalizing lures of Jewish Emancipation is thus put to rest in the name of universalist science. Freud, in his ambivalence, could, by means of this conceptual stratagem, remain a Jew and, at the same time, not a Jew. In this way, "being a Jew could develop from a politico-social *circumstance* into a personal, individual problem"[17] (my emphasis), as well as into a universal fate. Thus did Freud seek "hiddenly" to transform a misfortune of history into a universalist science of man. The "Jewish problem"—the ancient *Judenfrage*—had been kicked upstairs.

CHAPTER 6

THE ANCIENT *JUDENFRAGE*

Freud came out of the Jewish Middle Ages only to enter the Jewish middle classes. Entering a highly developed and developing Europe, coming from behind, like Marx—and all the other intellectuals of the nineteenth-century Diaspora—he developed a modernization "complex." The very "backwardness" of *shtetl Yiddishkeit* gave its sons a kind of perspective from behind, *à rebours,* on the civilization of Europe. If you will, a "lead of the retarded" took the form of the "punitive objectivity" of the nonmember. To accept the achievement of Western modernization at its own self-estimation would have been to downgrade themselves. And who enjoys doing that? *Shtetl* ascriptivities, as they prolonged themselves into the Europe of Jewish Emancipation, revealed surprising and embarrassing staying power. What was normal in the *shtetl Gemeinschaft* looked bad in the West. Jewry, in general, was making a "scene" in *Gesellschaft,* and everybody knew it, though few would admit it: the Jews were too ashamed, the liberal Gentiles too "nice." Marx had declared it openly from the start, using it as the fulcrum of his "Marxism." (He was rewarded by being called a "self-hater," a Jewish anti-Semite.)

The problem renews itself again and again, as "Jewish Emancipation" occurs again and again. Freud's critique of the developmental vicissitudes of the sexual instinct in the European modernization process was structurally equivalent to Marx's critique of the proud boast of European "civil society" (as Hegel had rendered it) to have overcome the egoism of bourgeois economic self-interest after its emancipation from feudal controls. Marx unmasked this false universalization, claiming that the state had not "assimilated" these egoistic interests—had not "refined them behind their back," so to speak—into identification with the Common Good of the political community, but that, on the contrary, these individual- and group-particularistic interests were using the "universal" state as a means to their end. The tail was wagging the dog. For Marx, Jewish "pariah capitalism" was "exhibit A" in the failure of the state to "assimilate" bourgeois society, and for him it revealed, in coarse and unmistakable form—more "honestly," so to speak—the very greed that the more "spiritual" Christian businessmen concealed beneath the proprieties and civilities of their economic and social exchanges.

Freud faced in Western Europe, analogously, what Weber calls the "erotic sublimation of sexuality." Instead of seeing in it what Durkheim in Paris and Simmel in Berlin were to see—a social-institutional "transsubstantiation" of the psychological—Freud saw only sentimentality and moral hypocrisy, Western-Christian efforts to refine the irredeemably coarse, a tender-minded "looking the other way." *Freud's critique of the claims for the development of the sexual instinct becomes a metaphor for his critique of Western development generally.* "The coprophilic elements in the [sexual] instinct have proved incompatible with our aesthetic ideas. . . . A considerable proportion of the sadistic elements belonging to the erotic instinct has to be abandoned," he concedes, but, lest we mistake his thrust, he adds:

> All such developmental processes, however, relate only to the upper layers of the complicated structure. The fundamental processes which promote erotic excitation [for Marx read: economic exploitation] remain always the same. Excremental things are all too intimately and inseparably bound up with sexual things; the position of the genital organs—*inter urinas et faeces*—remains the decisive and unchangeable factor. . . . The genitals themselves have not undergone the development of the rest of the human form in the direction of beauty; they have retained their animal cast.[1]

"And so," Freud concludes, "even today love, too, is, *in essence* as animal as it ever was"[2] (my emphasis). Freud, looking at sexual activity in the West (as Marx had looked at economic activity) finds all its social institutionalization to be so much sublimation, so much "superstructural" disguise of coarse "nature" underneath. He asks of his followers that they not be "taken in by" this superstructure, that they not be suckered by appearances. "The basis of all this," Max Weber notes, "is to be found in the naturalism of the Jewish ethical treatment of sexuality."[3] To the economic naturalism of Marx, emergent Western capitalism was mere greed all dressed up in Sunday clothes; to the sexual naturalism of Freud, "love in the Western world" (de Rougemont) is "id" tricked out as "Eros," is like a "Yid" trying to "pass" as a *goy*. This is the fundamental metaphor. Freud finds the sexual instinct in the West "essentially" untransformed, unassimilated. It is stuck between pariah and parvenu much as the Jew, socially, is between pariah and parvenu. Freud is, so to speak, ego—between id on one side and superego (Gentile sociocultural demands) on the other. He warns against assimilation, against "conversion." The id-"Yid" is essentially untransformable (in Jew as in Gentile). One cannot—one must not—replace the id by the superego (the Jew by the Gentile); one can—one should—replace the id by the ego: "Where Id was, there shall Ego be." Freud sets himself a twofold task: to mediate "his own" people from the "darkness" of *Yiddishkeit* to the "enlightenment" of science (ego)—that is, to modernize them—but warning them against going all the way over to the superego (against becoming Gentiles)—that is, to prevent their becoming "civilized" in the Western sense. His other task is to unmask the gentility of the Gentile. Freud, as a transitional figure, a kind of New Moses, will "take apart" the package of the modernization process offered to "his people" by the new Egyptians among whom they sojourn, and separate the modernization process from the (Western-Christian-sublimational) civilizational process. He will use the naturalism of his own subculture as a knife to cut this Western package in two.

In the West, the ascetic ethic of Protestantism was in the process of penetrating, mastering, and transforming both the public world of economic and social intercourse (where one "performed contracts" and "exchanged civilities") and the private world of sexual intercourse. Innerworldly restraint was to be the great instrument of this transformation. Coarse greed and lust were being "gentled." "Love taught him shame, and shame, with love at strife, / Soon taught the sweet civilities," wrote England's seventeenth-century poet laureate John Dryden in *Cymon and Iphigenia* (line 133). The fierce giants of Diaspora intellectual Jewry scorned all this emergent bourgeois-Christian "niceness" as so much hypocrisy, as a lure, ultimately, to conversion to that "pale Galilean" who had taught—so Matthew Arnold was saying—"sweetness and light." The Western-Christian claim to have linked decisively the outer with the inner, to have integrated outer conduct—economic, social, and sexual—with the inwardness of feeling and conviction, was rejected by the descendants of Judaism in *Galut*. Diaspora in the West forced a bitter choice on the emancipated Jewish intelligentsia (ultimately, also, on the Jewish "masses"): either *Yiddishkeit* lacked something and the West had something to offer, or *Yiddishkeit* had something and the West had nothing (essentially) to offer. In the former case, assimilation or conversion was in order, to acquire that "something"; in the latter case, reduction rather than conversion was indicated—that is, an essentially reductive analysis that would strip the apparently "superior" culture of its apparent superiority (thus elevating the apparently "inferior" and marginal subculture). In part, such a "confrontation" of cultures is a special case of the general theme of "the spiritual antagonism," Yvor Winters writes, "between the rising provincial civilization and the richer civilization, . . . an antagonism in which the provincial civilization [read: the subculture of the *shtetl*] met obviously superior cultivation . . . with a more or less typically provincial assertion of moral superiority." * [4]

* We shall return at other places to this "moral" theme in the encounter of Diaspora Jewry with the West. Generically we call it "Hebraism," and its "mission to the West" is to convict its decadent "civilization" of corruption by confronting "their" manners with "our" morals. (Trotsky would later write *Their Morals and Ours.*) This is a version of "the international theme." Susan Sontag notes that "every sensibility is self-

Max Weber, for his part, finds the differences in the Diaspora encounter to be ultimately structural and religious in origin:

> Above all, what was lacking in Judaism was the decisive hall-mark of that inner-worldly type of asceticism which is directed toward the control of this world: an integrated relationship to the world from the point of view of the individual's proof of salvation (*certitudo salutis*), which proof in conduct nurtures all else. Again in this important matter, what was ultimately decisive for Judaism was the pariah character of the religion and the promises of Yahweh. An ascetic management of this world . . . was the very last thing of which a traditionally pious Jew would have thought. He could not think of methodically controlling the present world, which was so topsy-turvy because of Israel's sins, and which could not be set right by any human action but only by some free miracle of God that could not be hastened. . . . The Jew's responsibility was to make peace with this recalcitrancy, while finding contentment if God sent him grace and success in his dealings with the enemies of his people, toward whom he must act soberly and legalistically, in fulfillment of the injunctions of the rabbis. This meant acting toward non-Jews in an objective or impersonal manner, without love and without hate, solely in accordance with what was permissible.[5]

Freud's stance vis-à-vis "this recalcitrancy" of the id is not to recommend its transformation (assimilation) but precisely "to make peace with it." This is Freud's well-known "stoicism," and here we find its non-Greek provenance. Freud the Jew rejected the claims of Protestant alchemy to have turned this base sexuality into the gold of love. Lust, no more than greed, could not be set right by any human action, "but only by some free miracle of God [in which Freud, of course, no longer literally believed] that could not be hastened." [6] The delayed Parousia had caused the Calvinists to retract from the "end of days" the magic of the messianic event —in a kind of reversal of prolepsis—back into the present where it became attenuated into the everyday magic of secular Protestant self-control. Freud was a principled disbeliever in the transformative claims of this Protestant magic; sexuality is better left with a professional marriage broker (*Schadchen*) than to the uplift of a Protestant minister. The *Schadchen* "quite explicitly rated, bargained for, and exchanged all human qualities as if they were commodities which could be given an exact price." [7] Sexual activity, for Freud, remained its old, coarse, recalcitrant

serving to the group that promotes it. Jewish liberalism is a gesture of self-legitimization. . . . The Jews pinned their hopes for integrating into modern society on promoting the moral sense." "Notes on 'Camp,'" in *Against Interpretation and Other Essays* (New York: Farrar, Straus & Giroux, 1966), p. 290.

self. In economic activity, for Marx (until the Revolution comes), selfish greed, despite its sublimated appearance, remains selfish greed. Max Weber's Quakers and Baptists, who believed that "by such practices as their fixed prices and their absolutely reliable business relationships with everyone, unconditionally legal and devoid of cupidity,"[8] they had become "spiritual," who believed, in a word, that by ridding themselves of "Jewish" haggling they had rid themselves of "Jewish" cupidity, were—to Marx—only kidding themselves. Their New Testamentary economic behavior *spiritualiter* barely concealed beneath its decorum the old *carnaliter* of the Old Testamentary double ethic. The cupidity remained essentially the same, despite the "universalism," the fastidiously fixed prices, the vaunted "reliability" (predictability). "I had to laugh at these *goyim* and their politeness, . . ." the character Harry Bogen remarks in *I Can Get It For You Wholesale.* "They act like gentlemen to each other. They're polite all the time so they can be sure one won't screw the other. Well, thank God I didn't need any substitutes for smartness. I didn't have to be polite, except for pleasure."[9] *Dutiful* politeness, universalistic, equable, reliable even-handedness, the belief of the Calvinist in the certifiably religious merit of such economic (as of such sexual) performances does not alter one jot or tittle the rank concupiscence and avarice they serve to conceal. Bourgeois-Protestant love may have eliminated haggling from courtship, as bourgeois-Protestant capitalism eliminates haggling from economic exchange, but sexuality and avarice endure unchanged.

From Solomon Maimon to Normon Podhoretz, from Rahel Varnhagen to Cynthia Ozick, from Marx and Lassalle to Erving Goffman and Harold Garfinkel, from Herzl and Freud to Harold Laski and Lionel Trilling, from Moses Mendelssohn to J. Robert Oppenheimer and Ayn Rand, Gertrude Stein, and Reich I and II (Wilhelm and Charles), one dominating structure of an identical predicament and a shared fate imposes itself upon the consciousness and behavior of the Jewish intellectual in *Galut:* with the advent of Jewish Emancipation, when ghetto walls crumble and the *shtetlach* begin to dissolve, Jewry—like some wide-eyed anthropologist—enters upon a strange world, to explore a strange people observing a strange *halakah* (code). They examine this world in dismay, with wonder, anger, and punitive objectivity. This wonder, this anger, and the vindictive objectivity of the marginal nonmember are recidivist; they continue unabated into our own time because Jewish Emancipation continues into our own time.

CHAPTER 7

SEXUALITY AND CHRISTIANITY: THE REFINING PROCESS

Sublimation "is what Nietzsche calls the transformation of coarse drives into refined ones," writes Karl Jaspers.[1] But sublimation can take place only as a result of *inhibition,* Nietzsche argued, and "this provides a clue to the explanation of the paradox that precisely in Europe's Christian period . . . the sex drive became love (*amour-passion*) as a result of sublimation."[2] This is the bone that stuck in Freud's throat. Christian Europe, the *goyim,* had a corner on "romance." The whole phenomenon of courtship and its rituals, as well as courtesy itself, descended from the feudal court. Freud was deeply ambivalent about this sublimation. Herbert Marcuse would later say what Freud never did—that sublimation *is* repression. The whole program of revolution as derepression would have been abhorrent to Freud. And yet he felt that he himself was coarse, and that Jews were coarse, and that Christian refinement (sublimation) was hypocrisy.

All the Christian deferences to women, all the obliquities and courtesies and cunning delays in gratification *converted* the sex drive into Christian-bourgeois love. Or did it? Was the "conversion" only skin-deep? Freud concedes, though grudgingly, that "the ascetic tendency of Christianity had the effect of raising the psychical value of love in a way that heathen antiquity could never achieve."[3] Freud looked on sublimation, the conversion of the id, much the way he and other Jews looked on the conversion of the "Yid" to Christianity, namely, with considerable scepticism. Much of psychoanalysis can be seen as an elaborate device for catching the refined id *in flagrante delicto.* Like Augustine before him, but with a different "inner meaning," Freud was forever reminding us of the location of our genitals *inter urinas et faeces.* "Everything preceding or following the sexual act," Emil Ludwig writes, "was pretty much of a closed book to Freud."[4] No one ever called Freud "sexy."

I look at it this way: In the eighteenth and nineteenth centuries, the Industrial Revolution under (ultimately) Calvinist auspices took hold of European avarice (one of the "seven deadly sins") and organized it in rational-bureaucratic forms in such a way that avarice was transubstantiated into something else. Marx, using the premodern pariah capitalism of his own people as his model, unmasked the whole thing as disguised greed and egoism. Similarly, feudal Catholicism and, later, bourgeois Protestantism took hold of lust (another of the "seven deadlies") and institutionalized it, in the course of a long sociocultural revolution, into love. Freud, entering the West in the late nineteenth century, using a premodern, coarse, pariah model of the sex drive, proceeds to unmask the whole thing as at best a pious fraud.

Ultimately, the spirit of bourgeois-Christian love—i.e., choice of partner, courtship, leading to monogamous marriage—depends on delayed consummation the way the spirit of bourgeois capitalism depends on delayed consumption. Freud paid scant attention to sexual foreplay. It either maneuvered the partners toward orgasm, or it was perversion. To Freud's *shtetl* puritanism, forepleasure—like courtship, essentially, or courtesy—was a form of roundaboutness, of euphemism. To play with sexual stimulation, to postpone the intense endpleasure of orgasm, was a form of *goyim naches*, of games goyim play, endlessly refining themselves. Freud had a choice here. If the rules of that game genuinely transformed the old coarse "fuck" into something "rare and strange," then he, Freud, was missing out on something. "They" were *experiencing* something he wasn't. He, most of the time, bore a grudge against their claim.

It was another "lie" of "theirs," he felt. In the 1960s the Supreme Court of the United States declared that something *apparently* pornographic (read: coarse) is *really* not pornography if it has "redeeming social value" (where "redemption" can be thought of as "refinement"). To redeem is to save; to save is to refine what is coarse, to give it "meaning," to "make a silk purse out of a sow's ear." To Freud, and to the generality of Diaspora Jewry in nineteenth-century Europe, to become refined—which was what was happening to them—was to become spiritualized. They identified spirituality in the West with refinement, and both with the stigma of "assimilation." No wonder they were of two minds about it. To the Eastern European Jew this was Reform Judaism (covert or overt); and Reform Judaism, in Eastern European conviction, could no more refine the (Orthodox) "Yid" than bourgeois Christianity could refine the (primordial) id.

Max Weber goes to the heart of this animus against sublimation when he argues that the

> ascetic aversion of pious Jews [and, we may add, of certain of their descendants in the era of Jewish Emancipation] toward everything esthetic was *originally* based on the second commandment of the Decalogue. . . . But another important cause of aversion to things esthetic is the purely pedagogic and jussive character of the divine service in the synagogue, even as it was practiced in the Diaspora,

> long before the disruption of the Temple cult. . . . Thus among the Jews the plastic arts, painting, and drama lacked those points of contact with religion which were elsewhere quite normal. This is the reason for the marked diminution of secular lyricism *and especially of the erotic sublimation of sexuality,* when contrasted with the marked sensuality of the earlier Song of Solomon. The basis of all this is to be found in the *naturalism of the Jewish ethical treatment of sexuality.*[5] [My emphasis]

The concept of marrying because one had "fallen in love," Freud's disciple Theodore Reik assures us, was inconceivable to the older Jewish generation in his boyhood Vienna: "Love is to be found only in novels and plays," was their conviction. Love, "which was not considered a necessary condition to marriage within the ghetto and which became so highly valued in the period of the emancipation," [6] was a highly problematic matter to Freud in late nineteenth-century Vienna. "No," Reik says decisively, "love or romance had no place in the Judengasse. Meeting and mating was the Schadchen's (matchmaker's) doing." [7] A whole genre of Jewish wit turns on the ways the *Schadchen* would "mislabel" his product as a broker in the give-and-take of matchmaking. No "individual object choice" is legitimated within the *shtetl* subculture. The love-death linkage of the "romantic love complex" occurred only at the turn of the century, in authors like Arthur Schnitzler.[8] With Jewish Emancipation, there were earlier figures "such as the highly romantic Heinrich Heine. But these were emancipated Jews. Unemancipated Jews even today," writes Ernest van den Haag, "are characterized by a nonesthetic, utilitarian attitude toward the body, whether they are religious or not." [9] Alfred Kazin's parents, van den Haag writes (commenting on Kazin's memoir *A Walker in the City*) "regarded love as a goyish invention," [10] and so, in fact, did Freud—and so, in fact, as it happens, it was.

Eros, of course, means intermarriage. Freud was not about to become the legitimator of assimilation, yet he was being so used twenty years after *The Interpretation of Dreams*. Ludwig Lewisohn would write *Don Juan* in 1923, Ben Hecht *A Jew in Love* in 1931. Whereas Abraham Cahan's concerns in *The Rise of David Levinsky* (1917) had been social and Marxian, "the secular Jewish prophet honored by Hecht and Lewisohn," Leslie Fiedler writes, "is not Marx but Freud. . . . Psychoanalysis seemed to them one more device for mocking the middleclass, one more source for arguments in defense of sexual emancipation." [11] It was also a device for pitting the putative "honesty" of sexuality against the "hypocritical" propriety of bourgeois social decorum. If Hecht's own Freudianism was of the "vulgar" variety, at least one of the preoccupations of his hero Jo Boshere (né Abe Nussbaum) was quintessentially Freudian. Boshere, who had changed his name, who had surrounded his self "with such delicate mannerisms . . . that his personality has almost lost its Semitic flavor," [12] was a Don Juan who delighted for a night or two in his physical conquests, so long as one thing held his interest: "The varying mannerisms with which women surrendered their bodies fascinated him. He studied their disrobings and listened avidly to their first *honest* murmurings of passion. Then their slow return to *planes more polite* was a process which also held his studious eye. For the brief *humanizing* and revelatory phase of sex . . . he felt a deep *social* delight. [Then] Boshere lost most of his interest in copulation" [13] (my emphasis).

Freud disbelieved in romantic love. There is an old Yiddish proverb—"*Zey hobn zikh beybe lib—er zikh un zi aikh:* They are madly in love—he with himself, she with herself" [14]—that expresses his scepticism. For Freud, *courtoisie* is a decoration of sexual intercourse in the same way that courtesy decorates social intercourse. His deepest urge was to strip both of their courtliness. He experienced both as a hypocritical disguise—analogous to Marx's superstructure—that must be stripped away, like any "appearance," exposing the "reality" underneath.

In bourgeois-Western lovemaking, foreplay—"love play"—foreshortens the ritual of courtly love into the space-time requirements of the bourgeois bedroom. Freud and his psychoanalytical heirs make short shrift of the "rules" of courtly love: in the pathos and longing of such love they see the practice of *coitus interruptus.* They see "the courtesy and gentleness, which were the essence of the Courtly attitude, serving as a reaction-formation against underlying sadism. . . . The culture of which Courtly Love was symptomatic," concludes one analyst, "had not achieved full genitality." [15]

Both Marx and Freud unmasked the "sublimation" that was courtly love. Both had a *ressentiment* against it. It was so "refined," so "spiritual," so un-Jewish. The young Leslie Fiedler, commuting daily from Bergen Street in Newark to the Bronx campus of NYU, would carry his "dissent into the classroom itself by writing Marxist interpretations of Courtly Love." [16] Fiedler's *Love and Death in the American Novel* (1966) continues those early "Marxist interpretations" under the auspices of Freudianism. "One senses from the start in the verse of courtly love," he writes, "a desire to mitigate by ritualized and elegant foreplay a final consummation felt as brutal [read: coarse], or else a desire to avoid entirely any degrading conjunction with female flesh." [17]

Love as "an esthetic exhilaration and as a romantic feeling," Ernest van den Haag notes, "never made much of a dent on Jewish attitudes toward the body or toward the opposite sex. Love as 'sweet suffering' was too irrational. If you want her, get her. . . . All forms of courtship which do not end in marriage are seen not as pleasures in themselves, but rather as exploitations, misuses: 'she takes his money,' or 'he is just using her.' " [18] This tradition continues. One senses, for example, that it is with considerable relief that sociologist Peter M. Blau eventually finds a way, in his "Excursus on Love," of translating—as he believes, without residue—the whole "romantic love complex" into the tough-minded, Homansian, utilitarian exchange system.[19]

Courtship is the act of paying court or wooing. It involves the attentions and tendernesses of a man to a woman whom he desires to marry.* Read Freud's deeply beautiful letters courting Martha Bernays from 1882 to 1886: "The Courtship of Sigmund Freud," as it might be called.[20] His *practice* of love far outruns the legitimations available in his subculture. Yet, is it not apostasy to give "their" meanings to his "experiences"? So, with Martha safely in the marriage bed, he "cuts back" to the essentials of ancestral *Yiddishkeit: "Entia non multiplicanda praeter necessitatem."*

It is a claim of this analysis that Freud had considerable awareness of the interrelations among the institutions of Western culture. "Romantic marriage" is one institution, along with the institutions of capitalism and liberal democracy, to which Christianity—especially Protestant Christianity—gave strong religious sanction.[21] Freud sensed, I think, the inner "meaning-nexus" between European "love" or romantic sexual intercourse and European "civil society" or courteous—later, "civil"—social intercourse. In both types of intercourse—sexual and social—distantiations are introduced that are absolutely foreign to earlier, premodern *Gemeinschaft*-types of sociosexual "withness." For three generations in the twelfth and thirteenth centuries troubadours and minnesingers sang of a faithful "love service" to a "high-minded" and exacting lady by a frustrated and sorrowful lover: she does not grant him the amorous "reward" he covets but only approval, reassurance of his worth: "The great lady accepts him as a being worthy of her attention," Herbert Moller writes, "but only at the price of behavioral restraint and refinement of manners, that is, at the price of 'courtois' behavior. As contemporaries put it," he adds, "'courtoisie' is the result of courtly love."[22] The full meaning of this "restraint" is not revealed until the nineteenth century, when the thesis-antithesis dualism of the eighteenth-century Enlightment is "sublated" in Hegel's Enlightenment-romantic synthesis: Christianity, by secularizing itself into refinement, emerges as a "secularized spirituality." "By refining substance into subjectivity," Karl Löwith claims, "Christianity produced a revolutionary reversal in world-history."[23]

* Consider, for example, Longfellow's *Courtship of Miles Standish.*

CHAPTER 8

ROOTING OUT ROUNDABOUTNESS

Even today when Cynthia Ozick writes her story "Envy; or, Yiddish in America," with Edelshtein of Minsk enraged at the American-born sons of suburban Jewry, she depicts assimilation as a seduction to the values of courtly love: "Mutes, Mutations. What right had these boys to spit out the Yiddish that had bred them, and only for the sake of Western Civilization? Edelshtein knew the titles of their Ph.D. theses: literary boys, one was on Sir Gawain and the Green Knight, the other was on the novels of Carson McCullers." [1] And Edelshtein's great rival Ostrover, who has such a good press, whose Yiddish "translates well," and who draws crowds to his poetry readings at the "Y," gets the ultimate put-down: "Ostrover was courtly." [2] Edelshtein in a letter writes: "Please remember that when a goy from Columbus, Ohio, says 'Elijah the Prophet' he is not talking about '*Eliohu hanovi.*' Eliohu is one of us, a *folksmensh,* running around in secondhand clothes.* Theirs is God knows what. The same biblical figure, with exactly the same history, once he puts on a name from King James, COMES OUT A DIFFERENT PERSON." [3]

The late Susan Taubes noted that "the Old Testament has had the benefit of the most sublime spiritualization † through centuries of Christian interpretation." [4] Bourgeois-Christian love is just such a "spiritualization" of coarse sexuality. This literal level is the unspiritual level; it is the coarse, "given" Old Testament. It is like the id, understood "carnally" (*carnaliter*); but, as a "preparation" for the New Testament, it is read "spiritually" (*spiritualiter*). To refine, in psychoanalytic tradition, is to repress, to "aim-inhibit." "The repressed impulse, which was now *unconscious*, was able to find means of discharge and of substitutive gratification," writes Freud, "by circuitous routes and thus to bring the whole repression to nothing." [5] These byways and divagations of lust and rage must be found out in their secret places and exposed to the full light of day and human reason.

* "How could I have explained to Mrs. K," writes Norman Podhoretz, "that wearing a suit from dePinna would for me have been something like the social equivalent of a conversion to Christianity?" *Making It* (New York: Random House, 1967), p. 26.

† As Irwin Edman writes, "more and more cruel and crude appeared the Old Testament in comparison with the New." "Reuben Cohen Enters American Life," *The Menorah Journal*, 12, no. 3 (June–July 1926): 252.

This "Enlightenment" streak in (especially) the early Freudian movement is caught at the full tide of its animus against the embourgeoisement of the Jew by the heroine of Susan Taubes's novel *Divorcing.* Of Sophie Blind's father, Rudolf Landsmann, M.D., a leader of the movement in Budapest, we read:

> "It is wrong to teach a child to say thank you!" Papi always said, raising his index finger if anybody in the family or the maid or the shopkeeper asked her to say thank you. Omama was no exception. Sometimes Papi stopped in the middle of a sentence to correct himself, just as he stopped to correct anybody else. Papi belonged to a movement dedicated to rooting out hypocrisy and roundaboutness whose leader was a man called Freud. When you asked for something you mustn't say, "Do you have . . ." or "Could you give me . . ." or "I would like to ask you . . ." No, there was no getting around Papi; Sophie wouldn't get that piece of chocolate till she said, "Give me . . ." She cried. "Why is it so difficult?" Papi laughed. "I want some chocolate," she said sullenly. "Is that so?" Papi said and walked on, pokerfaced . . . . Her father believed that the discovery of this new science was the most important event in human history; he was doing something that would change all mankind.* [6]

The first Freudian parental generation was at considerable pains to see to it that their children remained untempted by the "forbidden fruit" of the Diaspora. Sublimation, courtesy, romance—none of these had an inner rationale in Freudianism. Sublimation was stopgap, furtive, evasive, hypocritical, roundabout subterfuge. But gradually, as the children of the pioneers began breaking the taboo and discovered *trayf*—"the things that can reach us only through the beautiful circuit and subterfuge of our thought and desire" [7]—enormous inner conflicts were set going and cultural tragedies occurred.

In Berlin, at the time, the circle of Georg Simmel's interests included the handling of precisely such nonkosher stuff as was under Viennese ban. Simmel (1858–1918) explored the *trayf:* salon society, sociability, coquetry, Goethe, discretion, manners, the stranger, conversation, Christian love, tact, social games, (social) parties, hierarchy, the aristocratic motive, faithfulness and gratitude, fashion, adventure, "the esthetic significance of the face" (1901), social importunity,[8] the pathos of ruins. If Freud in Vienna was writing sentences that began, "But if the patient observes the

* See also the magnificently rendered scene on p. 200 of *Divorcing* (see note 6), which ends the following section. It concerns the only patients of her father about whom Sophie liked to hear him talk: two Kafkaesque sisters, the whole of whose lives is exhausted without residue in the sheer exchange of social civilities ("Good morning," "Good-bye," "How are you?" etc.) and sequelae to the civilities—which are more civilities of the same order. Bourgeois-Christian civility (obliquity) here carries the burden of nihilism.

rule [of free association] and so overcomes his reticences. . . ," [9] Simmel in Berlin, intermarried, "emancipated," was interested precisely in the rules of reticence and how *they* could be observed.

Simmel leaves the mainstream of the Diaspora intelligentsia and becomes the "father" of "the phenomenological family," of those Diaspora intellectuals who, sick unto death of unmasking the *goyim,* decide to abstain, for a time, from the *ivresse des grandes profondeurs* in order to take on faith the system of appearances *goyim* take at face and that are constitutive of their everyday lives. The "phenominological family" includes Husserl, Scheler, Landsberg, Dietrich von Hildebrand, Kraus, Max Jacob, the Steins (Edith, Husserl's secretary; and Gertrude, Leo's sister), Berenson, Bergson, Susanne Langer, Wittgenstein, Schütz, Gurvitch, Gustav Ichheiser, and their present-day intellectual heirs: Maurice Natanson, Richard Gilman, Susan Sontag, and Harold Garfinkel. More will be said in another place about *this* "family" of Diaspora intellectuals.*

* In Simmel, the tragedy of his acculturation, which went hand in hand with his (social) assimilation, grounded his brilliant insights into the "Tragödie der Kultur." In this tragedy, the autonomy of the cultural, of the stockpile of Western "objective spirit"—including cultural appearances—when assimilated as "Bildung," ends by converting the cultural aspirant to the exigencies of its own symbolic forms. See "Theory and Tragedy of Culture," in Rudolph H. Weingartner, *Experience and Culture: The Philosophy of Georg Simmel* (Middletown, Conn.: Wesleyan University Press, 1962), pp. 71–84.

CHAPTER 9

THE TEMPTATION SCENE

Freud in Vienna tries mightily to remain neutral between his Gentile Swiss followers under Jung, on the one hand, and Karl Abraham of the Berlin Psychoanalytic Society on the other. But clearly he regards Abraham as "one of our own" and Jung and the Swiss as "guests" of the movement whom he needs but suspects. With the publication in 1965 of the Freud-Abraham letters all this was confirmed, despite the fact that some letters were omitted and most were abridged—"censored, to put it less politely," [1] Susan Sontag writes—for, as the editors say, "reasons of discretion." [2] The psychoanalytic movement was always discreet in public, in the "civil society" of the general culture. Still, we learn much. Abraham has sensed deviationism among the Swiss and desires to bring it into the open. Freud urges Abraham to exercise "courtesy" toward Jung, and asks him to

> please be tolerant and do not forget that it is really easier for you than it is for Jung to follow my ideas, for in the first place you are completely independent, and then you are closer to my intellectual constitution because of racial kinship, while he as a Christian and a pastor's son finds his way to me only against great inner resistances. His association *with us* is the more valuable for that. I nearly said that it was only by his appearance on the scene that psychoanalysis escaped the danger of becoming a Jewish national affair. I hope you will do as I ask.[3] [My emphasis]

Gentile proselytes were extremely important to Freud for another reason: only they could shore up his self-doubts that psychoanalysis might not be, as its adherents claimed, a "science" at all (having discovered no new truth) but a social-cultural movement of Diaspora Jews who, as social pariahs, only dared *say* what Gentiles had *known* all along but, due to their gentility, had been unwilling or unable to mention. If the latter should be the case, psychoanalysis reduces in the end to what Freud half-feared it might be: a counterculture adversary to the bourgeois-Christian ethos of civility and respectability. The Abraham letters are valuable even in censored form, for with Abraham, unlike with Ernest Jones, as

Sontag notes, "Freud is able, without embarrassment, to refer to his sense of his Jewishness and the special vantage-point he felt it gave, and also to confide his fears that, without adherents among the *goyim* ['the people'], psychoanalysis would be just 'a Jewish science' and a casualty of anti-Semitism." [4]

Abraham, too, notes the ethnic kinship he feels with Freud, and, after identifying the "completely Talmudic" technique of apposition of a paragraph in Freud's book on wit which "strangely attracted" him, he remarks the staying power of pre-Emancipation modes of thought. "After all, our Talmudic way of thinking cannot disappear just like that." [5] By July 1908 Abraham writes that "Jung seems to be reverting to his former spiritualistic inclinations. But please keep this between ourselves." [6] Freud replies by again urging tolerance, since "on the whole it is easier for us Jews, as we lack the mystical element," [7] but reassures Abraham: "May I say that it is consanguineous traits that attract me to you? We understand each other." But still, Abraham should have "shown greater delicacy of feeling" by keeping his quarrel with Jung in a latent state. Freud speculates that "the suppressed anti-Semitism of the Swiss" is deflected from himself to Abraham, and assures Abraham that if he, Freud, had not been Jewish, his "innovations would have met with far less resistance." [8]

Here we come to an important matter, essential for the understanding of post-Emancipation intellectual Jewry and the kinds of ideology it generated (Marxism, Zionism, Freudianism): this is the conviction, as formulated by a Viennese contemporary of Freud, Theodor Herzl, that—on the whole—Gentiles come in two and only two varieties, namely, *verschamte und unverschamte Antisemiten*, overt and covert anti-Semites.[9] Any wide reading in Freud puts it beyond doubt that he too shared this conviction of the founder of Zionism, that he believed, as Bakan puts it, "that anti-Semitism was practically ubiquitous *in either latent or manifest form*" [10] (my emphasis). On November 7, 1938, in England, Freud received three visitors (Joseph Leftwich, I. N. Steinberg, and Jacob Meitlis) and told them: "Basically, *all are anti-Semites. They are everywhere*. Frequently anti-Semitism is latent and hidden, but it is there. Naturally, there are exceptions. . . .* But the broad masses are anti-Semitic here as everywhere" [11] (my emphasis). In the broad masses everywhere, as in the Polish and Ukranian peasantry of the pale, anti-Semitism is overt and takes the form of pogroms; in the middle classes, anti-Semitism is covert and takes the form of politeness. This is one root (there are others, equally important) of the ethnic-specific animus of Freud and Eastern European Jewry generally against Gentile civility: they *define it* as a (middle-class) mask concealing anti-Semitism. They define it as *refined* anti-Semitism, polite anti-Semitism, as a "reaction-formation" against the coarse anti-

* An exception Freud cited here was the Catholic Count Heinrich Coudenhove-Calergi.—J.M.C.

Semitic or hostile component of their own (Gentile) id (which defense against socially unacceptable anti-Semitism sometimes "refines" it all the way over into its opposite, that ideal mask for anti-Semitism, called "philo-Semitism"). And situations defined as real are real in their consequences. Thus we have Freud defining the resistance of the Swiss contingent to psychoanalysis as "suppressed anti-Semitism." Note that he chooses his words carefully: "suppressed" not "repressed" anti-Semitism —that is, an anti-Semitism consciously held in check by their . . . what? Perhaps prudence, fear, bourgeois-Christian "niceness," . . . what you will.

But the "Zurichers" took a long time performing their apostasy, and Freud hesitated to make the break open and irreparable (then only Jones would remain of the original Gentile members *). "If Jung wishes, he can be of extraordinary service to *our* cause † and I fully understand your wish to keep him" (my emphasis), Abraham writes Freud.[12] But the Jung-Abraham differences continue, and Freud hates to be forced to take sides openly: "Just because I get on most easily with you (and also with our colleague Ferenczi of Budapest)," he confesses, "I feel it incumbent on me not to concede too much to racial preference and therefore neglect the more alien Aryan." [13] (Twenty-six years later, in 1934, with the beginnings of Nazism looming, he writes Oskar Pfister: "Switzerland is not one of the hospitable countries. There has been little occasion for me to change my opinion of human nature, particularly the Christian Aryan variety." [14])

Then, once more, the troubling matter of formulating his differences with the "alien Aryan" Swiss comes up. After a visit from Eugen Bleuler, professor of psychiatry at the University of Zurich, and his wife, who spend a Friday evening with the Freuds, Freud writes that they both were "very kind, insofar as his unapproachability and her affectation permit. . . . They both tried to take me by storm and persuade me that I should not *talk of* "sexuality," but should find *another name for* what does not coincide with sexuality in the popular sense. All resistance and misunderstandings would then cease. I replied," Freud writes Abraham, "that I had no use for such household remedies" [15] (my emphasis). It is all there: the bourgeois, polite, social formality ("his unapproachability"), the hypocrisy ("her affectation"), the attempt of the bourgeois Gentile to "bribe" him to clean up his coarse language and settle on a polite euphemism for his "coarse Galatea," sexuality. This *Ostjude* would not convert (i.e., refine). He would remain unhousebroken. When four months after this "temptation scene" with Bleuler, in his second letter to Pastor Pfister (February 9, 1909), Freud remarks, almost parenthetically, that "you are aware that for us the term 'sex' includes what you in your pas-

* And Jones had "entered" the circle through his marriage to a Jewish woman.

† Note that Freud in his reply reassures Abraham by telling him that Jung "adheres unreservedly to *the* cause" (my emphasis). *A Psycho-Analytic Dialogue* (see note 1), p. 5.—J.M.C.

toral work call love, and is certainly not restricted to the *crude* pleasure of the senses" (my emphasis), the issue of sheer terminology becomes all the more revealing.[16] But suppose Bleuler had been right, suppose a "name change" would have made *all* the difference between resistance and acceptation? I am absolutely convinced, using all the *Verstehen* I can corral, that Freud experienced this visit and Bleuler's proposal as an invitation to a "sell-out," that he experienced it subjectively as an act of proselytization—religious proselytization: they were offering to perform rhinoplastic surgery on his id (the "sexuality" he discovered behind symptoms). What he *heard* from these awfully "kind" *goyim* was: "Only change your name, and we'll accept you. Let us do a nose-job on you, then we'll accept you [i.e., your id theory, your "Yid"]—please, that's all we ask, and it isn't much, really, is it?"

Freud could have said all or nearly all he had to say without creating trouble for himself, Stefan Zweig writes,

> had he but been willing to draft his genealogy of the sexual life in more cautious, roundabout, non-committal phraseology. Had he been prepared to hang a verbal fig-leaf in front of his indelicate convictions . . . they could have smuggled themselves into recognition without attracting disagreeable attention. It might have even sufficed had he been willing . . . to use instead of the blunt term "libido" the politer epithet "Eros" or "love." . . . But Freud, scorning the minor courtesies, and inspired with a detestation for half-measures, used the plainest possible words and would consent to no circumlocutions.[17]

Freud's proud and moving refusal was, *literally*, a refusal to apostatize from *Yiddishkeit* (and from the functional equivalents, in *Galut*, of *Yiddishkeit*). It is precisely here that we find the "inner link" between the earlier Freud and the later Freud of the "metapsychological" works of 1928 and 1930—*The Future of an Illusion* and *Civilization and Its Discontents*. Freud's sexual "fundamentalism" is legitimated by a religious fundamentalism. This latter indicts as dishonest Protestantism's—and, for that matter, Reform Judaism's—sublimation of Jehovah into a God without thunder. Freud writes,

> Where questions of religion are concerned, people are guilty of every possible kind of insincerity and intellectual misdemeanor. Philosophers stretch the meaning of words until they retain scarcely anything of their original sense; by calling "God" some vague abstraction which they have created for themselves, they pose as deists, as believers, before the world; they may even pride themselves on having attained a higher and purer idea of God, although their God

> is nothing but an insubstantial shadow and no longer the mighty personality of religious doctrine." * [18]

The id may not make itself acceptable by refining itself, nor must the Old Testamentary God by reforming Himself, nor should psychoanalysts by assimilating themselves.

It is only in this context that Freud's reaction to the death of Alfred Adler becomes intelligible. Adler had been born in the Viennese suburb of Penzing and raised largely among Gentiles. Freud's family, in moving from Freiberg to Vienna's ghetto district of Leopoldstadt (when he was four), had come down in the world. In Leopoldstadt Freud, unlike Adler, was socialized among other Jews, as a member of a minority group. Freud's son Martin writes that "the Jews who lived in Leopoldstadt"—in contrast, presumably, to Jews who lived in suburbs like Penzing—"were not of the best type. . . . But rents were low in this district and my father's family circumstances were poor." [19] When Adler died in May 1936 while on a lecture tour in Scotland, Arnold Zweig wrote Freud that he was touched and saddened by the news of Adler's sudden death. Freud wrote back on June 22—this letter is omitted from *The Letters of Sigmund Freud*—as follows: "I don't understand your sympathy for Adler. For a Jew boy out of a Viennese suburb a death in Aberdeen is an unheard-of career in itself and a proof of how far he had got on.† The world really rewarded him richly for his service in having contradicted psychoanalysis." [20] This letter has shocked the reading public who mistakenly find anti-Semitism in it (exactly as they find it, equally mistakenly, in Marx). But Freud is here attacking assimilation, which is to say, apostasy; or, to reverse this, Freud is attacking Adler's apostasy from *Yiddishkeit*, which is to say, his assimilation. He sees Adler as having yielded (in his break with classical psychoanalysis) to precisely those temptations the smiling Bleulers had dangled before him that Friday night long ago in Vienna. In Freud's view, Adler had traded fidelity to truth and to his own true identity for social acceptance among the *goyim*. He made the truth polite; he manicured the id in the same way he polished the "Yid," and "the world rewarded him richly." (For "the world" we must read "the *goyim*," just as in Freud's 1914 letter to Abraham—a letter also omitted, this time from the Freud-Abraham letters—where he hesitates to contradict Abraham's sus-

* We can see from this statement of Freud how wide of the mark the usually accurate Cynthia Ozick is, when, in "The Hole Birth Catalog," she declares that "Freud's *Selbsthasse* was of a piece with his hatred for his inherited faith. He despised Judaism . . . ; [he lacked] the courage of connection." *Ms.*, 1, no. 4 (Oct. 1972): 59, 60. Later, this slur becomes "that *apikoros* Sigmund Freud," in "Usurpation," *Esquire* 81, no. 5 (May 1974): 173.

† Rank's biographer, Dr. Jessie Taft, notes "Dr. Jones's careful inclusion"—(in vol. 2 of *Life and Work* [1955—see note 18 for other details], p. 160)—"of the fact that 'Rank came from a distinctly lower stratum than the others' " in the psychoanalytic movement. Jessie Taft, *Otto Rank: A Biographical Study* (New York: Pelican Press, 1958), p. 8—J.M.C.

picions of the Swiss Gentile Pfister inasmuch as Abraham had been so right before on Jung: "I have been warned against contradicting you in the judgment of the people." * [21]) The official historiography of both Marxism and Freudianism is consistently reformist: Bernstein refines Marx as Jones refines Freud (Jones's *Life and Work* is a devotional work). So to refine them, to "censor" them, is precisely to deny the social coarseness of these conscious pariahs and their coarse ideas, a coarseness to which they clung with religious fidelity because it alone was warranty against their embourgeoisement, their becoming respectable. Yet it has happened. In a 1971 *New York Times Magazine* piece on Alfred Adler, for example, in which Freud's letter (see above) to Zweig on Adler's death is quoted, Freud's reference to Adler as "a *Jew boy* out of a Viennese suburb" is bowdlerized into " a *Jewish boy* . . ." [22] (my emphasis).

Ease up on Jung, Freud again pleads with Abraham in 1909: "Our Aryan comrades are really completely indispensable to us, otherwise psycho-analysis would succumb to anti-Semitism." [23] By 1910 he writes that "our cause is going very well, and is no longer restricted to my four eyes only." †[24] Freud was suffering a version of the particularism-universalism dilemma that the post-Emancipation intelligentsia experienced: if this "evangel" (psychoanalysis) is accepted by the *goyim*, that proves that it is universally true; but if it is universally true, it is no longer "mine" or "ours." Like the Judaism that Paul diasporated among the *goyim*, it was universalized, upgraded, "beautified" with the help of Hellenism. But by then it no longer belonged to "us"; it was "theirs"—and, in fact, in that "spiritual" mirror we looked rather bad and carnal ("the letter against the spirit"). Freud did not want psychoanalysis to remain an in-group, intraethnic "secret" for "four eyes only." Yet he knew "in his heart" that, as it spread among the "nice" bourgeois-Christian *goyim*, it would be cleaned up. It would assimilate. "But not while I'm alive," he thought (he "must have" thought).

When Jung finally seceded from the psychoanalytic movement, all Freud's secret self-doubt was awakened—not his fear of anti-Semitism, but his personal fear that his movement might be, in fact, not a scientific but an ethnic, minority movement and hence, understandably, without much power to convert members of the bourgeois-Christian majority or to hold them after winning them over. Ernest Jones told J. W. Burrow that "after Jung's defection Freud never really trusted a Gentile again." [25] "I was struck," Freud writes to Abraham, "by the complete analogy that

* Of course, "The people" hardly carries the thrust of Freud's meaning. He intended something considerably less appetizing. E.g., "*A goy bleibt a goy*" means "Once an anti-Semite, always an anti-Semite." See Leo Rosten, *The Joys of Yiddish* (New York: McGraw-Hill, 1968), p 142.—J.M.C.

† The editors of the volume in which this letter appears inform us that the then-current German saying, originally from the Hebrew, was that a secret should be restricted "to four eyes only." Abraham and Freud, eds., *A Psycho-Analytic Dialogue* (see note 1), p. 92, n. 1.

can be drawn between the first running away from the discovery of sexuality behind the neuroses by Breuer and the latest one by Jung"; Freud then quickly draws the startling conclusion: "That makes it the more certain that this is the core of psychoanalysis." [26] But Freud knows that this observation cuts both ways: if the *opposition* ("resistance") to psychoanalysis on the part of the Swiss stems from sociology-of-knowledge factors such as their religion and ethnicity, is not the *advocacy* of psychoanalysis correspondingly particularistic, does it not stem from the same sociology-of-knowledge factors? To be evenhanded, one should ask whether the "sanctimonious Jung and his disciples" [27] (as Freud labeled the apostates) have not a right to their sanctimony equal to the right of Freud and his disciples to their unmasking of sanctimoniousness. But the inexorable logic of the meaning of each Gentile defection was not lost on Freud: it put in increasing jeopardy the plausibility of the claim of psychoanalysis to be a universally valid science and exposed it both to the charge of "vulgar" anti-Semites that it was a "Jewish science" and to the scientific explorations of sociologists and historians of ideas and culture with an interest in subcultural and countercultural movements.

The dilemma bugging Freud despite all his cocksureness, the dilemma underlying the question of whether psychoanalysis was to be considered a cultural movement like Marxism (Marx, after all, had decked out his *Weltanschauung* in the pompous scientificality of "scientific socialism") or a scientific enterprise, boiled down to the following: had Freud *seen* something others had not seen, or was he *saying* something others saw but would not say?

"For Feuerbach," Karl Löwith writes, "the fundamental exponent of sensuous-natural corporeality is that organ which is not mentioned by name in polite society, although by nature it has great significance in the history of the world: the natural sexuality of man." * [28] Was Freud revealing a secret of nature, or was he breaking a secret of polite society? Was Freud being truthful, or being vulgar? Odd as it may seem, Freud himself, I think, was never *really* sure of the answer. Why not? In part, because he never clearly formulated the question.

In his "Resistance to the Systematic Study of Multiple Discoveries in Science," Robert K. Merton draws an obvious parallel with the resistance to psychoanalysis when, he writes—adopting without cavil the Freudians' version of their own history: "When amply available facts, having far-reaching theoretical implications, were experienced as † unedifying or unsavory, ignoble or trivial and so were conscientiously

* After Hegel's synthesis, Löwith notes, Feuerbach's "massive sensualism" must have seemed a step backward, a "barbarization of thought." *From Hegel to Nietzsche* (see note 28), p. 80.

† Note the facile positivism Merton unexpectably falls into here: on one side we have the ample, available, pure social facts, waiting only to be "registered" on some indifferent sensorium; on the other side we have experience with its subjective value-bias for or against these autonomous facts (in this case, against).—J.M.C.

ignored. It is a little like psychologists having once largely ignored sexuality because it was not a subject fit for polite society. . . . A gentleman would pass by in silence." [29] Again, the issue is fudged: did the psychologists "largely ignore" what they already knew? Or were they "ignorant" of what they refused to know? What was the inner thrust of psychoanalysis: to *cherchez les faits*? or to *épatez les bourgeois*? to see a scientific fact or to create a social "scene"? to see human nature or to change Western society? to explore truth or to create meaning? The Jew of Emancipation (writes Howard Brotz), having deserted the synagogue but not being socially accepted by non-Jews, lived "in a kind of *demi-monde* with other Jews of his type. . . . The compensation was that their thought was uncontrolled, particularly by such social demands as a gentlemanly code. They were free to develop . . . psychoanalysis." [30] How is the lifting of the "social demands" of this "code" related to the content of psychoanalysis?

CHAPTER 10

FREUD'S JEWISHNESS

Many students of Freud have tackled the question of Freud's "Jewishness." The WASP philo-Semite (think of Edmund Wilson on Marx in *To the Finland Station,* for example) usually begins talking about Old Testament prophets in their lonely crusade against corruption and hypocrisy. Philip Rieff and Lionel Trilling transform this Jewish prophetism into a psychological moralism in their versions of Freud. Rieff, for example, considers him an ascetic, psychological Jew, with an "animus" against Catholicism,[1] whose objective, like Hannibal's, was "to bring down the mighty Romes of our ascetic civilization." [2] The "Semitic mystique" of this "great Jew manqué" was "an élitist mystique by which he turned an objective disadvantage into a subjective advantage." [3] This is all true, but too much lonely psychologism-prophetism, and too much French.

We learn much more about Freud's Jewishness if we turn to a product of the Bloch Publishing Company, Earl A. Grollman's *Judaism in Sigmund Freud's World* (1965). We would learn a good deal about post-Emancipation Jewish intellectual prophets if we were to take our cue from the recent scholarship on Old Testament prophetism. Studies show that if the Israelitish prophets were not exactly "company boys," they were nevertheless a good deal closer to the Jewish community than their reputation would lead us to believe.[4] Grollman, for example, suggests that the social location of Freud's prophetism, the "essence of his Jewishness," was his *convivium* with other Jews. *Yiddishkeit* is "life-is-with-people"—a social and sociological, and not primarily a psychological-moral, phenomenon. (The same applies, of course, to *"Irishkeit," Goyishkeit,"* etc.) Grollman speaks of Freud's "community activities with other Jews":

> Many of his important theories were delivered before the Fraternity of Jewish students and the B'nai B'rith organization. Most of the colleagues in his movement were Jewish, including Alfred Adler, Wilhelm Stekel, Max Kahane, Rudolph Loewenstein, Barbara Low, Van d'Chys, Sandor Ferenczi, A. A. Brill, Otto Rank, Paul Federn, Joseph Breuer, A. J. Storfer, Wilhelm Fliess and Theodor Reik. But whatever the reasons—historical, sociological,—group bonds did provide a warm shelter from the outside world. In social relations

> with other Jews, *informality and familiarity* formed a kind of inner security, a "we-feeling," illustrated even by the selection of jokes and stories recounted within the group. It is what Freud called "the clear awareness of an inner identity, the secret of the same inner construction." [5] [My emphasis]

If Jews are, as Max Weber observed that they were, "a ritually segregated guest people (pariah people)," [6] "a distinctive hereditary social group lacking autonomous political organization and characterized by prohibitions against commensality and intermarriage originally founded upon magical, tabooistic, and ritual injunctions," [7] then they remain faithful members of the community of *Yiddishkeit* even after Emancipation to the degree that they live their social lives among "their own," avoiding—consciously or unconsciously—commensality, connubium, and convivium with the *goyim*. The post-Emancipation embourgeoisement of the Jewish community, its life in the Euro-American *Gesellschaften,* forced their premodern identity to go psychologically "underground." Emancipation is at the root of the moral "Marranoism" that even "secular Jewish intellectuals," from Freud to present day figures like Harvard sociologist Daniel Bell, are constrained to practice. Even in the "universal otherhood" (the *societal* community of the *goyim*), Jews can recognize the "tribal brotherhood" of their lost convivium. "I was born in *galut* and I accept—now gladly, though once in pain—the double burden and the double pleasure of my self-consciousness,* the outward life of an American and the inward secret of the Jew," writes Bell. "I walk with this sign as a frontlet between my eyes, and it is as visible to some secret others as their sign is to me." [8] The American "outward" life, the "inward secret" of the Jew as "sign" between the eyes visible only to "some secret others" (presumably other Jews), etc., etc.: this is pretty heady stuff from a secular Jewish intellectual—a Harvard sociologist—in late twentieth century! But it is perfectly understandable as an account of the way the structural differentiation involved in the Emancipation-modernization process is *experienced* by an articulate member of the second generation of Eastern European Jewry. This differentiation is experienced, social-psychologically, as doubleness, as "the double burden and the double pleasure" of "self-consciousness," of "alienation." The Diaspora prescription runs: Be a man in the street, a Jew at home. The old unitary Jewish ethnic solidarity prolongs itself in *Galut,* but as a private experience sharable only with others who have the same "inner construction." Sometimes, *in partibus infidelium,* it is "magically," uncannily revived: in the very midst of the cool civil nexus that binds the *goyim* into their

* "Self-consciousness has become the humility of the Jews," Sonya Rudikoff notes in "Jewishness and the Younger Intellectuals: A Symposium," *Commentary* 31, no. 4 (April 1961): 352.—J.M.C.

solidarity of the surface, in the very heart of the sociable *Gesellschaft,* across a crowded room, you "know" that "somehow" you share a primordial solidarity of the depths. "I believe the links holding Jews together—in the words of Edmund Burke," writes Jacob L. Talmon, "to be as invisible as air and as strong as the heaviest chains, and the Jewish ingredient to be as imperceptible to the senses yet as effective in results as vital energy itself." [9] This isn't Henry Ford talking, come back to life, retooling the old *"Protocols of the Elders of Zion"* for another go-round. It is Professor Talmon, of Hebrew University, Jerusalem, trying to locate and define the staying power of an "uncanny" premodern nexus.[10]

Almost forty years earlier Freud, in a speech prepared for delivery at the B'nai B'rith Lodge in Vienna, explained his early joining of that group as the "irresistible" attraction, for him, of Judaism and Jews, of the "many dark emotional forces, all the more potent for being so hard to group in words, as well as the clear consciousness of our inner identity, the uncanny intimacy that comes from the same psychic structure [*die Heimlichkeit der gleichen seelischen Konstruktion*]." [11] The most common translation of *Heimlichkeit* in the literature of psychoanalysis is "the uncanny." In 1919, Freud wrote a thirty-nine-page paper entitled "The 'Uncanny' " [12] which exactly catches the psychological coefficient of the ambiguous sociological solidarity experienced by Jews in the modernizing period of the Emancipation—namely, an unfamiliar familiarity, an open secret, an "us-in-the-midst-of-them" uncanniness.

Everybody knows that Freud—and Bell and Talmon after him—are not talking of Judaism in some religious denominational sense (which is the only culturally legitmate—that is, respectable—definition of religious identity the West supplies). What is most inward in their Jewish self-definitions is precisely what cannot become outward and legitimately Anglo-American, namely, the particularist inwardness of the ethnic nexus. The Western value system refuses to legitimate publicly this primordial ethnic tie as ethnic tie. (As exotica, yes, it has cultural rights.) Hence its stubborn, residual reality is forced "underground," and, when it travels aboveground, it is forced to assume the fictive identity of a denominational religion (Conservative Judaism serves this function in America).* The Eastern European ethnic-"tribal" identity dissolves only when, as, and if the social structural milieux that maintain its plausibility dissolve. In the meantime, the rites of segregation, the magically derived taboos on connubium, commensalism, and convivium—listed in the order of their staying power—are more or less observed in *Galut.* In the meantime, Jews join the Vienna Lodge of B'nai B'rith (like Freud) or give lectures before the Jewish Graduate Society at Columbia or Hillel at Harvard and publish them in the American Jewish Committee's *Commentary* magazine (like

* See Marshall Sklare's analysis on p. 205.

Bell). In the meantime, Jews tend to marry other Jews, eat with other Jews, live among other Jews, socialize with other Jews.

Sociological studies indicate that this pattern continues to be the case. In measuring the relative degree of residential concentration of the major socioreligious groups in the United States, for example, Gerhard Lenski finds that while white Protestants rank with Catholics as the most widely scattered and the least concentrated, Jews and black Protestants are the most concentrated. "The fact that the coefficient for the Jewish group [.39] was even higher than for the Negro Protestants [.37] is especially remarkable," Lenski writes of this finding, "since Negroes are so severely limited in their choice of residential areas both by finances and by out-group hostility. . . . One can only conclude that the magnitude of the coefficient is one more indication of the strength of the communal spirit [among Jews]." [13]

If this is so in America in the latter half of the twentieth century, it was all the more so in Freud's Europe at the end of the nineteenth century. Jews, whatever their degree of occupational and cultural assimilation, lived—that is, socialized—apart from Gentiles. Social interaction on both sides of the Jewish-Gentile line took place with one's "own kind." Social cleavage persisted. This is the "Jewishness" into which Freud and other secular Jewish intellectuals were socialized. In twenty years (circa 1900) in his father's assimilated Berlin house, according to Gershom Scholem, the authority on Jewish mysticism, "he never met a non-Jew. The paradoxical coexistence of assimilation with social apartness seems to have struck him early." [14] It was this paradox of social apartness, of having no crosscutting social ties with the Gentile community, that encouraged Freud's audacity. When he lobbed psychoanalysis up over the social barricades of his Jewish enclave and into the precincts of the Gentile, opposition was inevitable. Social cleavage had preceded intellectual cleavage. "One of the reasons that Jews have been a major focal point of conflict," writes the author of the Coleman Report, "is that there have seldom been cross-cutting lines of cleavage which tied various segments of them to other persons in society." [15]

Freud preferred the company of other Jews. If, as Nathan Rotenstreich notes, "a Jew is a Jew when he is with other Jews," [16] then Freud remained a fairly full-time "observant" Jew. Freud's Jewishness was the company he kept.

CHAPTER 11

THE LOCUS OF FREUD'S ORIGINALITY

> [Freud] is, one keeps forgetting, the great liberator and therapist of speech.
>
> Steven Marcus [1]

Freud was at once proud and deeply troubled by the fact that it was he, a Jew, who had discovered the sexual etiology of the neuroses. He used this ambivalence effectively. Defending psychoanalysis against its enemies in his 1925 paper "The Resistances to Psychoanalysis," he concludes by saying, "Finally, with all reserve, the question may be raised whether the personality of the present writer as a Jew who had never sought to disguise the fact that he is a Jew may not have had a share in provoking the antipathy of his environment to psychoanalysis." One might expect Freud at this point to consider such a charge (which, in vulgar form, ran "psychoanalysis is a Jewish science") beneath contempt and to refuse even to reply. Instead, he goes on as follows: "Nor is it perhaps entirely a matter of chance that the first *advocate* of psychoanalysis was a Jew. To *profess belief* in this new theory called for a certain degree of readiness to accept a position of solitary opposition—a position," he concludes, "with which no one is more familiar than a Jew" [2] (my emphasis). Note that Freud here does not link the content of psychoanalytical theory to the fact of his Jewishness, but rather connects his readiness to "advocate" and "profess belief in" it to his Jewishness. The Jew, being a social pariah, stands, in a sense, outside "the condition of cultural hypocrisy" that prevents "the *ventilation* of the question" [3] of sexuality (my emphasis). For if psychoanalysis offends men's narcissism by its theory of the power of the unconscious over the conscious ego,[4] and if its theory of infantile sexual life "hurt every single person at the tenderest point of his own psychical development"—namely, in their private fantasies of their sexually innocent (asexual) childhood—then "by its theory of the instincts psychoanalysis offended the feelings of individuals insofar as they regarded themselves as members of the *social* community" [5] (my emphasis). The Jew, as a nonmember of such a community, and thus immune to its sanctions, could dare to be unrespectable. Freud, when he first professed the theory of sexuality, found himself, as Jones notes, "in increasing opposition to his 'respectable' colleagues and seniors." [6]

Freud was disturbed as well as proud that it was he, a Jew, who had discovered the sexual etiology of neurosis, for the following reason: it opened up the whole troubling question of his originality. Was he the first to *discover* this sexual etiology, or the first to publicly *mention* it? In a word, behind the question of Freud's scientific priority lies a prior question, which can be put as follows: Was he the first to *see* something or the first to *say* something? These are two very different kinds of priorities. In the former, a scientific discovery in the traditional sense has occurred. In the latter case, a sociocultural breakthrough has occurred (if you will, a "social invention" rather than a "scientific discovery"). If psychoanalysis is the former kind of discovery, it was made by a scientist who happened to be a Jew; but if psychoanalysis is the latter kind of event, it belongs to the history of society, not of science, and it will have been "no accident" that a social pariah was the first to "mention the unmentionable." Which was it: scientific discovery or social breakthrough? *

Freud broaches this "touchy" matter publicly and explicitly as early as 1914 in his paper "On the History of the Psychoanalytic Movement," in which he discloses the parentage of "this scandalous idea" of the sexual etiology of the neuroses [7] which provoked the reaction of "distaste and repudiation." [8] He had consoled himself for the bad reception of his idea by the thought that, anyway, it was a "new and original idea. But, one day," he recounts, "certain memories collected in my mind which disturbed this pleasing notion. . . . The idea for which I was being made responsible had by no means originated with me" but had been imparted to him by no less than three people whose opinion had commanded his highest respect: Breuer, Charcot, and Chrobak.[9]

Somewhere between 1881 and 1883, while Freud was walking with Breuer in Vienna, the husband of a patient came up to Breuer and spoke to him privately. Breuer remarked to Freud as they resumed their walk that "these things are always *secrets d'alcove!*" Freud continues: "Astonished, I asked him what he meant, and he answered by telling me the meaning of the word '*alcove*' (marriage-bed), for he did not realize how extraordinary his remark had seemed to me." † [10] Note in this remark the word "secret" and the fact that the information is conveyed by Breuer to

* A parallel exists to the sexual etiology problem: Was Freud's "discovery" of the "significance" of everyday slips of the tongue to be viewed as scientific acuity? Or as social deviance that broke the "gentleman's agreement" of the *goyim* to indulge, in Kenneth Minogue's words, "in a polite conspiracy to accept forgetfulness and slips of the tongue as insignificant accidents"? Kenneth R. Minogue, *The Liberal Mind* (New York: Vintage, 1968), p. 120.

† Breuer, a "respectable" member of the Jewish professional class in Vienna, could still write twenty-five years later, "I confess that plunging into sexuality in theory and practice is not to my taste," but adds, the Freudian "revolution" having intervened: "But what have my taste and my feeling about what is seemly and what is unseemly to do with the question of what is true?" Letter to Auguste Florel, quoted in Lucy Freeman, *The Story of Anna O* (New York: Walker, 1972), p. 192.

Freud by means of a metonym—"marriage-bed" *stands for* "sex problem" —and that this euphemism is itself *in French,* the language of the sexual and social class secrets (as though German were too "respectable" a language for "forbidden" things).

The second time Freud heard the sexual etiology idea mentioned was in 1885, while Charcot was explaining certain neurotic symptoms of a female patient to Brouardel: *"Mais, dans des cas pareils c'est toujours la chose génitale, toujours . . . toujours . . . toujours."* As he said this, Freud reports, Charcot hugged himself animatedly, "jumping up and down in his own characteristic lively way. . . . I know that for one second I was almost paralyzed with amazement and said to myself, 'Well, but if he *knows* that, why does he never *say* so?' But the impression was soon forgotten" [11] (my emphasis).* (In the light of such testimony from Freud, we see how precisely wide of the mark is the easy assertion of Susan Sontag that "the project of Freud and the early pioneers of psychoanalysis was to *see* something that had not been seen before (because it was not known to be there" [12] [Sontag's emphasis]. Freud thus undergoes a triple "amazement" upon hearing Charcot's remark: he is amazed at the genital etiology of neurotic symptoms, he is amazed that this etiology is "known" (by Charcot, anyway), and he is amazed that this knowledge is never *said,* publicly, loudly, by Charcot. And most importantly, the scientist's "why" is aroused in Freud *only* by this last astonishment—namely, "Why does he never *say* so?" On the basis of what Freud himself tells us here, we must not wonder that he questioned whether his essential contribution was in having *seen* something or in having *said* something.

A year later (1886), after he had begun medical practice in Vienna as a *Privatdozent* for nervous diseases, the distinguished Viennese gynecologist Chrobak sent Freud a note asking him to take charge of a woman patient of his. Later, he took Freud aside and informed him that after eighteen years of marriage she was still a virgin. The husband was impotent. The sole prescription for the malady, he added, "is familiar enough to us but we cannot order it. It runs:

Rx Penis normalis
dosim
repetatur!

* It is perhaps not insignificant that this was the period in which Freud developed a consuming interest in the neurology of aphasia. A year after Charcot's inability or reluctance to use words about what he knew, Freud was lecturing on aphasia to the Physiology Club in Vienna. In 1891, he published his first book, *Aphasia,* and dedicated it to . . . Breuer! (See Jones, *The Life and Work of Sigmund Freud,* vol. 1, *The Formative Years and the Great Discoveries, 1856–1900* (New York: Basic Books, 1953), p. 213. Regarding *Aphasia,* Jones notes that this remarkably original work "in many ways foreshadowed the psychological theories [Freud] was soon after to develop." *Life and Work,* vol. 2, *Years of Maturity, 1901–1919* (New York: Basic Books, 1955), p. 5.

I had never heard of such a prescription," Freud concludes, "and would have liked to shake my head over my kind friend's cynicism." [13] Once more, Freud hears the "secret." It is "said," but said privately, and in a cynical joking manner—and, once more, in a foreign language. Even here, euphemism and distantiation are at work.

Later on, in 1893, the same problem comes up. In a letter to Fliess, Freud had opened the whole topic of the sexual etiology of neurosis. Fliess's reply confuses him. Has he discovered something, or is he merely mentioning something already known but unmentionable? Has he found a scientific truth, or merely (merely?) violated the bourgeois code? "Now for the sexual question. I think you could express yourself more graphically on this. The way you refer to sexual etiology implies a knowledge on the public's part which it has only in latent form. It *knows*, but acts *as if it did not know*" [14] (my emphasis).

A year later (1894) Freud writes that he is regarded in Vienna as obsessed: "They regard me rather as a monomaniac, while I have the distinct feeling I have touched on one of the great secrets of nature." [15] Secret of nature? or secret of bourgeois society? Something deeply repressed? or civilly inattended to in "polite society"? In the sciences of man, are these two orders of secret separable? One thing we do know: Freud is in the process of using the antagonism of others as proof of the truth of his contentions. But how much of this "resistance" is merely a social bourgeois resistance to his having mentioned unmentionables in public, rather than resistance to disclosing a secret of human nature? Again, how separable are these two processes? "There is something comic about the incongruity between one's own and other people's estimation of one's work," he remarks to Fliess.[16]

By October 1895 he has become quite sure of himself, of his theory. "I recently perpetrated three lectures on hysteria in which I was very impudent," he writes Fliess. "I shall be starting to take pleasure in being arrogant, partcularly if you continue to be so pleased with me." [17] Do we hear the sound of *épatisme* in that disclosure? By March 1896 he is bogged down in his work on the neuroses. He is still less sure of the stature, if any, of the truths he has discovered than of the meaning of the hostility they arouse: "I am met with hostility and live in such isolation that one might suppose I had discovered the greatest truths." [18] What a strange remark! Freud was openly using resistance to his claims as an index of their nature and merit. Freud said that *after* he had gained an understanding of the functioning of resistance in psychoanalytical treatment, it was his environment's rejection of him that gave him insight "into the *full* significance of his discoveries" [19] (my emphasis). Three weeks later he lectures on dream interpretations to the young people of the Jewish academic reading circle. "I enjoy talking about my ideas at the moment"; nevertheless, "a void is forming around me." [20]

But the sexual etiology of neuroses, the "id behind the symptoms," has a companion problem in Freud's conviction that he had discovered a component of innate hostility in the id. This instinct, like sex, also violated the bourgeois optimism of liberal Christians and respectable Viennese. "I have found little that is 'good' about human beings on the whole," he writes the Swiss Pastor Oskar Pfister. "In my experience most of them are trash, no matter whether they publicly subscribe to this or that ethical doctrine or none at all." Then he adds, addressing Pfister personally as a Protestant minister: "That is something that you cannot *say aloud,* or perhaps *even think,* though your *experiences* of life can hardly have been different from mine" [21] (my emphasis). Here we have the same structural problem about the aggressive instinct as we had with sexuality. Has Freud made a scientific discovery here? It would seem not, for he asserts with confidence that Pfister's *experience* is identical with his own—namely, that people "are trash." The difference between Freud and others, between Freud and this Gentile Protestant who in a sense "represents" the Swiss or Gentile branch of the psychoanalytic movement, is that Freud allows himself to *say* the shocking things that all of them (presumably) have *experienced.* Perhaps, he speculates to Pfister, the bourgeois-Christian censorship goes so deep, perhaps you cannot "even *think*" the awful truth about people that you have undoubtedly *experienced.* Eight years earlier he had written to Pfister on the publication of the pastor's *Analysis of Hate and Reconciliation,* saying that it "suffers from the hereditary vice of . . . virtue; it is the work of too decent a man, who feels himself bound to discretion." [22] Freud was not bound to such discretion.* He could tell secrets forbidden in polite society. He is furious at what he himself believes to be the truth of Jung's statement about his (Jung's) secession from "the movement" (relayed by von Muralt through Pfister) that Jung "does not reject me, and graciously allows me my place, but merely corrects me and makes me 'fit for polite society' ['*Salonsfähig*']." [23]

For Freud, then, the question of the genuineness of his originality was entangled with doubts about the priority of his discovery of the role of sex in the etiology of neurosis. His obsessive concern over the race for scientific priority—who got there first?—is crossed by his anxiety over the nature of his scientific originality—who got *where* first? Has he merely rediscovered what Breuer, Charcot, and Chrobak had discovered earlier? Is his sexual etiology idea a case of cryptomnesia—that is, of unconscious plagiarism? Or is his priority simply a case of appropriating as his own intellectual property something everybody knew all along but

* It has been suggested that Jung's increased emphasis on the "collective" rather than the personal contents of his patients' productions may have been due to "a reluctance, on grounds of delicacy, to *publish* personal material" (my emphasis). Avis M. Dry, *The Psychology of Jung: A Critical Interpretation* (New York: Wiley, 1961), p. 297.

had the decency not to ventilate? ("Am I the last to know but the first to say?") The egregious concern exhibited so frequently by "pure" scientists in the matter of priority, a disconcertingly unedifying finding which Robert Merton brilliantly recoups to serve as the linchpin of his sociology of science, became, in Freud's case, an obsession. The lofty Freud of Ernest Jones's bowdlerized *Life and Work of Sigmund Freud,* who was "never interested in questions of priority, which he found merely boring," [24] is restored to historical reality by sociologists impudent enough to do some counting. "In point of fact," Merton relates, "Elinor Barber and I have identified more than one hundred and fifty occasions on which Freud exhibited an interest in priority." [25] In this interest, Merton contends, Freud exhibits a tension and ambivalence typical of the role of the creative scientist.

But Freud's abiding concern with priority, the fact that "he oscillates between the poles of his ambivalence toward priority," [26] is not reducible to the general case of the ambivalence of men of science, to the inner conflict bred in them by their commitment to two potentially incompatible values: the impersonal "humility" that promotes the advancement of science and the personal "vanity" that seeks the rewards of priority, of having their "priority of discovery recognized by peers." [27] Freud's ambivalence about his priority in discovering the sexual etiology of the neuroses is clearly "overdetermined," and this for a very curious reason: if Freud's originality stems uniquely from his Jewishness, as he more than suspects it does—"Why was it," he asks Pastor Pfister, "that none of all the pious ever discovered psychoanalysis? Why did it have to wait for a completely godless Jew?" [28]—then the recognition and validation of this priority is uniquely dependent upon the *goyim* who man the reward system of "establishment" science which he is trying to crash. In Freud's case, the ambivalence of the Jew thus coincides with the ambivalence of the scientist; the one reinforces the other. Freud hungers for recognition of his "scientific revolution" from the very custodians—the Swiss Gentile psychiatric establishment of Jung and his circle—of what, to Freud, is "normal science."

Once more, the problem recurs: what has been discovered here? Wherein lies Freud's originality? In his scientific contribution as a theorist or in his social location as a Jew? Has he discovered a hitherto unknown sexuality and aggression beneath the civil surface of the *bürgerliche Gesellschaft*? Or does his originality lie precisely in his vulgarity? in his committing the indiscretion—for those not "bound to discretion," like Jews and other social pariahs—of *speaking* the unspeakable truths that all *goyim* already latently know are so? If the former is the case, Freud the scientist, who happens to be a Jew, has *discovered* a secret of human nature. If the latter is the case, Freud the Jew, who happens to be a scientist, has *told* a secret of civil society.

The Locus of Freud's Originality

If, in the natural sciences, as Whitehead has said, "everything of importance has been said before by someone who did not discover it," [29] perhaps in the social sciences everything of importance has been discovered before by someone who did not say it.* The roots of Freud's "anxiety of influence" run deep. Priority in the social sciences, like creativity in the humanities, may be as much a matter of naming as of knowing. "The commodity in which poets deal, their authority, their property," Harold Bloom writes, "turns upon priority. They own, they are, what they beome first in naming." † [30] The impending defection of his Swiss *goyim* will push Freud's ambivalence over his originality to a personal crisis over his identity which, in its crude form, will echo the worst charges of the anti-Semites: "Am I an original scientist or am I just a vulgar Jew?" The "organized scepticism" of the scientist, however incompletely internalized in Freud, conspires with the corrosive self-doubt of the emancipated Jew to make the existence of actual anti-Semites all but otiose. Besides, the quality of the anti-Semitism supplied by the Gentile community—afflicted as it is with invincible *goyisherkopitude*—is inferior; secular intellectual Jews of stature are thus obliged, *noblesse oblige* —in this as in other matters—to provision themselves. "No anti-Semite can begin to comprehend the malicious analysis of his soul," Norman Mailer informs us, "which every Jew indulges every day." [31]

All this explains why Freud so needs his Swiss *goyim*. To Freud the scientist, they satisfy his need "for assurance that one's work really matters"; [32] to Freud the Jew, their allegiance is a continuing reassurance in which not only the outside world—as Freud contended—but Freud himself is reassured that psychoanalysis is not "a Jewish science." The presence of *goyim* in the leadership of psychoanalysis as ideology, *as a movement*, is important as a warranty that it transcends ethnic interests; in terms of public relations it is a "balanced ticket." But for psychoanalysis *as a science*, the "Gentile presence" is something more than a public relations strategy. It is a pledge, not least for Freud himself, of its scientific generality. For Freud, like most Diaspora intellectuals, is inwardly unsure as to just what part of his work stems from his being a Jew, and what part from his being a scientist. "Jews are always forced to generalize about their problems," explains a grandson of old Avrom Glickman in Dan Jacobson's novel *The Beginners*, "because they never know just how much is Jewish in them . . . and how much is common, ordinary, human, necessary," and, we should add, how much is *goyish*.‡ [33]

We learn from an earlier letter, in which Freud criticizes Pfister's

* I wish to thank Jeanne Wacker for help and influence in the formulation of this idea.

† The source of this quotation, Bloom's *The Anxiety of Influence* (see note 30), is a brilliant book. Read it. In Bloom, modernist poetry finds its Malraux.

‡ But, as to the indiscreetness of psychoanalysis, however, Freud betrayed no puzzlement over its parentage: it was of Jewish descent.

account of a psychoanalysis for omitting the "minute details," that when Freud asked Pfister why the discovery of psychoanalysis had to wait for "a completely godless Jew," what he meant by that phrase was "a completely indiscreet, impolite Jew." Freud writes: "Discretion is incompatible with a satisfactory description of an analysis; to provide the latter one would have to be unscrupulous, give away, betray, behave like an artist who buys paints with his wife's house-keeping money or uses the furniture as firewood to warm the studio for his model. Without a trace of that kind of unscrupulousness," he concludes, "the job cannot be done." [34] Psychoanalysis, it is clear, was designed to be socially unrespectable. But was that fact proof positive that it was scientifically respectable? Or, to push the problem to its deepest level: was the question of the scientific respectability of the *Geisteswissenschaften* in the bourgeois-Christian era ultimately separable from the question of their social respectability? Were social "appearances," in some unprecedented and troubling way, criterial of objectivity in the new sciences of man? That is, in the present case, was introspective evidence about the institutional meanings of bourgeois civil society scientifically "respectable" evidence if the introspector—Freud—was a self-proclaimed "outsider" to that society and unsuccessfully —i.e., inappropriately—socialized in it? In the experience of another Victorian, Charles Dickens, the social and the psychological were virtually indistinguishable. The close correlation of his person with his society and its cultural values made him "inward" to his age. This good "fit," in Dickens, between the social and the psychological, writes Michael Wood, "is why Dickens could read Victorian society by looking into himself." [35] What society did Freud read by looking into himself? Into a self early and appropriately socialized in the lingering values of the subculture of the *shtetl*? Did such introspection yield insight into personalities institutionally integrated with the modernizing values of the West? If the answer is no, then to accept Freud's introspective evidence as valid was, in effect, to accept the representation of what was *outside* civil society (the social pariah), by shifting to the vertical axis, as the psychological *underside* of civil society: Europe's social pariah, the "Yid," becomes in this way everybody's psychological pariah, the id.

With Jewish Emancipation, the ecological base of Judaism—its tribal "we-are-here-and-you-are-there" horizontal differentiation—was, in principle, subverted. "Desegregation" occurred,[36] and with it, among the "exception Jews" of the early generations of Emancipation, there occurred the transformation of Judaism into a personalized, marketable, monogrammed "Jewishness." [37] This shift was, in reality, a shift from the horizontal plane—"life-is-with-people"—to a vertical representation of Jewish identity, with the pre-Western *Ostjude* repressed, censored—in a kind of latter-day renewal of Marranoism—and stashed down at the lowest, earliest stratum of the self. Psychological "segregation" replaces social-geographical segregation, internal restraints replace external constraints. (Durkheim would incorporate the insights of this *assimilation* process into his sociology, as Freud did into his psychoanalysis; Parsons would late hail it as the discovery of "internalization.")

Freud took the next step: in a bold stroke, this "conquistador" overcame the subjective opaqueness of the "civil society" of the Gentile by installing an id-"Yid" in the personality system of each of its members. By this daring imputation, by this "forced conversion," so to speak, the outsider became insider—or, more exactly, the social outside which was Jewry became the psychological underside of gentility. In this way, Freud was able to bridge "the apparently contradictory propositions of [the Jewish "outsider"] Durkheim about the subjective opaqueness of social phenomena and of [the Gentile "insider"] Weber about the possibility of *Verstehen.*"[38] In one stroke, Freud, a new "Moses" in his own fantasy, "passes" his Jews into the Gentile *Gesellschaft* and "converts" his Gentiles into "honorary Jews."

CHAPTER 12

EXCURSUS: MODERNIZATION AND THE EMERGENCE OF SOCIAL APPEARANCE

Freud was cruel and brutal in the way he treated defectors from the psychoanalytic movement.* Significantly, if he theologized the Gentile defectors—Jung relapsed into earlier "spiritualism"—he became a sociologist when he explained the Jewish defectors—Adler was a "Jew boy from a Viennese suburb" who made good among the *goyim*. But to both sorts of secessionist he was unforgiving and incivil. Philip Rieff handles this "scandal" (Freud's coarseness must always be cleaned up) by saying that "Freud would not suffer the false civility of separating ideas from men." [1] But just such a differentiation of men themselves from the ideas they hold is exactly what civility is, true civility. It has an old theological pedigree in the Christian separation of the sin from the sinner ("Go, sin no more," Jesus said) and a Greek philosophical pedigree in the ban on the *argumentum ad hominem*. If this be not "true civility," what is? And besides, Freud knew exactly what civility was even though it was not part of his mental furniture and he was unable to practice it. Civility was a bourgeois rite observed by the *goyim*—and occasionally even useful against them. "I was delighted with your remarks about Groddeck," he writes the Protestant minister Oskar Pfister. "We really must be able to tell each other home-truths, i.e., incivilities, and remain firm friends, as in this case." [2] Later he bursts out, having minded his manners too long, with: "And finally,—let me be impolite for once—how the devil do you reconcile all that we experience and have to expect in this world with your assumption of a moral order?" [3] He admires the way Pfister handles the opponents of psychoanalysis: "Well, I admire your ability to write like that, in such a moderate, affable, considerate manner, so factually and so much more *for* the reader than *against* your

* Freud's attitude, Jung said in 1925, was "the bitterness of the person who is entirely misunderstood, and his manners always seemed to say: 'If they do not understand, they must be stamped into hell.'" Quoted in Henri Ellenberger, *The Discovery of the Unconscious,* (New York: Basic Books, 1970), p. 462.

opponent. . . . I could not restrain myself. But, as I am incapable of artistically [*sic*] modifying my indignation, of giving it an aura pleasurable to others, I hold my peace" [4] (my emphasis).

Freud's personality, formed in the Eastern European Jewish home and nurtured in Leopoldstadt, felt ill at ease in "society." He enjoyed the thrust and parry of "home-truths, i.e., incivilities." Society (the *Gesellschaft*) is the place where social *appearances* emerge ("respectability" is one such) and become autonomous (i.e., subjectively opaque) and where one is constrained to take account of them in one's behavior. Insofar as we internalize the constraints of social appearance into restraints, we become *members* of the *societal* community. Let us take a concrete example from one of Freud's letters to Abraham. On September 29, 1908, he writes Abraham in Berlin to confess a "transgression against you,"—namely, that "I actually was in Berlin for twenty-four hours without having called on you," since, what with crossing from England with his brother Emmanuel and seeing his sister Marie (Mitzi) who lives in Berlin, and "between the two camps of fond relatives I saw as little of Berlin as I did of you." And so he asks Abraham—and this is the crucial point—to "forgive the *appearance* of unfriendliness" involved [5] (my emphasis). Family and relatives, the primary *Gemeinschaften,* know all about one: where you are, why you are there, deed and motive for the deed or the nondeed. The stranger, even a relative stranger like Abraham, does not.

Freud passes through the *Gesellschaft* that is 1908 Berlin. He leaves a wake of appearances in his train. To make oneself accountable for one's appearances before strangers is the first step to social modernization. In the *Gesellschaft,* whether we will it or not, we create a new, nonintentional life around ourselves: the unintended appearances of our purposeful social action. There is a "between-period," when we try to shrug off these appearances: "I didn't intend that, so I don't care." But then Freud's thoughts might have run something like this: "I would have visited Abraham if I'd had the time. Indeed, I know that, but does *he*? Suppose Abraham hears from a colleague who passed you on the street, who says, 'Freud was in Berlin yesterday. I passed him on the street.' He might mistake your not seeing him for your not liking him." Gradually we are won over to a new stage, almost an ethical mutation: we own up to our accountability for our intentions, our actions, *and* the appearance of our intentions and actions. A whole new dimension—the appearance of the ethical—is born. It is a dimension trivialized by the rules of etiquette, but nonetheless real for all that.

To become modern, then, is to become civil, which is to say, caretakers of our social appearance, and at once we are in the (frankly) very odd business of writing letters to our Abrahams and begging them to "forgive the appearance of unfriendliness." We no longer shrug off these visual echoes of ourselves. This is the new "social reality principle" [6] that emerges with the modernization process as its social coefficient. Let us call it the "civilizational process." Freud was aware of the autonomy of social appearance to some extent, but it had no theoretical interest for the psychoanalytic movement. The whole realm of social perception as such, of the ethic involved in making appearances congruent, of the snobbery involved in perceiving discrepant appearances—think of Abraham characterizing one of his opponents in the Berlin Society for Psychiatry as "a very pushing member, B., whose conversion to Christianity has proved only partially successful," * [7] think of Freud's remark on the death of Adler—all of this mode of social perception was occurring but was never itself thematized.

To break into this mode of perception is, ipso facto, to break into the life of society (not polite society necessarily, though polite society carries these structures into their play-form, as Simmel was to show). These are the rituals of appearance, these are the *rites de passage* that carry us from traditionary into bourgeois-Christian modernizing consciousness. With this circumspection of appearance, this discipline of appearance, this practice of the presence of the generalized other as an inner-worldly ascetic, modernity is born. We intrude, we trespass by our nonintentional appearances into the lives of others in the *Gesellschaft*, as they intrude into ours. "Forgive us our appearances," Freud might as well have written, "as we forgive those who have appeared against us." This was the essential discipline of the Diaspora.

Moses Mendelssohn had preceded Solomon Maimon to Berlin in the mid-eighteenth century. Mendelssohn and his circle were busily trying to master the exigent appearances. For a long while they were poseurs. Maimon arrived straight out of the *shtetl:* "I was shy, and the manners and customs of the Berliners were strange to me," he writes. "The odd mixture of the animal in my manners, my expressions, and my whole outward behavior, with the rational in my thoughts, excited his † imagination more than the subject of our conversation aroused his understanding." [8]

With Freud the "discrepant profile" read the other way. Outwardly he was very controlled, but inwardly he was a wild *Galitzianer*. Freud's was the first generation of his family born outside Galicia (Austria took Galicia from Poland in the Partition of 1772). Martin Freud writes of his grandmother Amalia (Freud's mother) that she came from East Galicia, adding:

It might not be known that Galician Jews were a peculiar race, not

* This is the only piece of evidence we have that Abraham had a sense of humor. It must not be mislaid.

† Referring, not to Mendelssohn, but to one of the circle of his Berlin *Haskalah* (Enlightenment).—J.M.C.

> only different from any other races inhabiting Europe, but absolutely different from Jews who had lived in the West for some generations. . . . These Galician Jews had little grace and no manners; and their women were certainly not what we should call "ladies." They were highly emotional and easily carried away by their feelings. But, although in many respects they would seem to be untamed barbarians to more civilized people, they, alone of all minorities, stood up to the Nazis. These people are not easy to live with, and grandmother, a true representative of her race, was no exception. She had great vitality and much impatience.[9]

Freud, in marrying the cool Martha Bernays, a Sephardic Jew, was marrying "up" endogamously (as Marx married "up" exogamously in marrying Jenny von Westphalen). She brought status (*yichus*) into the marriage as the daughter of the chief rabbi of Hamburg.

Let us stand back and make some summarizing statements before we move on. We have seen the earliest works of Freud as outcomes of his encounter with Western civility: the "politeness" he is forced to observe every day becomes the agent of censorship transforming the wishes of his id into wish-fulfillments disguised so as to be acceptable to that more "assimilated" aspect of his self that has internalized the moral and taste norms of the bourgeois-Christian West. This insight becomes his great *Interpretation of Dreams.* The method or praxis for reaching this id and circumventing the vigilance of the *goyim* (always on the lookout for Jewish misbehavior) is the method of "free association." Freud creates a "social space" congruent with the practice of this therapy: the secret, neutral space of the "analytic situation," in which both the moral norms of a precedent dyad (the confessional, with priest and penitent) and the civil norms of everyday life are suspended to create an entirely new social relation. In this situation, verbal vice and social indecorum are encouraged as a privileged communication (the generic legitimating ceiling is science, the specialty, medicine). In this situation, *goyim manquées* can regress back to their precivil id-"Yid" and then come forward once more, in a controlled resocialization, a controlled reassimilation stopping short of any illusions of total change or conversion. For Freud these fifty-minute hours are the velleities of his wished-for *social* revolution, that utopian picnic of which he daydreamed where none of the ladies will have to excuse themselves with euphemisms in order to relieve themselves because there will be no euphemisms, no roundaboutness, and hence no need for excuses. The analytic situation inverts the social situation: "Freudianism was to be indiscreet on principle. . . . The therapeutic hour . . . puts an end to decorum."[10] Shortly after he had introspected his own dreams, Freud turned to the social *faux pas* of Diaspora Jewry, the awkward lapses and parapraxes that were to become *The Psychopathology of Everyday Life*. In the meantime, he had discovered through introspection, in the course of trying to make intelligible the curious bewitchment that the play *Oedipus Rex* exercised over him, the "Oedipus complex." He believed he had discovered that an early forbidden, incestuous desire for sex with his mother had been repressed into unconsciousness out of fear of his father, who would castrate him in punishment for that wish. Our socioanalysis of this theory itself finds its origin in Freud's repression of the forbidden shame and murderous rage he experienced when his father told him how he had meekly acceded to the command of "an enemy of his people" to "mind his manners" and had had his brand-new fur hat knocked into the gutter in the bargain. Reading and seeing Sophocles' play subsequently facilitates the reemergence of a forbidden "conquistadorial" wish in the culturally legitimate form of identifying with a Greek hero who responds to an exactly similar encounter in an exactly opposite way: the play supplies a kind of *rite de passage* for Freud, in which an identity change occurs through a new identification with a new "father figure"—Oedipus—who, as luck would have it, is also a son and who, further, *mirabile dictu*, kills his father in a rage. If, as Ernest Jones writes, Freud's father "never regained the place he had held in his esteem after the painful occasion when he told his twelve-year-old boy how a Gentile knocked off his new fur cap into the mud and shouted at him: 'Jew, get off the pavement,' "[11] first Hamilcar, son of Hannibal, and then Oedipus, son of Läius, were to replace this submissive father in Freud's campaign against Rome (the Holy Roman Empire).

Much of the material that Freud dredged up during the introspection of his "didactic" self-analysis was, clearly, misleading. He believed he could extrapolate universally to all other childhoods (the "Oedipus complex" was universal) and to all of Western social reality and institutions. His private introspection, he believed, gave him an unshakable *prise* on social reality. But introspection, as Peter L. Berger notes, is "a viable method for the discovery of institutional meanings . . . [and] the understanding of social reality [only] *after* successful socialization"[12] (my emphasis). (It is only after successful socialization—*successful* socialization, we should add—that "the apparently contradictory propositions of Durkheim about the subjective opaqueness of social phenomena and of Weber about the possibility *of Verstehen*"[13] can be bridged, Berger concludes. Durkheim's *homo duplex*[14] is, paradoxically, a good many leagues further down the road to assimilation—"successful socialization"—than is the *homo triplex* of Freud's three "psychic institutions.")

Freud and his descendants habitually extrapolate from the Eastern European Jewish case to "man in general." Stanley Diamond, for example, notes that, given Freud's conception of the *universal* function of ritual, it is of great interest that Freud was a Jew. As in so many other instances, Freud universalized on the basis of the socially particular. Nowhere is this more evident than in his brilliant hypothesis about the nature of ritual, applicable, when viewed functionally, to the traditional European Jewish milieu, but misplaced when applied to the primitive ritual drama.[15]

CHAPTER 13

REICH AND LATER VARIATIONS

Politically, Freud was a liberal. Diaspora liberalism may be defined as the endeavor to institutionalize "neutral" social territory between the Jew (the id) and the Gentile world (the superego). It was the ego—the putatively neutral instrumental ego—that would hold its own "neutral" scientific ground by playing off the id against the superego, the superego against the id. Freud had no desire to use psychoanalytic theory, much less the psychoanalytic situation—the decorum-free consulting room—as a staging area for launching a revolutionary drive against the Gentile civil society which was its milieu. In a long life, at the end of the first century of Jewish Emancipation, he had settled his accounts with the Gentile superego. There would be no revolution from below. The superego, he had found, as Donald Barr writes, "is as savage as the Id, but on the side of decorum." [1] Freud opted for a standoff.

Freud himself stood polarized between the subculture of the "Yid" (id) and the incompletely internalized culture of the *goy* (the superego), between pariah and parvenu. There was a small margin of self-determination which, as Philip Rieff has observed, "amounts merely to a skill at playing off against one another the massive sub-individual (id) and supra-individual (super-ego) forces by which the self is shaped." [2] Freud's famous formula—"Where Id was, there let ego be"—was both a call and a warning to Diaspora Jewry (and to non-Jews, by extrapolation) that they come "up from *Yiddishkeit*" but not try to assimilate to "*Goyishkeit.*" It was to be the "great compromise" of classical nineteenth-century liberalism, but retooled for emancipating Jewry. On Freud's theory of the psychoneuroses, every symptom making up the various syndromes of his neurotic patients involved precisely such a "compromise"; each of the ten "defense mechanisms" * (from "isolation" and "reaction-formation" to "projection" and "sublimation") was involved in the production of "compromises" that would disguise the id, enabling it to "pass" as "normal." [3] Modernizing Jewry had repressed the processes involved in the forced march into "normal" gentility that it had undergone upon entering Europe, when the unconditioned "wish" of a Maimon, or a Marx, collided

* It is Freud's daughter who finds that to his nine methods of defense "we must add a tenth. . . : sublimation, or displacement of instinctual aims." Anna Freud, *The Ego and the Mechanisms of Defense* (see note 3), p. 47.

with the demands of Gentile restraint-structures. Freud creates in the psychoanalytical situation a moratorium, a decompression chamber, an *epoché* of the Gentile attitude, in which these "defensive processes are reversed, a passage back into consciousness is forced for the instinctual impulses or affects which have been warded off and it is then left to the ego and the super-ego to come to terms with them on a better basis." [4]

Within the "scientifically" legitimated precincts of this psychoanalytic interstitial social situation, with the social pressure of Western civility provisionally abated (checked at the door of Freud's insulting room), with Gentile politeness suspended for the *Interimsetiquette* of an analytic hour of uninhibited yet institutionalized vulgarity, Freud's Jewish patients could take time out from the hard praxis of "passing" to let the air out of the thing; they could stop behaving and "live a little." Bracketed outside, of course, the public authority of the "real world" of the "reality principle" of the Gentile continued its reign unabated. Once out there again, plagued by Gentile exigency, all would be once more compromise —but conscious, knowing, illusionless compromise. You may suspend ethics and still have a tolerable world. But when you eliminate also the appearance of the ethical—namely, manners—nihilism is born. Freud was resentful enough to try this experiment, cautious enough to limit it. He compromised. James Joyce, analogously, broke the bourgeois novel's conventions with his version of "free association," namely, the *monologue intérieure*. What for Henry James had been the "terrible fluidity of self-revelation" became for Joyce a technique of deliberate vulgarity. Joyce and his Dubliners, like Freud and his *shtetl* Jews, coming "from behind" in the nineteenth century, had to make "a wilderness in the clearing" of bourgeois-Christian respectability so that their Irish and Jews could breathe. But both operated within a restricted context: the novel form and the form of the psychoanalytical situation. Both constructed "imaginary gardens with real toads in them" [5]—named "Anna O" and "Leopold Bloom."

Psychoanalysis was to be an ideology, a compromise strategy, for living-the-Diaspora: the price of Emancipation—repression and sublimation—was to be paid, and paid in full, but consciously, and without adopting any of the illusory ideologies that the Gentile needed to console himself with for the renunciations exacted by civilized life. This "hybrid" which is Gentile, civil society is no genuine synthesis of id and superego, of nature and values. Its mediations between these "hateful contraries"—like the mediations of Hegel's system which "reflected" them—were ilusions, lies that pretended to overcome the conflict. But like the ultimate "lie of salvation" that informs them all, they only paper over inescapable conflicts. We must live this compromise and not destroy it (we do not know what might erupt on its destruction), but we must live it consciously, as far as possible, and without illusion.

The inner, ethnic resonance of Freud's "liberalism" was twofold. On the one hand, he was playing the typical role of the advanced intelligentsia of a recently decolonized people: he was part of an eite, mediating them over the hill into modernity, sacrificing as little as possible of their traditional *shtetl* past (their id-*Yiddishkeit*); this is the culture-broker aspect of liberalism, with the "neutral" instrumental ego of the mediator negotiating between plural interests ("interest-group liberalism") within a given framework of public values (the "imperial," Gentile order). But also, like a lawyer, the analyst was a "double agent," representing both public Gentile authority—the "reality principle"—and the private, subcultural interests of his client (the "wishes" of the pleasure principle).[6] He stood, as I have said, between id and superego, between tradition and modernity, between pariah and parvenu. For all his fierceness, then, Freud represented the compromise that was to become Diaspora liberalism. He turned his face against the "wholeness-hunger" *—"a great regression born from a great fear: the fear of modernity" [7]—that covertly drove certain of the Diaspora intelligentsia to seek a radical *social* fulfilment of their premodern "wish": Marx, Lassalle, Rosa Luxemberg, Trotsky, Emma Goldman, Jerry Rubin, and Abbie Hoffman. Freud kept a close watch on the political radicals and revolutionaries. After all, his schoolmates Heinrich Braun and Victor Adler were both active in politics.[8]

It was not till the early thirties that Freud fully realized that his own movement contained an analyst, Wilhelm Reich, who had gone back to Marx and contracted "political fanaticism" [9] (as Jones calls it), a situation that led to Reich's estrangement and expulsion (in 1934) from the movement. In 1933 Reich had been expelled from the German Communist party for an "incorrect" view of the causes of fascism. Thus Reich's attempt to "marry" two of the Diaspora ideologues, Freud and Marx, ended in his separation from the two movements speaking in their names. Reich soon left for "exile" in Scandanavia (one thinks of Marx and Heine in Paris, then Marx in England) whence in 1939, due to the efforts of his American translator and friend the New York psychiatrist Theodore P. Wolfe, he left for the United States, settling in Forest Hills.†

Born in Bobrzynia, Galicia, in 1897 to middle-class Jewish parents—a mother who eventually killed herself and a father who raised cattle for the German government—Reich had an odd childhood. His was a parvenu family, "proud and much more identified with German culture than with their Jewish heritage. Neither Wilhelm nor his brother [Rob-

* The author of this concept (Peter Gay, "Weimar Culture"—see note 7) uses "wholeness-hunger" with a wider generality of reference than I do. I make it an analytical tool for understanding the Jewism Emancipation.

† I was myself for a short time a patient of Dr. Wolfe. The price then (late 1940s) was twenty-five dollars an hour. (I still have the cancelled check.)

ert]," David Elkind reports, "were allowed to play with the peasant children or with the Yiddish-speaking children of the ghetto." [10] After World War I, while still a medical student, he became a practicing psychoanalyst in Freud's circle in Vienna. He was soon to show his independence by innovating theory and technique which, while originating in Freud, ended Freud's conservative, stoic-liberal compromise and detonated the dynamite of social critique still "bound" in Freudianism. Reich became in his own eyes a revolutionary Prometheus: he considered himself "Freud unbound," and his appeal went well beyond psychoanalytical circles.

Reich appealed to many for several reasons: he combined the psychological and the sociological, depth psychology and radical politics. He was a theoretical materialist who created nevertheless a "formalist" therapy in which the "content" of analysis—dreams, free associations, slips—became less important than how content was expressed (the adverbs of content): handclasps, mannerisms, dress, gait, physiognomy, and so forth. But Reich's most important contribution (his most famous was his delusionary "discovery" of "orgone energy") was in therapy: he analyzed the latent "character" resistance *before* tackling the patient's symptoms. Resistance to "the primary rule" of psychoanalytic candor (the "ethic of honesty") Reich believed, took the form of character resistance: the defenses against insight into the infantile sources in the id of the patient's current pathology anchored themselves in the very physiology of the body, in "stiff upper lips," in the tendency to "grin and bear it," in evasive movements of the eyes, in shielding the genitalia by crossing the legs, in—the last stronghold of retreating anxiety—a rigid pelvis.

Most important of all in Reich's appeal to the "Freudian Left" [11] is the application he made of his idea of "character-armor." He called the rigid surface of the neurotic personality *"Charakterpanzerung"* (character-armor), a kind of hard cuticle defending the ego against the urgent, vital sexuality repressed within and clamoring for release through revolutionary praxis. The analogy here to Reich's namesake and heir—Charles Reich—is "no accident." In Reich II (Charles), the masculine genitality of Reich I's thirties protest has been tenderized into the soft androgeny of the American seventies, where ingenuous green shoots of "the greening of America" make their way up through the civilities of the Gentile *Gesellschaft* of "consciousness II." "Consider a social event among professional people—a dinner, cocktail party, garden party [remember Freud's picnic?], or just a lunch among friends," Reich II asks us. "Everything that takes place occurs within incredibly narrow limits," he continues. "The events are almost completely structured around conversation. No one pays any sensual attention to the food, the mind-altering experience of the drink, or to the weather, or to the nonverbal side of personality. . . . They do not strive for genuine relationships, but keep their conversation at the level of sociability." [12] In Reich II the grief of Reich I is audible once more. In 1947 Summerhill's A. S. Neill witnessed a social visit to Reich I at Organon, Maine, by former staff, down from Canada and "dropping by"; the guests depart: "Poor Reich sat silent in a corner with a face full of misery. When we were alone he said, 'Neill, I couldn't go through an afternoon like this again. *Gesellschafts*—conversation just means hell to me.' " [13] Years before (in 1912) Franz Kafka had written: "Conversation takes the importance, the seriousness and the truth out of everything, I think." [14]

The name Reich I gives to (Reich II's) "consciousness II" is "character-armor," and in his great work *Character-Analysis* his first and archetypal example of it is politeness. "If, for instance, a patient is very polite," Reich writes, "while at the same time he brings ample material, say, about his relationship with his sister, one is confronted with two simultaneous contents of the 'psychic surface': his love for his sister, and his behavior, his politeness. Both have unconscious roots. . . . Analytic experience shows," he maintains, "that behind this politeness and niceness there is *always* hidden a more or less unconscious critical, distrustful or deprecatory attitude" [15] (Reich's emphasis). So, he advises the therapist, do not interpret the incestuous material, but, seizing the initiative, go after the politeness itself. "Were one to wait until the patient himself begins to talk about his politeness and its reasons," one would wait forever; "the patient will never talk about it himself; it is up to the analyst to unmask it as a resistance." [16] It is Reich's contention that, since "politeness immediately turns into a resistance," all "content" passing through it takes the impress of its form. "To remain with the example of politeness," he writes—not, I should think, a difficult resolve for Reich—"the neurotic, as a result of his repressions, has every reason to value highly his politeness and all social conventions and to use them as a protection." [17] It is more pleasant, Reich concedes, to treat "a polite patient than an impolite, very candid one," since the latter tells the analyst the unpleasant things which politeness would otherwise censor. Reich goes on to give eight examples of the kind of aggressive utterance that remains hidden behind the armor of politeness: telling the analyst that he is "too young or too old, that he has a shabby apartment or an ugly wife, that he looks stupid or too Jewish, that he behaves neurotically and better go for analysis himself," [18] and so forth. One must avoid, he warns the therapist, any deep-reaching interpretations of the unconscious "as long as the wall of conventional politeness between patient and analyst continues to exist," [19] especially with obsessive-compulsive characters who have "converted their hatred into 'politeness at all cost.' " [20] In his descriptions of these latently—that is, characterologically—restrained patients, these " 'good,' over-polite and ever-correct patients," [21] Reich turns obsessively to the wearers of the all-pervading, nice, bourgeois "smile" (there are inner and outer "smiles"): "those who are always 'armored,' who smile inwardly about everything and everyone,"[22] and those whose resistance expresses itself in "formal aspects of the general behavior, the manner of talking, of the gait, facial expression, and typical attitudes such as smiling, deriding, haughtiness, over-correctness, the *manner* of the politeness or of the aggression, etc"[23] (Reich's emphasis). Both the inward smile of the bourgeois "interior" and the relentless social niceness of the bourgeois "exterior" were fair game for Reich's revolutionary therapy.

Freud's therapy had remained to the end a talk therapy. "Indeed," notes George Steiner, "Freud's raw material and therapeutic instrument are no less verbal, no less rooted in language, than the art of Balzac or Proust. This is such an obvious point that it was long overlooked. Psychoanalysis is a matter of words—words heard, glossed, stumbled over, exchanged."[24] Freud could only *ask* you in words to leave your good behavior outside the analytic situation. Reich's technique of "vegetotherapy" ended the verbal era in psychoanalysis: if "good behavior" had anchored itself in the body's musculature, Reich directly attacked it by literally laying his hands on it and trying to break this "armor plating" into little, free-floating pieces which would then stream toward the last line of defense—the pelvis.

Reich, like Freud before him (and like Charles Reich after him), constructs a tripartite model of man that recapitulates in its layering, once more, the historical "phylogeny" of Jewish Emancipation.* He begins at the end, with the cultured philistinism of the "passing" parvenu:

> Thus, what is called the cultured human came to be a living structure *composed of three layers*. On the surface he carries the artificial mask of self-control, of compulsive insincere politeness and artificial sociality. With this layer, he covers up the second one, the Freudian "unconscious," in which sadism, greediness, lasciviousness, envy, perversions of all kinds, etc., are kept in check, without however, having in the least any of their power. This second layer is the artifact of a sex-negating culture; consciously, it is mostly experienced only as a gaping inner emptiness. Behind it, in the depths, live and work *natural* sociality and sexuality, spontaneous enjoyment of work, *capacity for love*. This third and deepest, representing the *biological nucleus* of the human structure, is unconscious and dreaded. It is at variance with every aspect of authoritarian education and regime. It is, at the same time, man's only real hope of ever mastering social misery.[25] [Reich's emphasis]

*** This Reichian model of patriarchal, authoritarian man and family was influential among the Frankfort circle of Diaspora intellectuals: Erich Fromm, Theodor Adorno, and Herbert Marcuse.**

Here, in Reich's "third layer," we have the ancestor of Charles Reich's "consciousness III": "natural sociality" versus "artificial sociability."

Reich I carried Freud out of the consulting room and into the streets of the 1930s and 1940s, attacking the "insincere politeness and artificial sociality" of the "civil society" of the Gentile that Marx had attacked long ago with his call for a *Gemeinschaft* grounded in man's species-being. Reich refused the "brutal bargain" of assimilation, he rejected the price in "social misery" and social discomfort of becoming a member in good standing of bourgeois-Gentile Europe. "The cultivated European bourgeoisie of the 19th and early 20th century," he writes, "had taken over the compulsive moral forms of feudalism and made them the ideal of *human* behavior" [26] (my emphasis). Invited to become "citizens" at the time of Emancipation, lured by the promise of a kind of Greek *polis,* the emancipated Jew found himself in the meshes of a bourgeois and secularized Christian society defining itself in universalist terms. As Freud and Herzl before him, Reich sees Europe's civility and its bourgeois-Christian restraint as a hypocritical façade disguising anti-Semitism. "The forces which had been kept in check for so long by the superficial veneer of good breeding and artificial self-control," he writes, "now borne by the very multitudes that were striving for freedom, broke through into action: In the concentration camps, in the persecution of the Jews.... In Fascism," he concludes, "the psychic mass disease revealed itself in an *undisguised* form" [27] (Reich's emphasis).

The *Kulturkampf* latent in Freud assumes, in Reich, overt and undisguised form. The seeds of paranoid thinking in Reich, later to flower in his conviction of a ubiquitous "emotional plague," are already in evidence in the Reich of the thirties and forties. Herzl's dictum that all Gentiles come in two and only two forms—overt and covert anti-Semites—is reformulated by Reich into his 1942 declaration that "there is not a single individual who does not bear the elements of fascist feeling and thinking in his structure." [28] The seeds of paranoid thinking *begin*—and it is of the utmost importance that we understand exactly *where* they begin—in his violent encounter with that seemingly most superficial of things, the polite civil surface of Western social intercourse: "Hello," "Good Bye," "Nice to see you," "Beg your pardon," "Would you mind if I . . . ," "My view, on the other hand, is rather that. . . ." It is this *surface* of the *bürgerliche Gesellschaft* that bugs and infuriates each generation of *shtetl* Jewry emancipated into the West. Somehow, this civil surface is nothing, a mere appearance, a mere concern for how one "looks" before "someone" (anyone, a "stranger"); this civil, polite surface is nothing—yet, somehow, mysteriously, everything. It seems to carry, in secret, secularized form, the very meaning of European civilization. Reich's is a classical, almost textbook case, of the violent encounter of the "tribal" society of the *shtetl* with the "civil" society of the West as it takes bourgeois form in nineteenth- and twentieth-century Europe and Anglo-America. Freud had pulled his punches (his vaunted "bourgeois liberalism"). Reich refused; and his principled delict of incivility eventually became the tort for which he was imprisoned in March 1957 in the federal penitentiary at Lewisburg, Pennsylvania. (He died there of a heart attack on November 3, 1957.) Erving Goffman, in our own day, is the first to thematize, to raise to explicit consciousness, this inner link in the West between lunacy and public incivility.[29]

Reich paid the price of an ultimate testing of this link. Philip Rieff describes Reich's thrust in the following way:

> On the level of action there is the "sham social surface" of the super-ego, where the human *appears* "restrained, polite, compassionate and conscientious." But this hamming by the super-ego is the rubber glove with which repressions *maintain* their sterile grip on character. In Reich's terms the tragedy of being *moral* occurs because the *polite social surfaces* of character are separated from the "deep, natural core" by repressions masquerading as the very instincts that they repress. The lesson to be drawn was clear: abolish the repressions masquerading as the very instincts that they repress. This was the therapy and tactic of Reich's Freudo-Marxism. If, and only if, a therapeutic aim—the dissolution of the super-ego—could be added to a political aim—the dissolution of the state—could a revolution truly occur. The instincts and the proletariat must triumph together, or not at all.[30] [My emphasis]

Reich antedated the attempt of the Frankfort school to amalgamate sociology (Marx) and psychology (Freud), to play the game of relating ideological to psychological process: "He was," notes Rieff, "far more forthright than later players at the same game—say, Erich Fromm in *Escape from Freedom*."[31] Freud's ideology of the Emancipation—"liberalism"—wanted an elite management of the id so as to adjust it to a Gentile world, not a complicity with it to liberate it from that world. Thus for Reich, as Rieff tells it,

> liberalism was understood to function in society as the super-ego functioned in the psyche, *a sham of civility pulled over the reality of conflict*, and therefore powerless against doctrines of conflict once these break through the surface of social life. "Genuine" revolutionary doctrine, on the other hand, functioned in society, as the pure biological impulses do in the psyche. Reactionary impulses come straight from the middle level of the psyche, as reactionary regimes come from the middle classes of society. Fascism was the

most powerful expression of the political level of the repressed unconscious.[32] [My emphasis]

The sharp impression Reich wished to convey of our moral condition, of the fact that we proudly call our neurotic weaknesses "character," is an impression, concludes Rieff, "more politely conveyed by the Fromms and Horneys." [33] Reich's message, in other words, was the message of pariah affect, homeless in a "world it never made." A kind of integrity (and not merely compulsive contrariness) forced him to shape a medium appropriate to his message: the message was, naturally, impolitely conveyed. So the man was obviously "sick." (Is there a man in the house who will stand up and say right out that he *wasn't*?)

Character-armor begins in politeness, in civility. Character-armor, which ultimately (Reich maintains) obstructs the involuntary convulsion of orgasm from the complete discharge of sexual excitation in sexual intercourse, originates in the trivial, everyday exchange of civilities in social intercourse. The impoliteness of total sexual orgasm—its social "ostracism," so to speak—becomes with Reich the explicit metaphor—as it was more covertly with Freud—for the vulgarity and awkwardness of the Jew in the mixed company of "high" Gentile social intercourse. The "id" was, indeed, an unwitting code-word for the "Yid."

From the 1940s to the 1970s these ideas of Reich made their way into the texture of urban American culture. Jacqueline Susann in her novel *Valley of the Dolls* speaks of her WASP heroine as having lived with her good New England family in the same "orderly kind of house, . . . smothered with orderly, unused emotions, emotions stifled beneath the creaky iron armor called 'manners.' " [34] The hero of Stanley Elkin's "The Dick Gibson Show," on a bus late at night between Des Moines and Chicago, makes a pass at the girl in the seat beside him. She shrieks and slaps him, but quite soon they are having a couple of jolly orgasms together. Elkin draws the moral: "What a lesson! So much for your timidities and reservations, so much for your doubts and reluctances, your equivocations and hesitancies and *shields of decorum more heavy than the world.* Pah for your civilizing trepidations—how many words there are for it, I could go on forever! . . . One smash of passion and poof went appearance" [35] (my emphasis).

Many of the better writers of the second generation of the Eastern European immigration also found that Reich "spoke to their condition": Norman Mailer and poet Karl Shapiro, for example. Paul Goodman combined Reich with Kafka. The hero of Saul Bellow's *Henderson the Rain King* discovers on arrival that his African chieftain possesses the complete works of Wilhelm Reich. In Isaac Rosenfeld's haunting novel *Passage from Home,* published the year following the English-language edition of Reich's *Character-Analysis,* we read of the hero's stepmother hovering over her unwelcome guest, Minna, "armed with a smile." [36] Bellow recalls that it was only after Rosenfeld "had given up the Reichianism which for a time had absorbed us both" that he "no longer questioned people impulsively about their sexual habits or estimated the amount of character armor they wore." [37]

But in depth psychology itself, Wilhelm Reich's heir was clearly "Fritz" Perls. If Reich used Freud's analytic situation as a revolutionary laboratory and model to transform the Western social situation (much as John Dewey once wanted to use the school to transform, rather than reflect, the society outside), it was left to the late Dr. Frederick S. Perls to transform Reich's individual analytic situation into Reichian *group*-therapy sessions. In his Esalen Institute Gestalt Therapy sessions, he struggled to create a social situation that would have all the properties of both a (public) encounter with strangers and a primary, private living with (family-type) familiars. If Freud attempts to create in Diaspora the *shtetl* Jew on a temporary, regressive basis, Perls would recreate the *shtetl* as a group in all the dense "withness" of group affect.

If we turn to Perls's *Gestalt Therapy Verbatim,* all of which is extracted from audiotapes made at weekend dreamwork seminars conducted by Perls at the Esalen Institute in Big Sur, California, from 1966 through 1968, we see the original adversary thrust of the Diaspora intelligentsia reappearing once more. After the ritual references in his introduction—"At this moment it seems to me that the race is about lost to the Fascists" [38]—Perls goes down to the real business of "encounter therapy" by saying: "I'm not talking about ourselves as social beings. I don't talk about the *pseudo*-existence, but of the basic natural existence." [39] After assuring us (like Erich Fromm) that we are "living in an insane society" and insisting, "but I am *not* nice" (my emphasis), he goes on to distinguish three classes of verbiage production in his therapy sessions: "*chickenshit*—this is 'good morning,' 'how are you,' and so on; *bullshit*—this is 'because,' rationalization, excuses; and *elephantshit*—this is when you talk about philosophy, existential Gestalt Therapy, etc.—what I am doing now" [40] (my emphasis). Reich's three-layered personality has acquired two more layers in Big Sur. "The first layer is the cliché layer. If you meet somebody you exchange clichés—'Good morning,' handshake, and all of the meaningless *tokens* of meeting" (my emphasis). Behind the cliché layer is the role-playing layer, the V.I.P. role, the nice-little-girl and good-boy roles. "So those are the superficial, social, *as-if* layers. We pretend," Perls continues, "to be better, tougher, weaker, more polite, etc. than we really feel" [41] (Perls's emphasis). Beneath that is the third layer where we experience nothingness; we feel stuck and lost. Behind this impasse layer lies the fourth, "the *death* layer or *implosive* layer" (Perls's emphasis) which, when really contacted, explodes into the fifth or explosive layer: we become "authentic," capable of experiencing and expressing the four basic kinds of genuine explosive emotions: grief, orgasm, anger, and joy.[42]

By the end of 1968, Perls was coming to the conclusion that workshops and group therapy "are obsolete, and we are going to start our first Gestalt Kibbutz next year." The permanent membership of the kibbutz was to have been thirty, with the final differentiation—between staff and seminarians—eliminated. "The main thing is, the community spirit enhanced by . . . therapy." This *Gemeinchaft* was "meant to be a growth experience and we hope that this time we can produce *real* people"[43] (Perls's emphasis). We can gather the direction in which Perls would have taken his kibbutz from the following verbatim segment from an intensive four-week workshop at the Esalen Institute in the summer of 1968:

> Blair: I have an unfinished situation with you Fritz.
>
> Fritz: Yah.
>
> B: (quietly angry) I don't know what kind of Gestalt bullshit you were trying to pull last night, when I asked you for a match, but all I want is a simple yes or no when I ask you for a match, and not a bunch of verbal messin' around until I come up with the right combination of words and you come across with the match. And another thing, if I want *a damned sermon on social etiquette*, I'll ask you for it. As far as I am concerned, you enter my life space when I get up there on that damn chair and no other time. I'm not interested.
>
> F: (gently) So what should I do?
>
> B: Just don't mess up my mind when I ask you for a match. You can say a yes or no and that's enough. And I'll let you know when I want you, and that's up there on the hot seat.
>
> F: You made one mistake. You didn't *ask* me for a match.
>
> B: (loudly) Oh, yes, I did. Ninety-nine percent of the people in America, when you say, "Have you a match?"—those people who are over ten years old, that is—don't come up and say, "Yeah, I got a match," or some cute little fucking thing like that. You knew what I meant. Why did you fuck around?
>
> Dale: *Those are all dishonest people.*
>
> B: Ohh, don't give me that crap, Dale.
>
> F: Are you coming to my defense?
>
> Dale: Oh, nononono, I'm just telling him. (laughter) No, you do fine for yourself.
>
> B: (still mad) That's bullshit. That's the Gestalt game, that's what that is. And you can't look at me honestly and say you didn't know that I wanted a match.
>
> F: (coyly) Oh, I knew that you wanted a match.

B: Then why did you pull all that crap?

F: Because I pull all that crap. Because I am the *one per cent!* (laughter)

B: Ohh, brother, I want to get out of here.

F: That's a good resentment.

B: You know, I'm gettin' so I don't even resent you any more. (laughter) (Blair waves an admonishing finger at Fritz) You earn your money when you sit in that chair, and— (Fritz mimics Blair's pointing finger) Yeah. *"Bad boy."* (laughter) You are a–O.K., you play rules; I'll play mine. Just don't—My rules are, when I ask for a match, you know—just give it to me. (laughter) Give me a straight answer.

F: So can you also appreciate what I did?

B: Of course. Let me tell you, (laughter) I'm not alone on *that* jazz, Fritz. But that doesn't keep me from bein' damn pissed. The fact that—

F: The fact is that the blah, anemic guy you were two weeks ago is now coming out with the real anger.[44] [My emphasis]

As the 1970s got under way, title to Reich's "damned sermon on social etiquette" passed from Fritz Perls to Arthur Janov,* author of *The Primal Scream* (1970).[45] If to dress too loudly is a breach of taste, and if to talk too loudly is a breach of civility, to scream is tantamount to a revolution. In his portrait of Russian Jewish immigrants in England, Robert Kotlowitz in his finely observed novel *Somewhere Else* depicts the growing frustration of the Pilchik sisters as they find others unmoved by their arguments for revolutionary socialism: "So, boys," Anna said "in an unnaturally loud voice" to Zygmunt and Mendel one Saturday in the sisters' flat. "No use playing with theories. . . . You want to change the world, help us change it. Come to our meeting this week. We need young men like you. You don't know how much work there is to do. It won't be easy to socialize this country. Everyone has manners, everyone knows how to behave. Everyone is too nice. . . . They have to learn how to scream." † [46]

* In France, title passed in the 1960s to the anthropologist Claude Lévi-Strauss (as we shall see in Part II).

† In his memoir "Baltimore Boy," Kotlowitz (born in 1924) recounts how the old synagogues disappeared and how "the gnarled, crackling Hebrew of the Bible slowly began its transformation at services into the resonant dignity of English as even Orthodox congregations began to pray more and more in the national language; and with that has come a paling of Jehovah Himself into a neat, even-featured image of polite dignity; in short, an Anglo-Saxon God." This "polite dignity" is paralleled by the development in the Baltimore cantor's son of a "polite personality": "Aboveboard I was a neat, pleasant, well-mannered boy who paid attention to the rules; it was easier that way." "Baltimore Boy," Robert Kotlowitz, *Growing Up Jewish,* ed. Jay David (New York: Pocket Books, 1970), pp. 252, 243. The story originally appeared in *Harper's,* December 1965.

The secret inner bond between overthrowing property and outraging propriety was clear to the Pilchik sisters. It had not been obvious to Karl Marx. He had to learn the connection the hard way. Like Freud, Marx experienced civility as censorship. This fact supplies the inner link between two ideologies of the Jewish intellectual culture of the Diaspora: Freudianism and Marxism.

PART II

Karl Marx and Claude Lévi-Strauss

CHAPTER 14

FATHER AND SON: MARX VERSUS MARX

Karl Marx's father, Heinrich—his original name was Hirschel ha-Levi Marx—was a liberal, cultivated, "enlightened" lawyer, a convert to Evangelical Protestantism. At his bidding, on August 26, 1824, his son Karl and Karl's five sisters were baptized into the Evangelical Church. Shortly before graduation from the Trier Gymnasium, the seventeen-year-old Marx wrote a commentary on the Gospel of Saint John entitled "On the Union of the Faithful with Christ according to John XV, 1–14, described in its Ground and Essence, in its Unconditioned Necessity and in its Effects." Chief among the "effects" of this union with Christ, Karl Marx writes, is that heathen virtue itself is gentled; it is no longer gloomy, stoic, difficult, and dutiful. "Every repulsive aspect is driven out, *all that is coarse is dissolved*, and virtue is made clear, becoming gentler and more human"[1] (my emphasis). This early theological work of Marx, as important, in its way, for an understanding of Marxism as the publication of Hegel's *Theologische Jugendschriften* were for an understanding of Hegel,[2] is structured by the contrast between the highest achievements possible to pre-Christians—"crude greatness and untamed egoism"—and the higher world, which "draws us up purified to Heaven" made possible by the union with Christ described in the Gospel of John.[3] This dialectic of "the crude" and "the refined" is central to Marx's thought.

Once at the University of Bonn, the young Marx's behavior takes a decisive turn—in parental eyes anyway—toward the coarse and the crude. What has been called "The Struggle with the Father"[4] begins. The issue between them was clear: the son had repudiated his father's commitment to "the social art," to bourgeois conversation, respectability, and propriety. The smooth parental solution of the "Jewish problem" did not work for the more passionate and more fastidious son. Because of Marx's deeper acculturation, he was esthetically revolted by the "discrepant profile" the parental conversion had bequeathed to him; he "shuddered at the grotesque admixture in himself of the Prussian and the Jew."[5] To convert was for him to conceal, and to conceal, his high good taste informed him, was to be vulgar. "Coarseness reveals; vulgarity conceals," E. M. Forster has told us.

Karl Marx's behavior at Bonn University was the despair of his father. First it was his beer drinking, dueling, reckless spending, and general carousing. The son, after a time, ceases to violate the Protestant Ethic, only to commit a deeper offense. He reads all night, seeking answers; truth becomes more important than sociability; the strength of his convictions offends his friends and family; he is becoming a fanatic, violating the enlightened Protestant Esthetic. The aging father writes his son from Trier (December 10, 1837):

> God help us!!! Complete disorder, stupid wandering through all branches of knowledge, stupid brooding over melancholy oil-lamps. Going to seed in a scholastic dressing gown and unkempt hair as a change from going to seed with a glass of beer. Repellent unsociability regardless of all propriety and even of all feelings for your father. The limitation of the social art to a filthy room. . . . Meanwhile the common crowd slip ahead undisturbed and reach their goal in a better or at least more comfortable way compared with those who despise their youthful joys and destroy their health in order to snatch at the shadow of erudition, which they would come to possess more easily through an hour's talk with some competent person, and in addition they would have enjoyed the social pleasure of conversation.* [6]

Six years later Marx in his first public article attacks the Prussian bureaucrats who, while allowing him to publish any convictions he pleases, insist on their right to censor the manner of expression of these views. In an enlightened bourgeois liberal era, civil society enjoins its members to be moderate. Obsession as such has become disreputable. This form of adverbial censorship is, as we shall see, particularly costly for the secular Jewish intellectual.

* Another father would later write a son who was in the course of developing strong convictions quite other than those of Marx: "Your mother and I like very much your attitude of having strong convictions and of not being too bashful to express them. What I meant was that you would have to learn to be more moderate in the expression of your views and try to express them in a way that would give as little offense as possible to your friends." Memo of William F. Buckley, Sr., to William F. Buckley, Jr. (age fifteen), quoted in L. Clayton Dubois, "The First Family of Conservatism," *New York Times Magazine*, August 9, 1970, p. 28.

CHAPTER 15

CENSORSHIP: PERSECUTION AND THE ART OF WRITING

In February 1843 the first political article Marx ever wrote, on censorship, appeared in the Swiss magazine *Anekdota.** Significantly, Freud's first great work appearing at the century's end, *The Interpretation of Dreams,* was also to deal with censorship: Freud discovered that, even in dream life, between the forbidden wish and the dreamwork falls the shadow of the censor. Freud correlated the role of the censor in dream life with the role played by the social censorship of manners in waking life: "The politeness which I practice every day is to a large extent dissimulation of this kind." [1] This work of Marx, his political debut, deserves close reading. In it the young Marx notes with fury that the latest "Prussian Censorship Instruction" demands that he observe "prior restraint"—not on his political views but on his manners and style of writing; not on what he says, but how he says it.

The new Prussian censorship instructions were a liberalization of the original edict of 1819; it instructed the censors not to construe the prior edict too substantively: article II of the prior edict was never intended to impede "any serious and restrained pursuit of truth," the instruction reads. Immediately, the word "restrained" triggers all of Marx's rage. Instantly, all the antinomies of Jewish Emancipation are set clanging: Jews are to vote as *citoyens,* but they must also "pass" as bourgeois; Jews are invited to act in the political arena, but they must behave in the social arena; Jews may do or say anything they wish in the West, with only this proviso: they must do or say it in a seemly and restrained manner. Marx writes:

> The pursuit of truth not to be impeded is qualified as being *serious* and *restrained.* Both modifications point to something outside the content of the pursuit rather than to the matter to be investigated. They detract from the pursuit of truth and bring into

* While this article was written in February 1842, it was not published until 1843, because the journal for which he had written his article on censorship, the *Deutsche Jahrbücher,* was censored!

> play an unknown third factor [alongside "pursuit" and "truth"]. If an investigation must constantly attend to this third factor, an irritation supported by law, will such pursuit not lose sight of the truth? Isn't the first duty of the person in search of truth that he proceed to it *directly* without glancing left or right? Don't I forget the substance if I must never forget to state it in a prescribed form? [2] [My emphasis]

The dream-censor imposes evasiveness on the id, Freud later says; the id must learn euphemism, obliquity, and circuitousness to "pass" the vigilance of the censor. In this way the id is refined, sublimated, civilized. Only as such may it qualify for admission to the consciousness of "civil society." Marx is in the toils of his first collision with bourgeois society and its doctrine of expressive "prior restraint." He continues:

> Truth can be as little restrained as light, and in relation to what should it be restrained? In relation to itself? *Verum index sui et falsi* [Truth alone measures truth and falsehood—Spinoza]. Hence, *in relation to falsehood?*
>
> If restraint shapes the character of inquiry it is a criterion for shying away from truth rather than from falsity. It is a drag on every step I take. [cf.: "The politeness which I practice every day is . . . dissimulation of this kind."—Freud] With inquiry, restraint is the prescribed fear of finding the result, a means of keeping one from the truth.[3] [Marx's emphasis]

Heinrich Marx had criticized his son's social behavior and had invoked the exigencies of bourgeois social form. The father had himself graduated in a generation from civil society to polite society. He feared his son might become a *déclassé*. Meanwhile, the son was exploring a frontier: he was discovering that, *in practice*, the line between civil and polite society, between morals and manners, between the "how" of a thing and the "what" of a thing, was a very difficult line to draw. He was depressed and infuriated by the fact that, however *analytically* distinct they might be, the roles of "good citizen" and "respectable bourgeois" interpenetrated each other. Bourgeois society even had prior tests—"restraints"—on how the truth you were researching should "look" when you found it, its *"bonne mine"*:

> Furthermore, truth is universal. It does not belong to me, it belongs to all; it possesses me, I do not possess it. A *style* is my property, my spiritual individuality. *"Le style, c'est l'homme."* Indeed! The law permits me to write, only I am supposed to write in a style different from *my own*. I may show the profile of my mind, but *first* I must show the *prescribed mien*. . . . The prescribed mien is

> nothing but *bonne mine à mauvais jeu*. . . . I may be humorous, but the law orders that I write seriously. I may be forward, but the law orders my style to be restrained. *Grey on grey* is to be the only permissible color of freedom, . . . the *official color*. . . . The essence of mind is *always truth itself*, and what do you make its essence? *Restraint*. Only a good-for-nothing holds back, says Goethe, and you want to make the mind a good-for-nothing? [4] [Marx's emphasis—except on "*first*"]

Marx was being asked to "hold back," to restrain himself. He was unwilling, or unable, it is clear, to do so. Marx, like Freud, with lingering Enlightenment optimism, believed he could interpose a neutral "free zone" between the unrestrained importunity of emancipating Jewry and the restraint system of the Gentile society in the West. Between the Jew and the Gentile superego Freud was to later interpose the "neutral" instrumental ego of the psychoanalyst. Marx said something analogous earlier by insisting that true restraint does not lie "in the language of culture permitting no accent and no dialect. Rather," he writes, turning to the language of universalist rationalism, "it speaks the accent of the substance of things and the dialectic of their nature. It is a matter of forgetting restraint and unrestraint [read: Gentile and Jew], and of crystallizing things. The general restraint of the mind is reason, that universal liberality which is related to *every nature* according to *its essential character*" [5] (Marx's emphasis).

But, this ritual bow in the direction of the Enlightenment over, Marx returns to the fray and to what really concerns him: the inherent tension in bourgeois society between truth itself and the problem of saying it "like it is." He perceives accurately that the civic society of bourgeois culture will yield on everything except procedures; it will concede all nouns, if it can retain control of the adverbs. Marx returns to the question of the Prussian censorship instruction, its censorship of appearance, rather than reality, of form rather than content, and tries to tear it to shreds. It instructs us, he says, in its mildness, in its assertion that the 1819 edict was not intended to impede any "serious and restrained pursuit of truth." Ridiculous! says Marx. The ancient lure to the *maskilm* of Jewish Emancipation, the promise of freedom, is held out once more. But Marx this time will read the small print in the "brutal bargain" of Emancipation: "Be free *citoyens*," it proclaims, "come in any stripe, pursue and speak any truth, only"—the bourgeois caveat reads—"be serious and restrained." *Timeo Danaos et dona ferentes:* I fear Greeks bearing gifts, he writes, quoting Virgil.[6] "For I treat the ridiculous seriously when I treat it as ridiculous," runs the savage pilpulism of Marx, "and the most serious lack of intellectual restraint is to be restrained about a lack of restraint." Then he continues:

> Serious and restrained! What wavering and relative concepts! * Where does seriousness end, and where does levity begin? Where does restraint leave off, and where does lack of restraint start? We are dependent upon the *temperament* of the censor. Prescribing a temperament for the censor would be just as wrong as prescribing a style for the writer. If you wish to be logical in your esthetic criticism, prohibit the pursuit of truth in a *too serious* and *too restrained* manner, for the greatest seriousness is the most ridiculous thing, and the greatest restraint is the bitterest irony.[7] [Marx's emphasis, of course]

Marx then goes for the jugular of the Prussian Censorship Instruction: its implicit claim that, at the end of the road of social research, there sits patiently a value-free "truth" waiting to be formulated in the "official" prose of a value-neutral and "civil" civil servant. "All this," Marx declares, "proceeds from a completely wrong and abstract view of truth. . . . Even if we disregard the *subjective* side," he continues,

> namely that one and the same object appears differently in different individuals and expresses its various aspects in as many various intellects, shouldn't *the character of the object* have some influence, even the slightest, on the inquiry? *Not only the result but also the route belongs to truth.* The pursuit of truth must itself be true; the true inquiry is the developed truth whose scattered parts are assembled in the result. And the nature of the inquiry is not to change according to the object? When the object is humorous, inquiry is supposed to appear serious? When the object is touchy, inquiry is to be restrained? Thus you injure the rights of the subject. You grasp truth abstractly and make the mind an *inquisitor* who dryly *records the proceedings*.[8] [My emphasis on sentence "*Not only . . .*"]

Here we see the matrix of Marx's essay, written in 1843 and published in 1844, on the "Jewish question." "When the object is *touchy*," he asks, disbelievingly, "inquiry is to be *restrained*?" Of course not, is the obvious answer. Such restraint is exactly the sort extorted by the "neutral" civil service bureaucrats of a bourgeois state thinking itself to be the "Universal Idea" of Hegel. It is with the current essay behind

* Note how, with his exclamation marks and numerous italicizations, Marx is already *enacting* the unrestrained mode of expression frowned on by bourgeois writing codes. This is the first of three *manifestoes* in which Marx makes a public declaration of motives latent (hidden) in most of the Diaspora intelligentsia. It proclaims: Jewish Emancipation has failed. Liberal reform, gradualism will not work. There must be revolution. (Marx's other manifestoes are "On the Jewish Question" and *The Communist Manifesto.*) Freud's interest, on the other hand, was in the disguises forced on the latent wishes of assimilating Jewry.—J.M.C.

him that Marx will tackle—in his long-postponed essay on the Jewish Question—the two works in which Bruno Bauer wraps the "touchy" subject of the Jews in a hieratic prose of genteel academic restraint.

What then, for Marx, is the status of this new censorship instruction? Is it *political*? Clearly not, in the old sense of "political," anyway. The new norms go, not to the political content of the ideas expressed, but to the restraint of their manner of expression. Is the new censorship instruction, then, *moral* censorship, legislating morality? The old censorship edict, Marx notes, includes within the purpose of censorship "the suppression of 'whatever offends *morality* and good conduct.' The Instruction *quotes* this from Article II. But . . . the [new] *commentary* . . . contains omissions in regard to morality. To offend *morality* and *good conduct* is *now* to injure 'discipline, morals, and outward loyalty.' One observes," Marx continues, in his careful exegesis of the new instruction, "that *morality as morality,* as the *principle of a world* with its own laws, has disappeared," and thus the new censorship does not invade this inner realm (whose autonomy it does not recognize in any case). If the norms of the new censorship instruction do not bear on the old matter of political-moral behavior, what realm is it legislating for? What has taken its place? *"Police-regulated honorability* and *conventional good manners* have taken its place,"[9] replies Marx—that is, respectability and public propriety (Marx's emphasis). It is fanaticism, it is obsession that has been tabooed by bourgeois civil society. "The qualities of reasonableness, moderation, compromise, tolerance, sober choice —in short, the anti-apocalyptic style of life brought into the world by the middle class" is experienced by Marx as an "iron cage." * A man obsessed, he attacks bourgeois civil society whose "great cultural triumph is," as Podhoretz observes, "*precisely* that it brought obsession into disrepute"[10] (my emphasis).

Since truth is decreed by the governmental censors, the reference to the search for truth—"inquiry"—is mere ritual. Marx asks:

> Is *truth* to be understood in such a way that it is constituted by *governmental order*, and is *inquiry* a superfluous and obnoxious third element which cannot be entirely rejected *for reasons of etiquette*? . . . For inquiry is understood a priori as being *opposed* to truth and appears therefore with the suspicious official patina of seriousness and restraint a layman is supposed to display before a priest.[11] [Marx's emphasis]

Marx then breaks into a metaphor that not only reveals the nature of

* I am reinterpreting here, of course, the famous passage of Max Weber: "But fate decreed that the cloak should become an iron cage." Max Weber, *The Protestant Ethic and the Spirit of Capitalism,* trans. Talcott Parsons (New York: Scribner's, 1930), p. 181.

the censorship instruction but betrays the hidden way he and his colleagues among the Jewish exiles in the Diaspora had experienced all the "tolerance instructions" of the nineteenth-century social emancipation: "You are to write freely, but *every word is to be a curtsy* before liberal censorship, which lets your serious and restrained words *pass*. By no means should you lose," he concludes, "a consciousness of humility" [12] (my emphasis). The "serious and restrained" words of your liberal-Reform Jews will "pass," but the mocking impudence of your *schlemiels*, like Heine, will not pass. The "serious and restrained" words of your revisionist Marxists will pass, but the savage vulgarity of your pariahs, like Marx himself, will not "pass" into respectable, bourgeois-Christian society. In theory, Marx could differentiate the cultural from the social, but in practice, not unlike his follower Mike Gold, he "was a hater of refinements of thought, partly because he *could not* distinguish them from refinements of manners, which he *knew* to be a petty-bourgeois lure" * [13] (my emphasis), and partly because he *would not* so distinguish refined thoughts from gentle manners, and partly because he knew such thoughts to be indistinguishable from such manners, and hence a petty-bourgeois lure. To incorporate mental restraints and discriminations into the personality system went together with internalizing the social-behavior constraints of the social system, making up one modernization-civilizational "package." In the modernization process the finesses of one system become the nuances of the others; intellectual distinctions breed personal distinction (and vice versa); personality, social, and cultural systems all—allowing for ascertainable "lags"—play suavely into each other. As discrepancies in intersystem "profiles" are surmounted, a "drift to consistency" remorselessly sets in: the cunning of the modernization process is at work "refining substance into subjectivity." † [14]

"Every word is to be a curtsy," wrote Marx. The ancient idea of "charity," feudalized into "chivalry" in the Middle Ages, secularized into "courtesy" (and "curtsy") in the seventeenth and eighteenth centuries, undergoing a final metamorphosis in the nineteenth century into the "civility" of the emergent civil societies in the nation-states of the West. This ancient value-package was the "collective representation" hovering over the secularizing Christian West that rubbed emerging Jewry the wrong way. It caused in them what Eastern European Jewry called *tsuris:* trouble, aggravation. For Jews of the Emancipation, whether

* The authors quoted here (see note 13) apply this quotation only to Gold, precisely to distinguish his "vulgar Marxism" from Marx's. I, of course, see the matter somewhat differently.

† This is Karl Löwith's phrase describing the world-historical "revolution" introduced by Christianity (see note 14). I see this revolutionary theological input of Christianity continuing its "work of refinement" in the secularized incognito of the modernization-civilizational "package" exported to the Third World.

observant or inobservant, "the core concept that embodies and integrates the whole Jewish experience in the Diaspora," writes Ben Halpern, "is the idea of Exile, . . . a ban of penance, . . . living in expiatory subjection to the Gentiles." [15] With the dissolution, at the time of Emancipation, of the formal, sacral institutions embodying this subjection—namely, ghetto and *shtetl*—informal, de facto institutions of segregation appeared, "sponsored" by both Jew and Gentile. Separate-but-equal facilities were the rule for rank-and-file Jews. In the "neutral" spaces of the literary-social salons, Masonic lodges, and financial operations—and among bourgeois converts to the Evangelical Church like Heinrich Marx and his family—there was "passing." But questions of capacity, qualifications, "civil betterment," and "passing readiness" were always only just out of sight. The bourgeois question, Had they arrived (socially)? was always more salient for both sides than the citizens' question, Had they voted? The new historical situation of Jewish Emancipation "took the majority of Jews by surprise," writes Jacob Katz, "and confronted the Jewish community with unprecedented tasks. The *practice* of the newly attained political rights required of them cultural and social adjustment" [16] (my emphasis). In my terms: social interaction ritual—i.e. bourgeois-Christian *rites*—were prerequisite to the practice of civil *rights* and, ultimately, a condition of access to them. They were, at once, rites of passage and rites of "passing." But if the Jew's consuming interest was in acculturation, the bourgeois Gentile observed him for the signs of assimilation (social). It was the Gentile superego that presided over the Committee on Admissions, that set all the qualifications and passed on whether Jews "passed," and held all the blackballs in its hand. The theological antipathy of the Middle Ages had yielded to the complaints of debtors and creditors of the seventeenth and eighteenth centuries; in the nineteenth century, with the emergence of the social category, social antipathy was mixed with economic antipathy and gradually displaced it among the middle classes. The question stood: are Jews to be admitted to bourgeois *society*?

Like someone importunate for admission to a select private club, one is never quite sure just what are the admission qualifications, or who are the members of the admission committee, or—strange as it seems—whether one *really* wants to belong in the first place: one does not need to be possessed of *echt* Jewish "self-hate"—the "normal" garden variety of social uneasiness will do just as well—to say with Groucho Marx: "Any club that'll have me isn't worth joining." An earlier Marx complains to the Gentile Prussian censors: "You demand restraint and you proceed from the enormous unrestraint of making the civil servant a spy of the heart, an omniscient person, philosopher, theologian, the Delphic Apollo. On the one hand, you force us to acknowledge unrestraint, on the other, you forbid us unrestraint." [17] "Offensive utterances and defamatory judgments on individuals are not suitable for print," Marx quotes from the instruction. "Not suitable for print!" he exclaims. "Instead of this gentle phrasing we should have liked to receive objective definitions for what is considered offensive and defamatory." [18] Marx quotes the hope of the instruction that political literature and the daily press will "gain a more dignified tone" through the good offices of its censors' vigilance and attacks the "romanticism of the spirit, . . . the *romantic* indefiniteness [and] sensitive inwardness" (Marx's emphasis) of such ambiguous norms of "preventive prudence." * [19]

The last matter Marx turns his attention to is the clause of the censorship instruction urging the appointment of censors "who can overlook with self-confidence and tact minor objections" in a piece of political writing "which are not justified in view of the purport and direction of the entire article." Marx fairly explodes: "The *content* as a criterion for censorship already disappeared, as we have observed; now the *form* disappears too. . . . All *objective norms* have been abandoned; the *personal* relationship is left; and the censor's *tact* may be called a guarantee. What [norm] can the censor violate, then?" Marx asks (his emphasis). "Tact. But tactlessness is no crime." [20] (Of the Nazi "final solution," Trevor-Roper writes that "it was a dirty business, everyone agreed, . . . [but] it was bad form—contrary to the German, 'inborn gift of tactfulness'—to discuss the details." [21])

Marx, himself fabled for a tactlessness verging on the heroic, has, in this, his first public article, worked his way to the structural elements of the problem of nineteenth-century Jewish Emancipation: on the one side we have the petitioning emigrant from (ultimately) the back country † of the *shtetl* seeking to "pass" into the West, into its political and social systems by means of education and interpersonal skills, into its streets and public places, into its professions (as, in this case, Marx inaugurating his career as a political journalist), and everywhere urged to show "restraint" in his pursuits (of career, of money, of—in this case —"truth"); on the other side we have the "immigration" officials staffing the "customhouses," the censors, the Gentile Western superego, "instructed" to use "tact" in what it will allow to "pass." Tact, the dictionary tells us, is "delicate perception of the right thing to say or do without offending." [22] To Marx, such a directive, couched in terms of "restraint" and "tact," is the ultimate in arbitrariness, "based on haughty conceit of a police state. . . . The censor . . . is prosecutor, lawyer, and judge in one person." [23] A curious "police state," nevertheless, it legislated not criminal laws ("But tactlessness is no crime"), nor civil laws, nor morals, but manners. Marx had been emancipated into the modern, bourgeois-liberal era of "civil society." Not having undergone in his upbringing

* "Prior restraint," as we say today in freedom-of-the-press litigations.

† The late Sir Lewis Namier called the Russian pale the "hinterland" of world Jewry.

the blessings of a properly installed Protestant Ethic, he would encounter and experience the informal sumptuary legislation of a Protestant Etiquette as a heteronomous tyranny.

Later, in another battle over censorship, Marx replies to an attack on his critique, in the *Rheinische Zeitung,* of the debates in the Rhenish Diet on freedom of the press. The *Kölnische Zeitung* in turn attacked the Left Hegelians for their assaults on Christianity and reproved the censors for the "blameworthy forbearance" they had shown in allowing the newer philosophical school—and I quote from Marx's reply—"to make the most *unseemly* attacks upon Christianity in public papers and other printed writings not intended exclusively for scientific circles." * [24] Marx makes short work of the assumption of this "liberal leading article" that science is on the side of Christianity and that the religious faith of the ordinary reader should not be exposed to the doubts aroused by public religious controversy. In fact, he writes, "the truly believing heart of the 'great masses' is probably more exposed to the corrosion of doubt than the *refined* worldly culture of the 'few' " [25] (my emphasis). This cryptic remark—one more example of the onslaught of pariah Jewry against refinement *as such*—means that while the "crude" religious beliefs of the masses (in miracles, etc.) are in open collision with scientific findings, thus creating real crises of faith, the "refined" liberal Protestantism of the "elite" enables it to escape such a real clash and hence to escape the anxiety of real doubt. But the liberalism of the Cologne paper is in the end, according to Marx, less concerned with whether the investigations of Christianity in the public papers be scientific or unscientific than it is with another requirement; in Marx's words: "Even if it is attacked by unscientific investigations in all the papers of the monarchy it must be discreet and quiet." Marx once more brings the matter of seemliness to center stage: it is decorum, and concern for appearances, and fear of scandal, and deference to "good taste" that prevent philosophical and religious ideas from entering the so-called "unsuitable terrain" of newspapers. Attention must be paid, Marx insists, to "the cry of life of ideas which have burst open the orderly, hieroglyphic husk of the system to become citizens of the world." [26]

One more time Marx will turn his attention to censorship and the special meaning it had for him (and shortly thereafter his paper, the *Rheinische Zeitung*, is suppressed and Marx goes into exile in Paris). On the day he becomes editor-in-chief, he replies to charges by an Augsburg paper that, as he writes, "makes the *faux pas* of finding the

* See a parallel attack by Irving Howe on Hannah Arendt for printing her *unseemly* attack on the Eichmann trial in a public magazine not intended exclusively for intellectual circles. Irving Howe, "*The New Yorker* and Hannah Arendt," *Commentary* 36, no. 4 (October 1963): 318 ff.

Rheinische Zeitung to be a Prussian *communist*. . . . The reader may decide," Marx rejoins, "whether this *ill-mannered fancy* of the Augsburger is fair . . . after we have presented the alleged *corpus delicti*" [27] (my emphasis). He counters their charge that his paper has presented "dirty linen with approval" by asking whether his paper should maintain that communism * is not an important current issue because it "wears dirty linen and does not smell of rose water." Marx recalls that the Augsburg paper itself, in the person of its Paris correspondent, has been seeking to assimilate certain socialist-communist ideas to monarchy itself and, in the process, of course, laundering communism. This correspondent is "a convert who treats history as a baker treats botany." The real offense then, of Marx, is thus understandable: the Augsburg paper "will never forgive us for revealing communism to the public in its *unwashed* nakedness. Now you understand the dogged *irony*," Marx tells his readers, "with which we are told that we *recommend* communism, which had the happy elegance of being discussed in the Augsburg paper" [28] (Marx's emphasis). To "seek to appropriate socialist-communist ideas" [29] into bourgeois liberalism, Marx holds, much more into monarchy, is to refine away all their coarse power, to endow them with "the happy elegance" of bourgeois chit-chat in the family newspaper. Communism *is* "dirty linen," Marx declares, which must indeed be laundered if it is to "pass" in respectable journalistic circles.

We know already, in outline anyway, what will happen when Marx puts his hand to writing "On the Jewish Question": we know that he will "wash dirty linen in public" and that, in so doing, he will violate not only the Gentile commandment of public decorum—opening himself to the charge of vulgarity—but he will also violate "a powerful though unwritten commandment of Jewish life: 'Thou shalt not reveal ingroup secrets to the *Goyim*' " † [30]—opening himself to the charge of anti-Semitism. In one stroke, he will have become a double pariah: unfit by reason of vulgarity for the polite society of Gentiles—*vulgar* anti-Semitism, after all, was not *salonsfähig*—and persona non grata with the Jewish community because he had told "truth in a hostile environment." ‡ [31]

In October and November 1842 he published his analysis of the cruel wood-theft laws passed by the Rhenish Diet (sitting in Düsseldorf) against peasants who gathered fallen branches in the forest to use as fuel. Then, in early 1843, he began a series of articles on the economic distress

* Marx is not by any means a Communist at this time.

† Thus did Professor Seymour Leventman, coauthor of *Children of the Gilded Ghetto,* liken, in a letter to *Commentary* magazine (see note 31), attacks on Philip Roth's *Goodbye, Columbus* to earlier attacks on his book for having violated this taboo.

‡ This is Hannah Arendt's explanation of why the organized (and the not-so-organized) Jewish community came down on her hard for her *Eichmann in Jerusalem:* "What I had done according to their lights was the crime of crimes: I had told 'the truth in a hostile environment,' as an Israeli official told me" (see note 31).

of the Moselle vintagers. Later, he was to recall these two articles as his first "embarrassed" effort to deal in detail with "material interests." [32] Finally, on March 18, the following announcement appeared in his paper: "The undersigned declares that as from today he has resigned from editorship of the *Rheinische Zeitung* due to present censorship conditions." [33] The paper shuts down on April 1, and on June 19, 1843, Marx marries Baroness Jenny von Westphalen in the Protestant church at Kreuznach. After a honeymoon trip to Rheinpfatz, Switzerland, the couple return to the home of his mother-in-law at Kreuznach. There Marx works on "On the Jewish Question" and the *Critique of Hegel's "Philosophy of Right."* As he writes, he is preparing his departure from Prussia. Why will he leave? Because, he writes Ruge that summer, he is allowed only to use "pins instead of a sword" in his fight for liberty: "I am tired of this hypocrisy and stupidity, of the boorishness of officials, I am tired of having *to bow and scrape and invent safe and harmless phrases*" [34] (my emphasis).

The expressive norms of verbal propriety embodied in the Prussian Censorship Instruction were experienced by Marx as a form of persecution—persecution by propriety. To have continued to write would have been "to bow and scrape and invent safe and harmless phrases," that is, to practice the bourgeois form of what Leo Strauss has called "writing between the lines." [35] This technique of esoteric writing, in which a hidden truth is deliberately concealed like a stowaway among the plausible baggage of exoteric opinion shipped to the "vulgar," was repugnant to Marx. Besides, the form of censorship emerging in the liberal era addressed itself more to the manner of statement than to its content. In a man constitutionally incapable of understatement, such censorship was intolerable. He refused this form of moral Marranoism as his "ticket of admission" to the cultural system of bourgeois-Christian Prussia.

"How rare the fortunate times," Marx had concluded his article on the Prussian Censorship Instruction, quoting Tacitus, "in which you can think what you wish and say what you think." The months at Kreuznach with the Westphalens following his honeymoon with Jenny were to be one of those fortunate times. Taken up with working on his 150-page *Critique* and his reply to Bauer on the "Jewish Question," these months in 1843—prior to the Paris manuscripts of 1844—are *the* decisive months in Marx's intellectual development. His practical experience for the first time flows directly into a theoretical critique. Just as "his own struggles with the censors . . . provided Marx with at least part of the experience which underlies his long and bitter attack on the bureaucracy in the *Critique*," [36] so his observations of newly emancipated Jewry entering civil society—the *bürgerliche Gesellschaft*—gave him the empirical grip which underlies his long and bitter attack on Hegel's presumed "reconciliation" of *bourgeois* and *citoyen* in the modern state in the latter's *Philosophy of Right*. Intending to revise his *Critique,* Marx wrote an introduction to it and published it in the same issue of the *Yearbook* in which he published "On the Jewish Question."

The "original motivation-nexus" (to use a phrase of Leo Strauss) of Marx's call for the abolition of private property lies in this early struggle with public propriety. "Cultural education spread," Horkheimer and Adorno write, "with bourgeois property."[37] Bourgeois propriety spread in the wake of bourgeois property. Bourgeois *Bildung*, in the large sense of the restraints of the Protestant expressive esthetic, with its sense of "mine" and "thine," with its spheres and privacies, the whole envelope of precious space enclosing each differentiated bourgeois individual like a sacred mandala, ticketing him against intrusion—all of this Marx experienced as emasculating, domesticating, taming. France, at least, he had learned, allowed one to say the unsayable. He would take his heterodoxy there. There, in self-imposed exile from Germany, he would address himself to the "Jewish question," the ancient *Judenfrage*. Decisions made in coming to terms with the "Jewish question" could then be used in settling his accounts with the bourgeois-Christian West. In October 1843 he left with Jenny for Paris.

"On the Jewish Question" was published in Paris, in February 1844, in the only issue ever to appear of the *Deutsch-französische Jahrbücher* that was edited by Marx and his friend Arnold Ruge.[38] In that issue Parisians read the opinions that were to become an abomination to Marx's fellow Jews, a delight to anti-Semites, and a source of continuing embarrassment to members of the revolutionary Marxist movement, both Jew and Gentile:

> Let us consider the actual, secular Jew—not the *sabbath Jew,* as Bauer does, but the *everyday Jew.*
>
> Let us look for the secret of the Jew not in his religion but rather for the secret of the religion in the actual Jew.
>
> What is the secular basis of Judaism? *Practical* need, *self-interest.*
>
> What is the worldly cult of the Jew? *Bargaining.* What is his worldly god? *Money.*
>
> Very well! Emancipation from *bargaining* and *money,* and thus from practical and real Judaism would be the self-emancipation of our era. . . .
>
> Christianity arose out of Judaism. It has again dissolved itself into Judaism.
>
> From the outset the Christian was the theorizing Jew. Hence, the Jew is the practical Christian, and the practical Christian has again become a Jew.
>
> Christianity overcame real Judaism only in appearance. It

> was too *refined,** too spiritual, to eliminate the crudeness of practical need except by elevating it into the blue.
>
> Christianity is the sublime thought of Judaism, and Judaism is the vulgar * practical application of Christianity.[39] [Marx's emphasis]

Even though in 1843 the bourgeois taboo against revealing in public —even presuming such a revelation were true—the ignominious group behavior of minorities (including one's own) was much less strong than it was to become subsequently, nevertheless, Marx's essay, as we have noted, embarrassed his friends, pleased anti-Semites, and enraged Jews. Yet for all its shock value, Marx's "book review" of Bauer's two works on the "Jewish question" merely reargued in mid-nineteenth-century form a question that had been publicly argued in the previous century: "Are the Jews congenitally unsociable and rude, or are they this way as a result of having been segregated into ghettoes?"—"such was the form of the question," notes the Franco-Jewish historian Léon Poliakov, "over which argument raged in the Eighteenth Century, on the eve of the Emancipation." [40]

Was Marx an anti-Semite (i.e., a Jew-hater)? Was he a self-hating Jew? Was what Ben Halpern calls "the vulgarity of Marx's references to Jews" [41] and Edmund Silberner Marx's "anti-semitic vulgarism" [42] truly anti-Semitism? or vulgarity? or both? If both, was it vulgar anti-Semitism as opposed to polite anti-Semitism? Was Marx vulgar? Were the Jews Marx referred to vulgar? Suppose they were—then are Marx's vulgar references to them and their vulgarity anti-Semitism? or vulgarity? or both? Suppose on the contrary, that the Jews Marx referred to as vulgar were not vulgar but that, believing them to be vulgar, he made vulgar references to them and their presumed vulgarity? Was he in that case an anti-Semite? or vulgar? or both? These questions carry us to the core of Marx and Marxism and place in our hands the key to his savage assault on the bourgeois-Christian taboos of "respectable" nineteenth-century European civilization, an assault renewed in its savagery, if not in its thrust, by another intellectual of the Jewish Diaspora at the end of the nineteenth century, Sigmund Freud.

In that very fourth decade in which Marx published "On the Jewish Question" a teenage Ferdinand Lassalle was also struggling with the "Jewish question" as framed in the public discussion of "Jewish Emancipation." Lassalle had a strong interest in Reform Judaism, and his desire was strong to make the Jews a respected people.[43] He wanted to be their Maccabean vindicator.[44] At nineteen he writes to his mother

* Following Robert Payne's translation—in *Marx* (New York: Simon & Schuster, 1968), pp. 93, 95—I have changed "noble" and "common" in the version quoted here (see note 39) to "refined" and "vulgar," respectively.—J.M.C.

that Jewish "misfortune, however, as it appears here, namely as brokenness and inconsistency of the human spirit, is the esthetically ugly." [45] The choice Lassalle was to make, between left-wing revolution and Reform Judaism's liberalism, was governed by his answer to a prior question: was the sorry social "look" of Jewry in the West the outcome of long confinement and persecution by the surrounding Gentile culture, or was it the product of largely indigenous forces working within the Jewish subculture? Lassalle thus struggled to make up his mind about his own identity: was he, in the West, to be a pariah or a parvenu? All his life he wavered in his answer. Marx never did. While Marx's decision to be an outlaw took final intellectual form only in the years 1843–45—the years of his marriage to the aristocratic Gentile Jenny von Westphalen, his critique of Hegel, and his manifesto on the "Jewish question" (the years which were "the most decisive in his life," Isaiah Berlin writes [46])—this decision itself has earlier roots. As with Hobbes, as Leo Strauss notes—or with any great thinker, for that matter—the later formulations of Marx tend "to disguise the original motivation-nexus," the fundamental attitude that lies at the core of his doctrine.[47] Marx's father, long before Karl read Hegel, had presented his son with the essentials, on a behavioral level, of what Karl Löwith calls *"das Problem der bürgerlichen Gesellschaft"*: the problem of bourgeois society.[48]

CHAPTER 16

THE MARXIAN *URSZENE*: PROPERTY AND PROPRIETY

Marx's "primal scene" was thus very much a Jewish *Urszene,* rooted in his Jewish experience. Just as the core of Freud's psychoanalytic theory, the "Oedipus complex," is a universalization of his father's social humiliation, so, I contend, the core of Marx's "scientific socialism"—the insight that the determining realities of the socioeconomic "substructure" are masked by the cultural ideology of the "superstructure"—was "discovered" as a Jewish experience. When he attacks Bauer's theological interpretation of the "Jewish question," Marx does so as a debunker: "Let us consider the actual, secular Jew—not the *sabbath Jew,* as Bauer does, but the *everyday Jew*" [1] (Marx's emphasis). Here we have the earliest version of the substructure/superstructure dichotomy. It is not a spatial, higher/lower dichotomy, but a temporal, longitudinal dichotomy: the workaday weekday Jew versus the Jew of the hieratic seventh day or Sabbath. Gentiles like Bruno Bauer who defined "the Jewish question" in terms of religion were ideologists, they were "idealizing" the problem, just as Hegel had done in his reconciliation of state and civil society. Even Left Hegelians like Bauer had fallen for the romantic solution embodied in Hegel's system.

Hegel's system was an elaborate theodicy, a secularized Christian theodicy, papering over the contradictions of the liberal civic era it was designed to legitimate. Chief among the "accursed contradictions" veiled by the Hegelian "speculative identity"—as first Feuerbach, then Marx, was to note—was the supposed synthesis of civil society and the modern state. Instead of the state assimilating private interests to its "common good," private interests—individual and group interests—were using the state to further their own ends. Feuerbach and later Marx saw Hegel's idealization as an attempt to "remove this contradiction from sight" [2] through the techniques of sublimation, obnubilation, and idealization. Marx decided to reverse this process: taking the "group interest" most familiar to him—that of emancipating Jewry—he brought to light the contradiction between its bourgeois commitment to its own aggrandizement and its citizen's commitment to the "common good" and the "public interest." What to liberalism (especially as it became pluralistic liberalism) might have passed for an ardent ethnic narcissism, to

Marx was an unsightly discrepancy between official ideology and the self-serving fact. He refused to allow Hegel's romantic liberal idealism to remove this contradiction merely from sight: he was to propose radical revolutionary praxis as a way of removing it from reality. The "Jewish question" was thus to serve Marx as a model in his demonstration of the failure of the bourgeois state to transform its bourgeois members into universalistic citizens. The contradictions in Hegel's system reflect the contradictions in the Prussia of his time. In 1843 Marx was engaged in unmasking Hegel's *Philosophy of Right*—writing his *Critique*—concurrently with his exposing the realities of the "Jewish Question." There was an inner connection between Hegel's political pseudosynthesis and Bauer's theological idealization of the "Jewish question": both studiously avoided the reality of vested *collective* interests—at the level of ethnic and class interests—running counter to and exploiting the public interest. This was to be the enduring "problem of bourgeois society" (*das Problem der bürgerlichen Gesellschaft*). It is thus that historian Gertrude Himmelfarb can maintain that Marx's essay "On the Jewish Question" is neither a youthful aberration nor an eccentricity but that if one reads "the whole of the essay rather than snippets and quotations, it becomes a formidable argument . . . integrally related to the rest of his thought. . . . It is a horrendous and odious essay," she adds, "but it is also an intellectually impressive statement of his vision." [3] The empirical ingredient in this vision was the stubborn staying power of Jewish particularism; it was this that first revealed Hegel's "beloved community" to be *eine illusorische Gemeinschaft,* an illusory halfway covenant.

Jewry, then, rebutted Hegel's dream of the state assimilating and sublating into itself all egoistic interests (individual, family, guild), transforming civil society into a new community. It wasn't just the enduring *golus*-Jew [4] with his haggling and "sharp practices" nor "the phenomenon of social dissociation even when Jews enjoyed political equality" [5] that troubled Marx. What enraged him was ideology—that is, the fact that particularistic interests could be masked by abstract and universalistic legitimations, whether political, religious, or economic—and that academic theorists such as Hegel and Bauer could be taken in by these ideologies. Marx's first debunking job was to debunk the "Jewish question," to divulge the everyday Jew beneath the Sabbath Jew of the liberal-academic discussions of the "Jewish question." This, I believe, is the ethnic provenance of Marx's concept of "ideology." As Helmut D. Schmidt writes:

> Jewish interests were firmly entrenched on the side of the Manchester school of laissez-faire. As a group the Jews had nothing to gain from state interference in private enterprise and they stood to lose a good deal by the fall of liberals from political power. So they fought back mainly through the press [1848–1874]. Their

> power was not exactly measurable but recognizable. What made their power appear sinister to their enemies was the fact that the Jews were anxious to hide it for fear of arousing yet greater hostility. Thereby they increased the impression of all sharing in a conspiracy particularly as they defended their interests *in the name of lofty principles not as Jews but as Germans.*[6] [My emphasis]

The Enlightenment, the French Revolution, and the Emancipation had presumably liquidated all group and corporate interest, in principle anyway. The Jewish *kehillah* was over. Collective existence was at an end. All men were only individuals. Schmidt writes:

> By the terms of the Jewish emancipation it was impossible for Jews to defend their political or economic interests *as Jews.* The reality of their *collective* existence was never adequately taken into account by the political philosophy of nineteenth century Europe in whose political categories there was no real place for them.[7] [My emphasis]

Liberalism could never handle the de facto existence of Jewry as a collective problem. All through the nineteenth and twentieth centuries secularized Jewish intellectuals arrived at an identical choice-point: either to legitimate this observed de facto ethnic "segregation" of emancipated Jewry via nationalism—the Zionist ideology—or to delegitimate it by subsuming and universalizing it under a class variable—the communist and socialist ideologies. (Bundist socialism would try to do both.) Even slight shifts in the factors involved could convert a Communist into a Zionist, as happened in the case of Moses Hess. But in almost every case, whether the road taken was communism or Zionism, the *initial* quarrel of the secular Jewish intellectual was not with the larger society, but with the behavior—or misbehavior—of his fellow Jews. "The anti-Jewish denunciations of Marx and Börne," Hannah Arendt writes, "cannot be properly understood except in the light of this conflict between rich Jews and Jewish intellectuals." [8]

Oftentimes the "rich Jews" were relatives, and then the "conflict between rich Jews and Jewish intellectuals" was a family quarrel. Two examples of this are Helene Deutsch and Hayim Zhitlowsky. In the case of the pioneer psychoanalyst Helene Deutsch, who moved from the ideology of socialism to Freudian ideology, the quarrel began as a family quarrel. "First let me confirm what the reader must already suspect," she writes, opening the chapter on her mother in *Confrontations with Myself:* "For most of my childhood and youth I hated my mother." [9] Many pages later we learn why: "I hated my mother's bourgeois materialism." [10] Helene Deutsch's ability publicly to confess hatred for her Jewish mother was, it seems evident, a factor in her *not* having to transfer that hatred to Western bourgeois society (that is, in her not becoming a Communist). This is suggested by Dr. Deutsch herself when later she tells of meeting Rosa Luxemburg at the International Socialist Congress in Stockholm in 1910:

> I found out that Rosa Luxemburg was born into a Polish-Jewish bourgeois family, as I was, and that throughout her life she had maintained a close, typically Jewish attachment to her relatives. But when she was only fifteen, burning with indignation against the evils of society, she had joined the Socialist Party. It is interesting to note how she transferred her adolescent rebellion from her family to the whole of bourgeois society. . . .
>
> . . . Rosa's rebellion was transferred outside the family circle.* [11]

Hayim Zhitlowsky left his little Jewish village of Ushach, in Russia, when he was sixteen. Why? He was a young socialist revolutionary and he wished to be a Russian among Russians, one of "the people," in Tula. Also, he wanted to extricate himself from "the bourgeois atmosphere which caused conflicts between my parents and me" and where "each year the desire for worldly pleasures grew" and Orthodox observance receded: "My mother uncovered her hair and my father began to wear his coat shorter. In place of the old spiritual ideals came the thirst for luscious living and luscious earnings. Material wealth became their idol. . . . From this bourgeois atmosphere I had to escape." But in the summer of 1883, the year Marx was buried in Highgate, he returned to his natal village of Ushach, where the "Jewish question" confronted his universalistic socialism in a form Marx never encountered: in the form of his own family, loved ones, and relatives. "In the foreground emerged the Jewish question," he writes, "confronting me like a Sphinx: Solve my riddle or I will devour you." [12] The riddle was, as Zhitlowsky realized, that while the philo-Semitic liberal solution to the "Jewish problem" only led to Jewry's further embourgeoisment, the socialistic solution was "objectively anti-Semitic" and would destroy his people. We quote him at length:

> The philosemitic solution of the Russian-Jewish press, demanding equal rights and justifying Jewish merchantry and its achieve-

* It is perhaps a researchable hypothesis that in a Gentile environment, insofar as one's family and ethnic group are forbidden objects of public criticism and hostility, aggression will to a corresponding degree be transferred to the (Gentile) out-group, where it is permitted, even legitimated, by ancestral adversary categories; and that where, on the contrary, one can openly detest and be ashamed of one's parents for being vulgar—for this is the burden of Dr. Deutsch's chapter on her mother—one is freer to espouse more individualistic ideologies, such as psychoanalysis.

> ments for Russia, could not impress me. In fact, it revolted me. I sensed it as an absolute contradiction to my socialist ideas and ideals, which had a pronounced Russian populist, agrarian-socialist character.
>
> Samuel Solomonovich Poliakov built railroads for Russia. Those railroads were, according to Nekrasov's famous poem, built on the skeletons of the Russian peasantry. My uncle Michael in Ushach distilled vodka for the Russian people and made a fortune on the liquor tax. My cousin sold the vodka to the peasants. The whole town hired them to cut down Russian woods which he bought from the greatest exploiter of the Russian peasant, the Russian landowner. . . . Wherever I turned my eyes to ordinary, day-to-day Jewish life, I saw only one thing, that which the antisemites were agitating about: the injurious effect of Jewish merchantry on Russian peasantry. No matter how I felt, from a socialist point of view, I had to pass a death sentence not only on individual Jews but on the entire *Jewish* existence of individual Jews.[13] [Zhitlowsky's emphasis]

Zhitlowsky, like Marx, turned his eyes to "ordinary, day-to-day Jewish life"—to the *alltag* Jew, not the Sabbath Jew—and saw there much that Marx had seen a generation earlier. And he realized that universalistic socialism was a version of assimilation, and that it meant the complete disappearance of the Jewish people, and that Marx's was the most logical and consistent solution to the "Jewish problem"—"the most logical, yet for me," he adds, "psychologically impossible. I was happy and comfortable in my Jewish world. Jews were closer to me, more my own kind, than many Russians with whom I was good friends and closely associated because of our common views. Why fool myself? After all," he concludes, "I was a Jew."[14] Zhitlowsky had answered the riddle of the Sphinx. Liberalism was a poor ideological solution to the "Jewish problem" because of its elision of the "open secret" of its de facto collective dimension. Socialism and communism, recognizing the collective problem, omitted its particularist Jewish dimension. Combining his two loves, Zhitlowsky opted for Yiddishist socialism.

Unlike the observant Jew, the secular Jewish intellectual—Moses Hess, Rahel Varnhagen, Lassalle, Marx, Freud, Herzl—knew how the emancipating Jews—especially the pariah *Ostjuden,* the *golus*-Jews—"looked" to the average bourgeois Gentile. And he cared. And he was embarrassed and ashamed. How *did* they look? Let us follow the Fabian Mrs. Sidney Webb (née Beatrice Potter) as she makes her way into London's East End in 1889, there to observe the "look" of newly arrived Polish Jewry. It is six years after Zhitlowsky returned to his Russian village. It is *Shabbes:*

> You enter; the heat and odor convince you that the skylight is not used for ventilation. . . . [You see] the swaying to and fro of the bodies. . . . Your eye wanders from the men, who form the congregation, to the small body of women behind the trellis. Here [i.e., in the women], certainly, you have the Western world, in bright-colored ostrich feathers, large bustles, and tight-fitting coats of cotton velvet or brocaded satinette. At last you step out, stifled by the heat and dazed by the strange contrast of the old-world memories of a majestic religion and the squalid vulgarity of an East End slum.[15]

As her study concludes, Beatrice Potter turns to East End business practices, of which she lists many, and finds them shocking. The Eastern European Jew keeps the laws and keeps the peace and performs his contracts, but nevertheless something is missing. "The reader will have already perceived," she writes, "that the immigrant Jew, though possessed of many first-class virtues, is deficient in that highest and latest development of human sentiment—social morality. . . .* He totally ignores all social obligations other than keeping the law of the land, the maintenance of his own family, and the charitable relief of coreligionists." [16]

What Beatrice Potter here sees as a Jewish social "deficiency," an ethnic delict, Marx—only six years dead—transformed into a "symptom" of a *general* deficiency: bourgeois capitalism. This is Marxism's "primal scene," the Jewish economic *Urszene* which Marx had incorporated into his essay on the "Jewish question" forty-six years earlier (1843). Marx had universalized it; Beatrice Potter reparticularized it. Both turn their thoughts to the Anglo-Jewish economist David Ricardo. For the English Fabian, Ricardo is suddenly seen, in a startlingly new perspective, not as the supposed economist of her own decorous bourgeois English business people, but as an economic anthropologist of the "pariah capitalism" of the Eastern European Jewry of Whitechapel:

> Thus the immigrant Jew seems to justify by his existence those strange assumptions which figured for *man* in the political economy of Ricardo—an Always Enlightened Selfishness, seeking employment or profit with an absolute mobility of body and mind, without pride, without preference, without interests outside the struggle for the existence and welfare of the individual and the family. We see these [strange] assumptions verified [not in the behavior of Englishmen, much less mankind, but] † in the Jewish

* It is significant, in this connection, that Moses Rischin devotes over one-third of his famous book on the migration of Jews to New York City to what he calls "Learning a New *Social* Ethic" (Part IV) (my emphasis). Moses Rischin, *The Promised City: New York's Jews 1870–1914* (New York: Harper Torchbook, 1970), pp. 169–257.

† The material in brackets of course is my own, not Miss Potter's.—J.M.C.

> inhabitants of Whitechapel; and in the Jewish East End trades we may watch the prophetic deduction of the Hebrew economist actually fulfilled.[17]

Marx, on the other hand, reveres Ricardo for building his economics on precisely this type of market "scene," namely, a purely contractual, purely utilitarian "cash nexus" disembedded from every social ethic and moral sentiment. Ricardo is *the* scientific economist of bourgeois capitalism: "Ricardo's theory of value is the scientific interpretation of actual economic life," he declares against the French utopian socialists, who try to prove their superiority over the English economists—as the English Fabian has just done?—by "seeking to observe *the etiquette* of a 'humanitarian' phraseology," reproaching Ricardo and his school for their "cynical language" because "it annoys them to see economic relations exposed in all their *crudity* [read "Jewishness"], to see the mysteries of the bourgeoisie unmasked" [18] (my emphasis).

It is most significant that the great historian of the *shtetl* and of Eastern European Jewry, the late Maurice Samuel, a Roumanian non-Marxist Jew settled in Scotland, should converge with Marx in an identical analysis of Gentile economic behavior. "Apart from the necessities of the law, you [Gentiles]," he writes, in a book called *You Gentiles*, "attempt to bring into the field of business the curious punctilio of the fencing master—courtesies and pretenses, slogans and passwords, which mitigate only in appearance the primal savagery of the [business] struggle." [19] Here again, the elements of the Diaspora critique make their appearance: the observation of punctilios, courtesies, and mitigations, the relegation of these to the moralist category of "pretense" or hypocrisy, and, finally, the by-now-conventional contrast of the "primal savagery" with the misleading "appearances" (think of Freud's "primary process" underlying the superego; think of Marx's ideology concept).

For Maurice Samuel, it is clear, the *goyim* embed their economic exchange of goods and services in a social exchange of civilities * because, good hypocrites that they are, they refuse to *admit* the "primal savagery" of what is actually occurring between them. As with Marx, the civil nexus is an ideology, a figleaf for the cash nexus. *Goyim* have this hang-up. The civilities are a kind of games *goyim* play. Leave them to their *goyim naches*.

Marx's ideology, scientific socialism, is (as we shall see) an odd kind of "apology" for the emancipating Jewry of nineteenth-century Europe. It looks like anti-Semitism, but it isn't. It is anti–philo-Semitic. It annoyed both liberal Gentile and assimilating Jew that the *Ostjude* should provide the occasion, create the actual social scene, in which they were forced

* Just as, on the level of theory, Gentile economists such as Adam Smith—unlike Ricardo and Marx—embed their theory of capitalism in a prior theory of moral sentiments.

"to *see* economic relations exposed in all their crudity, to *see* the mysteries of the bourgeoisie unmasked." Bourgeois-Christian democracy, the whole edifice of refined bourgeois Gentile civility and "social ethics," was but a superstructure, a cunning obnubilation designed to conceal the rank materialism of bourgeois capitalism underneath. Both Marx and Freud viewed bourgeois modernization as a vast *ecclesia super cloacam.** The scandal of the *Ostjude* was that he exposed to full view, openly, the dark underside of European society.

At the very time Beatrice Potter visited London's East End, the Danish-American Jacob A. Riis visited New York's Lower East Side to see "how the other half lives." He writes of the Eastern European Jewry he sees there: "Money is their God. Life is of so little value compared with even the leanest bank account. In no other spot does life wear so intensely *bald* and materialistic an aspect as in Ludlow Street. . . . *Proprieties* do not count on the East Side; nothing counts that cannot be converted into hard cash" [20] (my emphasis). Throughout the nineteenth century the contrast keeps cropping up: "bald," "bare," "naked," "materialistic," "cash-nexus" on the one hand; "propriety," "social sentiment," "civility" on the other. The social behavior of emancipating Jewry becomes an *experimentum crucis* for the nascent social sciences. In these Jews, the pariah was not yet hidden in the parvenu. The *Ostjude* becomes for Marx his *Unterbau,* his substructure. All the rest is "propriety" (i.e., bourgeois social and legal "formalism").

Scarcely a generation after Riis, the "socialist phase" of Walter Lippmann, as a German Jew, typically began with his intense preoccupation with the problem of the "behavior in public places" of newly rich American Jewry. Lippmann's socialism was not driven by any passion for redistribution. His was not a socialism that would give with one hand to Mike Gold's *Jews Without Money* what it took with the other from *Our Crowd.* No; Lippmann's was a sumptuary socialism designed to curb the ostentation of bourgeois Jewry.† The ideologies of intellectual Jews are their ways of settling their accounts with the "Jewish question" (as they see it) and only derivatively universalist manifestoes addressed to "Mankind." We quote at length from Lippmann's analysis of a half-century ago. He writes that while there are not among Jews

> more blatantly vulgar rich than among other stocks, sharp trading and blatant vulgarity are more conspicuous in the Jew because he himself is more conspicuous. . . . He needs more than anyone else

* Kenneth Burke's definition of art. Personal communication.

† Leo Strauss, in another context, notes the connection of the "classical aversion to commercialism" with "the traditional demand for sumptuary laws." "Preface to the English Translation," *Spinoza's Critique of Religion,* trans. E. M. Sinclair (New York: Schocken, 1965), p. 16.

to learn the classic Greek virtue of moderation; for he cannot, even if he wishes to, get away unscathed with what less distinguishable men can. For that reason the rich and vulgar and pretentious Jews of our big cities are perhaps the greatest misfortune that has ever befallen the Jewish people. They are the real fountain of anti-Semitism. They are everywhere in sight, and though their vices may be no greater than those of other jazzy elements in the population, they are a thousand times more conspicuous.

Moreover, they dissipate awkwardly. It happens that the Jews, for good or evil, have no court or country-house tradition of high living, and little of the physical grace that just barely makes that mode of life tolerable. When they rush about in super-automobiles, bejeweled and be-furred and painted and overbarbered, when they build themselves French chateaus and Italian palazzi, they stir up the latent hatred against crude wealth in the hands of shallow people: and that hatred diffuses itself. They undermine the natural liberalism of the American people. . . .

I waste no time myself worrying about the injustices of anti-Semitism. There is too much injustice in the world for any particular concern about summer hotels and college fraternities. . . . I worry about the Jewish smart-set in New York. . . . They can in one minute unmake more respect and decent human kindliness than Einstein and Brandeis and Mack and Paul Warburg can build up in a year. I worry about upper Broadway * on a Sunday afternoon where everything is feverish and unventilated. . . . And as a Jew writing in a Jewish weekly to Jews I say that there is a very serious danger of failure. . . . The Jew is conspicuous, and unless in his own conduct of life he manages to demonstrate the art of moderate, clean and generous living, every failure will magnify itself in woe upon the heads of the helpless and unfortunate. The Jew will have to display far better taste than the average if he is to discount for the purpose of sympathetic understanding with the rest of the American people the fundamental fact that he is conspicuous." [21]

Lippmann's socialism betrays its roots. Closer in inspiration to Marx's

* A dozen years earlier he had worried about Washington. In "The Discussion of Socialism: Politics and Meta Politics" in the *Harvard Illustrated Magazine*, the "Ballinger scandal"—a kind of Jewish "Teapot Dome" (which was an Irish scandal. See Stephen Birmingham, *Real Lace: America's Irish Rich* [New York: Harper & Row, 1973], pp. 103–34) during Taft's incumbency—motivates Lippmann's socialist call: "If you support Ballinger and the Guggenheims," he proclaims, "you are consistent with nineteenth century unsocialist theory; if you support Gifford Pinchot, you are a supporter of an essential part of the Socialist program." *Harvard Illustrated Magazine*, April 1910, pp. 231–32. Lippmann will later move, as he acculturates to the "culture of civility"—and as Jews assimilate—from the advocacy of public property to his final phase of the "public philosophy" (namely, civility).

communism than he would be pleased to admit, this apostle of puritan "plain living and high thinking" clearly constructs his socialist ideology as a prophylaxis for what he takes to be Jewish ostentation. When Eastern European socialism is urged by Eastern European Jews, it is urged for the sake of the Jews; Eastern European Zionism also. They are auto-emancipations. But the provenance of German-Jewish socialism, as of German-Jewish Zionism, is different. Lippmann's was a sumptuary socialism as Brandeis's was a sumptuary Zionism. "For it was clear to those who did not seek the way of individual escape by means of conversion," Jacob Katz writes of post-Emancipation Jewry, "that, as Jews, they would always be judged by the collective and it was to their advantage to see that the lowest type of Jew, who seemed to provide a model for the stereotype, should disappear altogether." [22]

CHAPTER 17

MARX AND THE EUPHEMISTS

The whole of the nineteenth century can be viewed as a search for the proper set of euphemisms with which to talk about the "Jewish question." The stage was set in 1781 with the publication of Christian Wilhelm von Dohm's pamphlet *Uber die bürgerliche Verbesserung der Juden: On the Civic Betterment of the Jews*. But what did this well-intentioned Gentile Dohm—"the outstanding advocate of Jewish emancipation in eighteenth century Prussia," according to Hannah Arendt [1] —mean by his phrase "civic betterment"? Logically, Jacob Katz points out, the "subject of the implied verb *verbesseren* is society, the Jews themselves, or probably both." [2] And this, indeed, was Dohm's proposal: for civic improvement to occur, both society and Jewry would have to mend their ways. Dohm "accepted the prevailing evaluation of the Jews," Katz writes, "as a politically incapacitated and morally degenerate group." He had not written, Dohm replied to his critics, an apologia for the Jews as they *are* but—*vide* the title—as they *will be*.* [3] Thus, the idea of self-improvement as a precondition for civil rights—a debate that was revived in the form of "functional prerequisites for a stable democracy" only at the end of World War II with reference to decolonization (and after 1950 with reference to civil rights for American blacks)—was being publicly debated at the end of the eighteenth century in reference to Jews.

Thus, Jews and non-Jews alike who in the decades following Dohm's work fought for the betterment of Jews' civic and social situation did so, Katz notes, "under the assumption that at the same time a civic and moral *self*-improvement on the part of the Jews was necessary." Thus the "objective" appraisal that the access of Jews to Western bourgeois civil society would require a goodly amount of "adjustment and self-adaptation," to use "value-free" terminology, was actually "couched in terms of moral judgment, stating that the Jews must become not only different but better." Not a little of this transposition of the "Jewish

* A parallel in the 1950s was the growing resentment of militant blacks in the United States toward the second *A* in the acronym NAACP: National Association for the *Advancement* of Colored People. The more militant leaders were more exteropunitive, blaming white American society, insisting that *it* must "advance."

question" into the key of morals is due to Dohm's *"Verbesserung,"* a term remaining in use for almost half a century.[4]

But not everyone was equally pleased at that way of talking about the "Jewish question." There is the pathos of Jews like Moses Mendelssohn who welcomed Dohm's initiative in behalf of Jews yet found his estimate of the current "cultural depravity" of the Jew difficult to swallow. In hailing Dohm's book, Mendelssohn "characteristically dropped the term *bürgerliche Verbesserung,* substituting in its stead *bürgerliche Aufnahme*: that is, civil acceptance. Inadvertently, perhaps," Katz adds, "he interpreted Dohm's term as referring to the state, which had to improve the Jews' status." [5] Here we see, not some inadvertence, as Katz suggests, but an early form of a structural element in the "Jewish Emancipation problematic" that recurs throughout its history.

The discoveries in science of Copernicus, Darwin, and himself, Freud wrote in 1917, by toppling man from his privileged position at the center of things (things cosmological, biological, and psychological, respectively), wounded "the general narcissim of man." [6] If the self-love of Gentile humanity was, these three times, severely wounded by discoveries in science, the ethnic narcissism of the Jew suffered all at once a grievous trauma by its discovery of nineteenth-century European civilization. In the pre-Emancipation era, Jewry could maintain the illusion of its privileged position by maintaining the plausibility of its expectation of the long-deferred messianic reversal. A credible theodicy was always ready to hand to explain "the problem of evil"—namely, the present (and hence apparent) inferiority of the Jewish people vis-à-vis the present (and hence apparent) superiority of the surrounding *goyim.* Solomon Maimon, for example, recalls an incident from his Polish boyhood (he was later to visit, and embarrass by his behavior, Mendelssohn and his circle in Berlin). One day, Prince Radzivil, a great lover of the chase, came with his daughter Princess Radzivil and his whole court to hunt in Maimon's neighborhood. The young princess, needing rest, came with the ladies and servants of her court "to the very room," Maimon writes in his celebrated *Autobiography,*

> where as a boy I was sitting behind the stove. I was struck with astonishment at the magnificence and splendor of the court. . . . I could not satisfy my eyes with the sight. My father came in just as I was beside myself with joy, and had broken into the words, "Oh, how beautiful!" In order to calm me, and at the same time to confirm me in the principles of our faith, he whispered into my ear, "Little fool, in the other world the *duksel* will kindle the *pezsure* for us," which means, In the future life the princess will kindle the stove for us.[7]

"No one can conceive the sort of feeling this statement produced in me," recalls Maimon, supplying precious testimony on the waning of the Jewish "middle ages":

> On the one hand, I believed my father, and was very glad about this future happiness in store for us. . . . On the other hand, I could not get it into my head that this beautiful rich princess in this splendid dress could ever make a fire for a poor Jew. I was thrown into the greatest perplexity on the subject.[8]

Jewish Emancipation in the next century consists in a humiliating series of such encounters of the theodicy of Jewish Exile with the West. On every such contact, the plausibility of the explanation of why the people of the Covenant need "betterment," and why the surrounding *goyim* are riding so high, comes under considerable strain. "Little Jewish boys," Margaret Mead writes, "read the stories of Polish heroes, with admiration as well as with the required disapproval, covert admiration" coexisting uneasily with overt disapproval of the lure of the "world more attractive" existing beyond the pale of the Eastern European *shtetl.*[9] "The core concept that embodies and integrates the whole Jewish experience in the Diaspora," writes Ben Halpern, "is the idea of Exile, . . . a ban of penance, . . . living in expiatory subjection to the Gentiles."[10] Emancipation puts this core concept under increasingly more strain. Traditional ethnic self-esteem eases this tension and maintains Jewry's morale by the stance it takes up toward the past, the present, and the future. (The matter might be put as follows: Jewish secularization takes place in three tenses.) As far as the condition of the Jews goes, at any given time the need for "betterment" due to "degradation," "inferiority," (call it what you will) can be either affirmed or denied. If it is affirmed, then it will be explained by the past. The traditional, observant Jew will explain it as part of sacred salvation history—that is, it is a punishment for Israel's sins. The secularizing, intellectual Jew will turn this theodicy inside out, forging it into an instrument with which to blame the Gentile. The older, intrapunitive theodicy becomes an exteropunitive sociodicy: "You made us what we are today," the secularist intelligentsia of the Diaspora will insist, indicting the Gentile West, creating what Salo Baron calls the "lachrymose" historiography of the Jews.[11] The culture of the West being what it is—Christian—the victim-status carries considerable prestige. This victim-status, derived from the Christ-figure,* becomes for Jews almost irresistible when to its pathos is added the attraction of the fact that it is liberal Gentiles of impeccable status like Dohm who themselves offer past anti-Semitism as the overall explanation for the present Jewish "condition." Historically, Katz writes, Christian Dohm "lays the blame for the civic and moral deterioration of Jewry on Christian society, which debarred Jews from using their abilities and exercising their innate moral qualities. But his diagnosis of the fact of deterioration, or perhaps even

* See pp. 211–212.

degradation, was accepted with little hesitancy."[12] Dohm's description of the present degradation of the Jews was "accepted with little hesitancy" precisely because—and this is another recurring feature of the problematic of Jewish Emancipation—it was coupled with the anti-Semitism explanation of the origin of this degradation. It was coating on a bitter pill. This "package"—conceding Jewry's ignominy, pledging betterment, explaining it by Jew-hate—is the formula for both the classical liberal Jewish adjustment to the Diaspora and its counterpart among the *goyim*, liberal Gentile philo-Semitism. This Diaspora liberalism divides once more into two varieties: the militant activist liberalism whose provenance is among Eastern European Jewry and which, throwing over the passivity of the rabbinical *halakah*, organized for autoemancipation; and the more assimilated liberalism of Western Jewry, which threw off the traditional legal system only to replace it with the restraints of the Gentile *halakah* of civility. (To this day, the thrust of the former type of liberalism is reflected in the American Jewish Congress, as the latter is in the American Jewish Committee.*)

The liberal Jewish adjustment for living-the-Diaspora, then, was to concede present Jewish shortcomings contingent upon Gentile admission of Christian shortcomings both past and present. In the Diaspora ideology of liberalism, in other words, anti-Semitism was not a phenomenon of interaction, a "tragic but inevitable" outcome of "Jews in a Gentile world," but was almost entirely an input from the Gentile side of the line, gratuitous, willful, unnecessary. The Diaspora ideologies of Zionism and radical Marxism directly challenged Diaspora liberalism's diagnosis of the past and the present and its hopes for the future. Zionists, for their part, "held to a sociological doctrine that Jew-hatred was *necessarily caused* by Jewish homelessness and would disappear when the national home was built and the exiled Jewish masses were gathered in." The symmetrical ideology of universalistic Marxism was identical in this respect to Zionism: "Jewish radicals analyzed anti-Semitism *as incidental* to the class struggle and expected it to disappear in the ruins of the capitalist system. Those who made a *direct attack* on anti-Semitism," Halpern concludes, "were Jewish liberals"[13] (my emphasis). In this way, the disesteem and "self-hate" structural to the experience of dispersion into the West could be muted. Zionists planned to heal at one stroke the wound to national self-esteem by leaving Europe—and by leaving behind the invidious comparisons fatal to remaining there. Marxists planned to kill the "Jewish question" by revolution, not emigra-

* Ben Halpern contrasts the frankly ethnic politics of Eastern European Jewish activist liberalism with the Central and Western European passive and individualistic liberalism. *Jews and Blacks* (see note 8), p. 125. The former liberalism was in a kind of preestablished harmony with the pluralistic liberalism of melting-pot politics needed for survival in metro-America.

tion: at one stroke, all would be changed, changed utterly, as a species-humane community is born. The ideology of Diaspora liberalism was essentially a decision and a utopian dream: it was the decision to remain in the West (neither emigrating nor revolting); it was the dream that, by dint of *nudzhing* and *kvetching*, litigation and voting, education and modernization, a neutral society might awake from the nightmare of history, offering neutral spaces and public places where Jew and Gentile might mingle civilly and socially, a social system in which differences in culture made no difference in society.

But the question that remained for Diaspora liberalism was how best *to talk about* those differences between Jew and Gentile that persisted. The search for the proper set of euphemisms with which to talk about the "Jewish question" continued unabated. Mendelssohn, as we have seen, dropped (not so inadvertently) Dohm's term "civic betterment" (*bürgerliche Verbesserung*) for "civil acceptance" (*bürgerliche Aufnahme*). Mirabeau journeys from Paris to Berlin. He had read and was duly impressed by Lessing's *Nathan the Wise,* arriving in Berlin just after the death of its real-life hero, Mendelssohn. He attends the salon of Henriette Herz, intervenes with Frederick II in favor of her people, and reads Dohm's *Civic Betterment.* Emulating Dohm and C. F. Nicolai, the comte de Mirabeau soon publishes his own apologia for the Jews, *Moses Mendelssohn et la reforme politique des Juifs.*[14] "Civic betterment" has taken on a French accent and been politicized into "political reform." But in Germany the idea of the self-improvement of the Jews as a precondition for full civil rights gains more and more currency after the Congress of Vienna in 1815; Dohm's very term is used in its documents.[15] Finally, by way of the public discussion of Catholic Emancipation in England, the term "emancipation"—not used prior to 1828 in Germany—begins to take hold as a way of talking about the "Jewish question" and, in the end, expropriates all others. "Emancipation" as a euphemism for talking about the "Jewish question" defeats all its rivals because it gets rid of any notion of self-improvement as a precondition for civil rights on the part of Jews, and, by being a political term purely and simply, it rids the "problem" of any lingering suggestion that there might be nonpolitical qualifications—bourgeois qualifications—for political citizenship. It cuts off in advance any idea that there might be a possible connection between the rudimentary political rights of civil society and the bourgeois social rites of polite society. "Emancipation" has the additional advantage, from the side of Diaspora liberalism, of implying that the pre-Emancipation status of Jews in the Gentile world—accounting for all their subsequent disabilities—was one of slavery. Sir Isaiah Berlin merely draws out the implications of the term itself when he writes, in 1961, his *Jewish Slavery and Emancipation.*[16] European Jewry, then, in its non-Zionist, non-Marxist mainstream, becomes—in both its own and in liberal Gentile eyes—the earliest of those "belligerent communities of pathos" of which Renate Mayntz speaks.[17] With the emergence of this pathos of the victim a mystique is born; henceforth, Gentile liberalism will be inseparable from bourgeois-Christian philo-Semitism.*

It is a revealing cultural circumstance that so many of the Diaspora ideologies begin their "revolutions" in revolt against euphemism. Freud's psychoanalysis deeuphemizes sex, the id, which represents, as we have seen, the pre-Emancipated Jew. The "civilized" sexual morality of Western civil society, Freud argues, inclines us "to concealment of the truth, to euphemism, to self-deception, and the deception of others." [18] Theodore Herzl's Zionism really began on January 5, 1895, when, as correspondent for the Vienna *Neue Freie Presse* covering the public degradation in Paris of Captain Dreyfus, he heard the mob scream "Death to Jews!" (*"A mort! A mort les juifs!"*) The liberal Jewish editors of the *Neue Freie Presse* altered the text of Herzl's dispatch in their Sunday edition, universalizing, that is, euphemizing it to read: "Death to the traitor!" "Even if we grant, on insufficient grounds," Herzl's biographer, Alex Bein writes,

> that it was really a traitor who was being condemned and degraded, the attitude of the crowd was—according to the report—a strange one. We read, in the *Neue Freie Presse,* that the crowd shouted: "Death to the traitor!" This is quite comprehensible—but there is something incomplete about it. We cannot avoid the impression that Herzl's telegrams were edited before they were printed, and it was fear that motivated the excisions. It is unlikely that Herzl . . . had himself colored the report. Four years afterwards there still rang in his ears the shouts of the crowd, which left him shattered: *"A mort! A mort les juifs!"* [19]

Politeness, perhaps even more than fear, motivated the excision and the resulting euphemism (the substitution for "Jews" of the more abstract "traitors"). There was a contradiction between the coarse bluntness of Herzl's dispatch and what Hannah Arendt calls in another context "the hypocritical politeness which surrounded the Jewish question in all respectable quarters." [20] This politeness and euphemism existed in Marx's time, in all respectable quarters. In fact, such politeness and euphemism defined respectability. It is this cultural situation that will make it all but inevitable that the anti–philo-Semitism of Marx's essay "On the Jewish Question" will be misread, when it appears in 1844, as unadulterated anti-Semitism.

* Liberal ideology's concept of "suffering situations" links it with the cultural pathos of the Jew and with philo-Semitism. See Kenneth R. Minogue, *The Liberal Mind* (New York: Vintage Books, 1968), pp. 1–13.

CHAPTER 18

CLAUDE LÉVI-STRAUSS: THE RUDE, THE CRUDE, THE NUDE, AND *THE ORIGIN OF TABLE MANNERS*

Claude Lévi-Strauss belongs with the founding patriarchs of Jewish intellectual culture in the Diaspora, with Marx and Freud. He is to anthropology as they are to sociology and psychology. Structural anthropology is the last of the classic ideological "remedies" for the cultural status-wound inflicted on intellectual Jewry by its emancipation into the West. In comparison with Western modernity, Lévi-Strauss—his religion, his people—appeared backward, "primitive."

His revered teacher, Émile Durkheim, believing in historical development, had founded French scientific sociology with his first great work in 1893, *The Division of Labor in Society*, in which he analyzed the modernization process as a development from tribal or mechanical solidarity—which he illustrated chiefly (as a son of rabbis) by copious Old Testament references *—to modern civil societies in the West, which he called "superior societies." It is significant, recalling the old dispute over the word "betterment" (*Verbesserung*) in Dohm's title, that the subtitle of the first edition of Durkheim's *Division of Labor*—namely, *Étude sur l'organization des sociétés supérieures*—was subsequently dropped. Lévi-Strauss experienced such "developmentalism" as demeaning, much as today in Latin America Marxist intellectuals derisively reject the whole "developed-underdeveloped" paradigm of modernization by calling it *desarrollismo.*[1] All our teachers, Lévi-Strauss recalls, were "obsessed with the notion of historical development."[2] Experiencing the same status-wound that would later lead members of the Jewish community to bitterly resent Arnold Toynbee's reference to observant, Orthodox Judaism as a "fossil," Lévi-Strauss, though an "unsynagogued," secular Jewish intellectual, turned decisively against the whole idea of social evolution, even

* Forty-five explicit references to Deuteronomy, Exodus, Joshua, Leviticus, Numbers, and the Pentateuch are indexed in *The Division of Labor*, more than to any other single topic or person. Professor Benjamin Nelson once remarked in a lecture that the index to Max Weber's *Economy and Society* contained more references to Jesus than to Marx.

in its modern and "relativized" form (what is now called "the new evolutionism"). His deeply oral imagination—he castigated the "cannibal-instincts of the historical process," [3] as he would later code myths under the categories of "the raw and the cooked" [4]—spat out Western civilization and the vaunted meaningfulness of *historical* experience. "My intelligence is neolithic," he announced; "to reach reality we must first repudiate experience." [5]

Lévi-Strauss attributes this fundamental insight to Karl Marx—who also repudiated appearances—to whom he considers himself to be in pupillary succession. Falling back on the anthropological language of "initiation," he writes:

> When I was about seventeen I was initiated into Marxism by a young Belgian socialist whom I had met on holiday. . . . A whole new world was opened to me. My excitement has never cooled: and rarely do I tackle a problem in sociology or ethnology without having first set my mind in motion by reperusal of a page or two from the *18 Brumaire of Louis Bonaparte* or the *Critique of Political Economy*.[6]

Lévi-Strauss, by thus rooting his ahistorical structuralism in Marx, inadvertently unpacks the historicism and idealism at the root of Marxism. Historicist idealism is an ideological strategy, used by both the old aristocratic "insiders" and the new ethnic "outsiders," for recouping from the status-humiliations of modernity. Cultural and subcultural dispossession are a "wound in the heart." Structuralism, like Marxism, is an ideology of subcultural despair, an uneasy melange of cognitive relativism and ethical absolutism.

The component of positivism in Marx—his hard-boiled, hard-nosed "materialism"—is small indeed compared to the logicism—his "contradictions" talk—and idealism. It is not for nothing that Talcott Parsons, after briefly analyzing Marx as part of the positivistic tradition, breaks off his analysis: "Further discussion of Marx will therefore be postponed until his relation to idealism can be taken up [in chapter 18, "The Idealistic Tradition"]. He is one of the most important forerunners of the group of writers . . . to be dealt with under the heading of idealism." [7] The curious paradox of Marxism which Michael Polanyi has identified as constituting the secret of its appeal, namely, "sceptical fanaticism"—characteristic also of that other product of Jewish intellectual culture in the Diaspora, Freudianism—is itself rooted in large part in the fact that Marxism is a theoretical "conceit" *—that is, a violent yoking together of theoretically unmediated components (positivism and idealism) which

* Using "conceit" as it is used in literary criticism, the way Coleridge in *Biographia Literaria* used "fancy," pitting it against "imagination" (only the latter "melds" components into new wholes).

appeals to an intellectual clientele at once cynical about the "situation of social action" and utopian about the "ends of social action."

Thus, the allure of these ideologies for a dissociated theoretical sensibility consists in their appeal to moral passion in the language of social science. A passionate social conscience is licensed as dispassionate cognitive science. In "scientific" socialism as in "scientific" psychoanalysis, the normative and the cognitive are conflated; "the fire and the rose are one." A pitilessly punitive and sceptical objectivity unmasks a given world of fact; a homeless revolutionary longing projects a new world of value.* Members of the Frankfurt Institute for Social Research, for example—Adorno, Horkheimer, Marcuse, and others—considered their effort to combine elements of Marxism with Freud's psychoanalysis in developing "critical theory" to be the work of "unattached" and "universalistic" radical intellectuals. The Frankfurt Institute members are famous for their indignant repudiation of all sociology-of-knowledge attempts to relativize their radicalism by exploring its possible connections with their cultural marginality and ethnicity.

Members of the Frankfurt circle, its historian Martin Jay notes, "were anxious to deny any significance at all to their ethnic roots. . . . [Felix J.] Weil, for example, has heatedly rejected any suggestion that Jewishness—defined religiously, ethnically, or culturally—had any influence whatsoever on the selection of Institut members or the development of their ideas. What strikes the current observer," Jay continues, "is the intensity with which many of the Institut's members denied, and in some cases still deny, any meaning at all to their Jewish identities." † [8] In this "vehement rejection of the meaningfulness of Jewishness in their backgrounds" on the part of Frankfurt's "critical theorists," in this insistence on their own "total assimilation," Jay argues, "one cannot avoid a sense of their protesting too much." [9]

It is important to note here that, excepting the case of Walter Benjamin, there was no open break, by Frankfurt circle members, with their parents or with the Jewish community. On my analysis, there existed all the shame and anger at the vulgarity of the parental "bourgeois materialism" as there had been in the case, for example, of Helene Deutsch; but—unlike Deutsch, and like Rosa Luxemberg—this hostility

* Jean-Richard Bloch in a brilliant essay (translated by Lionel Trilling) was the first to identify this subcultural syndrome, what Bloch calls a "combination of skepticism and fanaticism" in the secular intellectual Jews of modernity. "Napoleon, the Jews, and the Modern Man," *Menorah Journal* 18, no. 3 (March 1930): 219.

† Jay notes the intensity of the disclaimers of Weil, "the financial sponsor of the Institut and other leftwing ventures such as the Malik Verlag and the Piscator Stage." He writes: "In more than a score of letters, Weil exhorted me to ignore the Jewish question entirely in my treatment of the Institut; to bring it up once again, he contended, would play into the hands of earlier detractors who had 'explained' the Institut's radicalism by pointing to the cosmopolitan roots of its personnel." Martin Jay, "Anti-Semitism and the Weimar Left," *Midstream* 20, no. 1 (January 1974): 44.

was displaced from Jewish bourgeois society to the permitted target of the larger Gentile society. It is highly significant that the radicals of the Frankfurt Institute (again, with the exception of Benjamin) precisely did *not* carry their rejection of "the commercial mentality of their parents," [10] to use Jay's phrase, into outright *personal* rebellion. Of equal significance is the obverse fact: these well-to-do business-oriented Jewish parents of the Weimar '20s and '30s did not, for their part, rebel against the radical mentality of their sons but, on the contrary, generously supported them —as affluent suburban parents were later to support their New Left activist offspring in the American '60s [11]—in their "higher" calling.

What had been published by Marx openly and publicly in 1844 on the "Jewish question" would be written discreetly in 1946 by Horkheimer in a private letter to Leo Lowenthal: "The Jew is the pioneer of capitalism." [12] The difference is that the Marxism of the Frankfurt circle is a refined or bourgeois Marxism. Frankfurt Marxists, as Edward Shils notes, are "*Edelmarxisten.*" [13] Marx's "bad taste" was his insistence on saying in public things others would only say in private. He repudiated, in other words, the core differentiation of bourgeois society, that "division of labor" it had institutionalized as its "solution" to the discontents of modernity: the bifurcation of life into private and public "spheres." [14]

A private solidarity with the close-knit bourgeois Jewish family (*pace* Marx's revilement of "bourgeois familism") was dutifully protected; the Marxian strictures of "critical theory" were conspicuously reserved for, and publicly directed against, the larger bourgeois Gentile society, where estrangement and "alienation" were both normal and subculturally "normative," being defined as "exile." There was, for example, some transient "initial friction" between father and son, Jay relates, when Max Horkheimer, the Frankfurt Institute's most important director, decided not to follow his father into manufacturing:

> The one real period of estrangement that did occur between them followed Horkheimer's falling in love with his father's gentile secretary, [Maidon], eight years his elder. He married her in March, 1926, at about the same time that he began teaching at the university. . . . It was apparently much harder for his parents to get used to the idea that Horkheimer was marrying a gentile than that he was becoming a revolutionary." [15]

It is the ironic fate of Marx's communism, as of Freud's psychoanalysis, that they came to embody and express the normative and cultural differences they were designed to deny and transcend. "Both systems," in Stanley Rothman's view, "deny the reality of cultural differences, affirming instead a universal ideology applicable across cultures and across ethnic lines. What better way to end one's marginality than by undermining the categories that define one as marginal?" [16] It was relatively late in his intellectual life that Lévi-Strauss was to settle on an intellectual tool, structuralism, that would put an end to the trauma of status-loss inherent in Jewry's entry into the modernized West in the nineteenth century. "Anthropological analysis tends, admittedly," Lévi-Strauss writes toward the end of *Tristes tropiques,* "to enhance the prestige of other societies and diminish that of our own: in that respect," he concedes, "its action is contradictory." [17]

To escape from this contradiction, Lévi-Strauss constructs the anthropological ideology of "structuralism." In this way he tackles the contradiction inherent in the anthropological version of the paradox of "sceptical fanaticism," namely, that while fiercely critical—even culturally subversive—of Western usage (*moeurs*) and modern society, he became, in the face of other, exotic, and earlier cultures, uncritically accepting, whatever their defects. "At home," he writes in *Tristes tropiques,* "the anthropologist [read: Claude Lévi-Strauss] may be a natural subversive, or convinced opponent of traditional usage: but no sooner has he in focus a society different from his own than he becomes respectful of even the most conservative practices. . . . How shall we have the right to fight [these conservative abuses] at home if, when they appear elsewhere, we make no move to protest? The anthropologist who is a critic at home and a conformist elsewhere is therefore in a contradictory position" [18] since, in terms of his "cultural relativism" ("scepticism") there can be no privileged or absolute values ("fanaticism"). "There is only one way," he concludes—going back through Marx to Rousseau, "our master and our brother"—"in which we can escape the contradiction in the notion of [the] position of the anthropologist, and that is by reformulating, on our own account, the intellectual procedures which allowed Rousseau to move forward from the ruins left by the *Discours sur l'origine de l'inégalité* to the ample design of the *Social Contract,* of which *Emile* reveals the secret, . . . and [thus] discover the unshakable basis of human society" in "the neolithic age, . . . that myth-minded age." [19]

Soon after writing *Tristes tropiques,* Lévi-Strauss underwent a kind of conversion. The whole normative status his teacher Durkheim had given to the societies of historical, modernizing, Western civilization, calling them *"sociétés supérieures,"* was repudiated. The tetralogy of Lévi-Strauss completed in 1971, *Introduction to a Science of Mythology,* seals that repudiation.* In the first volume, *The Raw and The Cooked* (1964), an ancient theme of Diaspora intellectuality puts in its appearance (recalling Freud, Marx, and others)—namely, Part 2, which begins by

* The four volumes are: vol. 1, *Le Cru et le cuit* (Paris: Librairie Plon, 1964); vol. 2, *Du Miel au cendres* (Paris: Librairie Plon, 1967); vol. 3, *L'Origine des manières de table* (Paris: Librairie Plon, 1968); and vol. 4, *L'Homme nu* (Paris: Librairie Plon, 1971).

coding Bororo myths, with high Parisian irony, under the category of "The 'Good Manners' Sonata" (pp. 81–133), with a subdivision on "Childish Civility" (pp. 108–20). Echoes of Marx and Freud can be heard in Lévi-Strauss's obsession with the raw, the coarse, the vulgar, the naked, and their transformation-mediation-sublimation into the cooked, the refined, and the clothed.

In 1968 Lévi-Strauss published the third volume of his *Mythologiques*. Its 475 pages carry an astonishing title: *L'Origine des manières de table: The Origin of Table Manners*. Replete with references to the *De Civilitate Morum Puerilium* of Erasmus, the volume culminates in a seventh part, "*Les Règles du savoir-vivre*", in which the neolithic "know-how" of living (*savoir-vivre*), which is the morality encoded in myths, is pitted against the modern Western "know-how" of behaving (*savoir-faire*).

If the first two volumes of his *Introduction to a Science of Mythology* unpack the "secret logic" at work in mythical thought, Lévi-Strauss's third volume reveals the morality that also lies hidden in mythology—a morality, Lévi-Strauss tells us, "as remote, alas, from our morality, as its logic is from our logic." [20] True morality, the morality "immanent in the myths" of "savage peoples," is based on a "deference toward the universe." Our morality, the morality of "mechanical" civilization, is a code of "good usage" (*bon usage*) based on our fear of the impurity outside ourselves.[21] Modern Western *savoir-faire* inverts the true order of savage *savoir-vivre*. We must quote at length the concluding sentences of Lévi-Strauss's *Origin of Table Manners* in which Sartre is made the spokesman for the Western civilization the anthropologist contemns:

> If the origin of table manners or, to speak in a more general fashion, the origin of good usage, is to be found, as we believe we have demonstrated, in that deference toward the world which constitutes *le savoir-vivre*, namely, to respect our obligations to it [i.e., the world], it follows that the morality immanent in myths runs exactly opposite to the one we profess in our time. It instructs us, in any case, that our formula "Hell is the others" is not a philosophic proposition but an ethnographic testimony on a civilization. From infancy, we are socialized to be afraid of impurity coming from outside ourselves. When savage people proclaim, on the contrary, that "Hell is in ourselves," they offer us a lesson in modesty which one wishes we were still capable of understanding. In this century in which man has made it his business to destroy countless living species, so many societies whose richness and variety have constituted from time immemorial his most splendid heritage, never has it been more necessary to insist, as the myths teach, that an integral humanism begin not with man, but by putting the world before life, and life before man, and respect for other beings before the love

> of self. . . . [Man] must cease appropriating the earth as a thing and behaving in relation to it with neither shame nor reserve.[22]

French ethnologists and anthropologists were unprepared for such a book, with such a theme, bearing such a title: *The Origin of Table Manners*. An obsessive theme of Diaspora intellectuality—morals versus manners, the hypocrisy of civility, the triviality of etiquette—surfaced once more and, once again, became the target, both as fact and as symbol, for that *ressentiment* harbored by emancipating Jewry against the complex code of interaction ritual which governs the "relations in public" (as Erving Goffman calls it) of the members of Western bourgeois society. "I am often struck," an American Jewish literary intellectual writes,

> by how eager we are to reveal all sorts of ugly secrets about ourselves. We can explain the hatred we feel for our parents, we are rather pleased with the perversions to which we are prone. We seem determinedly proud to be superior to ourselves. No motive is too terrible for our inspection. Let someone hint, however, that we have bad table manners and we fly into a rage.[23]

If we allow "table manners" to stand as a synecdoche for propriety, good usage, and civility in general, as Lévi-Strauss does, the anthropologist, at this not uncommon charge against "his people," did a slow burn which resulted in the magnificent *Origin of Table Manners*.

The work culminates with a sermon, addressed to the West, on the nature of true deference and demeanor, in which the rules of "how to live" of so-called *peuples sauvages* are put into the lists against the rules of "how to behave" of so-called civilized peoples. Lévi-Strauss has managed to extract from his descriptive "science" of mythology a normative morality in terms of which he grades our civilization. He gives it a zero for conduct: *zéro de conduite*.

As early as 1959 Lévi-Strauss had laid out his program for the *Mythologiques* in a discussion with Georges Charbonnier broadcast over French radio. If, he said then, "we want to understand art, religion or law, and perhaps even cooking or the rules of politeness, we must imagine them as being codes formed by articulated signs, following the pattern of linguistic communication."[24] But of greater interest is Lévi-Strauss's alleged reason for turning the relation of savage "good usage" and civilized "good usage" into a relation of "hateful contraries."[25]

The criterion used is the differentiation of the Western, presumably Christian, abhorrence of *"l'impureté du dehors,"*[26] of dangerously impure natural substances coming in from the outside (*de dehors*), in contrast to the modesty of the savage, who is in mortal fear of contaminating nature and men with the impurity inside himself. There are two directions of defilement, then: pollution can come from within (*de dedans*) or from without (*de dehors*).[27] It is exactly here that we make a decisive discovery about the origins of the Lévi-Straussian fascination with table manners and table etiquette. In one of those rare passages in which he speaks of his early youth, Lévi-Strauss writes:

> My only contact with religion goes back to a stage in my childhood at which I was already an unbeliever. During the First World War I lived with my grandfather, who was the rabbi of Versailles. His house stood next to the synagogue and was linked to it by a long inner corridor. Even to set foot in that corridor was an awesome experience; it formed an impassable frontier between the profane world and that other world from which was lacking precisely that human warmth which was the indispensable condition to my recognizing it as sacred. Except at the hours of service the synagogue was empty; desolation seemed natural to it, and its brief spells of occupation were neither sustained enough nor fervent enough to overcome this. They seemed merely an incongruous disturbance. Our private religious observances suffered from the same offhand quality. Only my grandfather's silent prayer before each meal reminded us children that our lives were governed by a higher order of things. (That, and a printed message which hung on a long strip of paper in the dining-room: "Chew Your Food Properly: Your Digestion Depends On It.") [28]

The desolation, the absence of fervor, the "incongruous disturbance" are not surprising. It is the long strip of paper that arrests our attention. On it, a kind of dietary law of propriety stares down on the dining room table. A hygienic imperative instructs the children in the *bon usage* of eating and chewing. Moreover, the food is seen under the aspect of its potential endangerment to the digestion, if not the health of those who consume it.

This is the earliest cited case in Lévi-Strauss's own life of "that complete inversion" he speaks of in *The Origin of Table Manners*, in which good manners become a hygiene of self-protection against external threat.[29] The analysis must be pursued to its final term. The very criterion Lévi-Strauss uses to castigate Western table manners—and its good usage in general—is identical with that which Jesus first used in castigating the ritual purity of the Jewish Pharisees. By declaring that it is not the evil that comes into man from the outside (*en dehors*) but that which comes from within (*de dedans*) that defiles, Jesus made the decisive break with Judaism. Thus Max Weber—and this is the only case known to me where he lays aside his *Wertfreiheit*—writes in *Ancient Judaism:*

> Precisely with regard to ritualistic (Levitical) purity, even Jesus' message took quite a different course [from the Essenian ethic]. The monumentally impressive lordly word, "not that which goeth into the mouth defileth a man; but that which cometh out of the mouth" and out of an impure heart (Math. 15:11, 18f.) meant that for him ethical sublimation was decisive, not the ritual surpassing of the Jewish purity laws. And the anxious segregation of the Essenes from the ritualistically impure is contrasted by his well-ascertained unconcern in having intercourse and table community with them.[30]

In the concluding passage to Lévi-Strauss's masterwork, *The Origin of Table Manners,* we thus find ourselves in the presence of an episode of unusual significance in the intellectual culture of the Diaspora. In this passage the "lesson in modesty" taught by the myths, and which the great Franco-Jewish structuralist puts in the mouths of his neolithic savages to be leveled as an indictment against Western, modern, Christian civilization is identical to the "monumentally impressive lordly word" that Jesus first raised against the Torah of the very Judaic civilization to which Lévi-Strauss, by descent, belongs. Contemporary biblical scholarship validates Weber's identification of the distinctive element in the mission of the historical Jesus. Ernst Käsemann, a post-Bultmann "form critic" writes of the same text Weber refers to (Matt. 15: 11, 18ff.) that

> Matthew obviously thought that Jesus was only attacking the rabbinate and Pharisaism with their heightening of the demands of the Torah. But the man who denies that impurity from external sources can penetrate into man's essential being is striking at the presuppositions and plain verbal sense of the Torah and at the authority of Moses himself. . . . For Jesus, it is the heart of man that lets impurity loose upon the world. . . . By this saying, Jesus destroys the basis of classical demonology which rests on the conception that man is threatened by the powers of the universe and thus at bottom fails to recognize the threat which is offered to the universe by man himself.[31]

Lévi-Strauss has, in effect, transformed the experience of religio-cultural inferiority into an incognito: in the *persona* of his suppositious savages he castigates the West for "habituating us from infancy [*dès l'enfance*] in the fear of impurity from outside [*de dehors*]"[32]—much as his grandfather's dining room injunction and his rabbi grandfather's kosher laws had instructed him in the ritual fear of the impurity of certain foods. We may repeat here about Lévi-Strauss what Etienne Gilson says of his Sorbonne philosophy teacher of long ago, the idealist Léon Brunschvicg: "What he objected to in Christianity was what it had retained of Judaism."[33] This strain of secular Jewish Marcionism runs strong in French intellectual Jewry, from Bergson and Brunschvicg through Simone Weil to Lévi-Strauss.*

Lévi-Strauss's master, Durkheim, had written that "Judaism, in fact, like all *early religions,* consists basically of a body of practises minutely governing all the details of life and leaving little free room for individual judgment" [34] (my emphasis). Lévi-Strauss could perhaps live with the fact that Durkheimian modernization theory had turned his ancestral religion into a species of "early religion." What he could not live with was that which Durkheim actually wrote—and which is bowdlerized from the original in the preceding, standard translation: "Le Judaïsme, en effet, commes toutes *les religions inférieures* . . ." [35] (my emphasis). The essential thrust of all the work of Lévi-Strauss, as much for the educated lay reader as for professional colleagues, is put in lapidary form by Sanche de Gramont: "There are no superior societies." [36]

The demeaning status-implications of Western modernization theory, the place it assigned to Judaism and, by implication, to Jews, was the bullet Lévi-Strauss could not or would not bite (in common with all the classical Diaspora ideologists). This fact, I believe, is what sent him (*a*) *back* to the primitives, and (*b*) *up* into the platonic heaven of ahistorical structuralism. It is the conviction of Talcott Parsons, voiced at the August 1973 meeting of the American Sociological Association, that Lévi-Strauss's structuralism, by leaving both social structure and history behind, and by analyzing the culture-value system alone—the element of "myth"—constitutes a "regression" from the more full-bodied theory of human action of Durkheim. The above analysis places that "regression" in the sociology-of-knowledge context of Jewish Emancipation as a status-ordeal.

There is a respectable tradition that views great works of art as issuing from the psychological traumata of their creators (this is the view of Edmund Wilson's *Wound and the Bow,* for example). Sociocultural wounds, it is my hypothesis, lie behind the ideological creations of the giants of the Jewish Diaspora. In Freud and Marx, as we have seen, the "inferior" Jew loses his inferiority and the mighty *goyim* are brought low. The "final triumph" of the Freudian hermeneutic, with its remedial reading of social delicts as medical symptoms, is its transvaluation—"the implication," Goffman tells us, "that *socially improper* behavior can be *psychologically normal* . . . and *socially proper* behavior can be *truly sick*" [37] (my emphasis). The "final triumph" of Marxism is Marx's refusal to give a remedial and apologetic reading of the economic behavior of the Jews, describing it with unembarrassed bluntness, only to turn around

* Spinoza had set the precedent. In what Hermann Cohen was later to call a "humanly incomprehensible act of treason" Spinoza had exhorted the Christians, as Leo Strauss recounts, "to free essentially spiritual Christianity from all carnal Jewish relics. . . ." In the modern era, Spinoza had reopened an old status-wound. Leo Strauss, "Preface to the English Translation," *Spinoza's Critique of Religion,* trans. E. M. Sinclair (New York: Schocken, 1965), pp. 19, 20.

and make this crude *Judentum* * the very stuff (*Unterbau*) of the bourgeois civilization of the *goyim*. It is a failure of understanding that sees in Marx's conviction—that stripped of his sublimations and refinements a Gentile is as avaricious as a Jew—an offense only to Jews. "Christianity," Marx writes, "overcame real Judaism only in appearance. It was too *refined,* too spiritual, to eliminate the crudeness of practical need except by elevating it into the blue. Christianity is the sublime thought of Judaism, and Judaism is the vulgar practical application of Christianity." † [38] Like theodicies, the sociodicies of the Diaspora giants cope with the problem of pain, suffering, and evil. Each bestows meaning, and thus "solves" the *tsuris* of *Galut,* the status-loss of Emancipation, the humiliations of "assimilation" ("imitation"), the embarrassment of being defined as "primitive." If, as E. M. Forster said, "Coarseness reveals; vulgarity conceals," Freud, Marx, and Lévi-Strauss struggle to redefine the post-Emancipation situation in terms of the Jewish pariah, the *Ostjude:* He becomes—like Rousseau's "natural" man—an instrument of critique of the Jewish (and Gentile) parvenu. He may be a "primitive" and crude; he is not hypocritical (Freud's "ethic of honesty").

A sociocultural status-humiliation of this character provides the motivation-nexus, the subcultural climate and provenance, of the work of Lévi-Strauss. Clifford Geertz, in attempting to understand the dramatic transformation that took place in the work of Lévi-Strauss between the personal and elegiac *Tristes tropiques* (1955) and the "high science" of *La Pensée sauvage* (1962)—which led into his science-of-mythology tetralogy—asks: "Is the transmutation science or alchemy? Is the 'very simple transformation' which produced a general theory out of a personal disappointment real or a sleight of hand?" Is Lévi-Strauss writing science, Geertz concludes by asking, or is he, "like some uprooted neolithic intelligence cast away on a reservation, shuffling the debris of old traditions in a vain attempt to revivify a primitive faith whose moral beauty is still apparent but from which both relevance and credibility have long since departed?" [39]

* "*Judentum,* the German word for Judaism, had the derivative meaning of 'commerce,'" David McLellan reminds us. *Marx Before Marxism* (New York: Harper & Row, 1970), pp. 141–42.

† I have substituted, for "noble" and "common" in the Easton and Guddat translation (see note 38) the words "refined" and "vulgar," respectively, from the Robert Payne translation—in *Marx* (New York: Simon & Schuster, 1968), pp. 93, 95. Note that in this early formulation of the "kingdom of *necessity*" ("need") from which communism will finally free us, Marx, while defining necessity as "practical *need*," appears to accept the same goal he takes to have been Christianity's—viz., "to eliminate *the crudeness of* practical need" (my emphasis). Easton and Guddat, *Writings of the Young Marx,* p. 247. Christianity is faulted only for having failed to attain this goal (because it used the wrong means). Only by eliminating practical need as such, Marx maintains, can its crudeness be eliminated. Public impropriety (crudeness) will end only when private property is abolished. It is in this sense that Marx's socialism, as noted earlier, starts out as a "sumptuary socialism." Beginning with particularist shame, it becomes in the end universalist and motivated by genuine passion for justice.

In the final chapter, "Finale," of the final volume (1971) of his tetralogy—*L'Homme nu* (*Man Nude*, or *Naked Man*)—Lévi-Strauss, in a moving and eloquent passage, claims that all the binary oppositions in the myths that his four volumes have disclosed and inventoried derive in the end from a "fundamental, generative opposition," an "*antinomie première*"—that, namely, voiced by Hamlet: "To be or not to be, that is the question." [40] Again we witness here a metaphysicization of his masters, Émile Durkheim and Marcel Mauss. Their famous work of 1903, *Some Forms of Primitive Classification: A Contribution to the Study of Collective Representations,* was a kind of epistemological study of the origin of the universal fact that all peoples classify, divide, and arrange the world into categories: classes, genus, species, varieties, equivalences, binary oppositions. They found the origins of classifications—even logical and ontological ones, like being and nonbeing—in the social arrangements that constitute a society both within itself and vis-à-vis other peoples and societies. Here we see once more what Talcott Parsons remarked as Lévi-Strauss's "regression" from Durkheim. By rooting all the social and natural oppositions in the "primal antinomy" (*antinomie première*) of Hamlet's soliloquy, Lévi-Strauss bids a final farewell to the stubborn empirical dimension of the social sciences, a dimension that defines and entraps man into history and its rebuking artbitrariness and humiliating reversals.

By means of the universal and ahistorical "idealism" of the ideology of structural anthropology, the early involvement of Lévi-Strauss with the fact of his Jewishness, the ancient "Jewish problem," has disappeared. The "primal antinomy," the primary "*donnée*" of the socialization of Jews in the West in the post-Emancipation era—namely, the "primitive classification" of the world into "*goyim*" and "ourselves"—has been swallowed up and assimilated, sublimed into the lofty binary oppositions of nature and culture, raw and cooked, night and day. Taking our cue from Lévi-Strauss, who concludes with a citation from a hero of literature, Hamlet, we end this section with a quotation from Alexander Portnoy, not the least of whose *kvetches* to his parents concerns the "primitive classification" or "*antinomie première*" they had instilled into him: "The very first distinction I learned from you, I'm sure, was not night and day, or hot and cold, but *goyische* and Jewish!"* [41]

*For a remarkably convergent analysis of the role of Levi-Strauss's Jewishness in his structuralism—his transformation of marginality into "a recognized and prestigious immunity" (p. 305)—see anthropologist Stanley Diamond's *In Search of the Primitive: A Critique of Civilization* (New Brunswick, N.J.: Transaction Books, 1974), pp. 321–331. The book was published after the above was written.

PART III

The Demeaned Jewish Intellectuals: Ideologists of Delayed Modernization

CHAPTER 19

JEWS AND IRISH: LATECOMERS TO MODERNITY

If there are unique elements in the story of the Jewish struggle with modernity, there are, nevertheless, parallels with other peoples. Reasoning is the act of comparing and connecting, as well as of contrasting and distinguishing. I share the rationalist hope of which Alfred North Whitehead speaks: "That we fail to find in experience any elements intrinsically incapable of exhibition as examples of general theory, is the hope of rationalism." [1] There follow, accordingly, two exploratory probes in comparative analysis: Jew and Irish will be compared as latecomers to modernity, and secular Jewish intellectuals will be viewed as a modernizing elite, involving a comparison of Jewish Emancipation and the "new nations" of the post-World War II period.

It is the fate of latecomers to modernity among "new nations" entering an already stratified international community to suffer, especially in the person of their leaders, the self-disesteem of what Gustavo Lagos calls "*atimia.*" *Atimia* is the loss of status or honor relative to other nations experienced by "underdeveloped" countries on entering the international "modernization-stratification" system of post-World War II.[2] The self-disesteem of the atimic process was experienced earlier in the "delayed modernization" of nations like Japan and Germany, but also, I contend, in the delayed modernization of minorities *within* the modernizing nations of the West such as Eastern European and Russian Jewry and the Irish Catholics. The story of the Irish famine of the 1840s which killed a million Irish and drove them into the rapidly modernizing world of Anglo-American Protestantism is a case study in the phenomenon of "delayed modernization." [3] The story of the Russian pogroms of the 1880s which killed thousands of Eastern European Jews and drove them out of their Middle Ages into the Anglo-American world of the *goyim* "beyond the pale" has yet to be told as a case study in the phenomenon of delayed modernization.*

* That "the European Jews were the last community to emerge from the Middle Ages," as Sir Isaiah Berlin notes in *Jewish Slavery and Emancipation* (New York: Herzl Press, 1961), p. 5, is eminently true of the Jewry of the *shtetlach* in the twenty-five provinces of the Russian "pale of settlement."

Once in the world of the modern West, the Irish and the Jews set about constructing social organizations and engineering conceptual apologia that would shelter themselves, their *Yiddishkeit* and *"Irishkeit,"* from the subversive lure of the massive American Thing. The Irish defined their enemy as a religious heresy and called it the Americanist heresy. The Jews, using their own word for apostasy, called it assimilation. The Irish Catholics, convinced that to maintain their cultural belief and value system *in partibus infidelium* implied retaining control of the machinery of secondary socialization, constructed their far-ranging parochial school system. The Jews, convinced that to maintain their *shtetl* subculture intact in *Galut* required life with their own people,[4] "constructed" their teeming Lower East Side system. Churches and seminaries were built, diocesan weeklies printed; *shuls* and *yeshivoth* were built, Yiddish newspapers appeared. To retain their subjective plausibility, Berger and Luckmann write, subcultures "require subsocieties as their objectivating base, and counter-definitions of reality require counter-societies." [5]

This whole story has been told and retold to death as an interreligious cowboy story, the good guys against the bad, Catholic versus WASP, Jew versus Christian. To say this is, to be sure, to grasp a valid dimension of what actually happened, but to recount it exclusively as a *Kulturkampf* —of minority culture against majority culture, minority religion against majority religion—is to throw history out of focus, to skirt sociology altogether, and to debar oneself from exploring the possibility that these essentially minority reports of what happened are themselves self-serving interpretations, weapons in the status-politics of subcultures, part of the problem to be analyzed and not the solution to it.

To open out this story of the immigrant minorities and the proverbial melting pot to a larger perspective and a comparative approach, I view these two subsocieties with their countercultures as underdeveloped societies bearing relatively traditional cultures, as societies within the West and only recently granted independence (Jewish Emancipation, Catholic Emancipation), as forced to undergo the special pathology of "delayed modernization" right under the proper nose of their erstwhile "colonial" overseer, the Puritan WASP modernist core culture. For example, David Riesman has said that it is the special peculiarity of America that it "happens to have colonials—Negroes and other ethnic minorities—*within* its borders. . . . Upon the Jewish minority, this situation operates with special force" [6] (my emphasis).

It does indeed, and this chapter spells out a number of parallels between Diaspora Jewry and the phenomenon of delayed modernizers. Perhaps the deepest atimic affinity is on the level of culture and consciousness: Jewry is defined by Christendom as having been a *praeparatio evangelica,* a preparation for the Good News of Christ's coming, a foreshadowing, a herald—in the words of Erich Auerbach, a *figura*. Christendom calls its Covenant and its Testament "New," Jewry's Covenant and Testament "Old." Jews, both before their emancipation in the nineteenth century and after, had to learn from others a form of the consciousness of underdevelopment. Western academic philosophy and anthropology of religion created their own version of this in the concept of the "*higher* religions." For someone identified with the theologically "lower" status-value, self-contempt—the word is that of Jules Isaac—will be learned even if it is not, in any conventional sense, taught.

There is a second related but different parallel between Jewry dispersed in the West, exiting from its Middle Ages only in the eighteenth and nineteenth centuries, and nations, old or new, entering the international stratification system and discovering their underdeveloped "backwardness": ghetto Jewry at the time of Jewish Emancipation *was* "backward," and everybody was agreed that it was "backward," but no one was agreed as to why it was so "backward." During the Enlightenment period, when the question was debated, advocates of emancipating the Jews, both Jewish and Gentile, said that the present state of the Jews was due to the persecution and segregation that had been enforced upon them during the Middle Ages in the West, and not due to biology or any indigenous failings of Jewish culture. This theory of the involution of Diaspora Jewry upon contact with the destructive if more evolved West came to be called by Salo Baron (the famous Columbia University historian of Jewry) the "lachrymose conception" of prerevolutionary Jewish history.[7] In this conception, Jewish woes and degradations due to the Diaspora milieu are exaggerated by Reform Jews, Zionists, and others because in this way it could be argued that Jews, despite appearances, were—in the words of Rabbi Schorsch—"culturally qualified for the rights and responsibilities of citizenship."[8] The sociological reason for concentrating on medieval persecutions, he continues, was "the desire to attribute the defects of Jewish life, so often cited to justify the denial of emancipation, to the intolerance of a hostile Christian majority."[9] This attribution struggle, as it may be called, goes on when new nations receive independence: to whom do we attribute a given failing? To the colonial powers? To our own indigenous tradition? To both?

Another parallel is this: the shock of the occupying Western powers on premodern societies placed acute pressure especially on traditional religious symbols, Robert Bellah claims, "because Christian missionaries were among the shock troops of the modernization process, quick to point out the barbarous and unprogressive consequences of traditional religious beliefs and practices."[10] The reverse parallel is true in the Jewish case: Orthodox Judaism "occupying" modernizing Europe in the nineteenth century suffered the same assaults.

Another parallel is the condition of being caught between tradition and modernity. Edward Shils, in his brilliant monograph *The Intellectual Between Tradition and Modernity: The Indian Situation* (1961) details the social-psychological and other consequences of being trapped between the tug of tradition and the lure of modernity. In a similar case, Stanley Burnshaw recounts the situation of the pioneering Hebrew poets and intelligentsia of the 1890s. These "enlighteners," born and reared in the tradition-bound *shtetl,* were suddenly plunged into the secular world of prerevolutionary Russia: "While accepting a modern view of man intellectually, they remained emotionally bound to their strictly Jewish experience. Thus we find in the lyrics of the greatest of these poets, Bialik, . . . a constant struggle between Judaism and Western secularism." Bialik's younger contemporary, poet Saul Tchernikovsky, took a different tack: railing against the Talmudic "interlude," he extolled the prebiblical Canaanite cults and in his famous poem "Before the Statue of Apollo" depicted the Jewish people as "rebels against a Nietzschean god of life." [11]

The nineteenth-century "revolution" that was Jewish Emancipation is like the twentieth-century revolutions described by historian R. R. Palmer. These revolutions, whether in Russia or China or in formerly colonial areas, are alike in "having been precipitated by contacts with an outside or foreign civilization, and by the stresses, maladjustments, feelings of backwardness and other ambivalences ensuing thereupon," Palmer writes. The French Revolution, on the other hand, he writes, "grew directly out of earlier French history. The French were untroubled by any feeling of backwardness, they did not have to strain to keep up in a march of progress." [12] The almost continuous immigration of Jews into Western Europe and Anglo-America from the culturally "backward" areas of the pale has brought it about that they have lived a revolutionary situation of the twentieth-century type from the nineteenth century on up to our own day. This mixed chronological profile, this mixture of anachronism and progressivism, is, according to Mary Matossian, a characteristic of delayed modernization.[13] Discrepant traits are exhibited by any people who are committed to a crash program of modernization, who are leapfrogging over centuries, syncopating long developmental processes.

Another parallel is the affinity to Marxist ideology. Frank Lindenfeld, noting that the Russian Revolution was precisely not a revolution spearheaded by a proletarian uprising but a modernizing movement led by native intellectuals who adopted a Marxist ideology, goes on to observe that "revolutions" carried out by groups calling themselves Marxists have occurred, significantly, *only* in underdeveloped countries like Russia, China, and Cuba.[14] Indeed, Talcott Parsons notes, "evidence has been accumulating which would appear to indicate that the appeal of the radical left in a given society bears an inverse relation to the degree of industrialization of that society." [15] This is true, but in the frame of analysis I propose, Marxism and other ideologies do appeal, even in the developed countries, to certain subcultures—ethnic, religious, and regional—undergoing the excruciation of delayed modernization. In this respect, progressivism for midwestern "Bible Belt" Protestantism, Coughlinism and McCarthyism for Irish Catholics, and Stalinism-Marxism-Trotskyism for Eastern European Jews all perform the same latent function: they appeal to the premodern *Gemeinschaft*-type past of these subcultures. Parsons interprets Communist ideology as a "statement of the symbolic values of modernization in which symbolic *covert* gestures of reconciliation are made toward both the past and the future" [16] (my emphasis). The first of these covert gestures, he goes on to say, involves the attempt to preserve "the integrity of the premodern system; and I believe that this is the primary significance of the symbol, socialism. In essence, the purpose of this device is to assure us that the process of differentiation which is inherent in modernization need not jeopardize the integrity of preindustrial community solidarity . . . . Communist ideology," he concludes, is "primarily defensive and protectionist in character." [17] This covert neotraditionist appeal of Marxism for the Eastern European Jewish intelligentsia is paralleled by the more overtly neotraditionalist appeal of Father Charles Coughlin in the thirties and Senator Joseph McCarthy in the fifties for their "natural" constituency, the urban Irish Catholics. In large part, writes Jack Newfield in his memoir of and apologia for Robert Kennedy, "it was Kennedy's cultural conditioning as a Boston [Irish] Catholic that made it so easy for him to make a mistake of the magnitude of working for—and admiring—Joe McCarthy. For Kennedy to drift into the atavistic subculture of McCarthyism was as logical as for a proletarian Jew at [New York] City College in the 1930s to become a Marxist." [18] Father Leonard Feeney, S.J., of the famous Boston heresy case in the 1950s, was expressing the cultural-theological aspect of this same problem of the delayed modernization of the Irish in modernized, Protestant America. His yearning was for the past. Walking in the North End of Boston in the Italian Catholic section, vividly aware of the persisting close-knit *Gemeinschaft* infrastructure of Italian, as against Boston Irish, Catholicism, he exclaims: "I wish to God that we could replace the thing we call culture with this. These people really live. Look at the children!" [19] (Not a few members of the Abraham Lincoln Brigade felt similarly about Spain. German fascism represented, among other things, modernization; communism seemed to promise a *Gemeinschaft*. The love affair of the Left with Spain has many roots.)

The late Irish-American novelist Edwin O'Connor memorializes this phase of Irish Catholic modernization in his novels *The Last Hurrah* and *On the Edge of Sadness*. The late Isaac Rosenfeld's *Passage from Home* (1946), a beautiful autobiographical memoir, is the Jewish elegy on passing from the *shtetl* tradition. Thomas Wolfe's *You Can't Go Home Again* renders the rural Protestant version of the same process in classic form. As for the black community, after Richard Wright's *Native Son* and Ralph Ellison's *Invisible Man* and the traditional figure of James Baldwin, it now sees the "Zionism" of its "Black Moses," * Marcus Garvey, resurrected in Malcolm X's *Autobiography* and Eldridge Cleaver's *Soul on Ice*. Black nationalism is in its phase of high revolt against the era of its Uncle Toms (as *Yiddishkeit* revolted against the Reform Judaism of the earlier German assimilationists). It sees its task today as ridding itself of its consciousness of underdevelopment, as one of knocking that humiliating second *A* out of the acronym NAACP—National Association for the *Advancement* of Colored People—and taking the offensive against the so-called advanced white core culture from whose values, as spelled out in its norms, it learned self-contempt and experienced shame. The tradition of black "Marranoism," outward compliance accompanied by inner resistance, gives way to the cry for "Freedom now!" The conspiracy tradition of "inner emigration" yields to the integrity of an avowed and open struggle.

In all of this we see the first stages in the politics of the intellectuals of the underdeveloped countries anticipated in nineteenth-century Europe and repeated in twentieth-century America. In the underdeveloped countries, the intellectuals first drive for constitutional liberalism and the moral renewal of their people (think of India up to World War I). Here the colonized, in the person of their representatives, meet the colonizers with the decorum of bourgeois Victorian liberals and request positions in the civil service, appointive offices, and "balanced tickets." This first stage is the stage of "the notables," according to Edward A. Shils.[20] It is, in our comparative frame, the era of the *shtadlan*, when Jewish notables represented as-yet-unemancipated Jewry in the courts and councils of Europe. "The court Jews and their successors, the Jewish bankers and businessmen in the West," writes Hannah Arendt, "were never socially acceptable"[21]—and, what is more, never wanted to be. The generations of political intellectuals that followed, however, were much more ambivalent about their identity. The Jewish notables had no desire to leave the Jewish people, she writes, "while it was characteristic of Jewish intellectuals that they wanted to leave their people and be admitted to society."[22]

In the second stage, a fervently politicized nationalism—the product, paradoxically, of the identity-ambivalence of the native intelligentsia—gets under way. India was the first of all the underdeveloped colonial countries to go through this phase in which the older generation of liberal constitutionalists and piecemeal reformers is regarded as "excessively subservient to the foreign rulers and as excessively bemused by their

* This is the title of Edmund David Cronon's biography of Marcus Garvey (1887–1940), founder of modern African nationalism.

foreign culture and their foreign forms of government. . . . The politics of cultured and urbane gentlemen, speaking French or English to perfection, was not for this generation," concludes Shils.[23] We see parallel developments later in Egypt, East Africa, Syria, Iraq. We see the same pattern repeated in Europe for the Irish and the Jews, and repeated—and foreshortened—in America for Irish Catholics, Eastern European Jews, and blacks. We see the nationalism, the fanaticized consciousness, the socialism, the populism, the oppositionalism and moralism, the rejection of a civil for an ideological politics.

The sheer fact of the more advanced societies constitutes a "culture shock" for the less advanced when, in the person of their modernizing intellectual elite, culture contact is established. What Kelsen calls "the normative power of facticity"[24] adds up to a demeaning "assault." The values and life-style of the colonial power—or, for the indigenous minorities within a more general core culture, the meanings and beliefs of the "oppressive majority"—constitute a status-wound to the normal narcissism of peoples and nations. The defense (apologia) against this "assault" we call ideology.

Assaulted *in* the West *by* the West and its modernity, Jewish intellectuals produce the full spectrum of required ideology: the Zionism of Hess and Herzl; the communism of Marx, Lassalle, Trotsky, Luxemburg, and Bernstein; the cultural apologetics of the Society for Jewish Culture and Learning; and the ideology called "Hebraism." Hebraism is the tactic of admitting one's inferiority in terms of power in order to claim moral superiority in terms of indigenous spirituality and simplicity. It is a standing temptation for the modernizing intellectual. It is an ideology of delayed modernization.

"Hebraism" was for the unsynagogued, secular Jewish intellectual what Reform Judaism was for the German Jew still committed to "formal" membership in a Jewish—albeit a "reformed" Jewish—community. Both these ideologies elided the "shameful" Talmudic "interlude" of *Yiddishkeit*. Both recurred to the Hebrew Bible, traded on its high prestige in the West, and glorified their ancient ancestors as the "seedbed" of all that was noble in the West. (Unlike the Soviet Russians, they never claimed to have invented baseball.) Using invidious comparisons, the "assaulted intellectuals" of Reform Judaism and Hebraism thus launched their *mission civilizatrice* to Gentile Europe.

A recent manifesto by Philip Rieff, couched in the tradition of cultural "Hebraism," on the "transgressed Jew of culture" can be seen as another variation on the theme of the "assaulted intellectual": torn between primordial, traditional identity and the universalizing solvent of the modernization process, a "modernizing elite" endures, in its own person, proleptically, like a shaman, all the agonies eventually in store for the peoples from whom it has emerged. For the more brilliant of the intellectual "Jews of culture" the modernization process has always been experienced as a "package"—i.e., to assimilate modernity was ipso facto to assimilate Christianity, *more incognito;* modernity is thus experienced as secularized Christianity, as an assault, a transgression. In "Fellow Teachers," Rieff writes that "for the sake of law and order, justice and reverence inseparable from their god-terms, we mere teachers, Jews of culture, influential and eternally powerless, have no choice except to think defensively: how to keep ourselves from being overwhelmed by that unique complex of orgy and routine which constitutes modernization and its totalitarian character type." * [25]

Modernization, indeed, if not a "totalitarian" phenomenon, is at least what Marcel Mauss called a "total phenomenon." It discourages eclecticism and syncretism (*bricolage*). While Rieff enlists his Arnoldian "Jews of culture" against the current anarchy, he assures us at the same time that no reactionary clerisy can claim him:

> I am no advocate of some earlier credal organization. In particular, I have not the slightest affection for the dead church civilization of the West. I am a Jew. No Jew in his right mind can long for some variant of that civilization. Its one enduring quality is its transgressive energy against the Jew of culture; those transgressions have been built so deeply into the church-organized interdicts that they survive even now, after the main interdictory motifs of Christendom are dead. . . . The Jews continue to resist their assigned roles and worst gall, refuse to disappear into the universalist future of "Man." The gospels were not good news; the ungospelled present has its supremely pleasant feature, the death of the church.[26]

This is the traditional language of a modernizing elite vis-à-vis the ex–colonial powers. The particular historical *texture* of such traditional "emancipation talk"—Rieff's identification with "the proud, elitist culture of [ancient] Israel" † [27]—must not mislead the student of modernization; *structurally* the ideology of "Hebraism" is identical with the function performed by the status-talk of a Gandhi, a Coomaraswamy, an Ataturk, a Chester-Belloc, or, more recently, a Qaddafi. As Professor Mary Matossian writes:

> The "assaulted intellectual" works hard to make invidious comparisons between his own nation and the West. He may simply claim that his people are superior, as did Gandhi: "We consider our

* Editors Robert Boyers and Robert Orrill of *Salmagundi,* in which "Fellow Teachers" appeared (see note 24), describe Rieff's book-length article on "culture and barbarism" as "a major cultural document of the greatest significance" ("Editor's Note," p. 5).
† In this case, Rieff is defending Israelitic culture against Nietzsche.

> civilization to be far superior to yours." Or he may hold that his ancestors had already rejected Western culture as inferior. But these assertions can elicit conviction only among a few and for a short while. More often the intellectual says, "We are equal to Westerners," or "You are *no better* than I am." Around this theme lies a wealth of propositions: (1) "In the past you were no better (or worse) than we are now." (2) "We once had your good qualities, but we were corrupted by alien oppressors" [the Chinese use the Manchus as scapegoat, Arabs blame Ottoman sultans, Russians blame Mongols]. (3) "We have high spiritual qualities despite our poverty, but you are soulless materialists" [e.g., Sun Yat-sen]. (4) "Everything worthwhile in your tradition is present or incipient in ours" [e.g., the Koran favors parliamentary rule].[28] [My emphasis]

The Celtic revival was an example of this sort of subcultural status-politics. So was the social construction of Reform Judaism and its self-assignment of a moral "mission to the Gentiles." Early in the century, in America, the Irish Catholics and the Jews established—within a year of each other—their American Irish Historical Society and American Jewish Historical Society, respectively. Each has put out its own quarterly for generations. The Irish, under the urgings of their subcultural status-seeking, as they rummaged about among the old lists and deeds of heroes, early took to ignoring the difference between Scotch Irish and Irish Irish. Thus they could even claim Woodrow Wilson for their team. There is no end to stuffing these quarterlies with dreary proofs that the Irish poured all that tea into Boston harbor or that Columbus and Lincoln were Jews. Arthur Cohen has recently written a book called *The Myth of the Judeo-Christian Tradition* (1969), but this, apparently, is a myth with so many pressing functions to perform that he is finding it virtually undebunkable.

It is hard for the "assaulted" intellectual in the countries of delayed industrialization—or for his counterparts in the advanced world—to take up a stable attitude vis-à-vis the West. Partly Westernized himself, he is deeply ambivalent, wavering between *odi* and *amo,* xenophobia and xenophilia. Appalled, frequently, by the discrepancies between the standard of living of his own culture and that of modern Western nations, he may, like Sun Yat-sen, a trained physician, deplore "such Chinese habits as spitting, letting gas loudly, and never brushing the teeth, as 'uncultured.'"[29] He is not altogether sure just what he thinks of that curious "process" Norbert Elias calls "civilization" or of the disturbing entanglement that he senses may obtain between the civilizational process and the modernization process.

Kemal Ataturk of Turkey was an early master of international stratification and status politics. He discovered unknown strategies of nihilation and self-enhancement in his bouts with the emerging atimic process. He used the technique of "encouraging an import by calling it indigenous," Mary Matossian notes, and complemented this by the technique of "eradicating the indigenous by calling it imported. For example, [he] pointed out that the fez was a headgear imported from Europe a hundred years before." [30] Kemalist intellectuals discovered in the remote past of their people the very virtues which are supposed to make a modern nation great: they "glorify their ancestors as brave, tolerant, realistic, generous, peaceful, and respectful of women; in short, 'spiritual' exemplars of the well-bred Western European gentleman" who were temporarily 'corrupted' by the 'imperialism' of Arab-Persian-Byzantine culture." [31] Matossian points out that if the manifest content of Kemalist ideology is archaistic, its latent content is futuristic. Marxist ideology, on my reading, is the mirror opposite: a "progressive" manifest content is the carrier of a premodern, "secret" latent content appealing to the "wholeness-hunger" endemic in modern man.*

The concern of both nationalists in underdeveloped countries and minority intellectuals in the developed countries for vernacular languages and peasant folk arts brings us to our final comparison—the problem of the "assaulted" intellectual's relationship with the uneducated "masses" of his own people. It is not a simple relationship, one may be sure. Intellectuals like Nehru wonder if the peasants are not the "true" Indians and they (the intellectuals) the phonies.[32] The Russian Narodniki go "back to the people" to learn of them that are meek and humble of heart. Or the intellectual's attitude toward his own uneducated, "backward" masses may take the form of: "He looks up to 'the people' and down on 'the masses.'" [33] This is the kind of strategy that keeps many left-leaning "mass culture" theorists in business today: the indigenous folk-people endure beneath the "mass," which is an artifact of business enterprise and mass media. Ideologies of delayed industrialization often both "condemn the peasant for his backwardness, and praise him for being a *real* representative of indigenous culture," [34] thus applying both a stick and a carrot to move him to industrialization.

Here again the case of Diaspora intellectual Jewry is paradigmatic and parallel: their "backward" Masses were called *Ostjuden,* and assimilating "exception" Jewry felt all the contradictory emotions for them that successful bourgeois feel for a down-at-the-heels poor relation knocking at the door at midnight, or what I personally feel when I pass rheumy-eyed "Bowery bums"—typically, Irish (all stereotypes are, more or less, accurate)—suffering the misery and degradation of alcoholism: sympathy, fear, shame, dishonesty, a "There but for the grace of God go I" feeling.

* The term *wholeness-hunger* comes from Peter Gay's book on *Weimar Culture: The Outsider as Insider* (1968).

CHAPTER 20

SECULAR JEWISH INTELLECTUALS AS A MODERNIZING ELITE: JEWISH EMANCIPATION AND THE NEW NATIONS COMPARED

If the morally ambiguous stance of the intellectual in the new "underdeveloped" nations is analogous to that of the new ethnic intellectual in the old "developed" nations, this is a result of an analogy of situation. The Jewish intellectual who today theorizes about the modernizing new nations is frequently someone whose family and ethnic situation, not more than a generation or so ago, bore striking resemblances to that of the new nations. Thus these theorists of modernization recall their situation among the *goyim* of Galveston, Texas, as Marion Levy, Jr. does.[1] Or, remembering the demoralization and vulgarity that frequently accompanied modernization, they write, as Daniel Lerner does, a dedication

For My Mother
Louetta Lerner
Who Passed from Traditional Ways
To a Modern Style
With Grace and Dignity.* [2]

Or, the empathy of their situation takes them on a "passage to India" where, like Edward Shils, they write brilliantly of *The Intellectual Between Tradition and Modernity: The Indian Situation* (1961). Or, as with Irving Louis Horowitz, years of modernization analysis funds itself into an exploration of the situation of Israel and the Diaspora in *Israeli Ecstasies/Jewish Agonies* (1974).

* Contrast this dedication with that of an earlier generation: "To the memory of my mother whose natural resistance to the current of assimilation has preserved for her son vistas of a receding culture. . . ." Abraham Aaron Roback, *Curiosities of Yiddish Literature* (Cambridge, Mass.: Sci-Art Publishers, 1933), p. 5.

It behooves us, then, to spell out in more detail the "modernization" parallels between *shtetl* and ghetto Jewry, from the time of emancipation until the present, and the situation of other peoples and nations.

Most obviously, the Jews were something like a colony. They were self-governing—with *kehillot* and super-*kehillot*—only up to a point. They were segregated, and self-segregated. The nineteenth century was "the century of emancipation," as it is called: Jews in Europe, Catholics in England, blacks in America, muzhiks in Russia—all were formally "emancipated." Jews were decolonized, entitled,* granted civil rights.

Another parallel: they were, on the whole, a "backward" and "barbarous" people, in the unembarrassed language of the early nineteenth century. We are talking here largely of the phenomenon of Eastern European Jewry, the proverbial *Ostjude*. He has always been premodern, "underdeveloped," precivil. In France, as in Germany, the fundamental factual assumption of the Emancipation debate—the underdeveloped state of the Jewish communities—was never itself in question. "But while the friends of the Jews argued," writes Miriam Vardeni, "that the Jews' negative characteristics were a result of persecution, their enemies argued that these characteristics were innate." [3] Moses Mendelssohn became Exhibit A in this nurture/nature argument that framed the Jewish Emancipation Proclamation of Napoleon. Lessing told the Germans that, in effect, one of his best friends was a Jew. Mirabeau considered Mendelssohn his most persuasive argument on behalf of Jewish Emancipation. "May it not be said that his example," he asked the French, "especially the outcome of his exertions for the elevation of his brethren, silences those who, with ignoble bitterness, insist that the Jews are so contemptible that they cannot be transformed into a respectable people?" [4] The need for Jews to be "advanced" was openly admitted on all sides of the debate. No one demurred when, later in Saint Petersburg, a group of Western-educated Jews formed the Society for the Advancement of Culture Among Jews.

I call all this to mind to point up what may be a profound analogy between the Jewish community in the nineteenth century emerging into autonomy in the European system and the Third World nations decolonized into the international system of today: the earliest ideology, the proto-ideology of Diaspora Jewry, was the "lachrymose" story of their own history. An intellectual or priestly class, we learn from history, emerges with the differentiation of the culture system and its beliefs and values from the social system. Their job is to legitimate the social facts by means of the cultural myths and values. If there is a gap, they bridge it. The "lachrymose" ideology of Jewish history was created by Jewish intellectuals and their Gentile allies to justify the civic emancipation of Jews to the

* Harry Golden's *You're entitl'* (Cleveland: World, 1962) reminds us that, for Jews, America symbolized the end of European Jewry's feudal life of "privilege" and "underprivilege." The era of rights, of entitlement before the law, had begun.

Gentile community. Only a Middle Ages rife with persecution could legitimate the gap between the Jewish cultural-religious self-conception of superiority, with its customary dose of ethnic narcissism, and the sorry socioeconomic "look" of the actual Jewish communities. Before Emancipation, Diaspora Jewry explained its Exile—i.e., the discrepancy between its essential chosenness and its "degraded" condition—as a punishment from God for its sins. After Emancipation, this *theodicy*, now turned outward to a new, Gentile status-audience, becomes an *ideology*, emphasizing Gentile persecution as the root cause of Jewish "degradation." This ideology was so pervasive that it was shared, in one form or another, by all the ideologists of nineteenth-century Jewry: Reform Jews and Zionists, assimilationists and socialists, Bundists and Communists—all became virtuosos of ethnic suffering. In the ideologies of Marx and Freud, the blame is "impersonalized" and directed toward the "system."

Of course, there had been massacres and pogroms and Christian anti-Semitism. The point is that these Diaspora groups were uninterested in actual history; they were apologists, ideologists, prefabricating a past in order to answer embarrassing questions, to outfit a new identity, and to ground a claim to equal treatment in the modern world. The result was a predictable division of labor: the story of Christian Jew-hatred was written by anti-Christian Jews, while the story of Jewish *goy*-hatred was turned over to Christian anti-Semites. You can be sure that neither worked the other's territory. A kind of "gentleman's agreement" prevailed. "It was Jewish historiography," Hannah Arendt writes,

> with its strong polemical and apologetical bias, that undertook to trace the record of Jew-hatred in Christian history, while it was left to the anti-semites to trace an intellectually not too dissimilar record from ancient Jewish authorities. When this Jewish tradition of an often violent antagonism to Christians and Gentiles came to light, "the general Jewish public was not only outraged but genuinely astonished," so well had its spokesmen succeeded in convincing themselves and everybody else of the non-fact that Jewish separateness was due exclusively to Gentile hostility and lack of enlightenment. Judaism, it was now maintained chiefly by Jewish historians, had always been superior to other religions in that it believed in human equality and tolerance. That this self-deceiving theory, accompanied by the belief that the Jewish people had always been the passive, suffering object of Christian persecutions, actually amounted to a prolongation and modernization of the old myth of chosenness . . . is perhaps one of those ironies which seem to be in store for those who, for whatever reasons, try to embellish and manipulate political facts and historical records.[5]

The point of the parallel here is that with many new nations the charge of "imperialism" as an explanation-legitimation of their present "degraded condition" is often a functional equivalent of the Jewish community's charge of "anti-Semitism." The statement is frequently doing many jobs of work other than the ostensible one of stating facts. Needless to say, colonialism, like anti-Semitism, has worked its ugly will on defenseless peoples. Just as the problems of the modernization of latecomers indigenous (like the Jews) to the West have almost uniformly been discussed in contexts such as anti-Semitism, so now the modernization problems of latecoming new nations have almost uniformly been discussed in the context of imperialism. "Like most people today," Marion Levy writes, "I happen to detest imperialism as it has existed and have no desire to deny its evils. I do wish, however, to point out that the morals of imperialists are essentially irrelevant to the problems faced by members of relatively nonmodernized societies in contact with modernization." [6] The effects of contact and collision between premodern and modern societies and premodern and modern consciousness have been obscured, Levy maintains, by the fact that this contact took the political form of imperialism. It is understandable, therefore, "that it is exceedingly difficult to get discussions of the phenomena apart from resentments about, guilt feelings about, or defensive attempts to reinterpret the myriad situations associated with the term 'imperialism' throughout the world." [7] Again, the paradigm here has been the difficulty of disentangling the phenomena of Jewish premodernity's contact with Western-Gentile modernization apart from resentments about, guilt feelings about, or defensive attempts to reinterpret the myriad situations associated with the term "anti-Semitism" in the West. If, even with the revolution of our choice, the problems of the collision of premodern with modern are still with us, so, even with the ecumenism of our choice, the problems of Jewish-Gentile collision would still be with us, in part because they are a special case of—and prefigure—the modernization collision.

There is an embarrassment of parallels. In the nineteenth century, with the dispersed new Jewish nation struggling to be born—as later with the ingathered Israel—there were many Gentiles in the West who "lent a hand," as today underdeveloped nations have many ardent sponsors in the developed countries. What were Gentile Zionists and philo-Semites but an early form of "foreign aid." *

Before the present century was born, communities of post-Emancipation Jewry were exemplifying Boeck's "lead of the retarded," with their

* A form of benevolence drenched, as always, in the moral ambiguities of a politics of altruism. Leonard Stein's *The Balfour Declaration* (London: Vallentine-Mitchell, 1961) unfolds the curious history of Gentile Zionism, in which the covert anti-Semitism of Gentile political Zionists like Lord Balfour and Wickham Steed carries the day against the sincere if hysterical anti-Zionism of establishment Anglo-Jews like Edwin Montagu. A more appalling tragicomedy of cultural ironies is difficult to imagine.

ethnic-ascriptive solidarities crisscrossing the lonely differentiations of the urban nonkinship *Gesellschaften* (analogous in this way to class solidarities). Talcott Parsons tends to underobserve the staying power of ascriptive nexuses in the modern world. (Because ascription and achievement are analytically distinct and polar variables in a long-term evolutionary sense, he fails to see the functions of residual ascription as it prolongs itself into modern, differentiated societies.)

Modernization occurred indigenously and over a long period of time in the West—and, it appears, indigenously only in the West. Western Jewry exhibits many of the advantages and disadvantages of latecomers to that process, for whom modernization was an import or, in the case of the Jews, what the late J. P. Nettl called "an inheritance situation." In *Modernization and the Structure of Societies* (1966), Levy lists five advantages and three disadvantages. The principal advantage of latecomers is that the process of modernization is "no longer the sort of *terra incognita* it was for the indigenous developers" and that they thus have some sense of the transition problems involved. Secondly, there always exists for the latecomer the possibility of borrowing (expertise in planning, capital accumulation, machines, and skills). The problem here, of course, is exactly *what* do you borrow when you borrow? A tractor, or a form of consciousness? A way of dressing, or a cast of mind? The problematics of the package problem always went, for Jews, under the heading "assimilation." The latecomer's third advantage is that of being able "to skip some of the early stages associated with the process of modernization as developed indigenously and gradually." By taking over the latest inventions, accumulated capital formation is acquired at one stroke (with initial obsolescences avoided). Borrowers are possibly advantaged over developers in taking over social inventions, too (for example, teaching methods). Post-Emancipation Jewry early exhibited the advantages of a telescoped modernization. The intellectuals among them especially—think of Solomon Maimon—came out of the ghetto at a dead run [8] and hurtled themselves proleptically into, if not modernity, then certain of its aspects. (As with Prussia and Japan, there were drawbacks to being in such a hurry.) A fourth advantage of the latecomer is knowledge—sketchy as it may be—of where the modernization scenario may lead. He can point to certain possible fruits, outcomes, results. The mediating intellectual can activate his people—in the case at hand the Jewish masses, the *Ostjuden*—with the charm of prospects and possibility. Levy's last advantage is simply the advantage of the modernized society to latecomers: they are able to help.[9]

Among the disadvantages for the latecomers to the modernization process is the problem of scale. Levy is thinking here of the generally high levels of literacy, for example, necessary in large proportions of the population if the modernizing facilities (schools, communications, government) are to be effectively staffed. This disadvantage—or dilemma—may be transposed into the dilemma faced by the socially mobile nineteenth-century Jewish intellectual: "Should I assimilate as an 'exception Jew,' " he asked himself, "improving myself, wending my private way in bourgeois society, making my 'separate peace'? Or will I never be really 'emancipated' and modernized unless I enlarge the public scale of my latecoming modernization so as to include my fellow *Ostjuden*, sunk in the traditionary, Orthodox past?" Gradual, indigenous development usually mitigates this painful choice between self-enhancement and group enhancement, egoism and altruism, liberty and equality.[10]

A second special disadvantage and frustration for latecomers is the scandal of the continuing gap between what indigenous members of highly modernized societies have achieved and what even the successful latecomers are able to attain. Even if closed in relative terms, this gap may continue to grow rather than lessen in absolute terms with the passage of time. Thus we have here a form of relative deprivation on an international scale. Nations today are internationally stratified on a modernization scale the same way individuals within a modern nation—as well as the groups to which these individuals belong—are ranked by domestic stratification systems. Lateral entry into this stratification system generates painful self-disesteem.

The final disadvantage singled out by Levy brings us to our deepest level of comparison between post-Emancipation Jewry and the decolonialized Third World and simultaneously brings us directly to what Peter Berger calls the *bricolage*–versus–the "seamless robe" scenarios of the modernization process.* "The members of a relatively nonmodernized society," Levy writes, and we must apply this to the Jews from the time of Emancipation until now, "see before them many and various results of the process in which they are, or are about to become, involved. These appeal to them in varying degrees, and almost inevitably the popular leaders, the influential persons, or the society's members in general are obsessed with the belief that they can take what they please and leave the rest."[11] They know something about the results of modernization; they may have seen Leningrad or Indianapolis; they know what they *don't* want; they believe themselves thus advantaged over the indigenous developer. But they are thus likely to be quite sure that they think they know where they are going and not going. They assume willy-nilly the posture of the consumer of modernity. They imagine them-

* *Bricolage* means that modernization comes as a "package" that one can take apart, picking and choosing what one wants. If modernization is a "seamless robe," however, it must be accepted or rejected in toto. See the brilliant analysis in chapter 4, "Modern Consciousness: Packages and Carriers," of *The Homeless Mind* in which, by means of a Weberian *Denkexperiment*, Berger, Berger, and Kellner endeavor to discriminate the intrinsic from the extrinsic elements in the empirical package of modernity. Peter L. Berger, Brigitte Berger, and Hansfried Kellner, *The Homeless Mind: Modernization and Consciousness* (New York: Random House, 1973), pp. 97–115.

selves in a supermarket. They will pick and choose. "The result is likely to be an interplay among old and new factors of a particularly explosive character," writes Levy. "The very discrepancy between their planning and their results constitutes a special disruption for them." [12]

Levy, though not opting for the extreme version of the "seamless robe" theory, nevertheless finds the keynote of relatively modernized societies in "the fact of general interdependence itself." The core of interdependence, in turn, he finds in "the diminished levels of self-sufficiency" that go with the modern division of labor in specialized organizations and subsystems. With modernization, the older "relatively high levels of self-sufficiency of the various organizations is lowered" and "the mere fact that [the newcomer] is aware of more alternative organizations to his own family makes a difference." The "density of avoidant * relationships per person per day" radically increases.[13]

Levy vigorously attacks the *bricolage* theory as romantic: "The myth of easy independent selectivity from among the social structures of highly modernized societies," he writes, "must be recognized for what it is and has always been—a hybrid of wishful thinking and sentimental piety." [14] Questions such as private and public ownership, concepts like capitalism, communism, or socialism, get us nowhere, since these differences do not touch on the strategic factors differentiating the structures of modernized from relatively nonmodernized societies. The structures of modernization "can never simply be imported piecemeal. That is to say," Levy explains, and this is what makes the hope of ethnic pluralism as utopian, ultimately, as the wish for total assimilation, "the members of relatively nonmodernized societies . . . can never simply take over what they want or what fits in well with the rest of their social structures and leave the rest. This is the fatally romantic element best propounded by F. S. C. Northrop. He holds that a good and proper state of mankind inheres in a combination of what he seems to regard as a sort of combination of the best of the East and the West." [15] Modernity for Levy is "subversive" of traditional societies, disintegrating them. His preferred image of modernization is of a "solvent"—he refers, e.g., to a "peculiarly solvent effect" that "invades" and "erodes" with "explosive subversion" the structures of relatively nonmodernized societies; "a sort of universal solvent"; and a sort of universal *social* solvent" (my emphasis) that dissolves premodern social structures.[16]

Despite the appearances of a formidable functionalist scholasticism, Levy's 855-page *Modernization and The Structure of Societies* is a very personal testament and should be read as such.† He tells us on page 79

* Levy's term for Parsons's "affective neutrality."—J.M.C.

† Surely I am the first person ever to have read Levy as a *cri de coeur!* See Professor Levy's more recent, briefer exposition in *Modernization: Latecomers and Survivors* (New York: Basic Books, 1972).

that "I grew up in Galveston, Texas, a member of a family long of that place," and of the "dramatic" discrepancy between his particularist, premodern upbringing, with its fixed horizons and closed future, and the structures of modern American society. He experienced the crisis of modernity in his own person, as well as the havoc it wreaks on traditionary, particularistic values. He came to see the need for socializing his own children into modernity, into an open future. "In this context," he writes, "it is easy to understand the importance of a predominantly universalistic ethic." [17] And it is in this context also that he dedicates his book to—among others—Talcott Parsons, "from whom," he writes, "one could always learn without having to agree." [18]

Right or wrong, Levy's thesis sums up some of the hard-earned experience of post-Emancipation Jewry in its encounter with the structures of the modernizing West. The modernity of the West acted as a solvent upon the premodern structures of *shtetl* Jewry: it tended to dissolve their culture system, their social system, their personality structures. Levy sums up all of this experience in two significant sentences: "The structures of relatively modernized societies can never be imported entirely piecemeal," he writes. "Whether introduced by force or voluntary means, more is introduced than is bargained for or understood." [19]

You get more than you bargained for or understand. Here we have an echo of the "contract theory" of Jewish Emancipation: "We did not read the fine print," the complaint runs; "we only wanted the right to vote and walk your streets as free men: 'men in the street, Jews at home.' Emancipation doesn't mean having to marry you, or eat with you, or become like you. And now, look at our children and grandchildren: they're all beginning to wear your seamless robes."

This is "The Brutal Bargain," as Norman Podhoretz entitles the first chapter of *Making It*. Looking back on the Gentile Mrs. K of his Brownsville boyhood, who took him in hand as the psychopompess of his initiation into "high" Gentile taste, he writes: "What seemed most of all to puzzle Mrs. K., who saw no distinction between taste in poetry and taste in clothes, was that I could see no connection between the two. . . . How could she have explained to me . . . that a distaste for the surroundings in which I was bred, and ultimately (God forgive me) even for many of the people I loved, and so a new taste for other kinds of people—how could she have explained that all this was inexorably entailed in the logic of a taste for the poetry of Keats and the painting of Cézanne and the music of Mozart?" [20] In that oil company in Kuwait, in that steel mill set down in India, or in the more generalized forces of modernity, in the rationality immanent in technology, in the arbitrariness and functional specificity immanent in bureaucracy, in urbanization with its "world of strangers," in social pluralization as such, in, finally, modernity's very differentiatedness, is there not entailed a logic as inexorable as that entailed in Keats, Cézanne, and Mozart? [21]

From the earliest days of Emancipation, the Jewish intelligentsia in Diaspora used for its own purposes versions of the conservative distinction between the *"pays légale"* and the *"pays réel."* The advent of the French Revolution disembedded the legal system from its premodern matrices much as the Industrial Revolution disembedded—at least in theory—a purely market nexus from its feudal and mercantile capitalist matrices. To appeal from the actual culture, where it all hangs together—the *pays réel*—to the rights of the citizen—the *pays légale*—may be seen as an early form of the refusal of the total Western package. Was it a kind of practice session in *bricolage*-theory? (The ACLU carries on this tradition today, forcing logically legal test cases that take prayers out of public schools and Christmas crèches off village greens, with the American Jewish Congress a frequent amicus curiae.) Is there a difference between trying to disassemble components of the modern West *in* the West and importing its already disassembled parts into a noncontiguous foreign country? That is, being already in the West, near the area of technological production, was it more difficult for the Jewish community to take the modernizing package apart than for a people farther away? Can one buy the industrial package without the Western European civilization package? Are hopes and dreams of such a differentiation utopian? Which elements are differentiable? Is industrialism a kind of importable *Unterbau,* with social modernization a relinquishable superstructure?

In the meantime, though, post-Emancipation Jewry had to live with the whole package, they had to live the Diaspora. Ideologies were cognitive strategies for doing this. We have spoken of the "lachrymose" ideology of their own history. Nevertheless, the very presence of the modernizing West constituted what Matossian calls an "assault." "Many of our ancestors," writes Michael Polanyi, "recognizing themselves as disgracefully backward, were overwhelmed by the contact with a superior civilization." [22] They had imported, in other words, the consciousness of underdevelopment, what Jules Isaac calls "the teaching of contempt." Out of this, I believe, came early the ideology of Hebraism—namely, that whereas "you may be a superior civilization (whatever that is), we, in our political and economic impotence, are a superior moral heritage." There is Hellenism, which is pagan, perhaps civilized, and with an eye to beauty, but greater still is Hebraism, with its concern for justice and its superior morality. From Luzzatto to Heine (from whom Arnold got it) and beyond to Hermann Cohen (1842–1914) and the Marburg neo-Kantians, this is a major theme of alienated Diaspora intellectual Jewry. It is the "moralistic style" of the modern oppositional intelligentsia. If earlier intellectual strata emerged as a *priestly* caste to legitimate by fudging the embarrassing gaps between culture and society (between profession and practice), the later, "outsider" *prophetic* intellectuals emerged to widen these gaps, to expose them, to delegitimate the relation of the culture's values to its social system practice. Like Max Weber's double theodicies, Hebraism as ideology gave meaning to Jewish civilizational inferiority and moral superiority at one stroke. In his great essay "Maule's Well, or Henry James and the Relation of Morals to Manners," the late critic Yvor Winters speaks of the spiritual antagonism between a rising provincial civilization—he is thinking of nineteenth-century America—and a more central, richer civilization—he is thinking of nineteenth-century Europe. In this contest, he writes, as we have noted previously, "the provincial civilization met the obviously superior cultivation of the parent with a more or less typically provincial assertion of moral superiority." This theme, he says, obsesses James, Cooper, and Mark Twain.[23]

When Jewry was physically peripheral to Europe, locked into its *shtetlach* in the pale, this provincial assertion of moral superiority, of moral purism, was that of a spatial outsider, a geographical provincial. With Emancipation into Europe, the axis of this moralism shifted from a horizontal to a vertical plane, splitting into the toplofty "mission to the Gentiles" of Reform Judaism on the one hand and, on the other, into Marx's underclass of society and Freud's underside of personality. In each case, proletariat and id were invested with a subversively pure moral critique of the hypocritical, if superior, civilization of the West. (In passing, it may be said that the attempt of Jurgen Habermas to find in what he chooses to call "the Jewish sensibility in Marxism" a heritage of Jewish "cabbala and mysticism" is as misguided as David Bakan's earlier attempt to tie Freud to the Jewish mystical tradition.[24] These mystical interpretations cry out for demystification.)

It is here, I think, that we have a far-reaching convergence of the role of the Jewish intelligentsia for 150 years within the European system and the modernizing elite of many of the new nations: the moral passions become the ruling passions, become special pleaders. Lionel Trilling once wrote, in a Burkean essay entitled "Manners, Morals, and the Novel," "that the moral passions are even more willful and imperious and impatient than the self-seeking passions."[25] It is Susan Sontag, we recall, who notes that "the Jews pinned their hopes for integrating into modern society on promoting the moral sense."[26]

A final parallel between the modernizing elite of the new nations and the modernizing intelligentsia of Diaspora Jewry will close this exploration in comparative analysis: the members of each of these mediatorial elites were burdened with the necessity not only of taking moral stances but of choosing a language in which to express them. The immigrant intellectual issuing from the Yiddish-speaking world of Eastern Europe, like the black African today, faced the crisis of cultural loss involved in the loss of the home language, the *mama-loshen*. As John Updike writes,

> The black African moved to literary expression confronts choices a Westerner need not make. First, he must choose his language—the

> European language, with its alien tradition and colonial associations, or the tribal language, with its oral tradition and minuscule reading audience. Unless his mother and father came from different tribes and used a European tongue as lingua franca in the home, his heart first learned to listen in the tribal language, which will forever then be more pungent and *nuancée;* but English and French command the far broader audience, across Africa and throughout the world. So he must choose his audience.[27]

"For whom does one write?" is a question that forces itself with maddening insistence on the literary intellectual representatives of a modernizing "underdeveloped" people, trapped in the moral and cultural ambiguities of "delayed modernization."

"We were in some ways, . . ." Leslie Fiedler writes of his Freshman Composition class at City College of New York in the late thirties, "like a class in an occupied country, a group of Alsatians or Czechs, say, under a German master." "We were forbidden Yiddishisms as we were forbidden slang; and though we had our censors outnumbered, our ignorance and shame kept us powerless." Thus were urban Jews force-fed a language "whose shape was determined by antiquated rules of etiquette (usually called 'grammar'), . . . a language capable of uttering only the most correctly tepid Protestant banalities no matter what stirred in our alien innards." Fiedler enlisted in a *kulturkampf* against these WASP "standards of an established alien taste. . . . I would know," he writes, "what I wrote against as well as for: against their taste as well as for our own." [28]

Not unconnected with this question about what sociologists call "the institution of language" is another, about social and cultural institutions: How does one behave? In life? In literature? "Can you explain," novelist Philip Roth asks himself, "why you are trying to come on like a bad boy—although in the manner of a very good boy indeed? Why quarrel, in decorous tones no less, with decorum?" [29]

PART IV

Children of the Founding Fathers of Diaspora Intellectuality: The Contemporary Scene

CHAPTER 21

A TALE OF TWO HOFFMANS: THE DECORUM DECISION AND THE BILL OF RITES

Readers of the *New York Times* for Wednesday, April 22, 1970 were greeted on page one with the following headline: "Panthers' Apologies Free Two Jailed for New Haven Contempt; Seale Vows Decorum." There it was, page-one news, the very thing Hegel and Marx had fallen out over: Is the modern state possible without modern bourgeois society and behavior (*bürgerliche Gesellschaft*)? There it was on page one: Bobby Seale, the national chairman of the Black Panther party: " 'We understand the necessity for peace and decorum in the courtroom,' Mr. Seale told Judge Harold M. Mulvey. 'We will maintain decorum in the courtroom,' he added at another point," using, as the article later notes, "a moderate tone." There it was, the very issue at the root of all the internal differences among Diaspora intellectual Jewry for the past 150 years of Emancipation: Is political emancipation tied to social assimilation? Does access to the political *rights* of the *citoyen* hinge on our prior performance of the social *rites* of the *bourgeois*? Must we prove ourselves *gentle*men before claiming the rights of men? Must we behave before we can act (politically)? Is decorum a "functional prerequisite"—to speak Parsonsese—to the Bill of Rights? to public assembly, free speech, fair trial? Is civil society—more particularly, is civility itself—in this, the bourgeois liberal era, necessary to the state? Has it become a *raison d'état* that we mind our manners? To explore the implications of these questions we shall turn to the 1969–70 trial of the "Chicago Seven." It was a kind of "everyday life" experiment, a case study crucially relevant to the questions raised by Lenin in *State and Revolution.* Today we can frame the same issue more relevantly under the "law and order" rubric of "State and Decorum."

The riot-conspiracy trial of the "Chicago Seven," * arising from

* The original group, of course, was the "Chicago Eight": the eighth defendant was, ironically, Bobby Seale, who was gagged and manacled in court in order to silence his protests against being denied the right to defend himself and whose case was finally separated from that of his codefendants.

demonstrations at the 1968 Democratic national convention, reached its climax in the sentencing of Abbie Hoffman, by federal district court Judge Julius Hoffman, to eight months in jail for contempt of court. On hearing the sentence, the Judge's Yippie namesake declared: "When decorum is [political] repression, the only dignity that free men have is to speak out." [1] With this declaration in early 1970, Abbie Hoffman had finally surfaced and articulated the latent issue that had been secretly at work all along in the civil rights agitation of the two preceding decades. With this declaration as its manifesto, the civil rights movement came to self-consciousness: in discovering that it was a counterculture and consequently a counterpolitics, the movement demonstrated—*ambulando*—the inherently bourgeois nature of civil liberties, the real meaning of "bourgeois civil liberties"; decorum was experienced as political repression. What *you* define as public decorum, Abbie Hoffman told Julius Hoffman, *I* define as political repression. On that conflicting definition of the situation, the trial came to its furious end.

In the sit-ins on buses and at lunch counters in the fifties in the South, the attempt to disentangle civil liberties from social civilities achieved some measure of success. Where radical differentiation failed, the decisions of the federal court system—culminating in the Supreme Court—seemed to give substance to the growing conviction among activists that only regional and local "backwardness" delayed the final splitting of social rites from civil rights, of the sociocultural from the political. In the sixties, new types of public places were chosen for the demonstration of probing "misbehaviors." The streets became the chosen scene for a disconcerting mix of legal misdemeanor and social misbehavior that troubled public officials responsible for the public order. Semipublic places like university plazas and classrooms were the subsequent scenes of agitation and takeover. ACLU types, alarmed and recalling their high school civics texts, told the young activists to take their cause off the streets and out of the classroom and into the voting booth. So, in August 1968, they went to the convention of the Democratic party in Chicago, and everybody knows what happened there: all hell broke loose. The activists claimed they were denied the civil right of peaceful assembly in the public parks and were repressed by Mayor Daley's police. The public authorities claimed that the activists used their right of free speech and assembly to foment riot in public places and thus deny the rights of others. Above the noise of claim and counterclaim, the voice of the liberal civil libertarian was heard again in the land: take this fight out of the parks and into the courts. The federal prosecutor in Chicago did just that, and that's how Abbie Hoffman, Jerry Rubin, and others of the now-famous Chicago Seven ended up testing the limits of deference and demeanor in their final public testing place, the federal courtroom of Judge Julius Hoffman. This terminal setting was almost contrived to spell out the issue precisely as Abbie Hoffman would, indeed, in the end, spell it out. The interaction ritual of the Anglo-Saxon adversary proceeding is intricately choreographed. The substantive rights of the defendant are meticulously shored up in this proceeding, it is contended, by the procedural rites of due process. Returning to Chicago to stand trial, defendant Rennie Davis announced: "We came to Chicago in August, 1968, to disrupt the ritual and sham which is ordinarily put over as the democratic process. Now we are disrupting the ritual and sham which Judge Hoffman calls the judicial process." [2]

The tactic by which *this* tactic was effected involved a kind of ceremonial profanation ritual, a defrocking of Judge Hoffman and a vandalizing of legal decorum. If, as Goffman observes, "spite actions" at law and vandalism (in the usual sense) represent ways in which "the substantive order is abused for ceremonial purposes," [3] the legal "black mass" at Chicago became a kind of behavioral vandalism in which decorum was abused for substantive—i.e., political—purposes. But the Chicago trial provided an arena not only for this general cultural attack on the impersonal judicial process and on Judge Hoffman as its representative, but also for an intra-Jewish fight, a play within a play, as the two Hoffmans acted out an ancient scenario: the socially unassimilated Eastern European Jew versus the assimilated German Jew who "passes" among the *goyim*. Throughout the trial the two Hoffmans conducted reciprocal vendettas against one another. J. Anthony Lukas of the *New York Times* notes that what he calls the judge's "efforts to escape his own Jewishness" and his eagerness to win "social acceptance among the *goyim*" may explain not only his (initially) gentle condescension to "*schwartzes*" like black defendant Bobby Seale, but also "his real rage . . . reserved for the Jews who misbehaved." [4] What Lukas does not care to note is the other side of this ancient *Kulturkampf* among Jews in Diaspora, namely, that if Julius Hoffman's real rage was reserved for the Jews who misbehaved, Abbie Hoffman's real rage was reserved for the Jews who "behaved"—German Jews (either authentic or "honorary" *) like Julius Hoffman.

To get perspective on this tale of two Hoffmans, this trial within the trial, we must go back a few years. In the 1960s in New York Paul Krassner began publishing a monthly called *The Realist* (the grandfather of the subsequent "underground press"). It was daring, scatological, curiously apolitical; its specialty was irreverant satire and impolite reportage (as in its monthly feature, "An Impolite Interview with . . ."). In late 1967, editor Krassner met with Jerry Rubin and ex–civil rights worker Abbie Hoffman in New York and invented YIP, the Youth International Party, whose battle cry they declared to be "Yippie!" † An ab-

* Three partitions of Poland provided many *Ostjuden* with the opportunity to claim the *yichus* and status of a German Jew.

† I follow roughly in this account the chronology supplied by Gene Marine, "Chicago," *Rolling Stone*, April 2, 1970, p. 38.

surdist sensibility, derived from their own "outsider" experience (and perhaps from reading Camus) equipped them to bring together the "Yippie Ethic" (adversary to the Protestant Ethic), the youth culture, and the growing counterculture with elements of New Left politics and a psychedelic life-style (pot, rock, sex, "acid," long hair, "freaky" clothes). All of this was to bring about *Revolution for the Hell of It* (a later book by Hoffman). *Épatez le bourgeois* was retooled into "Fuck the System." [5] "It's all true," writes Gene Marine, "the new life-style *is* the Revolution, and the old order is dying." [6]

As was abundantly clear from its earliest protests, the New York–based Yippies derived a good deal of their inspiration from "sick" comedian-satirist Lenny Bruce and his "insider's" criticism of middle-class Jewish gentility. In protest at a preview of a dada exhibition at the Museum of Modern Art in early 1968, for example, a group of Yippies "saluted arriving guests by calling out, 'All you rich old ladies go back to Schraffts.' " * One held a placard reading "Bourgeoie Zoo." Another was garbed in a bedouin Arab robe "for no particular reason." [7]

It is this life-style that was brought twice to Chicago—first in protest and then on trial—and this life-style that was the novel element in both confrontations. It is significant that, at the trial, defendant David Dellinger's tilts with Judge Hoffman are those of a WASP square and seldom go beyond Puritan levelism. The following colloquy, for example, occurs between them:

> Mr. Dellinger: Mr. Hoffman.
> The Court: I'm Judge Hoffman.
> Mr. Dellinger: I believe in equality.
> The Court: Sit down.[8]

Bobby Seale's disruption was of a different order. Interruptions, shouts, sneers, refusals to obey the court's directives. Judge Hoffman had him bound and gagged, but it did no good. Seale was still able to disrupt the proceedings. Over the wild protests of his codefendants and their legal counsel, he was finally jailed for contempt.

From the outset the issue of decorum was placed, by Abbie Hoffman and Jerry Rubin, at center stage. The defense table itself was an "offense," littered with papers, candy wrappers, and books. It was a prop in Yippie Theater. "Across the narrow aisle," writes J. Anthony Lukas, who covered the trial for the *New York Times*, "the government's table reproached us all [*sic*] with its cool, efficient order." The defendants put their booted feet up on the black leather chairs and sometimes on the table. Their manners, writes Lukas, "weren't always nice." [9] Writing in *Liberation*

* Krassner of *The Realist* was present, as were people from the EVO (*East Village Other*) and listener-sponsored radio station WBAI.

magazine, Sidney Lens noted at the start of the proceedings that the trial's "true drama is in the character of the defendants. Abbie and Jerry, whatever their appearance to those who favored oxford grey, represent a new youth culture that has turned its back on the hypocrisy of an older generation." [10] As we were soon to learn, they also represented a new generation enlisted in an old intraethnic quarrel: the battle of the *Ostjuden* and the *Yahudim*, the alienated Eastern European outsiders and the manicured German Jewish assimilators who long to "pass." *

(Many years after writing his famous fictionalized account of the Leopold-Loeb murder case, *Compulsion* [1956], Meyer Levin owns up to a "secret motive" at work in his account of that trial. He calls it "the German Jewish theme." At the time of the murder, Levin writes, "there had reverberated all through our Chicago West Side, the neighborhood of Russian and Eastern European Jews, an undercurrent of vengeful satisfaction—these were the sons of German Jews, these two wealthy degenerates who had committed the vicious crime, and were even boasting of it!" [11] Well, an *Ostjude* named Levin would put the South Side Jew in his place! This animus surfaced publicly in the late sixties during the Chicago Seven trial.)

Lukas pinpoints an incident early in the trial as particularly revealing for the ethnic infighting that subsequently ensued between the two Hoffmans:

> The judge, a German Jew, seemed . . . testy about overt declarations of Jewishness. A young Orthodox Jew, wearing a *yarmulke*, tried repeatedly to get into the trial, but the Federal marshals turned him away. Mr. [William] Kunstler [chief defense attorney] took issue with the judge, who repeatedly refused to interfere. Always quick to exploit such opportunities, the defense managed to get Arthur I. Waskow, a radical historian from the Institute of Policy Studies, on the witness stand wearing a *yarmulke* and the following colloquy ensued: '*The Court:* Are you a clergyman, sir? *The witness:* No, sir. *The Court:* You will have to remove your hat. *Mr. Schultz*

* "*Yahudim*," the Hebrew word meaning "Jews," was applied by the Eastern European Jewish immigrants (the *Yidn*) during the period 1890–1920 exclusively—and derogatorily—to German Jews, also called "uptown Jews." *Yidn* worked in the *Yahudim*-owned garment sweatshops in the early days; Mike Gold attacked them in his famous novel *Jews Without Money*. The *Yahudim*, Judd L. Teller writes, did everything *sotto voce:* "They were fearful lest the untoward conduct of irrepressible *Yidn* jeopardize their American sanctuary. They established institutions to 'uplift' and 'Americanize' the *Yidn*. . . . The fact is," concludes Teller—and this is what the irrepressible Abbie knew about the repressed and decorous "Julie"—"that the *Yahudim* themselves were not really adjusted" to the America of the WASP upper class they tried to imitate. (*Strangers and Natives: The Evolution of the American Jew from 1921 to the Present* [New York: Delacorte Press, 1968], p. 46.) This insider's knowledge was Abbie's secret weapon in his war with Judge Hoffman. It was "Julie's" vulnerability, his Achilles' heel.

> [government prosecutor]: Your Honor, we don't object. I know that he—*The Court:* I object. . . .' Shuddering with anger, the judge repeatedly ordered Mr. Waskow to remove his *yarmulke* or get off the stand—relenting only at Mr. Schultz's repeated urgings. Sensing a vulnerability here Abbie Hoffman responded one day by yelling at the judge in Yiddish." * [12]

On February 4, 1970, when Judge Hoffman jailed defendant Dellinger for using an obscenity in court, Abbie Hoffman rose up in a rage and shouted at the judge, "You're a disgrace to the Jews, runt! You should have served Hitler better!" † following which "two marshals grabbed Mr. Hoffman by the shoulders and threw him into a leather chair." [13] Even more revealing than these angry outbursts was the insulting familiarity with which Abbie Hoffman constantly addressed Judge Hoffman: he always called him "Julie." ‡ Dellinger, as we have seen, addressed the judge as "Mr. Hoffman" instead of the standard "Your Honor," legitimating this by saying: "I believe in equality." Abbie Hoffman, on the other hand, in calling Judge Hoffman "Julie," forced on the judge the equality of ethnic origin. He was stripping him of his legal-judicial forms; he would not differentiate the man from the office. His needling was intended to get at the Jewish Hoffman beneath the respectable judge's garb. He succeeded only too well.

The day after jailing Dellinger for contempt for uttering an obscenity, Judge Hoffman cut off chief defense counsel William Kunstler in the middle of his argument for Dellinger's release. Abbie Hoffman then shouted: "Your idea of justice is the only obscenity in this court, Julie. . . . This ain't the Standard Club." This was a reference, Lukas notes, "to Chicago's major *German*-Jewish club [near the courthouse], where Judge Hoffman lunches" (my emphasis). Soon Abbie was telling Julie to "stick it up your bowling ball," adding, "How's your war stock, Julie?"—apparently "a reference to the Brunswick Corporation," Lukas explains with deflationary pedantry, "which makes bowling balls and in which Judge Hoffman's wife is reported to own stock." Lukas continues: "Then Mr. Rubin spoke: '. . . Adolf Hitler equals Julius Hitler.' Abbie Hoffman

* A kind of "cultural entrapment" takes place here. The judge is stuck with the very American (and Christian) definition of Judaism as a "religion" (this, the classical German Reform Jewish self-definition of Judaism). Waskow's *not* being a clergyman would thus have settled the matter. Everyone knows what is happening. The judge will be made to *seem* to be an anti-Semite if he retains his strictly American and Reform Jewish definition of Judaism as purely a religion! Lukas, it would seem, missed this dimension of the infighting.

† Almost all the media eliminated the Jewish infighting in their accounts of the trial.

‡ Abbie claimed he was "Julie's son" and wanted legally to change his first name to "Fuck" (Marine, "Chicago," p. 38—see note 5)—in order, presumably, to reply, when the Court asked him his name: "Fuck Hoffman." Also, he gave his address as "Woodstock Nation."

picked up the attack, spicing it with Yiddish. '*Shande fur de Goyim* [Disgrace for the Gentiles],' he yelled. Later, Mr. Hoffman gleefully translated the phrase as 'Front man for the WASP power elite.' "[14]

At the trial's end, when the jury filed in to announce its verdict (it cleared the seven of the conspiracy count, but found five guilty of making riot-inciting speeches) and the judge ordered the courtroom cleared, Abbie's wife Anita shouted to the defendants, "You will be avenged," and at Judge Hoffman, "We'll dance on your grave, Julie." * [15]

Convicted on Wednesday, the five were sentenced on Friday by Judge Hoffman. Each received a five-year sentence for crossing state lines with intent to incite a riot by inflammatory speeches during the 1968 Democratic national convention. But the real drama of the day came, wrote Lukas at the time, when each defendant rose to speak his final words, each giving vent to his personal style: "Mr. Davis, restrained but bitter; Mr. [Tom] Hayden [Irish, by the way], analytic and often cynical; Abbie Hoffman, theatrical and heavily ethnic; Mr. Rubin, flamboyant but bluntly angry."[16] Abbie Hoffman, huddled in a blue and green ski sweater, told Judge Hoffman: "Jail is not a nice place for a Jewish boy with a good education to be. . . . Tonight, after you sentence us, the gods are going to play Goliath and shave our heads. It's a technique perfected by the Nazis. They've waited [until sentencing] so we'd look nice."[17] According to the account in the *Times,* Abbie also told "Julie": "Well, I am an enemy of America spelled with a 'K.' We are outlaws in our own country. The government says I'm unpatriotic. I suppose I am. But the government says I'm un-American and I know I'm not un-American." As he sat down, Abbie, who had reserved his parting shot for the ethnic Judge Hoffman, "waved at the judge and cried: 'See you in Florida, Julie.' Judge Hoffman," Lukas appends," is scheduled to leave for a Florida vacation later this month."[18] No account of the last day in court, except that of the three authors in *RAT* (see note 1) reports the decisive declaration of Abbie Hoffman's final statement: "When decorum is repression, the only dignity that free men have is to speak out."

The trial of the Chicago Seven was ended, and suddenly, it seemed, the whole world was talking about etiquette and decorum and the way Judge Hoffman used his contempt power to punish the defendants for violating the proprieties of his courtroom. Anthony Prisendorf, describing courtroom decorum as a "loosely defined code of etiquette," traces the contempt power to pre–Magna Carta days, when the king's surrogates who presided at trials commanded the same degree of deference for themselves as that given the king himself; thus, to defy a court's power was to express contempt for the sovereign's authority.[19] Convinced that the punitively severe contempt citations would be vacated on appeal, most commentators speculated on the personalities of the parties in-

* This remark was mistaken by some people for a death threat.

volved, carefully avoiding mention of the particularistic intramural Jewish infighting the trial revealed.*

The *New York Post*'s Max Lerner, for example, observed that Judge Hoffman proved "human, all-too-human, thin-skinned, vain, vulnerable" under fire from the "resourceful" defendants and their lawyers, who "reached him in the soft underbelly of his self-esteem" and caused him to overreact vindictively.[20] M. W. Newman in the same publication described the Seven's lawyer, William M. Kunstler, as "a 'touch' type of person, always embracing someone or impulsively throwing his arm around a companion." [21] A letter from Irving Howe in the *Times* chided both sides for misbehavior: if Judge Hoffman had "behaved with fairness and restraint," defendant Hoffman and his brethren might have perforce "modulated their conduct." † [22] *Newsweek,* indulging in some comparative behavioristics of its own, noted that, unlike the Chicago riot-conspiracy trial, the earlier draft-law conspiracy trial against Dr. Benjamin Spock, the Reverend William Sloane Coffin, et al. had been "a model of deocrum." [23] The same issue of *Newsweek* wondered, in another piece, whether the trial system itself might have to be modified to cope with defendants and lawyers "who refuse to observe its fragile rules of decorum." [24] *Time* magazine observed that the defendants had "irked Hoffman by calling him 'Julie'" and revealed that defendant Rennie Davis had kept whispering to Assistant Prosecutor Richard Schultz while the latter was examining a witness, "You dirty fascist Jew!" [25] Two pages later *Time* speaks of the "impossible behavior" of the Chicago Seven and reminds them that "decorum can work in a defendant's favor by preventing unruly behavior that might prejudice the jury against him." [26] The same *Time* story also passes along attorney Kunstler's explanation that, for political cases, he has had to develop "a certain aggressiveness" even though it may run "counter to the rules the system has devised." [27] When, a short time after sentencing, Judge Hoffman denied bail to the Chicago defendants pending appeal, the *New York Times* editorialized that he had thus continued to act "as a man engaged in a personal vendetta" and found it fortunate that the case would now speedily move into "more objectively judicious hands." [28]

Clearly, people were, at this point, very confused. For the first time people were openly wondering whether the right to a fair trial might not always have presupposed the duty of deferential behavior—though

* David Gurin was an exception. In the course of reporting a "Freedom Seder" he alluded to the Chicago trial as repeating an ancient quarrel *within* the Jewish community: "It has been like all Jewish history: Moses vs. the worshippers of the golden calf, Marx and LaSalle [*sic*] vs. Disraeli and Julius Stahl (the arch-theorist of feudal reaction), Abbie vs. Julie." "A Hip Seder in Rocky's Land," *Village Voice,* April 23, 1970, p. 6.

† Howe, in the late '60s and '70s, is talking the Trilling "modulation" language he decried in the '50s. The New Left is getting to him.

nobody explicitly realized it until then. But if a functional prerequisite to the jury system is a normative "good behavior" system, is not that to legislate good behavior? Are not manners a social class affair? Have we eliminated other qualifications for voting and receiving a fair trial—property qualifications, religious qualifications, sex qualifications, residence, even literacy as a qualification—only to legislate good manners as an eligibility criterion for our right to exercise the rights listed in the Bill of Rights? Are the political rights of the *citoyen* to be enjoyed only by the bourgeois and not by the unruly underclass and the socially anomic? "Are we outlaws and guilty," the Chicago Seven were asking America and its legal system, "or are we merely outrageous and offensive?" When Vice-President Spiro Agnew in a 1970 speech in Saint Paul, Minnesota denounced the Chicago Seven for being, not "guilty as charged," but for being "anarchists and social misfits," he merely codified in flamboyant form the confusion and anger of all parties.

The *New York Times* in its editorial on the Chicago trial remained true to the old Ochsian Reform decorum when it contrasted the trial itself to the jury's verdict as follows: if the trial was "flamboyant," the jury's verdict stood as "a *quiet* justification" of the jury system (my emphasis).[29] Nat Hentoff wondered why political activists who were being (in his view) so obviously tried for their political acts and beliefs "should be expected to remain respectful" in such a courtroom. Hentoff chides Mayor John Lindsay of New York for saying that "there's no civil right to be uncivil" and asks: "Is civility an absolute value, to be adhered to at whatever cost to the sense of personal legitimacy each of these defendants so clearly possesses?"[30] Hentoff goes on to predict that in political trials to come there will be more defendants "who will not be civil and who will thereby offend those who value appearances—especially the appearance that justice is being done even when those put off by a style not their own *know* differently"[31] (my emphasis).

One such trial, in fact, was already in progress in New York as Hentoff wrote these words (in February 1970), and, indeed, the defendants' courtroom demeanor was offending those who value appearances. This was the pretrial hearings of the "Panther Thirteen" being held before U.S. district court Judge John J. Murtagh. Charged with a conspiracy to plant bombs in public places, they were now shouting in a public place: the courtroom at 100 Centre Street. The interruptions, contumely, and general indecorum reached such a point that on February 25 Judge Murtagh adjourned the hearings indefinitely, informing the lawyers of the Black Panther defendants that the hearings would remain in recess until he received, in writing, signed promises from all thirteen defendants that they would "conduct themselves in accordance with traditional courtroom decorum." The Panthers in turn refused, challenging Murtagh's right even to demand such behavior as a precondition for resuming trial, but then lost a habeas corpus action to make their point.[32]

Murtagh's action was without precedent. His decision, his opponents argued, violated the Fifth Amendment, since by promising to behave in the future the defendants would be incriminating themselves. The strongest objection was that his action made the defendants' constitutional right to a fair and speedy trial conditional. As a way out of the impasse the prosecutor in the case, Manhattan District Attorney Frank Hogan, proposed to use closed circuit TV to get the hearings going again: the defendants in a room adjacent to the courtroom would follow the proceedings of their own trial, conferring with their lawyer over an intercom. Defense lawyers contested the prosecution proposal on three grounds, arguing that (1) it would deprive the defendants of the right to confront their accusers, (2) it would prejudice the jury against them, and (3) it would deprive them of the close-hand contact with their lawyers required by law.[33]

Jane Alpert (later herself to be tried on a bombing charge *), covering the Panther Thirteen trial for the underground newspaper *RAT*, reported that the Panthers "carry on loud conversations in open court" and contended that they had already won some significant legal points by "simply demanding them loudly enough." [34] She agreed with the Panthers that "there is no justice for black people in white men's courts" and, rehabilitating an old saying of Jews about Gentiles, wrote: "Scratch a white liberal and find a racist." Greil Marcus, identifying politics with activism, wrote that to really "act on" the American freedoms embodied in the Bill of Rights (free speech and assembly, due process, privacy) in a *political* context is to run into the political culture of the self-righteous "silent majority" and its distaste for and distrust of politics. Vote and keep quiet: "Other sorts of political behavior are anti-social." [35] Once more, as in Agnew's "social misfit" charge, the relation of political behavior and social behavior are at the center of contention: is behavior that is actively propolitical ipso facto antisocial?

Debate raged for weeks on Judge Murtagh's controversial ruling. Is the Sixth Amendment right (of physical confrontation with one's accuser) a right of physical copresence? Does a defendant in a criminal proceeding have the *unqualified* right to be personally present at all stages of his trial? What exactly is the constitutional status of a written "pledge of good behavior"? [36] Each pundit fit the controversy into his own framework. Anarchist Paul Goodman saw the content of the shouted demands —"Constitutional Rights!," "Power to the People!," "Socialism!"—as ir-

* Convicted as an accessory, Alpert jumped bail and is now a fugitive and militant feminist in the Weatherwoman underground. See Edward Grossman, "Jane [Alpert] & Sam [Melville]: A Requiem for Two Bombers," *Midstream* 20, no. 3 (March 1974): 26–42.

relevant to their meaning, namely, a "response of life in over-structured and dehumanized institutions; it is not aimed at the courts as such but at all authority." [37]

Few cared to entertain the possibility that the provo tactics were exposés, experimenting probes aimed at demonstrating that every civil right has, as hidden proviso, a bourgeois rite, and that all civil rights are alienable with the nonperformance of civic rites. It is as though it had taken 150 years to isolate and surface the ultimate—and sole indefeasible—eligibility qualification *assumed* in the Constitution of the United States: you have to be nice. This had never been fully realized till our time. Obvious things must become odd before people notice them. In our time, with everyday normative expectation-systems under attack, it was only a matter of time before the critique of behavior as behavior, of the West's social appearances, would get under way. Much had to happen before incongruity procedures could be introduced programmatically into this dimension of the ordinary.* The *New York Times* quotes Harry Kalvin of the Chicago Law School: "We're a little puzzled now as to why defendants behaved so well in the past." [38]

About the time the Black Panther lawyers were challenging the constitutionality of Judge Murtagh's ruling, it became known that the Supreme Court was soon to rule on a case in which a Chicago judge had ordered an uncontrollably unruly defendant from the courtroom and went on with the trial, contending that the defendant had waived his right to be present. The trial judge had been upheld by the Supreme Court of the State of Illinois, and later by a federal district court that had considered Allen's petition for habeas corpus. This decision was in turn reversed by the federal court of appeals, which ruled that the Sixth Amendment's guarantee of an accused's right of confrontation with his accusers is an *absolute right* that cannot be infringed. By agreeing to review the case, the Supreme Court had joined the issue. Many expected the court to rule that such an absolute right cannot be waived. (Justice Hugo Black, for example, had a well-earned reputation as a Bill of Rights absolutist.)

On March 8, 1970, while the Court's decision was being awaited, Judge Irving R. Kaufman told a Fordham Law School Alumni Association gathering that the courtroom conduct of the Chicago Seven and the New York Thirteen threatened to become a "major epidemic" and could obliterate both fair trials and the judicial system itself. He called for

* Many "finite provinces" of cultural meaning have come under the pitiless gaze constituted by the unwillingness to suspend disbelief: think of Julian Beck's and Judith Malina's Living Theater attack on the decorums of the "bourgeois theater" in the '60s and '70s. Abbie and Jerry did the same thing in the Chicago courtroom: they ended the *epoché* of the natural attitude and did—rather deliberately—what comes naturally, namely, practiced certain strategems of profanation. These, as always, resulted in bewilderment, hostility, and mistrust.

its legal rejection, before other defendants respond to the siren call, believing that "absence of manners and disruptive conduct are effective trial tactics. Have defendants who place the trial on trial," he asked, "forgotten the lessons of history? . . . What would they substitute for our public trial conducted by adversaries and circumscribed by rules of evidence, rules of orderliness, courtesy and dignity? Would they honestly prefer the violence of an ordeal by combat or the spectacle of a Roman circus?" [39] For the first time, appellate judges were speaking of a trial's public, adversary character and its rules of evidence in the same breath, in the same sentence, with "its rules of orderliness, courtesy and dignity." Would Supreme Court judges do the same?

Finally on March 31, in a landmark opinion written, ironically, by Justice Hugo L. Black, the Supreme Court ruled on unruliness by unanimously reversing the court of appeals' ruling in the Allen case. Black's opening argument reads: "It is essential to the proper administration of criminal justice that *dignity, order, and decorum* be the hallmarks of all court proceedings in our country. The flagrant disregard in the courtroom of elementary standards of proper conduct should not and cannot be tolerated" [40] (my emphasis). In this, what may be called the "Decorum Decision" (in the "Good Behavior case"), Black listed three "remedies" available to a trial judge in handling an obstreperous defendant: (1) bind and gag him, (2) cite him for contempt, and/or (3) remove him "until he promises to conduct himself properly." (With this last, the Supreme Court had put its stamp on Judge Murtagh's method.) Black then considers the pros and cons of each "remedy" for courtroom indecorum. The first technique is itself something of an "affront to the very dignity and decorum of judicial proceedings that the judge is seeking to uphold." Citing or threatening to cite for contempt is approved. And, finally, removal is justified: "We hold that Allen lost his right guaranteed by the sixth and fourteenth Amendments to be present throughout his trial." Our courts cannot be permitted, Black wrote, to be "bullied, insulted, and humiliated and their orderly progress thwarted. . . . The record shows that the Illinois trial judge conducted himself with that dignity, decorum and patience that befits a judge. Deplorable as it is to remove a man from his own trial, even for a short time, we hold that the judge did not commit legal error in doing what he did. The judgment of the Court of Appeals is reversed." [41]

Legal rights, then, are not absolute but relative to social rites of decorum; one can forfeit the former by nonperformance of the latter. At last the West had taken up a certain type of social behavior * and had built it into the legal system as its essential precondition. If, then, legal rights are not an absolute, what of social decorum in public places? To Nat Hentoff's question, "Is civility an absolute value, to be

* It had, in Parsons's language, made a norm into a value.

adhered to at whatever cost?"[42] the Supreme Court seems to have replied with a decisive yes. How odd that civility and its rites should turn out to be an absolute value and legality and its rights a relative one. The Supreme Court was putting America on notice that the political culture of civility—the civic culture—was a functional prerequisite to the working of its democratic infrastructures.

The next day a *New York Times* editorial went to the heart (for a change) of a Supreme Court decision. In "Order in the Court," it noted that while the Supreme Court decision obviously could not insure decorum in every court, the decision has made clear that the constitutional right to a fair trial *"is contingent on* respect for those procedures without which a fair trial is impossible [and] that the rights of a citizen cannot be separated from the duties of citizenship"[43] (my emphasis). In other words, the Supreme Court had "put the burden on the defendant . . . to 'respect elementary standards of proper conduct' in the courtroom or to forfeit his right" to be present at his own trial.[44] These "elementary standards of proper conduct" constitute our Anglo-American "civility" or the "elementary forms of our religious life," the precontractual community values that are ex officio party to all the "social contracts" performed in the *Gesellschaft.* We are, the Supreme Court was saying in effect, a societal community. The solidarity sui generis to our kind of society is (paradoxically) a solidarity of the surface. The Supreme Court had taken bourgeois behavior up into the Constitution, reinstitutionalizing it as a Bill of Rites.

It is against the background of this Supreme Court decision that New York and New Haven Black Panther trials resumed, and exactly three weeks after its decision a headline in the *Times* (referred to earlier) reads: "Seale Vows Decorum." Presumably, Bobby Seale's vow was performed with tongue in cheek. Clearly, his codefendant David Hilliard's apology was so, for we read in an accompanying story from New Haven that the latter told a rally of Yale students that, by means of the apology that released him from his six-month sentence for scuffling with a deputy sheriff in court, he had been "crafty enough to outwit the system."[45] As a later account quoted him, he said that his apology to Connecticut Superior Court Judge Harold M. Mulvey "was necessary because we're crafty enough to outwit the stupid people who are trying to oppress black people."[46] But Seale's and Hilliard's craftiness have not "outwitted the system," because the system (at its limits, anyway) exacts only appearances; we are required not to respect, but to *show* respect. What *motivates* us to show respect is our own business. We are not required to like the law or even to believe in it; only to observe it. To observe it out of fear or even out of contempt may not be the best thing; nevertheless, even the delights of *Schadenfreude* belong to the private sector and are numbered among the things that are not Caesar's.

In America the classic Western "solution" to the modernization problem—the excruciating bifurcation of life into public and private spheres, of the self into "behavior" and "experience"—approaches full institutionalization. The decisive differentiations issue from the early debate of New England Puritanism with itself. In the famous "Half-Way" Synod of 1662, when Congregationalism passed from religious utopia to a legalized societal community, Perry Miller writes, "religion was practically confined to the inner consciousness of the individual. . . . The churches were pledged, in effect, not to pry into the genuineness of any religious emotions, but to be altogether satisfied with decorous semblances."[47] So too with Anglo-Saxon common law; its development reinforced the bourgeois modern differentiation of private from public, inner from outer, thus completing the destruction of "tribal wholeness" of the earlier *Gemeinschaft.* "The ultimate task which Holmes the jurist set Holmes the historian," writes Mark A. DeWolfe Howe, "was to follow the evolution of common law doctrine toward its destined goal of externality."[48] Visible saints evolve, by the Decorum Decision, into decent and decorous citizens.

CHAPTER 22

JEWS, BLACKS, AND THE COLD WAR AT THE TOP: MALAMUD'S *THE TENANTS* AND THE STATUS-POLITICS OF SUBCULTURES

That Bernard Malamud passes as a Jewish author is a commentary on the cultural and theological illiteracy of our times. Jewish by descent, his literary themes and values are Christian, *echt* Christian, sometimes nauseatingly so. "Malamud's themes," Stanley Edgar Hyman informed us long ago, "are the typical themes of the New Testament: charity, compassion, sacrifice, redemption," adding that in Malamud "these Christian themes are thoroughly secularized." [1] Malamud's central theme is not merely redemption, but redemption through love, through sacrificial, universal, altruistic, agapic, Christian love. His heroes are Christ figures. But the decor of his novels and their characters are largely Jewish. And that's where the confusion begins. As a result, Gentile readers hail him, Jewish readers praise him, he gets prizes—and his books sell. And even ex-radical literary critics, like Philip Rahv and Lionel Trilling—who should know better—acclaim him a master. It is not merely, as Robert Alter notes, that there has been "a tacit conspiracy afoot in recent years to foist on the American public as peculiarly Jewish various admired characteristics which in fact belong to the common humanity of us all," with the Jewish people depicted as possessing "a kind of monopoly on vividness, compassion, humor, pathos, and the like." [2] No, the contemporary literary-cultural situation is characterized a good deal more by irony than by conspiracy.*

We have the curious cultural spectacle of Bernard Malamud, a teller of Christian tales, "passing" as a Jew. It is unhelpful in this regard to compare him to the painter Marc Chagall, as both Rahv and Trilling do. Hailing Malamud's "Magic Barrel" (1958) as perhaps the best story pro-

* Ancient Alexandria provides a precedent: "Philo claimed in the name of Judaism," Erwin Goodenough writes, "everything which he took from the gentiles." *An Introduction to Philo Judaeus* (New Haven: Yale University Press, 1940), p. 97.

duced by a writer in recent decades (predictably, and preposterously, he compares him to Dostoevski), Rahv goes on to note that the last sentences of this story are "like a painting of Chagall come to life." [3] Trilling, commenting on the same passage in the same story in the same year (throwing in a comparison to Hawthorne), also notes the "reminiscence of the iconography" of Chagall, "the great celebrator of the religious culture of the Jews of East Europe. It is this culture [that Malamud's character] Salzman represents." [4] But to establish Malamud's Jewish credentials by a comparison with Chagall * merely compounds the confusion, since Chagall himself, as the Jewish historian Judd L. Teller reminds us, has so completely succumbed to the imagery of Christian mysticism and Russian Orthodox iconography "that his dominant symbol of Jewish martyrdom is the Crucifixion, his Jewish family is the Holy Family, and the only thing Jewish about his work is the garb and facial features of his characters, but their destiny and posture are Christian." [5] Much the same could be said, *mutatis mutandis*, of many figures constituting the so-called American Jewish literary renaissence in American letters: they arrive on the literary scene by creating a Jewish character with a real Jewish Heart, "a true Jew, which," critic Robert Alter notes, "as one often discovers in American Jewish fiction, means that he turns out to be a true Christ." [6] The pages of contemporary American Jewish fiction swarm with incognito Christs passing as suppostitious Jews: more than one Jewish literary intellectual arrives by marketing his fictional characters under an incognito, saying, in effect, "*Incognito, ergo sum.*" [7]

The influence, then, of traditional Jewish experience "on American writers like Bellow and Malamud is for the most part peculiarly tangential, however conspicuous it may sometimes be in their work." [8] Take, for example, Malamud's novel *The Assistant* (1957). The Italian clerk, Frank Alpine, while peeling potatoes, asks the Jewish grocer, Morris Bober, about Jewish identity and why Jews suffer so much, suggesting that they like to suffer:

> "What do you suffer for, Morris?," Frank said.
>
> "I suffer for you," Morris said calmly.
>
> Frank laid his knife down on the table. His mouth ached. "What do you mean?"
>
> "I mean you suffer for me." [9]

Whereas in a Mauriac novel this Frank (François) would inevitably wind up on his knees in church, a Malamud novel moves to its

* The painter Rouault played the same role for Catholics like Maritain and neo-Thomism that Chagall does in the neo-Hasidism that descends from Buber. Both are wildly overpraised for extrapainterly reasons.

promised end: "One day in April Frank went to the hospital and had himself circumcised. For a couple of days he dragged himself around with a pain between his legs. The pain enraged and inspired him. After Passover he became a Jew." [10]

A sociologist of literature will see this universalistic fictional Judaism as a consolidation by Jewish literary intellectuals—on the level of what Talcott Parsons calls the cultural system—of a change in the social system: the war and postwar years are a time when grass-roots American Jewry undergoes a massive relocation of itself into suburbia. There, living for the first time as neighbors to Christians denominationally defined, the institution of Conservative Judaism comes into its own, legitimating the survival of the Jewish group as a strictly religious entity. Given American traditions, Conservative Judaism expressed a consensus among various segments of the Jewish community that, in Marshall Sklare's account, "ethnic solidarity would have to be perpetuated under religious auspices and that consequently a new type of religious institution [viz., Conservative Judaism] was required." [11] The post-World War II success of this "religious revival" among suburban Jewry is reflected in the invention of a new type of cultural institution: the new postwar fiction of Jewish religiosity. Both "institutions" reflect increased and deepening American-Jewish participation in the modernization process ("assimilation"). Both enact the "rites of modernization" in symbolic form.[12] What Jewish fictionists like Malamud do is to sublimate this social system redefinition into fictional form. The new definition of Jewishness as a religious identity, the new postwar redefinition of the descendants of the Eastern European Jewish group as a religious denomination, is, Sklare writes, "a highly convenient fiction which it is wise to cultivate." [13] Malamud and others, in short, construct their fictions on a fiction. This social "fiction" becomes the legendary, metaphorical Jew of the Malamudian Jewish fable. A further development occurs when Malamud relocates this suburban religiosity from the "gilded ghetto" back into the old *mise-en-scène* of the tenements of first settlement. This enables him to merge in his characters the new universalism of the assimilated suburbs with the "old-time religion" particularisms of fundamentalist, urban *Yiddishkeit.* Authentic and sometimes inauthentic ethnic detail functions in the syntax of his fictional creations the way *objets trouvés*—like newspaper clippings—function in the pictorial syntax of cubist collage: they lead what Susanne Langer calls a "virtual" existence in the work of art. These are what Alter calls "the palpably ersatz touches of Jewish local color that have been appearing with increasing frequency in recent novels and stories" [14] and constitute, for him, an element in a phenomenon growing since the mid-1950s—namely, "a new sentimental literary myth of the Jew has gained what appears to be general acceptance in American fiction and criticism." [15]

Why are the mythical literary Jews so *generally* accepted? For the Jewish community, they seal and celebrate the achievements and redefinitions of the postwar suburban "settlement." They make good on, and flesh out—on the cultural level—the Gentile expectation that Judaism is a "religion like any other religion," only more so. For the creators of these fictions themselves, as for their secular ex-radical Jewish appreciators—like Rahv, Trilling, Howe, and others—they solve the reentry problem. Having left the Jewish community in the '30s for political radicalism, and having moved from there to the esthetic, avant-garde radicalism of the '40s and '50s ("virtual revolution"), in the '60s and '70s they signal their homecoming: they celebrate "our country and our subculture." In the interval, the "idea of the Jew" had been raised by the Gentile culture and historical events (World War II) to unforseen heights of meaningfulness and pathos: the cultural availability of the idea of Jewishness becomes for secular Jewish intellectuals of the Old Left an irresistible temptation. Out of love, guilt, nostalgia, piety, and fear (for Israel, of the New Left) they find themselves in the uneasy position of trading on, of—to put it crudely—culturally cashing in on, their Jewishness.

The mid-50s is as good a date as any to mark this "identity crisis" of the secular Jewish literary intellectual, his move in the direction of particularism: Lionel Trilling vacillated between two titles (sociologically speaking, two legitimations) of his 1950 Wordsworth centenary address at Princeton: "Wordsworth and the Iron Time" and "Wordsworth and the Rabbis." The latter designation won out when he republished the essay in 1955.* [16]

But why did so many members of the *non*-Jewish literary-intellectual and religious community join in the general acceptance of "a new sentimental literary myth of the Jew"? They sentimentalized the Jew, it may be argued, for the same reasons that, during the same period, the romanticized Third World cultures, lionized black culture, patronized youth culture, coveted religious "dialogue," sought salvation in the secular city and sanity in the psychotic (R. D. Laing), and lately—among the ecololatrists—political solutions in the "natural" idea of wilderness: self-doubt, a self-lacerating, self-disesteeming cultural masochism, had undermined self-confidence, had reinforced their sense of the failure of a culture. Given such a "failure of nerve," redemptive "words" spoken out by "others" conventionally defined as "out-groups" and "marginal groups"—the other America, the other culture, the other world—alone qualified for a hearing as authentic, sincere, and "relevant." Only a heteronomous "word" could be salvific. "A sentimental literary myth," observes Robert Alter in his essay "Sentimentalizing the Jews,"

* At one point in this essay Trilling refers to "the *pensée* of Akiba which I have quoted. . . ." In *The Opposing Self* (see note 16), p. 128.

> usually represents the failure of a culture to come to terms with some vital aspect of its own life; most often, the culture responds to its own inadequacy by projecting its secret fears, its unadmitted desires or illusory fantasies of itself onto a patently unreal image of a figure from another culture. . . . Such myths are sentimental because they are not responses to any observable realities, but rather sets of contrivances—stock situations, characters, and images—intended to produce certain desired emotions or predetermined states of imagination.[17]

The importance of Alter's essays on modern Jewish writing derives from the fact that in a subdued and scholarly way he is engaged in what can only be called a cultural enterprise of grand larceny.* With malice aforethought, secure in his knowledge of what the Jewish tradition actually is, and of who the "modernizers" are, and of just what, culturally, they are up to when they come on as the indigenous "outsider," and equally secure in his knowledge of the American religiocultural disarray, its pathetic tropism toward the "outsider"—"our turning to the supposed aliens in our midst for an alternative to the true American" [18]—he loots us of our last, our archetypal "outsider-as-insider": the modern American-Jewish literary intellectual. This contemporary culture-hero, Alter informs us, is only residually or vestigially Jewish, if Jewish at all. Often, in fact, he is very American, very Christian, one of "our crowd." This is disturbing intelligence, a form of cultural subversion. But the charge is well documented.

Leslie Fiedler's Baro Finklestone, for example, the hero of his novel *Back to China* (1965), illustrates perfectly the sentimental myth, satisfies completely the Gentile fantasy of the mysterious outsider, the stranger as moral preceptor. Alter observes that

> like all Jews who are allowed to be the protagonists of novels, Finklestone is an inveterate *schlemiel*, but in his ineffectuality and muddle-headedness, he is also—Fiedler must insist—morally sensitive in a way that others are not. He is not just a well-meaning, perennially protesting liberal; he really cares about other human beings, he carries the world's guilt on his shoulders, and he is driven to a sort of self-immolation in an attempt to expiate that guilt. This last touch, incidentally, introduces the by-now-familiar motif of the Jew as Christ, which itself is a good indication of the degree to which the fantasy-image of the Jew in American fiction is American and Christian in its deepest imaginings.[19]

* So, more sensationally, and tendentiously—and with a more theological orientation—is Arthur A. Cohen in *The Myth of the Judeo-Christian Tradition* (1971—see note 22).

This cultural reversal results in "a kind of double sentimental myth: the Jew emerges from this fiction as an imaginary creature embodying *both* what Americans would like to think about Jews and what American Jewish intellectuals would like to think about themselves" [20] (my emphasis). The staying power of this "pious self-delusion," [21] the double sentimental literary myth, despite the efforts of critics like Hyman and Alter and in the face of mounting evidence to the contrary, is truly remarkable. As the literary-intellectual counterpart of the *general* cultural "myth of the Judeo-Christian tradition," [22] vested interests (cultural and otherwise) from both the Christian and Jewish communities "conspire" to keep the thing afloat. There is also always the understandable fear on the part of literary ecumenists that should the "positive" myth of Nathan the Wise and Daniel Deronda and of their contemporary literary descendants be unmasked, the "negative" myth of Shylock and Fagin and of their contemporary literary descendants might return in force and stage a kind of literary takeover. Nevertheless, myths are myths, whether products of negative or positive thinking.

All these considerations come to mind when we reflect on Malamud's most recent novel, *The Tenants* (1971). Why the vogue for Malamud's stories, rather than those incomparably better stories of Meyer Liben, for example? Liben's characters are precisely observed; they resist, with the stubbornness of stones, being blown up into Malamudian emblems. They are thus culturally unavailable; obviously, this is "minor fiction." * Why the vogue for I. B. Singer over his brother I. J. Singer? Because it is the former who works the vein of religiose piety that meets the exigencies of the sentimental myth. (The traditional sanctions against social assimilation are conspicuously absent in the case of successful literary assimilation.[23]) Why is the accuracy of Isaac Rosenfeld's hauntingly beautifully observed *Passage from Home* neglected in favor of Saul Bellow's fictions? Because, unlike Bellow's Augie, Henderson, Herzog, and Sammler, Rosenfeld's Bernard resists the cultural lure of representativeness, of cultural assimilation; he refuses to become a metaphor of the sentimental myth.†

In *The Tenants,* Malamud's "mythical" Jew is a New York novelist named Harry Lesser, occupying the top of a condemned East Thirty-first Street tenement with a "mythical" black writer named Willie Spearmint, both subjected to the harassments of a "mythical" landlord named Irving Levenspiel who wants them out so that he can tear down the building and set up a modern six-story apartment building. Lesser is

* See, for example, Liben's *Justice Hunger: A Short Novel and Nine Stories* (New York: Dial, 1967).

† Asa Leventhal in Bellow's novel *The Victim* and Tommy Wilhelm in Bellow's *Sieze the Day* put up considerable resistance to this metaphorical manipulation. Yet in the end they, too, are inflated into mythical "significance," they succumb to "literature."

trying to finish a novel he has worked on for ten years; Spearmint, trying to type raw black rage onto paper, is partly preoccupied with his mistress, Irene Bell. Willie, a subliterary Black Panther-type, brutally rejects all Lesser's advances. Lesser, we know from the outset, will end classically—"the victim" of his own fumbling, "liberal" good intentions. After Lesser takes Willie's Jewish mistress from him—the affair had all but petered out anyway—Willie in a rage burns both manuscript copies of Lesser's novel, *The Promised End.* Malamud's story ends with Lesser and Willie hacking one another to death while the landlord pleads over and over that they show mercy and compassion—*Hab rachmones*—for one another. So much for the bare bones of the plot.

The roots of Malamud's plot are in the urban social reality of the middle and late sixties in New York City. There were *two* wars going on between blacks and Jews then, as now: floating high above the hot war in the streets there exists a largely unacknowledged cold war at the top, waged between the black and Jewish literary-critical intelligentsia. There is, on the one hand, the social system war in the streets, fought out in terms of the politics of conflicting interests. And then there is a parallel "spiritual" war on the level of the cultural system—a *Kulturkampf*—waged in terms of cultural status-politics. The hot war in the streets is a struggle over real interests: scarce jobs, occupational eligibility criteria, the civil service merit system, community control of schools and, more recently, the "dual" and then "open" admissions policies for the City College. The other war, the one between black and Jewish intellectuals, is a struggle over symbolic interests; it is a cultural status war of several dimensions, a conflict equally savage—on its own terms—as the war going on "down below." (That Malamud chose the top storey of an old tenement as his scene for the cultural clash between black and Jewish literary intellectuals demonstrates his gift for inspired metaphor.)

The two struggles, social and cultural, are quite distinct, but occasionally—as when Norman Mailer ran in the primaries for mayor of New York in 1969—they overlap. Toward the end of the campaign Mailer and his runningmate, author Jimmy Breslin, endorsed a "dual admissions" program for CCNY (the City College of New York).* A Jewish literary intellectual had thus taken the "wrong" side in the hot war in the streets. Grass-roots voters in the Jewish community were up in arms. Taking the traditional campaign stroll through the Lower East Side, the

* The policy proposed was that in 1970 half of CCNY's freshman class be recruited from eleven black and Puerto Rican areas (in Harlem and the Bronx) while the other half be chosen according to traditional academic criteria. This meant that a number of academically qualified Jewish students would be refused admission. Incumbent John Lindsay and the other mayoral candidates denounced the plan as a "quota" system, "a word with dark roots in Jewish history." Flaherty, *Managing Mailer* (see note 24), p. 143.

Mailer entourage ate its fill at Ratner's dairy restaurant. "But despite the prodigious eating and the presence of Mailer's mother, who speaks Yiddish," his campaign manager recalls, "we were subtly damned with *goyishe* civility instead of being blessed with Jewish love. Eighty percent of the questions had to do with our stand on CCNY." [24]

The two struggles can overlap in other ways. If Mailer descended into the hot war of the streets, Midge Decter in a 1971 *New York* magazine article, "Is It Still O.K. to Hate Albert Shanker?" passed Mailer going in the other direction. Decter takes "hot war" members of New York's United Federation of Teachers (UFT) and their leader, Albert Shanker, up and off the street and includes them among the cultural intelligentsia at the top. These teachers do not really answer to the regnant image of the public schoolteacher, she maintains. She reconceptualizes them, in the interests of greater accuracy, as products of the Depression, as "aspiring members of the intelligentsia in the thirties" who, moved by the need for security, ended up in a profession a good deal beneath them. If the UFT membership is a kind of intelligentsia *manqué,* their leader Shanker is a full-blown intellectual. At some critical juncture in his life, for complex reasons, he turned "from the life and calling of a full-blown intellectual. In the very early 1950's," Decter writes, "he had been a graduate student of philosophy at Columbia, his particular field of interest being early Pragmatism." [25] The fields of the later pragmatism having become unmanageably alluring, Shanker apparently shifted his energies from philosophy to more palpable commitments. Kidding aside, we do see here, I believe, an attempt to carry Shanker and his UFT membership upward, making them ex officio participants in the debates of the cultural intellectuals at the top, rather than mere bread-and-butter warriors fighting an insurgent black subculture in a school decentralization battle.

Most of the time, however, the "high road" of the *Kulturkampf* doesn't intersect with the "low road" of the hot war in the streets. Herbert Gans has applied a sociological "succession model" to explain the interest-war in the streets: insurgent blacks, ill-equipped rural migrants from the South, struggle to start up the occupational ladder. The collision with earlier immigrant groups is largely a socioeconomic collision, despite the interethnic and interracial slurs that are hurled.[26]

The cold war at the top, that between the literary-cultural representatives of the contending groups, is a war for status: the status at issue is the culturally prestigeful one of "victim." Prior to the Supreme Court desegregation decision of 1954 and the civil rights movement of the 1950s and '60s, Jews by universal consent, especially since the Holocaust, had prescriptive and clear title to the victim-status. The prominence of blacks, with their own bitter history, their own outrage and importunity, has now clouded the Jewish title. The unacknowledged status-conflict "at the top" between Jewish and black intellectuals is a struggle over which victim is the "real" victim, over who is "really"—primogeniturially—entitled to the *privilegium odiosum* of Victim. (The "privilege" of this title is, in turn, an ambiguous gift of Christianity.)

As we read, for example, James Baldwin's 1971 "Open Letter to My Sister, Miss Angela Davis," in which he compares the aloneness of Miss Davis to that of "the Jewish housewife on the way to Dachau," and as we read the reply of *Midstream*'s editor Shlomo Katz, "An Open Letter to James Baldwin," the evidence is overwhelming that we are in the presence of what can only be called a skirmish in the continuing status-politics of two subcultures.[27] Genocide, "the most terrible word in the lexicon of the 20th century," Katz tells Baldwin, is made a mockery by his comparison of Davis to the Jewish housewife on the way to Dachau. Baldwin, by his comparison, is clearly engaged in an enterprise of cultural status-seeking; he is seeking, by this comparison, to equal, if not to expropriate, the cultural pathos of the Jew, substituting the cultural pathos of the black. And Katz is not about to let him get away with it. "Everybody," he writes, "tries to jump on each other's bandwagon without regard to fact, to meaning, to consequences, like rampaging children in a pillow fight." [28] Katz is at pains to translate his difference with Baldwin into factual differences: he insists on fidelity to historical fact and historical differences, on the literal versus the metaphorical meanings of words. But his language betrays him; the thrust of the struggle is clearly over status and values, not facts. When he tells Baldwin that genocide has happened, once and for all, in the literal sense, and not in the rhetorical misuse of it "by fly-by-night self-styled revolutionaries," [29] it is the term "fly-by-night" that gives him away: he considers himself to be addressing, clearly, cultural upstarts. Read the conclusion of Katz's *J'accuse:* "You try to take the thorny crown of martyrdom from 'the Jewish housewife in the boxcar headed for Dachau and attempt to place it on the head of Angela Davis. But this crown of martyrdom can only be earned in one way—the way of the chimneys of Dachau. On Miss Davis it doesn't fit." [30]

Katz, in the language of crowns and legitimacy, is addressing the cultural representative of a group engaged in what he considers to be cultural usurpation. What may be socioeconomic "turf" in Brooklyn is, manifestly, cultural "turf" in Manhattan. Eligibility criteria for advancing up the occupational status-ladder are here spelled out with finality for entry into the highest topdog status in the cultural value system: access to this title "can only be earned in one way," Baldwin is informed. Pretenders to this crown will be exposed as such. The "crown" is further described in such a way as to disclose the latent theological dimension of this prized and contested status: the crown that can never presumably fit Miss Davis but that does fit the Jewish housewife headed for Dachau is a "thorny crown." The status-struggle between Katz and Baldwin as representatives of two subcultures takes place, in the last analysis, within a Christian "definition of the situation." It is an exchange played out before a Gentile status-audience, for a symbolic cultural good—a crown of thorns—first worn by that Supreme Victim from whom our civilization takes its name. He it was who first established, for all time, for the West, that "reversal" of the Eros of Antiquity whereby the lowly, the ignominious, and the inconspicuous became the incognito for the highest. "Reverence for inconspicuousness is the final key," writes Ernst Bloch, the German-Jewish Marxist, "to this reversal of the motion of love. . . . This love has no parallel, therefore, in any previous moral faith, not even in the Jewish one, despite the 'Love thy neighbor as thyself' (Lev. 19, 18) that was received in Matthew 22, 39. Buddha leaps into the fire as a rabbit, to give a beggar a meal, but his love does not lead to the beggar, does not seek divinity in impotence." * [31] Jesus Christ, supreme Victim, superstar, first of the beautiful losers.[32]

This fact of our culture has important sociological consequences. If the direction of social mobility on the level of our social system is *upward*, defined by an increasing effort of access to power, money, and prestige, status-work on the highest levels of our cultural value system may be viewed as a form of *downward* mobility, a grim praxis designed to establish one's group credentials as more lowly than those of his rivals, entitling him to the "top" underdog status of undisputed and indisputable victim. The *cultural* credit-rating system, in other words, works on the principle of impecuniousness. It helps, even if we are not ourselves victims, if we can "claim relationship with" accredited victims. This can lead to comedies of intellectual manners. It can also lead to moving works of art (read, for example, the late Sylvia Plath's poem "Daddy").

John Galtung is a pioneer in spelling out the syntax of upward or social mobility. All of us, he maintains, occupy status sets of many, often discrepant, statuses, some of them defined as "Topdog" (or "T") statuses and some of them defined as "Underdog" (or "U") statuses. Take, for example, a black medical doctor and a white policeman in the South. In terms of being black, the doctor is defined as occupying an Underdog status; as white, the policeman is Topdog. But as a professional, the black doctor holds higher rank than the policeman. When these two interact—the black M.D. with his doctor's kit, for example, asking the white policeman in Brookhaven, Mississippi, if he can double-park while he makes a sick call—it is not at all unlikely that each will strive to define the interaction in terms of his own Topdog status and to force the other to define it in terms of his Underdog status. This would exemplify Galtung's "Axiom of Rank Equilibration," wherein interactors

* Bloch's indebtedness to Anders Nygren's *Eros and Agape* is patent.

strive to "equilibrate their status sets upwards, and only sets with equal ranks are stationary." [33]

We have no known authority to equal Galtung on the considerably more complex syntax governing the dynamics of the high enterprise of the deliberately downward cultural mobility we might call "underdogism." The highest norms of the expressive component of Western culture, what I call the Protestant Esthetic, legitimate only that form of expressive humility we call "good taste." The taboo on emotional incontinence and ostentation still holds in the highest quarters. The mix of these two status-systems, the one for the "real" and the other for the "cultural" world, makes for considerable moral ambiguity. Success must be disguised, money—especially when it accumulates and gets old—must turn itself into taste and purchase art, or else, forswearing even this vulgarity, must retreat, covering its face with shame in the dark vaults of the Morgan Guaranty Trust Company. Norman Podhoretz's *Making It* is a refreshing exploration of this form of double-entry moral bookkeeping.[34]

It is just here that we may socially locate the postwar cultural erosion in the plausibility of the claim of the Jewish group to the charisma of a continuing victim-status. The Jews, as a group, have "made it." "When one compares the Jew of Westchester and Nassau Counties with the Negro of Harlem," Rabbi Borowitz observes, "his concern with the problems of a Vatican Council and textbook writers seems to be utterly *luftmentshish*. . . . We are rich," he adds, "and reasonably well accepted." [35] A cultural "credibility gap" has opened up due to the discrepancy between the Jewish self-appraisal and how Jews look to others, especially to the insurgent black subculture. It is the black man, Rabbi Miller writes, "who, on the American scene, has been the persecuted. He is, in truth, the American 'Jew.'" [36] Diaspora—and, for that matter, Israeli—Jewry, by repeating the lachrymose rhetoric of the earlier immigrant generations, is acknowledging that Western civilization awards its highest cultural prestige to victims. But it is also exposing itself to the charge of the black intellectual Harold Cruse, who writes, in "My Jewish Problem and Theirs," that "having gained the cake . . . they would like to pretend that it is yesterday's bagels." * [37]

Jewish intellectuals, however, do not see themselves as black intellectuals and their allies see them—as powerful *goyim*, part of the "establishment," secure in the exercise of political and economic clout. They see themselves not as prisoners of some anachronistic self-image but as beset by a not-wholly-unfounded and nonparanoid anxiety that they may one day again be "victims" (even paranoids have real enemies, Delmore

* Cruse's essay (see note 37), part of the cultural "cold war at the top," is of course the black intellectual's retort to Norman Podhoretz's well-known "My Negro Problem—And Ours" (1963), reprinted in *Doings and Undoings: The Fifties and After in American Writing* (New York: Farrar, Straus, 1964), pp. 354–71.

Schwartz used to say). There is the well-founded fear of violence in the hot war in the streets, the fear of enforced socioeconomic retrenchment, of the demographic "takeover" of "their" city. But these real fears are confused with, and reflect, the "secret" fear of cultural status-loss, the fear of what Daniel Bell called, in another connection, "cultural dispossession" (in an essay in the 1963 "expanded and updated" edition of *The Radical Right*).[38] Only a status explanation, crossed with generational theory, can explain the complex phenomenon of the "Jewish dispossessed" and the move to the Right of the Jewish intelligentsia in the 1960s and '70s. A second "expanded and updated" version of *The Radical Right* is long overdue.

Malamud's *Tenants*, like Saul Bellow's *Mr. Sammler's Planet* (1969) before it, reenacts many of these issues in the "symbolic action" of the novel. Among reviewers of *The Tenants*, only the *New York Times'* Anatole Broyard appears to have detected the two dimensions of the black-Jewish collision: the old "liberal" role of the 1940s–1950s Jew vis-à-vis the black, the former sponsoring in a "Christ-like" way the latter's economic and political interests, and the very different dimension of rivalry "at the top," on the cultural level, for the stellar role—which I define as that of the cultural pathos of the Victim—which emerged in the 1960s. Willie Spearmint is culturally aggressive, Broyard notes, and "wants to stop understudying the Jew and take over the star's role in the drama of American society. In spite of all this, Lesser turns the other cheek." When the landlord, Levenspiel, smashes Willie's table and chair, Lesser, "like a liberal foundation giving a grant despite the hostility of the recipient, buys Willie new furniture. He suggests, at the same time, that Willie move down to a lower floor to avoid discovery. He himself lives on the top floor and we feel," the reviewer carefully notes, "that his real reason may well be his conviction that Willie's struggle is on a lower level than his own and should remain there. But Willie stays. He has been in the basement too long; he wants the view from the top."[39]

Contemporary themes appear in *The Tenants*, but themes also turn up from the 1930s to the 1950s. Wouk's Marjorie Morningstar reappears, almost in amber, out of the '50s. In a subplot, Willie's *meshuggeneh* mistress, Irene Bell (*née* Belinsky), is reclaimed from "self-hate," dyed blond hair, and the arms of Willie (Wouk's Noel Airman): Lesser "was sure her discontent was with herself"[40] (p. 52). "'Shalom,' he says to her in the street. She looks at him oddly, coldly. 'Why do you say that?' He fumbles, says he isn't sure. 'I never use the word'" (p. 113). Later, she wants to know why he had said, "Shalom" the day he met her outside the museum. He says, "I meant don't be a stranger." She responds with: "Be white? Be Jewish?" "Be close is better," he replies (p. 139). One reviewer who cannot fathom Lesser's interest in this "uninteresting" girl comments that "we are not led to believe he wants her because she is Willie's, yet we have no other explanation for a celibate man in desperate need of finishing his book suddenly becoming entangled like this, dreamily and dangerously."[41] "The intimate inner compulsions which underlie ethnic group attitudes," Harold Cruse writes, "are only partially understood in America."[42] As Lesser's mistress, Irene lets her black hair gradually grow back in (pp. 142, 146, 154): "She had redeemed her face, and perhaps something inside her, for she seemed kinder to herself" (p. 154). In the end, she leaves for San Francisco rather than for the Woukian suburban terrain of the '50s.

Another theme of the traditional American Jewish novel reappears here with reverse english: the WASP as mentor of the morals but especially the manners (linguistic and otherwise) of the Jew—*Hyman Kaplan*'s Mr. Parkhill, *Augie*'s Mrs. Renling, Podhoretz's "Mrs. K"—is now replaced by Lesser, who functions as caretaker of the morals, manners, and the novel of the black apprentice. As once WASP to Jews, so, now, Jew to black. As always, it is a thankless role.

Lionel Trilling's short story "The Other Margaret" reappears out of the '40s in a new version. In Trilling's story the black maid, the "other" Margaret, smashes the young white Margaret's "made present" for her mother's birthday: a green ceramic lamb with large, grave, black eyes à la Keane.[43] In *The Tenants* Willie burns Lesser's manuscripts. Moral and political issues of high moment are played out in terms of the sacred and significant forms of art. Rename this fable: "The Other Writer."

Malmud's tale also reproduces and updates in a curious way the literary class war of the '30s, when *Partisan Review* was born out of a struggle against the proletarian–social realism novel of Mike Gold's *New Masses*.[44] The Marxian matrix has of course vanished; Lesser struggles today to submit Willie's subliterary black id to the disciplines of the art-novel (read: the superego). Trilling's reworking of this theme in the mid-'40s, pitting the Jamesian art-novel against the cruder—and therefore presumably more "authentic"—naturalistic-confessional novel of Dreiser and "progressive liberalism" becomes, in retrospect, a kind of self-fulfilling prophecy of the core metaphor that will serve as the impersonation of a plot in Malamud's fable, *The Tenants*, in 1971. "Dreiser and James: with that juxtaposition," Trilling writes, "we are immediately at the dark and bloody crossroads where literature and politics meet."[45] "One winter's night," Malamud writes of Willie and Lesser, nature and fine art, "they meet on the frigid stairs" (p. 223).

Another theme, this one from the 1950s, reappears in *The Tenants*, but in ironically reversed form. In a now-notorious essay in the Autumn 1963 issue of *Dissent*, "Black Boys and Native Sons," Irving Howe, the magazine's editor, took it upon himself to scold Ralph Ellison and James Baldwin for deviating from the militantly black naturalistic "protest" novel of Richard Wright. Howe's final point, as summarized by Daniel Aaron, was that the black writer, if he is to "assert his humanity," must write "in protest and rage, even though he may have to discard the 'suave' and 'the elegant' (presumably derived from his white peers) for the 'harsh, clumsy, heavy-breathing' prose that is the appropriate vehicle for 'the part of suppressed bitterness.' By the same logic," Aaron continues, summarizing this chapter in the black-Jewish literary intellectual status-war, "the Jew was somehow betraying himself and Jewry in the act of transcending his Jewishness. Ellison insisted that he was not denying his race by designating Eliot, Malraux, Dostoevsky, and Faulkner as his literary ancestors rather than Richard Wright. . . . The irony of a white critic telling a Negro writer what he must do to be saved, both as a man and as a writer," Aaron concludes, "is not lost on any reader of the Howe-Ellison exchange." [46] James Baldwin got off rather more easily than Ellison because, as Howe detected from the non-"literary" sound of the Baldwinian voice in *Another Country,* Baldwin at least gave every promise of being "no longer held back by the proprieties of literature." [47] But Ellison, detecting *noblesse oblige* in Howe's "call to order," and perhaps sensing that he was being conscripted into Howe's esoteric vendetta against Trilling and the "Columbia liberalism" of the '50s,* refused to write of his own wounds and continued as he was.[48]

It is a subcultural irony that we should find Malamud's Lesser endeavoring to instruct Willie in the exigencies of "new critical" form, reversing the lessons black writers have so recently been hearing from critic Irving Howe. "If we are talking about art," he tells him, "form demands its rights." "Art can kiss my juicy ass," is the reply: "*I* am art. Willie Spearmint, *black* man. My form is *myself*" (p. 75). No, Lesser tells him, repelled by Willie's "funky manuscript" (p. 57) and the "mainly naturalistic confessional" form (p. 60) Willie seeks as the style "connatural" with his black protest. "You can't turn black experience into literature just by writing it down," Lesser insists, in this running argument at the top of the tenement (p. 74). "If you're an artist," Lesser explains, reaching for the ultimate contrast, "you can't be a nigger, Willie" (p. 51). The conflict over the nature of the novel and the importance of fictional form becomes, in the end, the chosen "vehicle" in Malamud's *Tenants* for playing out the literary-cultural status-war between black and Jewish intellectual. Black experience is eligible for registration in cultural terms only if it assumes proper fictional form. Lesser and his colleagues are the self-appointed custodians of these rubrical and civilized matters. "I am an expert of writing," Lesser explains. And Willie replies: "I hate all that shit when whites tell you about black" (p. 36). Willie is depicted by Malamud as experiencing these

* In the next decade, Howe was to make a complete about-face, repeating in the '60s with authority all the things Trilling had been at pains to tell him in the '50s.

lofty instructions in the mysteries of form as an obscure attempt to emasculate him and his experience. "Lesser," he says, "you tryin to fuck up my mind and confuse me. I read all about that formalism jazz in the library and it's bullshit. You tryin to kill off my natural writin by pretending you are interested in the fuckin form of it." (p. 165).

Lesser, in all this, never once levels with Willie. He never once identifies with his "pupil." He speaks from on high. It is a sign of Lesser's "underdeveloped heart"—as one used to say in the '50s—as well as a failure of Malamud's imagination, that Lesser never chooses to let Willie in on the "secret" that the Jewish writer—"Lesser," Malamud, Bellow, and others (and for that matter *all* the immigrant ethnics out of steerage)—has had to struggle with the very same ethnically emasculating exigencies of "that fucking form" (p. 224) that Willie does, on the levels of both social behavior and cultural performance. From Lesser's lofty instructions in the "rites of passage" to which he must submit his black experience if he is to enter the chosen precincts of the WASP novel—" 'if you're an artist you can't be a nigger, Willie,' he notifies him" [49]—Willie would never gather that "soul" shares a common predicament in this respect with *Yiddishkeit.* The resources of intimacy possible to shared subcultural "secrets" lie unused in Malamud's *Tenants.*

Milton Himmelfarb, for example, does break subcultural reticence by telling us of "a powerful and still operative Jewish tradition that most are probably not even aware is Jewish. That is the tradition of being attracted by the *edel* (cultivated) Gentile and repelled by the *prost* (common) one." [50] Well and good. And Willie is *prost* indeed. What Himmelfarb does not tell us—any more than Malamud's persona, Lesser, tells Willie—is of a latent and highly ambivalent component in this very attraction to the *edel,* to cultivated and even austere form: this is the other, especially Eastern European, Jewish tradition of knowing full well the ethnic price tag involved in submitting to the "elegant" allure of Western form and its attendant modernist sensibility.

For instruction in this Jewish predicament, analogous to that of the black writer, let us turn for a moment from Malamud to Saul Bellow. Unlike Malamud's fictional Lesser, Bellow knew the cost involved in the sacrifice to form. He, for one, as an apprentice novelist was hardly unambiguously delighted by his realization that every time he plugged his *Yiddishkeit* into the genre of the modernist "art" novel it came out *Edelkeit.*

The modernist idea of the novel, bequeathed to Saul Bellow in the early forties by Hemingway, was of a genre so fine that no Jew could violate it.* "Do you have feelings?" asks Bellow on the opening page of his first novel, *Dangling Man* (1944). Then "there are correct and incor-

* The allusion, of course, is to T. S. Eliot, who spoke of Henry James as having "a mind so fine no idea could violate it."

rect ways of indicating them," he replies, mocking the received code of novelistic propriety. Indeed, to indicate feelings without expressing them *is* the correct way of expressing them. Personal feelings are to be encoded in forms that do not mimetically "express" them. "Do you have an inner life?" he continues. "It is nobody's business but your own. Do you have emotions? Strangle them." [51]

With *Dangling Man,* purporting to be the journal of a young Chicagoan idling his time for six months as he awaits induction into the army, Bellow struggles to defy the received conventions of the well-made novel. The "shame" Joseph admits to in his opening entry, his embarrassment at recording his "inward transactions," represents Bellow's own ambivalence about offering this candid record of introspection as a novel. Such a novel is sure to be considered "a kind of self-indulgence, a weakness, and in poor taste." It will offend against that American inheritance "from the English gentleman—that curious mixture of striving, asceticism, and rigor." This code admits of a limited candor, to be sure, "a closemouthed straightforwardness. But on the truest candor, it has an inhibitory effect. Most serious matters are closed to the hard-boiled. They are unpracticed in introspection. . . . If you have difficulties, grapple with them silently, goes one of their commandments. To hell with that!" he concludes. "I intend to talk about mine" (p. 9).

Bellow is here struggling with the Protestant Esthetic and with the ways this WASP value-complex has institutionalized itself in high culture, shaping the ethos, sensibility, and taste at work in the canons of the modernist novel. *Dangling Man,* anchored in the milieu of Eastern European Jewry, is offered as being in an adversary relationship to this code. Bellow is engaged, in his own bold self-conception, in nothing less than an enterprise of cultural subversion. It is as though the revolutionary animus of his ex–radical hero Joseph, relinquishing the dream of overturning the societal world, had transposed its energies to the level of culture and was now engaged in toppling the tight little world of the novel, colonizing it with characters who could be expected to violate the norms of its decorum. (This transposition of political and societal concerns into the "key" of culture occurs as the Depression '30s pass into the war and postwar years, the "cultural" '40s and '50s.)

Clearly, the sons of Eastern European Jewry have had a hard time pouring their subculture of *Yiddishkeit* into Western Protestant culture patterns. What Robert Cohn becomes in Hemingway's *Sun Also Rises* is not a function, primarily, of the author's anti-Semitism. It is the value exigencies immanent in the craft and genre of the modernist novel itself and its attendant sensibility that make Cohn "look bad." Bellow's career as a novelist, basing itself on the central insight that Eastern European Jewry is not *"Romansfähig"*—not "fit" for the modernist novel—has been, from the outset, impaled on the horns of a dilemma: it could either remain within the conventions of the modernist novel—and thus be forced to do a cultural "nose job" on its Jewish characters, "assimilating" them—or break out of the WASP modernist novel, reverting, for example, to the picaresque form with its looser "admissions" criteria. Like all cultural dilemmas, this one is brutal.

Bellow has spent a lifetime trying to surmount it. Despite his bold intentions, mentioned above, *Dangling Man* and later *The Victim* (1947) turned out to be conspicuously well made and discreet. Even later, the will at work in what Frank Kermode calls the "*détente*" of *Augie March* (1953) was unable to do the work of the imagination, and Bellow was forced to retrench to the compromise of *Herzog*.[52] For Bellow, "letting go" would always involve "going back" to the earlier, given stratum of the culture of the *shtetl*.[53]

In *Herzog* (1964) Eastern European Jewish material returns to center stage in the form of a *luftmenschy* autodidact professor, vulnerable, harassed, importunate, enduring the messiness of a nervous breakdown. Nevertheless, all this "rawness" is very well cooked, and one is not surprised to find Jean Stafford in the pages of *Vogue* magazine "congratulating" Herzog on "the good taste in which he has conducted his crack-up" and declaring the novel "a work of elegance" about a "fastidious man." [54] What has become, one wants to know, of the manifesto that opens *Dangling Man*, with its brave declaration of independence for Eastern European Jewish expressiveness, with its implied insistence that the subculture of *Yiddishkeit* assert its rights to expressive elbowroom in the hitherto fastidious confines of the modernist novel? If we listen to the tale, and not the teller, to Bellow's accomplished and not to his avowed intention, we realize that he has "sold out" to the good-taste canon of Western modernism. His avowed intention, in the words of Theodore Ross, "to open doors on ways of feeling and living which differ from those of the tight-lipped Anglo-Saxon gentleman and his carefully preened code of values" and the proposal of "this contra-Hemingway writer" for accomplishing this—namely, to tap the sources of creative strength "which inhere in the style and society of the urban Jew"—this avowed intention has been abandoned.[55] As it turns out, according to Wallace Markfield, Bellow "doesn't write Jewish novels, but rather a highly intellectualized Jewish book. When he chooses to write about Jews he is very careful to stay away from bagels and lox and Ocean Parkway." [56] The current conflict in black novelists between "black feeling" and "white form" reenacts the conflict in Bellow between two sets of cultural values: the subculture of *Yiddishkeit* of his early socialization and the taste canons of the Western modernized culture he encountered later.

Deciding to write *Dangling Man* in the form of a journal was the initial collision in Bellow of these two value-patterns. Despite the high

Western Christian value placed on the individual, there is the equally strong prohibition on pride, vanity, and self-love. In practice, the potential contradiction between these two cultural values is "managed" by the expressive code of the culture which embodies the norms directing *how* personality is to be expressed. Talking about oneself in a diary is perfectly acceptable (the Puritan divines, after all, kept journals as a religious duty). But one must not indulge the perpendicular pronoun too much. All of decorum is reducible to a matter of adverbs. Bellow writes: "If you have difficulties, grapple with them silently, goes one of *their* commandments" * (my emphasis). Silently, as opposed to loudly, ostentatiously, sentimentally, complainingly, self-pityingly. The commandments of the *goyim* are a *halakah* of adverbs. Bellow is right that this code is not a code limited to literary decorum but pervades the entire culture. "To a degree," he notes, "everyone obeys this code" (p. 9). Thus, where T. S. Eliot writes that the progress of an artist is a continual self-sacrifice, a continual "*extinction* of personality" [57] (my emphasis), Emily Post writes equivalently that progress in good behavior is marked by unconsciousness of self, which she defines as the ability to "*extinguish* all thought of oneself" [58] (my emphasis).

In the face of these prescriptions for extinction emanating from the canonical cultural authorities on literary and social behavior, it is no wonder that Bellow pleads the "state of demoralization" of his protagonist, Joseph, as making it "necessary" for him to keep a journal, that is, to talk to and about himself (p. 9).† Only what Talcott Parsons calls the "sick role" can lift the curse of sentimentality off so much *chutzpahdik* self-regard. The exigencies of subject matter are pressed into service to legitimate a violation of form. "I do not feel guilty of self-indulgence in the least," Joseph protests (p. 10). What, indeed, one might ask, *is* so horrible in what Henry James calls "the terrible *fluidity* of self-revelation"? [59] (James's emphasis.) What exactly is at stake on the very opening page of *Dangling Man* where, as Marcus Klein observes, Bellow is pitting the Yiddish *shtetl* tradition of the "exercise of personality for its own sake" against the values of "American asceticism," which forbid "the exhibition of personality"? [60] The Protestant Ethic—impersonal service of an impersonal end—passes imperceptibly into the Protestant Esthetic of restraint and self-effacement. As self-importance

* Leslie Fiedler in "Chutzpah and Pudeur," as a myth critic, hurries this conflict between "*your* subcultural needs" and "*their* commandments" out of its socioreligious matrix of "Jew–WASP Gentile" up into a generalization characterizing all of Western culture. See *The Collected Essays of Leslie Fiedler* (New York: Stein & Day, 1971), 2: 516–42.

† Analogously, *Herzog* opens with the words: "If I am out of my mind, it's all right with me." In this prefatory "remedial interchange" (Goffman) with his readers, in which *Herzog*'s literary misbehavior is cognitively legitimated—as a mimesis of the "mental illness" of its own protagonist, Herzog—Bellow displays a ritual competence socialized in Freud's remedial strategy (psychoanalysis).

and vanity violate the Protestant Ethic, exhibitionism and ostentation are the core lapses in the Protestant Esthetic. The fierce puritanism of "high" good taste would see to it "that hardly any experience is recounted for its own sake"; [61] Bellow's "exercise of personality for its sake" commits the sin of ostentation. Deeply ambivalent over the nature of vulgarity, Bellow hedges, backing and filling. Thus, he initially conceives his personalist heroes as singing themselves with "nervy insolence" [62] (in Klein's words) in a manner fully sanctioned by Yiddish subculture. Then, reconceiving them in terms of the exigencies of the novel—dialogue, development, sensitivity, selflessness—he cuts their *chutzpah* to civilize them. They must be turned out as Reform Jews or Markfield's "highly intellectualized Jews" or Jews whose values are "comingled with the 'superior' values of Art and Sensitivity." [63]

This same revisionism of initial Yiddish impulse by subsequent WASP censorship may be observed at work in Bellow himself as a kind of self-censorship. His 1966 *Paris Review* interview with Gordon Harper took only about an hour and a half, taped in two sessions. But Bellow devoted "over five weeks" in a series of meetings—"up to two hours a day, at least twice and often three times a week throughout the entire five-week period"—to "the most careful revision" of the orginal tapes.[64] The typescript of each of the two sessions was carefully worked over by Bellow with pen and ink, "taking as many as three separate meetings to do a complete revision. Then another typescript was made, and the process started over." [65] Harper lists six types of changes made by Bellow: slight changes in meaning, language "tightened up," style improved, excursions deleted, colloquial substituted for literary diction, and, finally, "prunings." These last cultivations eliminated those few places in which Bellow, Harper writes, "came to feel he was 'exhibiting' himself, and these were scratched out." [66]

The better Jewish novelists, like Bellow and Malamud, have not put their black characters through any such "pruning" process. No one is asking that black Daniel Derondas start walking around in the novels of Jewish writers. But surely the black pickpocket of Bellow's *Mr. Sammler's Planet*, who pulls out and exhibits his penis in the West Side lobby, is not exactly representative. Nor is the black writer that Malamud transforms him into, taking him out of Bellow's lobby and putting him up a few flights, either a representative or a carefully observed, actual character. Willie could have had the benefit of a little "pruning," and, who knows, he might have begun to look like, say, Ralph Ellison.

Jewish nonliterary intellectuals are no more generous. Theodore Draper, for example, in *The Rediscovery of Black Nationalism* (1970), offers us a residual definition of the black nationalist movement: it is *not* an authentic nationalist movement (like, presumably, Zionism was). Draper sounds like nothing so much as a Reform Jewish spokesman lecturing the "downtown" *Ostjuden* of the thirties on the utter fantasticality of their utopian nationalist aspirations.[67] Ben Halpern, also, defines the black minority residually, and invidiously, spelling out for us in bleeding detail that they are not, and apparently never can be, an "ideological minority" like the Jewish subculture. They are only a "social minority, . . . no more than a mythic sub-culture" who aspire, like any group of upstarts, to a higher and culturally more meaningful status.* [68]

Subcultures tend to define each other residually. This problem for the theorist and novelist is a special case of a general social theory problem. "If, as is almost always the case," Talcott Parsons writes,

> not all the actually observable facts of the field, or those which have been observed, fit into the sharply, positively defined categories, they tend to be given one or more blanket names which refer to categories negatively defined, that is, of facts known to exist, which are even more or less adequately described, but are defined theoretically by their failure to fit into the positively defined categories of the system. The only theoretically significant [or, it should be added, imaginatively significant] statements about these facts are negative statements—they are *not* so and so.[69]

If a symptom of impending theoretical and imaginative change consists, as Parsons adds, "in the carving out from residual categories of definite, positively defined concepts and their verification in empirical investigation" [70]—or in the imagination, I would add—Malamud's *The Tenants* gives us no grounds for optimism for impending progress in the relations between our two classic minorities, blacks and Jews.

On the contrary, Malamud, as between Willie and Lesser, tries, perhaps, to be evenhanded. But he isn't. Willie is a residual category, ill observed, with no insides. The will—perhaps, especially, goodwill—cannot do the work of the imagination. Even in the very last line, as Willie and Lesser hack one another to death—"Each, thought the writer, feels the anguish of the other" (p. 230)—the Jewish writer tops the black. Each feels, but Lesser both feels and thinks; Willie only feels. Even as they die, Lesser is more.

* Stanley Diamond's touching elegy of Malcolm X, "The Apostate Muslim" (*Dissent* 12, no. 21 [Spring 1965]) is a notable exception to the prevailing subcultural status-politics. Though Diamond's general anthropology is wrongheaded, Jewish experience is here being used not to distantiate "Black Zionists" [p. 196] but heuristically, as *Verstehen*, the better to experience their effort to reverse the blocked black thrust toward assimilation, (p. 195).

PART V

Conclusion

CHAPTER 23

MODERNITY, JEWRY, CHRISTIANITY

> But the strangers we speak of are unique in retaining their peculiar attributes, especially their religious views, while stoutly denying that these peculiarities are of crucial importance, or relevant to their relationship to the society in which they dwell. This attitude rests on an illusion which is nevertheless, for the most part sincerely and honourably, accepted as a reality by both sides, but which, being half felt as delusive, communicates a sense of desperate embarrassment to those who seek to examine it: as if a mystery were being approached to the belief in the non-existence of which both sides are pledged, yet the reality of which both at least suspect.[1]
>
> *Isaiah Berlin*

Several ideas that run like an *obbligato* through this book must now, in the conclusion, be picked up and thematized for their own sakes. One of these is the curious, secret, adversary relationship of the secular Jewish intellectual to the Jewish bourgeoisie (that is, the ordinary, Jewish, middle-class community). The intellectual is sensitive and refined; the bourgeoisie, obviously, is vulgar. Undeniable as their vulgarity may be in his eyes, the secular Jewish intellectual almost never allows himself to come out and say so, explicitly. In this matter, all, excepting Marx, have observed, more or less faithfully, the eleventh or Diaspora commandment: "Thou shalt not reveal in-group secrets to the *goyim*." As a result of this self-censorship, this "secret," intraethnic war has been encoded in various ways in the literary and ideological product of the Jewish social critics of the Diaspora. Diaspora creativity is thus a form of "secret writing" enciphering covert Jewish "family understandings." The *opera omnia* of the Diaspora tradition constitute, in one degree or another, hermeneutic systems in which the Jewish *pays réel* must be read "between the lines" of the Jewish *pays légale*.

In earlier times, "when Jews spoke a language of their own, they could criticize and admonish each other without worrying about giving ammunition to their enemies," writes Milton Himmelfarb.[2] In a quite literal sense, Norman Denison notes, both Jewish German and Yiddish could serve "among other functions, as concealment codes." For Yiddish speakers, living mainly among non-German speakers, a German-derived linguistic structure in itself went a long way "towards meeting the need for concealment." Speakers of Jewish German, on the other hand, lived among German speakers and hence, for them, "an extensive special vocabulary was necessary. . . . Typical of the concealment function of Jewish German is the use of Hebrew numerals—of considerable importance to dealers discussing prices and wares in private."[3] After Emancipation, and writing in French, German, English, and other tongues, the fear by Jewish writers of being "overheard" built into secular Diaspora writing a subtler variety of "normal esotericism." A self-enforcing self-censorship, a taboo on the public ventilation of "tribal secrets" maintained in the name of prudence and "social responsibility," became common practice. The fear of "persecution," political and social, had created a "secret writing." *

What happened to what Professor Daniel Aaron in "Some Reflections on Communism and the Jewish Writer" describes as "the radical Jewish intellectuals' own hostility toward the vulgar Jewish philistine whose unashamed drive for social status struck them as *particularly reprehensible*"?[4] (my emphasis). Where did this hostility, this undeclared intra-ethnic war, go? It disappeared publicly, displaced and universalized—this is the nuanced meaning I give to "esoteric"—into a *general* indictment of bourgeois Western capitalism as a whole. The key phrase here is the "unashamed drive" of the Jewish bourgeoisie (Marx's and Lippmann's "primal scene"). It was the complex fate of the acculturated Jewish radical intellectual to feel the shame that ordinary, "unashamed" Jews were not feeling, and to perform on an intellectual-cultural level those rites of Goffman's "remedial interchange"—in the form of apology and explanation to the *goyim* (Marxism, Stalinism, Trotskyism)—that ordinary *prost* Jews were remiss in performing on the everyday social level.† The "vulgar Jewish philistine's" trip to Miami has, in a sense, created the Jewish intellectual "trip," the ideological pilgrimage to Moscow. The hidden injury of shame at "Miami," the fear of vulgarity by association, creates that "world elsewhere" which is "Moscow." Let us call it "the M & M phenomenon." "Miami" becomes a nightmare for the "refined" Jewish intellectual gen-

* The writing style of the late Professor Leo Strauss, "erudite, *elliptical,* abstract" as Irving Kristol notes (my emphasis), was a self-exemplifying instance of his own thesis in *Persecution and the Art of Writing.* Irving Kristol, "Social Sciences and Law," *The Great Ideas Today 1962* (Chicago: Encyclopedia Britannica, 1962), p. 243.

† Ironically, the more acculturated Jewish critics of the fifties were to attack, in turn, this "high-minded" thirties politics—the Rosenbergs were the target—to demonstrate, Morris Dickstein writes, its underlying "vulgarity of mind." For Leslie Fiedler and Robert Warshow "the vulgar middlebrow Jew is a cultural embarrassment who must be exorcised. . . ." This attack is "understandable, however unforgivable. . . . What was buried with the Rosenbergs . . . was two decades of American (and Jewish) Marxism. . . ." Morris Dickstein, "Cold War Blues: Notes on the Culture of the Fifties," *Partisan Review,* 41, no. 1 (1974): 48, 49.

erally. Robert Alter winces at "the hideous ostentation" displayed in Miami by the children and grandchildren of the Lower East Side.[5] Even in Tel Aviv, Cynthia Ozick finds "an arrogant row of Miami-like hotels. . . ." [6]

A striking parallel to the exasperated snobbery felt by the Jewish intellectual elite for its bourgeois Jewish community emerges in the way the British Left feels about its working-class vacation land, Blackpool. Blackpool maddens the English ideological Left, Peregrine Worsthorne notes, because it "shows the working class as it really is rather than as the Left would like it to be." It shows them to be

> resolutely old-fashioned, provocatively insular, shockingly low-brow, persistently racialist, . . . unashamedly vulgar, very easily pleased with very little . . . the very opposite, that is, of what socialism would wish them to be. . . . There they are, walking down the front, gawping, drinking, leering, having a wonderful time, *now,* in this unreconstructed capitalist hell, showing no awareness that they are living in a cultural desert, displaying no desire for higher standards, no concern about the Race Relations . . . behaving, in short, with brazen naturalness without the slightest reference to any canons of taste and propriety other than their own . . . a museum piece of genuine working class culture. . . . For the progressive Blackpool is a nightmare. They have got the rest of us on the run . . . but Blackpool refuses to budge.[7] [His emphasis]

This recoil from the vulgarity of their own Jewish community, in which we find the covert root of the social and literary creativity of Diaspora intellectuals, is not a matter confined to the West. One thinks of Russia and Babel's creative ambivalence about the Polish *Ostjuden.*[8] There are Tchernichovsky and Mandelstam. "But how offensive was the speech of the rabbi—though it was not ungrammatical," recalls Osip Mandelstam of a childhood trip to the synagogue in the Jewish quarter of Saint Petersburg, "how vulgar when he uttered the words 'His Imperial Highness,' how utterly vulgar all that he said!" [9] But synagogues were, in a sense, Jewish private places. In the West, with urbanization and the emergence of the "social" category, the "Jewish problem" was to become the problem of social appearance as such, the problem of creating "scenes" in urban public places like streets, parks, and public halls. It was no longer the charge made by anti-Semites of "hidden," behind-the-scenes manipulations by "Jewish financiers"; it was the anguish of acculturated Jews at the public behavior of their fellow Jews.

When in 1897—the same year as Herzl's first Zionist Congress—Walter Rathenau writes his pseudonymous manifesto, "Hear O Israel!," he opens by insisting on the visibility of "the Jewish problem." Whoever wishes to *see* it, he writes "should wander through the Tiergartenstrasse at twelve o'clock on a Berlin Sunday morning, or else look into the foyer of a theatre in the evening. Strange sight! . . ." [10] This aversion of the socially assimilating Jew to the loud and conspicuous public behavior of his fellow Jews is the functional equivalent of the disdain of the Jewish intellectual for the vulgarity of the Jewish community. The ancient "Jewish problem" had surfaced as a problem of behavior in public places, a problem of "relations in public" bequeathing to the Jewish intellectual his problem of "public relations." It was a problem of social esthetics.*

Nothing in the ethos of *Yiddishkeit* had prepared its sons for this demoralizing differentiation in social life of morals from manners.† And nothing in the ethos of *Yiddishkeit* had prepared them for the analogous ordeal of differentiation in the life of culture, namely, the distinction of fiction from legend and history. In the West, these two differentiations hang together. If your culture has "fiction," your social life will probably have "behavior," for behavior is a kind of fictive or ideal element in social interaction. C. S. Lewis pinpoints in the age of Sidney and Spenser the critical debate of sixteenth-century critics as the time of "the difficult process by which Europe became conscious of fiction as an activity distinct from history on the one hand and from lying on the other." [11] Not until some three hundred years later, as part of its "delayed modernization," did Diaspora Jewry take its first steps in that "difficult process." In 1853 there appeared a novel, or rather, a melodramatic Biblical "romance" written by a *maskil* of the Hebrew movement of enlightenment, *Haskalah.* Titled *The Love of Zion* and written by Abraham Mapu, it constituted for its Jewish readers their "first introduction to the very concept of literature as such." [12] But, in general, the idea of fiction has remained a stranger to the world of *Yiddishkeit.* East European Jews, Alfred Kazin notes, "have produced many stories, narratives, legends, but until our day, very little fiction." [13]

Like other modernizing peoples, the Jews, in moving from their towns and *shtetlach* into the urban public space of the modern city, were thrust among a world of strangers. In the small towns of their past, their personal and family worlds—and the world of their ethnic "family"—were

* This, for the sociologist in any case, is how one must construe Cynthia Ozick's statement that "the problem of Diaspora in its most crucial essence is the problem of aesthetics." ("America: Toward Yavneh," *Judaism* 19, no. 3 (Summer 1970): 273.

† And nothing had prepared them for that later Weberian "disenchantment," the differentiation of morals from politics. "If there is any lesson to be learned," writes Professor Danto, ruefully, about the Sorelian "general strike" at Columbia University (1968), "it is that flexibility and compromise, while morally repugnant, are the soul of politics." Arthur C. Danto, "II-Columbia-The Useless Lesson," *The New Republic* 160, no. 4 (January 25, 1969): 26. A review of *Up Against the Ivy Wall: A History of the Columbia Crisis,* by Jerry L. Avorn, Robert Friedman, and members of the staff of the *Columbia Daily Spectator.*

coextensive with their spatial worlds.[14] On opening the door in the *shtetl* they had been instantly surrounded by relatives, friends, enemies, neighbors, acquaintances, or, at the very least, by fellow Jews: "life-is-with-people." But when, in Vienna, Paris, Berlin, London, and New York, when Jewish city-dwellers (who had left their ethnic enclaves of first settlement) opened their front doors and stepped out into an urban public space belonging to no one in particular, they were instantly engulfed by strangers: "life-is-with-strangers." To tolerate the continued copresence of strange others without personally knowing them—that is, without coding them instantly as friend or foe—is a difficult feat for any still tradition-directed people. The social exigencies of behaving in a seemly way in a world of strangers, as a "stranger among strangers," require that one have in one's behavioral repertoire a certain "ritual competence," as Erving Goffman calls it,[15] that traditionally falls under the rubric of civility. For what, fundamentally, does "stranger" mean in the modern liberal era of the city of strangers but a "fellow user of a public place"? [16] And what kind of code did modern liberalism—which, at its best, Benjamin Nelson reminds us, "looks, at the very least, to the advent of a certain kind of Brotherhood, a Brotherhood in which all are brothers in being equally others" [17]—hope would replace the ancient brother-enemy code but a code that would transform otherness into the *tertium quid* of civility? Thus, out of an intolerance of the ambiguity of the surrounding stranger, to "travel in packs" in public places, to transform public space into private or semiprivate space, "privatizing" it by creating a mobile "home," is perceived by the copresent strangers as an intrusion, as "acting as if they owned the place, the space," as, in a word, creating a social delict that symbolically subverts liberalism's secret wish for the new equality of a purely civil kind of brotherhood. The depth of Walter Rathenau's acculturation to the core values of Protestant individualistic Calvinism is revealed by his "overreaction" to the unseemly group intrusion by his fellow Jews into the impersonal, public, "protestant" space of the modern *Gesellschaft*. He experienced their vulgarity religiously, that is, as a profanation.

The older question: Is Jewry *Salonsfähig*? that is, fit for the salon, passes into the later question: Is Jewry *Gesellschaftsfähig*? that is, fit for modern civil society? These social questions, as we have seen in our chapter on the entry of Jewish characters into the modernist novel—are Jews *Romansfähig*? that is, fit for the modernist novel?—are continuous to some extent with cultural problems. For questions of fitness, appropriateness, and propriety are all, in the end, matters of esthetic, not moral or political, judgment. And when, recently, Meyer Levin (in *The Obsession*) revealed to the public the quarrel with his rival dramatizers of Anne Frank's *Diary of a Young Girl, he* claiming they had bleached out her Jewishness, *they* claiming "that my work was unstageworthy, . . ." [18]

do we not hear the question: Are Jews *Bühnenfähig*? that is, fit for the stage? *

Everything, it would seem, has always "conspired" to maintain and justify the tradition of hidden self-censorship and the public relations orientation in the Diaspora: politeness, respectability, an era of political anti-Semitism and Holocaust, a time of cultural philo-Semitism, the fear by Jews of the label "self-hate" and by Gentiles of the label "anti-Semite" (both functioning as instruments of social control), everything, it seems, conspires to legitimate submerging whole dimensions of the experience of Diaspora Judaism where it does not actually falsify that experience itself. No Jew is free as long as telling the truth is *eo ipso* to become an informer to the *goyim*. Leslie Fiedler, after exploring Karl Shapiro's tergiversations in the attempt to "rewrite" his own past, confesses: "We are all spiritual Stalinists engaged in a continual falsification of our own histories, and we must pray for critics capable of pointing this out." [19] The nearest cultural parallel in this respect to the ideological "secret writing" of the Diaspora giants is, curiously, the writings of the Puritan divines, who were eventually to find their great critic in the late Perry Miller. To understand the Mathers, Miller maintained, it is necessary

> that we appreciate the habit of speech that grew up in New England as an inevitable concomitant to the jeremiads: references had to be phrased in more and more generalized terms, names never explicitly named, so that we are obliged to decipher out of oblique insinuations what to contemporaries were broad designations. When ministers [read: radical secular Jewish intellectuals—J.M.C.] denounced "oppression" and "luxury" they meant certain people whom they did not have to specify. . . . This habit of ambiguity, developed out of New England's insecurity, out of its inability to face frankly its own internal divisions, out of its effort to maintain a semblance of unity even while unanimity was crumbling—which became more elaborate and disingenuous as internecine passions waxed—was to cling to the New England mind for centuries. We look ahead to the decades in which an emerging Unitarianism swathed itself in terms of studied vagueness. . . . In Boston society today, matters may be fully discussed which, to an outsider, seem never to be mentioned at all.[20]

Miller was to crack the cryptogram of this "tribal reticence"—as he calls it in concluding the above passage—in the Mathers, in Jonathan Edwards, and in the New England mind generally.[21] A similar work of reclamation,

* Twenty-five years earlier, in his autobiographical *In Search*, Levin had performed the "self-criticism" he now asks of others: "I had tried to erase what was Jewish in my characters. . . . I was influenced by [Hemingway's] terse manner of writing. . . . I began to struggle with the Jewish element first by trying quite unconsciously to "pass," as in *Reporter* and *Frankie and Johnny,* where I eliminated the Jewishness of my characters." Meyer Levin, *In Search* (New York: Paperback Library, 1961), pp. 34, 472.

opening out the great secular Jewish "rabbis" and their covert jeremiads against "their own," is an idea whose time, I think, has come. For what is a Jewish intellectual in the first place but a person, in Bernard Rosenberg's definition, "who pretends to have forgotten his Yiddish." [22]

Are there broader implications to this "case study" of Freud, Marx, Lévi-Strauss, and Diaspora intellectual culture generally? It would seem that there are. But the "broad implications" are precisely indentured to the details. We find three conclusions growing out of our study:

1. In the first place, we learn that we learn nothing about our civilization from the Christian and Jewish celebrants of what ecumenist public relations insist on calling "Judeo-Christian" civilization. This factitious phrase with its facile hyphen is part of what I have called at the beginning of Chapter 22, "the cultural and theological illiteracy of our times." * To learn the nature of the civilization of the West we must go, not to the assimilators, not to our Chagalls and our Malamuds, nor to our Niebuhrs and our Neuhauses, but to the great unassimilated, implacable Jews of the West, to a Marx, to a Freud, to a Lévi-Strauss, to a Harry Wolfson, to those who exhibit a principled and stubborn resistance to the whole Western "thing." These proud pariahs *experience* Western civilization as an incognito or secularized form of Christianity, and they therefore openly resist it *as such*. Professor Harry A. Wolfson, the great Harvard scholar of Jewish philosophy and theology, puts the matter with unimpeachable authority. Looking back on a century of Jewish Emancipation, and writing in 1962, he openly declares of Western Jewry that

> a century of infiltration of Christian ideas into our life through all the agencies of education has robbed us of our essential Jewish character, of our distinctive Jewish philosophy of life. . . . In everything that guides our life and determines our view thereof, we have become Christianized, for we have *somehow* accepted Christ if not in the theological sense of a saviour at least in the historical sense of a civilizer. We have fallen in with the prevalent view that Christianity is essential to the progress of human civilization, which is, after all, another version of the Christian belief that Christ is necessary for the salvation of one's soul. . . . We proceed on the assumption that modern civilization is the fulfillment of the promises of Christ.[23] [My emphasis]

* The notion of a Judeo-Christian civilization was never, really, a *cultural* "myth"; it is a sociological "device." It is "a device—and here we must be frank—," writes Nathan Rotenstreich, "to convince the non-Jewish world that they share with Jews a common tradition. . . . It is also a device to convince the Jews that they share with the world not only the universal secular culture, but also the universal Christian 'cultian' culture." Nathan Rotenstreich, "Emancipation and Its Aftermath," in David Sidorsky, ed., *The Future of the Jewish Community in America* (New York: Basic Books, 1973), p. 52.

This study unpacks, somewhat, Wolfson's "somehow" in the preceding passage and endeavors to spell out some of the ways in which the "differentiated modernity" of the West is *experienced,* by its more profound Jews, as a matter of the acceptance or rejection of Christ, in Wolfson's words, as "a civlizer," if not as "a saviour." For them, the West is *experienced* as a standing "temptation scene" to religious apostasy: to universalize, to differentiate, to refine, to upgrade, to reform, is *eo ipso* to convert to "Christianity."

Some Jews turn back from the brink of this cultural conversion, deliberately reconverting to the Jewish community, becoming its spokesmen. A returnee (*baal teshubah*) in this little-known tradition of Diaspora intellectuality *—from Franz Rosenzweig to Cynthia Ozick in our own time—is converting, in effect, from the vulgarity which conceals to the coarseness which reveals, from Jewish parvenu-assimilation to Jewish pariah-*Ostjudentum,* from the refinement which is vulgarity to the coarseness which connotes the modern "authenticity." †

2. We have probed the question of the "primitivism" of the *shtetl* Jew and his resistance to modernization, in both belief and behavior. Peculiar as it may seem as a "finding," we find that a kind of predifferentiated crudeness on the culture system level, and a kind of undifferentiated rudeness on the social system level of behavior, is believed to be—by certain Jews themselves—not only an integral part of what it means to be a Jew, but integral to the *religious* essence of Judaism, and not an accidental result of Exile or of socioeconomic disadvantage. "How many Jews today," Michael Selzer asks in a recent analysis of Franz Rosenzweig's *Star of Redemption*—"How many Jews today, proudly identified during the past two or three generations with Western modernity, can join in Rosenzweig's *insistence* that the traditional primitivism and obscurantism of the Jews (in the eyes of their critics) is of 'the very essence of Judaism'?" [24] (my emphasis). It is with good reason, then, that in Chapter 9, The Temptation Scene, when Bleuler came from Zurich to visit Freud, we felt ourselves to be, in some obscure but unmis-

* This Diaspora ideology, which I shall treat at length in another book, is a variant of the tradition of the conscious pariah which Hannah Arendt discusses in "The Jew as Pariah: A Hidden Tradition," *Jewish Social Studies,* 6, no. 2 (1944).

† Thus, when Martin Kilson, Professor of Government at Harvard College, attacks Norman Podhoretz's espousal of the Jewish community's Zionism, he is specifically attacking the "revolting" intellectual taste of a Jewish intellectual who has sold out to the vulgarity of the Jewish community. "Though one is accustomed to a certain grossness in the sensibilities of the author of *Making It,*" he writes, "I was not quite prepared for the display in 'Now, Instant Zionism' [*New York Times Magazine,* February 3, 1974]. The nakedly crass and vulgar ethnic chauvinism surrounding his we-are-all-Zionists-now pronouncement to his fellow Jews is more than I expected, even from Norman Podhoretz. . . . [His] celebration of the new Jewish chauvinism is as politically dangerous as it is intellectually revolting." "Letters: American Jewish Loyalties," *New York Times Magazine,* February 24, 1974, p. 72.

takable way, witnesses to a *religious* confrontation: when Bleuler dangled the lure of *Edelkeit* before his eyes, it was *Yiddishkeit* that spoke through Freud and thundered its no.

Not only Freud's genius, but the genius of all the intellectual giants of the Jewish Diaspora has deep if "hidden" connections with their being consciously and deliberately, albeit helplessly, social pariahs. These "hidden transformations" occur not only with a Marx or a Freud in the field of the social sciences, but with an Einstein in the natural sciences as well. "He hated violence and ceremony equally," Howard Moss writes, in his elegy "The Gift To Be Simple." [25] Everybody knows the polarity that was Einstein: the social pariah with the crazy hair and the rumpled sweater, the subtle and fastidious rationalist exploring the secrets of the universe. "But if one probes deeper," Gerald Holton writes, "one will find that these polarities are essentially connected to his scientific genius. Einstein's *disinterest* in making quite sure he will not turn up incorrectly dressed for some formal occasion is not unrelated to his ability to adopt an unconventional point of view when it is needed to expose the key fault in some hoary old problem of science" [26] (my emphasis). But the inner connection runs deeper than this.* Einstein found the refinements and differentiations of Western social decorum and civility absolutely unfathomable, endlessly fascinating, and, personally, a torture. During Thomas Bucky's extended stay as a guest at Einstein's home, the physicist's only nonscientific reading "was Emily Post's book on etiquette. He read the book in his bed-room study in the evenings and his sharp laugh rattled through the house. Frequently he came downstairs with the book in hand and offered to read a particularly choice passage on the proper conduct of a gentleman." Einstein's friends, Bucky continues, "never expected him to behave in the conventional manner. . . . Since [my fiancée and I] knew how Einstein was tortured by formal occasions, we didn't invite him to [our] wedding in 1953 at the Plaza in New York. . . . He showed up," he concludes, "without being invited." [27]

Over the fireplace in Fine Hall at Princeton Einstein's famous line is inscribed: *Raffiniert ist Herr Gott, aber boshaft ist Er nicht*—God is subtle and refined, but He is not arbitrary or malicious. The social code of civility, also, is subtle and refined, and requires tact in its exercise. What we call "tact," Sartre notes, "is connected with *esprit de finesse*, a thing the Jew does not trust. . . . To base his conduct on tact would be to recognize that reason is not a sufficient guide in human relations and that traditional and obscure powers of intuition may be superior to it." [28] Einstein, we suggest, realized that the problem involved in the social

* Sociologist Lewis Feuer locates the social roots of Einstein's general theory of relativity in his membership in the turn-of-the-century Olympia Academy, a group recruited from the "counterculture of Zurich-Berne revolutionary students [which] was . . . a 'pariah culture,' " a circle "predominantly composed of students of Jewish origin—Einstein, Adler, Besso, Solovine." Lewis S. Feuer, *Einstein and the Generations of Science* (New York: Basic Books, 1974), pp. 54, 51.

assimilation of the emancipated Jew in the nineteenth century was, in a way (like God), *raffiniert*, subtle and refined, but that, unlike God's, society's refinement could be malicious and arbitrary. "The rationalism of Jews is a passion," Sartre writes, "the passion for the universal. . . . If reason exists," he continues

> then there is no French truth or German truth; there is no Negro truth or Jewish truth. . . . It is precisely this sort of disincarnation that certain Jews seek. The best way to feel oneself no longer a Jew is to reason. . . . There is not a Jewish way of mathematics; the Jewish mathematician becomes a universal man when he reasons. . . . He experiments with and inspects his intoxicating condition as universal man; on a superior level he realizes that accord and assimilation which is denied him on the social level.[29]

Experiencing himself as coarse and crude at the level of social system adaptation, the Jew as rationalist "escapes" upward into another order of subtlety and refinement at the level of the culture system. "He joins," Sartre writes, "crude sensibility to the refinements of intellectual culture." [30] Our analysis of Freud, Marx, and Lévi-Strauss, then, would seem to be applicable—*mutatis mutandis*—to other intellectual giants of the Diaspora.*

3. We may also conclude from this essay that socialization into modernity is, at best, a difficult matter. It is least difficult, perhaps, for the members of the WASP core culture descended from Calvinist Christianity. They, in a sense, are "ego-syntonic" to modernity. They alone were "present at the creation." For the rest of us, it is more or less costly, more or less rewarding. Part of the difficulty, as we see in the case of Freud, is the problem of *Gemeinschaft*-affect. Modernization invades our sentiency, demanding wider modes of feeling congruent with the civil modes of behavior needed for living among strangers. In this connection I once wrote, regarding modernization and differentiation in India:

> An important dimension of the tradition-modernity collision is located in the neglected domain of affect. The "magical" ties of blood and amoral familism, the given, ready-made intimacies of caste, ethnicity, and sect, indeed, all the old familiarities embedded in ascription render the Indian (of course, not alone the Indian) loath to trust himself to the cooler, more impersonal width-sentiments (such as respect and civility) ingredient in the processes of modernization. Affective modernization, in which traditionary affect is in part dissolved, in part relocated, is a traumatic though liberating

* This volume, in fact, is but a fragment of work completed and work in progress that deals with Kafka, Wittgenstein, Hannah Arendt, and many others.

> experience. For most people, it would seem, this emotional change [at the everyday life level] is what the "long revolution" of modernization is all about, is what it is *experienced* as (to use William James' formula for radical empiricism). To acquire the "affective neutrality" (Parsons) or "emotional asceticism" (Geiger) that civilizes one into modernity is to divest one's solidary sentiments of their sacred particularity. Nation building, the legitimation of *wide* public authority, the establishment of a civil politics, all fine things, can wreak havoc in the pre-civil emotional life of a familistic people. These changes are experienced inwardly as a kind of secularization of affect. Schooled in Calvinist Christianity, the modernizing West has undergone its sentimental education. Are there available in the East functionally equivalent values (operating fairly early in the socialization process) which can instruct the Indian in those curious innerworldly disciplines that promote, sanction and maintain the structures of generalized affect? [31] [Emphasis in original]

This same question, of course, applies with full force to all of us who strive to measure up to, or struggle against, the exigencies of modernity. Modernization is a continuous variable. All of us, any of us, are only relatively modern, be we Irish, Jewish, German, black, whatever. All of us are witness to the profanation of our sacred particularities; all of us suffer the pathos of the secularization process.

Our third conclusion is: the modernization process is "objectively anti-Semitic." But it is also, if much less so, "objectively anti-Catholic" and "objectively anti-Lutheran." The Catholic Counter Reformation is an early form of counter-modernization. The quarrel continues. The differentiations of modernity are "disenchanting."

We have noted the resistance movement to modernity, men like Marx, who create ideologies of dedifferentiation, at once nostalgic and utopian. For them, modernity's differentiations are "bourgeois contradictions" to be abolished by revolutionary action. We all know "the great hatred" of modernity and how deep its sources run. We have explored Freud's holding operation—an evasion, essentially, of the full thrust of modernism. We all know, also, those who willingly submit and who have made themselves a smoothly functioning part of modernity's *Apparat:* bureaucratic virtuosos of ascetic rationalism, "specialists without spirit, sensualists without heart." [32] We have most to learn, I think, from those heroic bourgeois who have a lover's quarrel with the modern world, exemplary men of the stature of Max Weber and Pastor Bonhoeffer.

In Max Weber the differentiations of modernity internalized themselves in the excruciatingly personal form of a human contradiction, a deep, inner value-conflict: the contradiction between man and specialist man, between diffuse human freedom and *disponibilité* on the one hand and, on the other, the "iron cage" of affectively neutral functional specificity, between two loves that have built two "cities." We must allow Karl Löwith, in his magnificent 1932 essay on Weber, to be our teacher—there is no better guide—on how a man of Weber's inordinate ethical passion lived this contradiction—for there is no "solving" it. We quote him at length:

> Weber never presented himself as an inseparable whole, but always as a member of a specific sphere—in this or that other role, as this or that other person: as an "empirical" individual scientist in his writings, as an academic teacher on the podium, as a politician on the rostrum, as *homo religiosus* in his most intimate circles. It is precisely in this separation of the life spheres—whose theoretical expression is value-freedom—that Weber's individuality in the uniqueness of its wholeness reveals itself. Even here the question for Weber was not the same as for Marx, namely, to find a way by which the specific human type of the rationalized world, i.e., the specialist man, can be abolished along with the division of labor. Rather, Weber asks, by which way can man as such preserve the freedom of self-responsibility, amid, and in spite of, his inescapable compartmentalized humanity. Here too Weber affirms this self-alienated humanity (as Marx puts it) because it was precisely this form of existence which, while not affording or offering it, *forced him* into an extreme "freedom of movement." To act in the midst of this specialized and indoctrinated world of "specialists without spirit, sensualists without heart" with the passionate force of negativity piercing now here now there through some structure of "bondage"—this was the meaning of "freedom of movement." . . . The salvation of the human individual as such means to him that it must take place within the ingrained attitude of specialist humanity and with regard to it. But submitting to his fate, he at the same time already opposes it. But this counter-position has this previous subjection as its inevitable presupposition. . . . Thus the individual as such . . . does not signify an indivisible whole above or outside the factual, compartmentalized mode of existence of the modern specialists. Rather, the individual is a "man" when he stakes his whole being in each and every separate role, great or small. . . . Thus Weber's deliberate renunciation of the "universal man" . . . is a renunciation which at the same time incorporates a great demand, namely, in spite of this "compartmentalization of the soul," man must ever be involved with his whole being—on the strength of passion—in all such acts which in themselves are isolated.[33] [My emphasis on "*forced him*"]

We see in this passage the kind of "secret," inner-worldly discipline "forced" on Weber by his inner assent to the modernization process: a kind of "role-distance" involving an ethicoreligious commitment to availability—that is, all of him would be there, if needed, in even the most trivial and routinized of roles, meeting the human needs of the most "ordinary" of persons whenever these needs might diffuse into "ultimate concerns" beyond the specified proprieties of patterned role obligations. Weber's ethic was an ethic of total human vulnerability concealed in the "divisions of labor."

Somewhere along the line this secret, inner-worldly ethic of Weber feeds off the Lutheran doctrine of condescension—in the christological sense of "condescension"—and reminds us of that other high, academic, German bourgeois, Dietrich Bonhoeffer, and the *Arkandisziplin* with which he "managed" the differentiations of modernity. It is in Bonhoeffer that the passionate ethicoreligious earnestness of Max Weber rediscovers itself in theological form. Weber, by withholding the "whole" man, by "condescending" to the inconspicuousness of specialized roles, by remaining deliberately in the penultimate, refusing the "triumphalist," flashy intimacy of pseudoeschatological "wholeness"-excitement, was practicing the inner-worldly asceticism of secularized Protestant Christianity. Religious motives maintained, for him, the meaningfulness of the "everydayness" of routine Western social life. Weberian motifs become audible as we listen to Pastor Bonhoeffer's instructions in the theological logic of insensitivity training:

> Let us ask why it is that precisely in thoroughly grave situations, for instance when I am with someone who has suffered a bereavement, I often decide to adopt a "penultimate" attitude, particularly when I am dealing with Christians, remaining silent as a sign that I share the bereaved man's helplessness in the face of such a grievous event, and not speaking the Biblical words of comfort which are, in fact, known to me and available to me. Why am I often unable to open my mouth, when I ought to give expression to the ultimate? And why, instead, do I decide on expression of thoroughly penultimate human solidarity? Is it from mistrust of the power of the ultimate word? Is it from fear of men? Or is there some positive good reason for such an attitude, namely, that my knowledge of the word, my having it at my finger tips, in other words my being, so to speak, spiritually master of the situation, bears only the appearance of the ultimate, but is in reality itself something entirely penultimate? Does one not in some cases, by remaining deliberately in the penultimate [read: the *alltag*], perhaps point all the more genuinely to the ultimate, which God will speak in his own time (though indeed even then through a human mouth)? Does not this mean that, over and over

again, the penultimate will be what commends itself precisely for the sake of the ultimate, and that it will have to be done not with a heavy conscience but with a clear one? [34]

Here we see the ancient Israelitish taboo on "direct reference" to the ultimate things—*ta eschata*—interiorized as theological taste; profanation is now inseparable from vulgarity. In the final count, Hanfried Müller writes, there is now, in Bonhoeffer, "no *visible* difference between Christians and heathens" (my emphasis); the church of the future should relinquish "every special ostentation." [35]

Here we witness Christianity "acting back" on Christianity itself, heterogenously refining out of existence its residual crudities and insensitivities.[36] All vulgar "triumphalism" must go. All the creaking, embarrassing, superannuated, supernatural *"deus ex machina"* machinery of revelation and miracle have become, literally, unseemly. Christianity lives now only through the *Arkandisziplin* of an incognito: the "hidden" Christ. To be inconspicuous, yet faithful. The secret discipline of the arcane. To perform the penultimate roles, holding fast and secretly to that which is good. Modernity, child of Protestant Christianity, "acts back" on its parent, secularizing it out of sight, offended by the unsightliness of its own visibility. The *Deus absconditus* of modernity: Thou art indeed a tasteful God, the depths of whose existence, Whitehead declares, "lie beyond the vulgarities of praise or of power." [37] Or of the rites of faith itself.

There is unbearable pathos in the figure of Pastor Bonhoeffer as he prepares to die: "Called to conduct his last worship service in prison shortly before his execution," Peter Berger writes, Bonhoeffer "held back, for he did not want to offend his neighbor, a Soviet officer." [38] A new offense has swallowed up the ancient *skandalon;* the rites of faith perform themselves in the rites of love; the *ius divinum* self-destructs; a new *ius civile* is all in all.

NOTES

Epigraphs

Lionel Trilling, "Afterword" to Tess Slesinger, *The Unpossessed* (New York: Avon Books, 1966), p. 316.

Erving Goffman, *Relations in Public: Microstudies of the Public Order* (New York: Basic Books, 1972), p. 157.

Léon Poliakov, "Anti-Semitism and Christian Teaching," *Midstream* 12, no. 3 (March 1966): 13.

Leo Strauss, *Liberalism Ancient and Modern* (New York: Basic, 1968), p. 268.

Erving Goffman, *Encounters: Two Studies in the Sociology of Interaction* (Indianapolis: Bobbs-Merrill, 1961), pp. 24, 25.

Norman Mailer, "Responses and Reactions VI," *Commentary* 36, no. 4 (October 1963): 320.

Harold Nicolson, *Good Behaviour, Being a Study of Certain Types of Civility* (London: Constable, 1955), p. 89.

Erving Goffman, *Interaction Ritual: Essays on Face-to-Face Behavior* (Garden City, N.Y.: Doubleday, Anchor, 1967), p. 91.

The character Harry Bogen in Jerome Weidman's *I Can Get It for You Wholesale* (New York: Modern Library, 1937), p. 236.

Erving Goffman, *Stigma: Notes on the Management of Spoiled Identity* (Englewood Cliffs, N.J.: Prentice-Hall, 1963), pp. 13, 101.

Albert Goldman, from the Journalism of Lawrence Schiller, "The Real Lenny Bruce Is Alive and Well in Brooklyn," *New York* (August 6, 1973): 38.

Émile Durkheim, *Socialism*, trans. Charlotte Sattler, ed. Alvin W. Gouldner (New York: Collier, 1962), pp. 41, 42.

John Searle, *Speech Acts: An Essay in the Philosophy of Language* (Cambridge: Cambridge University Press, 1969), p. 52.

Philip Rahv, "Lettuce and Tomatoes," *The New York Review of Books* 2, no. 11 (July 9, 1964): 6, 7. A review of George P. Elliot's *A Piece of Lettuce* and Leslie Fiedler's *Waiting for the End.*

Norma Rosen, "Symposium: Living in Two Cultures (II)," *Response* 6, no. 4 (Winter 1972–73): 110.

Talcott Parsons in *Max Weber and Sociology Today*, ed. Otto Stammer, trans. Kathleen Morris (New York: Harper Torchbook, 1972), pp. 197–98.

Anonymous, "An Analysis of Jewish Culture," in *Jews in a Gentile World: The Problem of Anti-Semitism*, ed. Isacque Graeber and S. H. Britt (New York: Macmillan, 1942), p. 253.

Thomas Hobbes, "Of the Difference of Manners," *Leviathan, Or the Matter, Forme and Power of a Commonwealth Ecclesiasticall and Civil*, ed. Michael Oakeshott (Oxford: Basil Blackwell, 1946), p. 63. I would like to thank Ronald Berman for this quote.

Michael Polanyi, "Jewish Problems," *Political Quarterly* (London) 14, no. 1 (Jan.–March 1943): 33.

Max Weber, "The 'Bernhard Affair' and Professor Delbrück," *On Universities: The Power of the State and the Dignity of the Academic Calling in Imperial Germany*, ed. and trans. Edward Shils (Chicago: University of Chicago Press, 1974), p. 13.

Hannah Arendt, "On Humanity in Dark Times: Thoughts about Lessing," trans. Clara and Richard Winston, *Men in Dark Times* (New York: Harcourt, Brace & World, 1968), p. 13.

Introduction

1. S. N. Eisenstadt, *From Generation to Generation: Age Groups and Social Structure* (New York: Free Press of Glencoe, 1956), p. 173.

2. Peter L. Berger and Thomas Luckmann, *The Social Construction of Reality: A Treatise in the Sociology of Knowledge* (Garden City, N.Y.: Doubleday, 1967), p. 28.

3. Erving Goffman's definition of "encounter" in *Relations in Public: Microstudies of the Public Order* (New York: Basic Books, 1971), p. 37, n. 13.

4. Philip Rieff, *The Triumph of the Therapeutic: Uses of Faith After Freud* (New York: Harper & Row, 1966), p. 240, n. 6.

5. George Lichtheim, "Socialism and the Jews," *Dissent* 15, no. 4 (July-August 1968): 333.

6. Erving Goffman, *Relations in Public: Microstudies of the Public Order* (New York: Basic Books, 1971), p. 109.

7. Martin Jay, *The Dialectical Imagination: A History of the Frankfurt School and the Institute for Social Research* (Boston: Little, Brown, 1973), p. 35.

8. Jaroslav Jan Pelican, *The Christian Tradition: A History of the Development of Doctrine,* vol. 1, *The Emergence of the Catholic Tradition,* 100–600. (Chicago: University of Chicago Press, 1971), pp. 30, 39.

9. Richard J. Bernstein, "The Frankfort School," *Midstream* 19, no. 7 (August-September 1973): 65.

10. Joseph Wortis, *Fragments of An Analysis with Freud* (New York: Simon and Schuster, 1954), p. 145.

11. Hannah Arendt, *Rahel Varnhagen: The Life of a Jewess* (London: East and West Library, 1957), p. 30.

12. Quoted in Milton Himmelfarb, *The Jews of Modernity* (New York: Basic Books, 1973), p. 23.

13. Jacob Katz, *Jews and Freemasons in Europe, 1723–1939,* trans. (from Hebrew) Leonard Oschry (Cambridge: Harvard University Press, 1970), p. 204.

14. J. P. Nettl and Roland Robertson, *International Systems and the Modernization of Societies* (London: Faber & Faber, 1968), p. 47.

15. Winston White, *Beyond Conformity* (New York: Free Press, 1961), p. 206.

16. David Little, "Max Weber Revisited: The 'Protestant Ethic' and the Puritan Experience of Order," in *International Yearbook for the Sociology of Religion,* vol. 3, *Sociology of Religion: Theoretical Perspectives (II),* ed. Joachim Matthes (Opladen: Westdeutscher Verlag Köln und Opladen, 1967), pp. 106, 111.

17. White, *Beyond Conformity,* pp. 163–64.

18. Lyn H. Lofland, *A World of Strangers: Order and Action in Urban Public Space* (Basic Books, 1973), p. 182, n. 6.

19. Kenneth E. Boulding, *The Meaning of the Twentieth Century: The Great Transition* (New York: Harper & Row, 1964), pp. 95–96.

20. Anonymous, "An Analysis of Jewish Culture," in *Jews in a Gentile World: The Problem of Anti-Semitism,* ed. Isacque Graeber and S. H. Britt (New York: Macmillan, 1942), p. 253. See also Talcott Parsons, "The Sociology of Modern Anti-Semitism," in ibid., pp. 108–11.

21. Max Nordau, "Speech to the First Zionist Congress (1898)," in *The Zionist Idea: A Historical Analysis and Reader,* ed. and trans. Arthur Hertzberg (New York: Meridian Books; Philadelphia: Jewish Publication Society of America, 1960), p. 239.

22. Erich Auerbach, "La Cour et la Ville,'" in *Scenes from the Drama of European Literature: Six Essays* (New York: Meridian Books, 1959), p. 164.

23. Norman Podhoretz, "Faulkner in the 50's," in *Doings and Undoings: The Fifties and After in American Writing* (New York: Farrar, Straus, 1964), p. 15.

24. Maurice Samuel, "Jews, Be Nice," in *Jews on Approval* (New York: Liveright, 1932), p. 9.

25. See Harold Laski, *The Danger of Being a Gentleman and Other Essays* (New York: Viking Press, 1940).

26. Maurice R. Stein, "The Poetic Metaphors of Sociology," in *Sociology on Trial,* ed. Maurice Stein and Arthur Vidich (Englewood Cliffs, N.J.: Prentice-Hall, 1963), p. 180.

27. Irving Howe, "Sholom Aleichem: Voice of Our Past," *A World More Attractive: A View of Modern Literature and Politics* (New York: Horizon Press, 1963), p. 215.

Notes

Chapter 1 The Matrix of Freud's Theory: The Jewish Emancipation Problematic

1. See *Writings of the Young Marx on Philosophy and Society,* trans. and ed. Loyd D. Easton and Kurt H. Guddat (Garden City, N.Y.: Doubleday, Anchor, 1967), pp. 67–92.

2. Sigmund Freud, *The Interpretation of Dreams,* trans. James Strachey (New York: Basic Books, 1958), pp. 141–42.

3. Ibid., p. 142.

4. Freud, *Interpretation,* pp. 142–43.

5. Ibid., p. 143, n. 3.

6. Ibid., p. 144.

7. Talcott Parsons, "The Superego and the Theory of Social Systems," in *Social Structure and Personality* (New York: Free Press, 1964), p. 23.

8. Freud, *Interpretation,* p. 144.

9. Erving Goffman, "Fun in Games," in *Encounters: Two Studies in the Sociology of Interaction* (Indianapolis: Bobbs-Merrill, 1961), pp. 24, 25.

10. James A. Sleeper, "Authenticity and Responsiveness in Jewish Education," in *The New Jews,* ed. James A. Sleeper and Alan L. Mintz (New York: Vintage Books, 1971), p. 122.

11. Story told by Solomon Litt, president of the Jewish Welfare Board, quoted in *The Jewish Digest,* September 1963, p. 70.

12. Sigmund Freud, *Jokes and Their Relation to the Unconscious,* trans. James Strachey (New York: W. W. Norton, 1960), pp. 80–81.

13. Ibid., p. 112.

14. Hannah Arendt, "Reflections on Little Rock," *Dissent* 6, no. 1 (Winter 1959): 51. Compare this passage, written in 1957, with the same placement of "society" that is found in Hannah Arendt, *The Human Condition* (Garden City, N.Y.: Doubleday, 1958), pp. 27, 28.

15. Quoted in Theodor Reik, *Jewish Wit* (New York: Gamut Press, 1962), p. 58.

16. Ibid., p. 189.

17. Ibid.

18. Ibid., p. 191.

19. Ibid., p. 192.

20. Ibid., p. 194.

21. Ibid., p. 290.

22. Ibid., p. 201.

23. Helene Deutsch, *Confrontations with Myself: An Epilogue* (New York: W. W. Norton, 1973), p. 25.

24. Ernest Jones, *The Life and Work of Sigmund Freud,* vol. 1, *The Formative Years and the Great Discoveries, 1856–1900* (New York: Basic Books, 1953), p. 22.

25. Freud, *Jokes,* p. 81.

26. Ibid., p. 81.

27. Ibid.

28. Reik, *Jewish Wit,* p. 34.

29. Freud, *Jokes,* p. 81.

30. Jacob Katz, *Out of the Ghetto: The Social Background of Jewish Emancipation, 1770–1870* (Cambridge: Harvard University Press, 1972), p. 86.

31. Ernest Jones, *The Life and Work of Sigmund Freud,* vol. 2, *Years of Maturity, 1901–1919* (New York: Basic Books, 1955), p. 171.

32. Émile Durkheim, *Suicide: A Study in Sociology,* ed. George Simpson, trans. John Spaulding and George Simpson (New York: Free Press, 1951), p. 168.

33. Katz, *Out of the Ghetto,* p. 86.

34. Henri Bergson, "Laughter" in *Comedy,* ed. and trans. Wylie Sypher (Garden City, N.Y.: Doubleday, 1956), pp. 146, 155.

35. Hannah Arendt, *The Origins of Totalitarianism* (New York: Harcourt, Brace, 1951), p. 59.

36. Ibid., p. 60.

37. Hajo Holburn, *A History of Modern Germany, 1640–1840* (New York: Knopf, 1964), 1: 307.

38. Freud, *Interpretation,* p. 142.

39. Sigmund Freud, "The Psychotherapy of Hysteria" (1895), in Joseph Breuer and Sigmund Freud, *Studies in Hysteria,* trans. A. A. Brill (Boston: Beacon Press, 1950), p. 201.

40. Sigmund Freud, "Further Remarks," in *Collected Papers,* vol. 1, *Early Papers: On the History of the Psycho-Analytic Movement,* trans. Joan Riviere (New York: Basic Books, 1959), p. 179.

41. Ibid., p. 181.

42. Sigmund Freud, "Screen Memories," in *Collected Papers,* vol. 5, *Miscellaneous Papers, 1888–1938,* pp. 52, 54.

43. Ibid., p. 63.

44. Ibid., p. 64.

45. Ibid., p. 69.

46. Philip Rieff, "Introduction" to Sigmund Freud, *The History of the Psychoanalytic Movement and Other Papers,* trans. Joan Riviere (New York: Collier Books, 1963), p. 13.

47. Quoted in Jones, *Life and Work,* vol. 1, p. 351.

48. Ibid., p. 191.

49. Ibid., p. 140.

50. Rieff, "Introduction" to Freud, *History of the Psychoanalytic Movement,* p. 9.

51. Hannah Arendt, *Rahel Varnhagen: The Life of a Jewess* (London: East and West Library, 1957), p. 183.

Chapter 2 The Matrix of the Method

1. Ernest Jones, *The Life and Work of Sigmund Freud,* vol. 1, *The Formative Years and the Great Discoveries, 1856–1900* (New York: Basic Books, 1953), p. 246.

2. Sigmund Freud, "Future Prospects," in *Collected Papers,* vol. 2, *Clinical Papers and Papers on Technique,* trans. Joan Riviere, ed. Ernest Jones (New York: Basic Books, 1959), p. 294.

3. Philip Rieff, *Freud: The Mind of the Moralist* (New York: Viking Press, 1959), p. 316.

4. Ibid., p. 317.

5. Rieff, *Freud,* pp. 317, 332.

6. Émile Durkheim, *The Rules of Sociological Method,* trans. George Catlin, ed. Sarah A. Solovay and John H. Mueller. (Chicago: Free Press, 1950), p. 14.

7. Donald M. Kaplan, "Psychoanalysis: The Decline of a Golden Craft," *Harper's,* February 1967, p. 43.

8. Hannah Arendt, "Preface" to *Rahel Varnhagen: The Life of a Jewess* (London: East and West Library, 1957), p. xiii.

9. E. M. W. Tillyard and C. S. Lewis, *The Personal Heresy: A Controversy* (London: Oxford University Press, 1939), p. 65.

10. Freud, "Future Prospects," pp. 294, 295.

11. Ibid., p. 294.

12. Ibid., pp. 293, 294.

13. Ibid., p. 293.

14. Norman Podhoretz, *Making It* (New York: Random House, 1967), p. 27.

15. George Steiner, "The Language Animal," in *Extraterritorial Papers on Literature and the Language Revolution* (New York: Atheneum, 1971), p. 85.

16. Mark Zborowski and Elizabeth Herzog, *Life Is With People: The Culture of the Shtetl* (New York: Schocken Books, 1962), pp. 226, 227.

17. Ibid., p. 420.

18. Rieff, *Freud*, p. 317.

19. Joseph Wortis, *Fragments of an Analysis with Freud* (New York: Simon & Schuster, 1954), pp. 49, 50.

20. Ibid., p. 59.

21. Ibid., p. 103.

22. Wortis, *Fragments*, p. 145.

23. See Christian Wilhelm von Dohm, *Concerning the Amelioration of the Civil Status of the Jews*, trans. Helen Lederer (Cincinnati: Hebrew Union College–Jewish Institute of Religion, 1957). Originally published in 1781.

Chapter 3 "Passing" into the West: The Passage from Home

1. Howard Morley Sacher, *The Course of Modern Jewish History* (New York: Dell, 1958), p. 400.

2. Ibid., pp. 400–401.

3. Philip Rieff, *The Triumph of the Therapeutic: Uses of Faith After Freud* (New York: Harper & Row, 1966), p. 46.

4. Peter Berger, *Invitation to Sociology: A Humanistic Perspective* (Garden City, N.Y.: Doubleday, 1963), p. 111.

5. Sigmund Freud, *The Psychopathology of Everyday Life*, trans. A. A. Brill (London: Ernest Benn, 1948), p. 4.

6. Norman Podhoretz, *Making It*, (New York: Random House, 1967), p. 161.

7. Freud, *Psychopathology*, pp. 10, 16.

8. Ibid., p. 136.

9. Ibid., p. 137.

10. Sigmund Freud, " 'Civilized' Sexual Morality," in *Collected Papers*, vol. 2, *Clinical Papers and Papers on Technique*, trans. Joan Riviere (New York: Basic Books, 1959), p. 82.

11. Ibid., p. 82.

12. Freud, *Psychopathology*, p. 77.

13. Philip Rieff, *Freud: The Mind of the Moralist* (New York: Viking Press, 1959), p. 308.

14. Hannah Arendt, *The Origins of Totalitarianism* (New York: Harcourt, Brace, 1951), pp. 56–68.

15. Reiff, *Freud*, p. 308.

16. Quoted in Max Brod, *Franz Kafka: A Biography*, trans. G. Humphreys Roberts (New York: Schocken Books, 1947), p. 113.

17. Freud, " 'Civilized' Sexual Morality," pp. 77, 78.

18. Norman Mailer, "A Talk-In on Vietnam," *New York Times Magazine*, February 4, 1966, p. 78.

19. Joseph Breuer and Sigmund Freud, *Studies in Hysteria*, trans. A. A. Brill (Boston: Beacon Press, 1950), p. 14.

20. Breuer and Freud, *Studies in Hysteria*, p. 23.

21. Lucy Freeman, *The Story of Anna O* (New York: Walker, 1972), p. 202.

22. Sigmund Freud, *The Interpretation of Dreams*, trans. James Strachey (New York: Basic Books, 1958), p. 142.

23. Erving Goffman, *Encounters: Two Studies in the Sociology of Interaction* (Indianapolis: Bobbs-Merrill, 1961), p. 25.

24. Quoted in Dora Edinger, *Bertha Pappenheim: Freud's Anna O* (Highland Park, Ill.: Congregation Solel, 1968), p. 69.

25. Ernest Jones, *The Life and Work of Sigmund Freud*, vol. 1, *The Formative Years and the Great Discoveries, 1856–1900* (New York: Basic Books, 1953), p. 223.

26. Freeman, *Anna O*, p. 150.

27. Jones, *The Life and Work of Sigmund Freud*, vol. 1, p. 223.

28. Freeman, *Anna O*, p. 146.

29. Edinger, *Bertha Pappenheim*, p. 38.

30. Ibid., p. 48.

31. Ibid., pp. 50, 51.

32. Ibid., p. 52.

33. Freeman, *Anna O*, pp. 32, 33.

34. George Steiner, *Extraterritorial: Papers on Literature and the Language Revolution* (New York: Atheneum, 1971), p. 84.

35. Ernest Jones, *The Life and Work of Sigmund Freud*, vol. 3, *The Last Phase, 1919–1939* (New York: Basic Books, 1957), between pages 78 and 79.

36. Helmut D. Schmidt, "The Terms of Emancipation, 1781–1812: The Public Debate in Germany and Its Effect on the Mentality and Ideas of German Jews," in *Leo Baeck Institute Year Book I*, ed. Robert Weltsch (London: East and West Library, 1956), p. 31.

37. Regarding this last point, see Marion J. Levy, Jr., *Modernization and the Structure of Societies* (Princeton: Princeton University Press, 1969), pp. 744 ff.

38. Erich Heller, Review of *My Youth in Vienna*, by Arthur Schnitzler, *Saturday Review*, January 16, 1971, p. 58.

39. Harold Lasswell, "Approaches to Human Personality: William James and Sigmund Freud," *Psychoanalysis and the Psychoanalytic Review* 47, no. 3 (Fall 1965): 54.

40. Ibid., p. 58.

41. Ibid., p. 64.

42. Ibid., p. 65.

43. Ibid., p. 57.

44. Ibid., p. 58.

Chapter 4 The Primal Scene

1. Sigmund Freud, *The Interpretation of Dreams*, trans. James Strachey (New York: Basic Books, 1958), p. 195.

2. Ibid., p. 196.

3. Ibid., p. 197.

4. Ibid., p. 197.

5. Ernest Jones, *The Life and Work of Sigmund Freud*, vol. 1, *The Formative Years and the Great Discoveries, 1856–1900* (New York: Basic Books, 1953), pp. 22, 24.

6. Sigmund Freud, *The Pyschopathology of Everyday Life*, trans. A. A. Brill (London: Ernest Benn, 1948), pp. 136–37.

7. Ibid., pp. 176, 178.

8. *The Letters of Sigmund Freud*, ed. Ernst L. Freud, trans. Tania Stern and James Stern (New York: Basic Books, 1960), pp. 3–4.

9. Jones, *Life and Work*, 1, p. 177.

10. Sigmund Freud, *The Origins of Psychoanalysis: Letters, Drafts, and Notes to Wilhelm Fliess, 1887–1902*, ed. Marie Bonaparte, Anna Freud, and Ernst Kris, trans. Eric Mosbacher and James Strachey (Garden City, N.Y.: Doubleday, 1957), p. 226.

11. See Aristotle, *The Poetics*, trans. W. Hamilton Fyfe (Cambridge: Harvard University Press, 1939), p. 57.

12. Freud, *Origins of Psychoanalysis*, p. 227.

13. Ibid., p. 232.

14. *Oedipus Rex*, trans. F. Storr, vol. 1 of *Sophocles* (Cambridge: Harvard University Press, 1951), p. 75, ll. 800–13; and *Oedipus the King*, trans. David Grene, in *Sophocles I*, eds. David Grene and Richard Lattimore (Chicago: The University of Chicago Press, 1954–57), pp. 45, 46, ll. 800–13. I have taken the liberty of conflating, here and there, words from Storr's translation with those of Grene.

15. Richard Jebb, ed., *The Oedipus Tyrannus of Sophocles* (Cambridge: Cambridge University Press, 1912), p. 89 (notes to lines 804–12, 808, and 809).

16. Aristotle, *Poetics*, p. 56.

17. C. M. Bowra, *Sophoclean Tragedy* (New York: Oxford University Press, 1944), p. 193.
18. Freud, *Psychopathology*, pp. 136–37.
19. Bowra, *Sophoclean Tragedy*, p. 193.
20. Freud, *Origins of Psychoanalysis*, p. 336.
21. Freud, *Letters*, ed. Freud, pp. 78–79.
22. Sigmund Freud, *Moses and Monotheism*, trans. Katherine Jones (New York: Knopf, 1939), pp. 45–46.
23. *Encyclopedia Britannica*, 11th ed., s.v. "Hannibal," p. 920, col. 2.
24. Ibid., s.v. "Lake Trasimene." I thank Professor Peter Berger for pointing out to me these parallels.
25. In Karl Abraham, *Clinical Papers and Essays on Psycho-Analysis*, ed. Hilda C. Abraham (London: Hogarth Press, 1955), pp. 72, 74.
26. Sigmund Freud, in Hilda C. Abraham and Ernst L. Freud, eds., *A Psycho-Analytic Dialogue: The Letters of Sigmund Freud and Karl Abraham*, trans. Bernard Marsh and Hilda C. Abraham (New York: Basic Books, 1965), p. 326.
27. Hannah Arendt, "Introduction" to *Illuminations*, by Walter Benjamin, trans. Harry Zohn, ed. Hannah Arendt (New York: Harcourt, Brace & World, 1968), p. 26.

Chapter 5 The Guilt of Shame

1. Peter L. Berger, "Excursus: Alternation and Biography," in *An Invitation to Sociology: A Humanistic Perspective* (Garden City, N.Y.: Doubleday Anchor, 1963), p. 60.
2. See Helen Merrell Lynd, *On Shame and the Search for Identity* (New York: Harcourt, Brace, 1958).
3. Ibid., pp. 53–54.
4. Ibid.
5. Ibid., p. 55.
6. Ibid., pp. 55–56.
7. See Kurt Riezler, "Comment on the Social Psychology of Shame," *American Journal of Sociology* 48, no. 4 (January 1943). I owe this reference to Lynd, *On Shame*.
8. Norman Podhoretz, *Making It* (New York: Random House, 1967), p. 27.
9. Lynd, *On Shame*, p. 59.
10. Regarding envy, see Helmut Schoeck, *Envy: A Theory of Social Behavior*, trans. Michael Glenny and Betty Ross (New York: Harcourt, Brace & World, 1969).
11. Lynd, *On Shame*, p. 58.
12. Ibid., p. 225.
13. Ibid., p. 58.
14. Leslie Fiedler, "The Jew in the American Novel," in *The Collected Essays of Leslie Fiedler*, vol. 2 (New York: Stein and Day, 1971), p. 76.
15. Ibid., p. 83.
16. Ibid.
17. Hannah Arendt, *Rahel Varnhagen: The Life of a Jewess* (London: East and West Library, 1957), p. 180.

Chapter 6 The Ancient *Judenfrage*

1. Sigmund Freud, *Collected Papers, Papers on Metapsychology, Papers on Applied Psycho-Analysis*, trans. Joan Riviere (New York: Basic Books, 1959), 4: 215 (written 1912).
2. Ibid.
3. Max Weber, "Judaism, Christianity, and the Socio-Economic Order," in *The Sociology of Religion*, trans. Ephraim Fischoff (Boston: Beacon Press, 1963), p. 257.

4. Yvor Winters, "*Maule's Well,* or Henry James and the Relation of Morals to Manners," in *In Defense of Reason* (Denver: University of Denver Press, 1947), p. 301.

5. Weber, "Judaism, Christianity, and the Socio-Economic Order," pp. 257, 258.

6. Ibid., p. 258.

7. Ernest van den Haag, *The Jewish Mystique* (New York: Stein & Day, 1969), p. 153.

8. Weber, "Judaism, Christianity, and the Socio-Economic Order," p. 252.

9. Jerome Weidman, *I Can Get It for You Wholesale* (New York: Modern Library, 1937), p. 236.

Chapter 7 Sexuality and Christianity: The Refining Process

1. Karl Jaspers, *Nietzsche: An Introduction to the Understanding of His Philosophical Activity,* trans. Charles F. Wallraff and Frederick J. Schmitz (Tucson: University of Arizona Press, 1965), p. 137.

2. Quoted in ibid., p. 137.

3. Sigmund Freud, "The Most Prevalent Form of Degradation in Erotic Life," in *Collected Papers,* vol. 4, *Papers on Metapsychology and Papers on Applied Psycho-Analysis,* trans. Joan Riviere (New York: Basic Books, 1959), p. 213.

4. Emil Ludwig, *Doctor Freud: An Analysis and a Warning* (New York: *Hellman,* Williams, 1947), p. 308.

5. Max Weber, *The Sociology of Religion,* trans. Ephraim Fischoff (Boston: Beacon Press, 1963), pp. 256, 257.

6. Theodor Reik, *Jewish Wit* (New York: Gamut Press, 1962), p. 99.

7. Ibid., p. 77.

8. Ibid., p. 100.

9. Ernest van den Haag, *The Jewish Mystique* (New York: Stein & Day, 1969), p. 150.

10. Ibid.

11. Leslie Fiedler, "Zion as Eros," in *The Jew in the American Novel,* Herzl Institute Pamphlet no. 10 (New York, 1959), p. 20.

12. Ben Hecht, *A Jew in Love* (New York: Convici-Friede, 1931), p. 4.

13. Ibid., p. 17.

14. Quoted in *Yiddish Proverbs,* ed. Hanan J. Ayalti, trans. Isidore Goldstick (New York: Schocken, 1949), pp. 120–21.

15. Richard A. Koenigsberg, "Culture and Unconscious Fantasy: Observations of Courtly Love," *Psychoanalytic Review* 54, no. 1 (Spring 1967): 46, 49.

16. Leslie Fiedler, *Being Busted* (New York: Stein & Day, 1970), p. 22.

17. Leslie Fiedler, *Love and Death in the American Novel,* rev. ed. (New York: Stein & Day, 1966), p. 49.

18. van den Haag, *Jewish Mystique,* pp. 149, 152.

19. Peter M. Blau, *Exchange and Power in Social Life* (New York: Wiley, 1964), pp. 76–85.

20. See *The Letters of Sigmund Freud,* ed. Ernst L. Freud, trans. Tania Stern and James Stern (New York: Basic Books, 1960), pp. 7–216.

21. Herbert W. Richardson, *Toward an American Theology* (New York: Harper & Row, 1967), p. 20.

22. Herbert Moller, "The Social Causation of the Courtly Love Complex," in *Sociology and History: Theory and Research,* ed. Werner J. Cahnman and Alvin Boskoff (Glencoe, Ill.: Free Press, 1964), p. 484.

23. Karl Löwith, "Hegel and the Christian Religion," in *Nature, History, and Existentialism and Other Essays in the Philosophy of History,* ed. Arnold Levison (Evanston, Ill.: Northwestern University Press, 1966), p. 191.

Chapter 8 Rooting Out Roundaboutness

1. Cynthia Ozick, "Envy; or, Yiddish in America," in *The Pagan Rabbi and Other Stories* (New York: Knopf, 1971), p. 45.

2. Ibid., p. 69.

3. Ibid., p. 82.

4. Susan Taubes, "The Riddle Of Simone Weil," *Exodus* 1, no. 1 (Spring 1959): 66.

5. Sigmund Freud, *An Autobiographical Study*, trans. James Strachey (New York: Norton, 1963), p. 55.

6. Susan Taubes, *Divorcing* (New York: Random House, 1969), pp. 195–96.

7. Henry James, preface to *The American*, reprinted in *The Art of the Novel: Critical Prefaces*, ed. Richard P. Blackmur (New York: Scribner's, 1934), p. 32.

8. See Georg Simmel, *The Sociology of Georg Simmel*, ed. Kurt Wolff (Glencoe, Ill.: Free Press, 1950), pp. 321, 325.

9. Freud, *An Autobiographical Study*, p. 76.

Chapter 9 The Temptation Scene

1. Susan Sontag, "Transmitting His Master's Voice," review of *A Psycho-Analytic Dialogue*, *Book Week*, April 3, 1966, p. 3.

2. Hilda C. Abraham and Ernst L. Freud, eds., *A Psycho-Analytic Dialogue: The Letters of Sigmund Freud and Karl Abraham, 1907–1926*, trans. Bernard Marsh and Hilda C. Abraham (New York: Basic Books, 1965), p. vii.

3. Sigmund Freud, in *A Psycho-Analytic Dialogue*, ed. Abraham and Freud, p. 34.

4. Sontag, "Transmitting His Master's Voice," p. 3.

5. Karl Abraham, in *A Psycho-Analytic Dialogue*, ed. Abraham and Freud, p. 36.

6. Ibid., p. 44.

7. Ibid., p. 46 (letter of July 20, 1908).

8. Ibid., p. 46 (letter of July 23, 1908).

9. Cited in Hannah Arendt, "To Save the Jewish Homeland," *Commentary* 5, no. 5 (May 1948): 401. Theodor Herzl, *The Jewish State*, trans. I. M. Lask (Tel Aviv: M. Newman, 1954), p. 53.

10. David Bakan, *Sigmund Freud and the Jewish Mystical Tradition* (New York: Schocken, 1965), p. 49.

11. Jacob Meitlis, "The Last Days of Sigmund Freud," *Jewish Frontier* 18, no. 9 (September 1951): 21.

12. Karl Abraham, in *A Psycho-Analytic Dialogue*, ed. Abraham and Freud, p. 49.

13. Ibid., p. 54.

14. Sigmund Freud, in *Psychoanalysis and Faith: The Letters of Sigmund Freud and Oskar Pfister*, ed. Heinrich Meng and Ernst L. Freud, trans. Eric Mosbacher (New York: Basic Books, 1963), p. 140.

15. Sigmund Freud, in *A Psycho-Analytic Dialogue*, ed. Abraham and Freud, p. 54.

16. Sigmund Freud, in *Psychoanalysis and Faith*, ed. Meng and Freud, p. 16.

17. Stefan Zweig, *Mental Healers: Franz Anton Mesmer, Mary Baker Eddy, Sigmund Freud*, trans. Eden Paul and Cedar Paul (New York: Viking Press, 1932), p. 331.

18. Sigmund Freud, *The Future of an Illusion*, trans. W. D. Robson-Scott (Garden City, N.Y.: Doubleday, 1957), p. 56.

19. Martin Freud, *Sigmund Freud: Man and Father* (New York: Vanguard, 1958), p. 19.

20. Quoted in Ernest Jones, *The Life and Work of Sigmund Freud*, vol. 3, *The Last Phase, 1919–1939* (New York: Basic Books, 1957), p. 208.

21. Jones, *Life and Work*, vol. 2, *Years of Maturity, 1901–1919* (1955), p. 105.

22. Maggie Scarf, "The Man Who Gave Us 'Inferiority Complex,' 'Compensation,' 'Overcompensation,' 'Aggressive Drive,' and 'Style of Life,'" *New York Times Magazine*, February 28, 1971, p. 47.

23. Sigmund Freud, in *A Psycho-Analytic Dialogue*, ed. Abraham and Freud, p. 64.

24. Ibid., p. 92.

25. J. W. Burrow, "Friction on a Rare Frontier," review of *Freud and His Early Circle*, by Vincent Brome, *Saturday Review*, June 1, 1968, p. 31.

26. Sigmund Freud, in *A Psycho-Analytic Dialogue*, ed. Abraham and Freud, p. 151.

27. Ibid., p. 186.

28. Karl Löwith, *From Hegel to Nietzsche: The Revolution in Nineteenth-Century Thought* (Garden City, N.Y.: Doubleday, 1967), p. 77.

29. Robert K. Merton, *European Journal of Sociology* 4, no. 4 (1963): 259.

30. Howard Brotz, "The Position of the Jews in English Society," in *Class, Status, and Power*, ed. Reinhard Bendix and S. M. Lipset, 2nd ed. (New York: Free Press, 1966), p. 350.

Chapter 10 Freud's Jewishness

1. Philip Rieff, "Freud's Jewishness," *Chicago Jewish Forum* 13, no. 3 (Spring 1955): 163.

2. Ibid., p. 164.

3. Ibid., pp. 162, 170.

4. See Peter L. Berger, "Charisma and Religious Innovation: The Social Location of Israelite Prophecy," *American Sociological Review* 28, no. 6 (December 1963): 940–50.

5. Earl A. Grollman, *Judaism in Sigmund Freud's World* (New York: Bloch, 1965), p. 41.

6. Max Weber, *Ancient Judaism*, trans. Hans H. Gerth and Don Martindale (New York: Free Press, 1952), p. 419.

7. Max Weber, *The Sociology of Religion*, trans. Ephraim Fischoff, introduction by Talcott Parsons (Boston: Beacon Press, 1963), p. 109.

8. Daniel Bell, "Reflections on Jewish Identity," *Commentary* 31, no. 6 (June 1961): 477. This article is based on a lecture delivered before the Jewish Graduate Society of Columbia University.

9. Jacob L. Talmon, "Uniqueness and Universality of Jewish History: A Mid-Century Revaluation," in *The Unique and the Universal: Some Historical Reflections* (New York: Braziller, 1965), pp. 69–70.

10. Cf. Leon Mayhew, "Ascription in Modern Societies," *Sociological Inquiry* 1, no. 5 (March 1946): 23, 24.

11. Sigmund Freud, "On Being of the B'nai B'rith," reprinted in *Commentary* (March 1946): 23–24.

12. Sigmund Freud, *Collected Papers*, vol. 4, *Papers on Metapsychology and Papers on Applied Psycho-Analysis*, trans. Joan Riviere (New York: Basic Books, 1959), pp. 368–407.

13. Gerhard Lenski, *The Religious Factor: A Sociological Study of Religion's Impact on Politics, Economics, and Family Life* (Garden City, N.Y.: Doubleday, Anchor, 1961), p. 79.

14. George Steiner, "Inner Lights," *New Yorker*, October 22, 1973, p. 152.

15. James S. Coleman, "Social Cleavage and Religious Conflict," *Journal of Social Issues* 12, no. 3 (1956): 46.

16. Nathan Rotenstreich, "Emancipation and Its Aftermath," in *The Future of the Jewish Community in America*, ed. David Sidorsky (New York: Basic Books, 1973), p. 56.

Chapter 11 The Locus of Freud's Originality

1. Steven Marcus, "Freud and Dora: Story, History, Case History," *Partisan Review* 41, no. 1 (1974): 102.

2. Sigmund Freud, *Collected Papers,* vol. 5, *Miscellaneous Papers, 1888–1938,* trans. Joan Riviere (New York: Basic Books, 1959), pp. 173–74.

3. Ibid., p. 170.

4. Ibid., p. 173.

5. Ibid.

6. Ernest Jones, *The Life and Work of Sigmund Freud,* vol. 1, *The Formative Years and the Great Discoveries, 1856–1900* (New York: Basic Books, 1953), p. 249.

7. Sigmund Freud, *Collected Papers,* 1: 296.

8. Ibid., p. 293.

9. Ibid., p. 294.

10. Ibid., pp. 294–95.

11. Ibid., p. 295.

12. Susan Sontag, "Transmitting His Master's Voice," review of *A Psycho-Analytic Dialogue: The Letters of Sigmund Freud and Karl Abraham,* ed. Hilda C. Abraham and Ernest L. Freud, *Book Week,* April 3, 1966, p. 13.

13. Sigmund Freud, *Collected Papers,* vol. 1, *Early Papers: On the History of the Psycho-Analytic Movement,* p. 296.

14. Wilhelm Fliess, in *The Origins of Psychoanalysis: Letters, Drafts, and Notes to Wilhelm Fliess, 1887–1902,* ed. Marie Bonaparte, Anna Freud, and Ernst Kris, trans. Eric Mosbacher and James Strachey (Garden City, N.Y.: Doubleday, 1957), p. 75.

15. Ibid., p. 85.

16. Ibid.

17. Ibid., p. 134.

18. Ibid., p. 163.

19. Ibid., p. 163, n. 167.

20. Ibid., p. 165.

21. Sigmund Freud, in *Psychoanalysis and Faith: The Letters of Sigmund Freud and Oskar Pfister,* ed. Heinrich Meng and Ernst L. Freud, trans. Eric Mosbacher (New York: Basic Books, 1963), pp. 61–62.

22. Ibid., p. 38.

23. Ibid., p. 74.

24. Ernest Jones, *The Life and Work of Sigmund Freud,* vol. 3, *The Last Phase, 1919–1939* (New York: Basic Books, 1957), p. 100.

25. Robert K. Merton, "The Ambivalence of Scientists" (chapter 18), in *The Sociology of Science: Theoretical and Empirical Investigations,* ed. (with an introduction) Norman W. Storer (Chicago: University of Chicago Press, 1973), p. 386.

26. Ibid., pp. 386–87.

27. Ibid., p. 399.

28. Sigmund Freud, in *Psychoanalysis and Faith,* ed. Meng and Freud, p. 63.

29. Quoted in Robert K. Merton, *Social Theory and Social Structure,* rev. ed. (Glencoe, Ill.: Free Press, 1957), p. 3.

30. Harold Bloom, *The Anxiety of Influence: A Theory of Poetry* (New York: Oxford University Press, 1973), p. 64.

31. Norman Mailer, "Responses & Reactions VI," *Commentary* 36, no. 4 (October 1963): 320.

32. Merton, *Sociology of Science,* p. 400.

33. Dan Jacobson, *The Beginners* (New York: Macmillan, 1966).

34. Sigmund Freud, in *Psychoanalysis and Faith,* ed. Meng and Freud, p. 38.

35. Michael Wood, Review of *Dickens from Pickwick to Domby,* by Steven Marcus, *Daily Spectator* (Columbia University) supplement, May 4, 1965, p. s-1.

36. See, e.g., Judd Teller, who entitles his chapter on Jewish Emancipation "Jewry's Desegregation," in *The Jews: Biography of a People* (New York: Bantam, 1966), pp. 186 ff.

37. The story of this psychologization is told by Hannah Arendt in *The Origins of Totalitarianism* (New York: Harcourt, Brace, 1951), pp. 66 ff., 80–88.

38. Peter L. Berger, *The Sacred Canopy: Elements of a Sociological Theory of Religion* (Garden City, N.Y.: Doubleday, 1967), p. 192, n. 21. The use I make of Dr. Berger's ideas here (including, of course, the bracketed interpolations) is strictly my own, and he is entirely without responsibility for my interpretation.

Chapter 12 Excursus: Modernization and the Emergence of Social Appearance

1. Philip Rieff, ed., "Introduction" to Sigmund Freud, *The History of the Psychoanalytic Movement and Other Papers* (New York: Collier, 1963), p. 10.

2. Sigmund Freud, in *Psychoanalysis and Faith: The Letters of Sigmund Freud and Oskar Pfister*, ed. Heinrich Meng and Ernst L. Freud, trans. Eric Mosbacher (New York: Basic Books, 1963), p. 82.

3. Ibid., p. 123.

4. Ibid., p. 33.

5. Sigmund Freud, in *A Psycho-Analytic Dialogue: The Letters of Sigmund Freud and Karl Abraham, 1907–1926*, ed. Hilda C. Abraham and Ernst L. Freud, trans. Bernard Marsh and Hilda C. Abraham (New York: Basic Books, 1965), p. 52.

6. I owe this phrase to Professor Benjamin Nelson, who uses it in a very different sense.

7. Karl Abraham, in *A Psycho-Analytic Dialogue*, ed. Abraham and Freud, p. 56.

8. *Solomon Maimon: An Autobiography*, ed. Moses Hadas (New York: Schocken, 1967), p. 76.

9. Martin Freud, *Sigmund Freud: Man and Father* (New York: Vanguard, 1958), p. 11.

10. Philip Rieff, *Freud: The Mind of the Moralist* (New York: Viking Press, 1959), pp. 317, 332.

11. Ernest Jones, *The Life and Work of Sigmund Freud*, vol. 1, *The Formative Years and the Great Discoveries, 1856–1900* (New York: Basic Books, 1953), p. 22.

12. Peter L. Berger, *The Sacred Canopy: Elements of a Sociological Theory of Religion* (Garden City, N.Y.: Doubleday, 1967), pp. 18; 192, n. 21. I have conflated two sentences here.

13. Ibid., p. 192, n. 21.

14. See Emile Durkheim, "The Dualism of Human Nature and Its Social Conditions," trans. Charles Blend, in *Essays on Sociology and Philosophy*, ed. Kurt H. Wolff (New York: Harper Torchbook, 1964), pp. 325–40.

15. Stanley Diamond, "Kibbutz and Shtetl: The History of an Idea," *Social Problems* 5, no. 2 (Fall 1957): 81n.

Chapter 13 Reich and Later Variations

1. Donald Barr, "What Did We Do Wrong?" *New York Times Magazine*, November 26, 1967, p. 134. Reprinted in Barr's *Who Pushed Humpty Dumpty? Dilemmas in American Education Today* (New York: Atheneum, 1971), p. 28.

2. Philip Rieff "Introduction" to Sigmund Freud, *Delusion and Dream and Other Essays*, ed. Philip Rieff (Boston: Beacon Press, 1956), p. 20.

3. See Anna Freud, *The Ego and the Mechanisms of Defense*, trans. Cecil Baines (New York: International Universities Press, 1946).

4. Ibid., p. 68.

5. Marianne Moore, "Poetry," *Collected Poems of Marianne Moore* (New York: Macmillan, 1951).

6. I owe this analogy—of the psychoanalyst as "double agent"—to Professor Benjamin Nelson of the New School for Social Research in New York City. Of course, I have put it to uses other than those for which he fashioned it.

7. Peter Gay, "Weimar Culture: The Outsider as Insider," in *Perspectives in American History*, ed. Donald Fleming and Bernard Bailyn (Cambridge, Mass.: Charles Warren Center for Studies in American History, 1968), 2: 68.

8. See Martin Grotjahn, "A Letter by Sigmund Freud with Recollections of His Adolescence," *Journal of American Psychoanalytic Association* 4 (October 1956): 644–52.

9. Ernest Jones, *The Life and Work of Sigmund Freud,* vol. 3, *The Last Phase, 1919–1939* (New York: Basic Books, 1957), p. 191.

10. "Wilhelm Reich: The Psychologist as Revolutionary," *New York Times Magazine,* April 18, 1971, p. 26.

11. See Paul A. Robinson, *The Freudian Left: Wilhelm Reich, Geza Roheim, Herbert Marcuse* (New York: Harper & Row, 1969).

12. Charles Reich, *The Greening of America* (New York: Bantam, 1971), p. 162.

13. A. S. Neill, "The Man Reich," in *Wilhelm Reich,* ed. Paul Ritter (Nottingham, England: Ritter Press, 1958), p. 22.

14. Quoted in Max Brod, *Franz Kafka: A Biography,* 2nd ed., trans. G. Humphreys Roberts and Richard Winston (New York: Schocken, 1960), p. 142.

15. Wilhelm Reich, *Character-Analysis: Principles and Technique. For Psychoanalysts in Practice and Training,* trans. Theodore P. Wolfe (New York: Orgone Institute Press, 1945), p. 29.

16. Ibid., pp. 29–30.

17. Ibid., p. 30.

18. Ibid.

19. Ibid., p. 32.

20. Ibid.

21. Ibid., p. 45.

22. Ibid., p. 46.

23. Ibid., p. 47.

24. George Steiner, "The Language Animal," in *Extraterritorial: Papers on Literature and the Language Revolution* (New York: Atheneum, 1971), p. 84.

25. "Fascist Irrationalism," in *The Function of the Orgasm: Sex-Economic Problems of Biological Energy* (New York: Farrar, Straus & Giroux, 1961), p. 204. The original American edition, translated by Theodore P. Wolfe, was published in 1942.

26. Ibid., p. 205.

27. Ibid., pp. 206–7.

28. Wilhelm Reich, "Preface to the Third Edition," *The Mass Psychology of Fascism,* trans. Vincent R. Carfagno (New York: Farrar, Strauss & Giroux, 1970), pp. xiii–xiv.

29. See, e.g., Erving Goffman, *Behavior in Public Places: Notes on the Social Organization of Gatherings* (New York: Free Press, 1969) and Erving Goffman, *Relations in Public* (New York: Basic Books, 1972).

30. Philip Rieff, "The World of Wilhelm Reich," *Commentary* 38, no. 3 (September 1964): 51.

31. Ibid.

32. Ibid., p. 51.

33. Ibid., p. 54.

34. Jacqueline Susann, *Valley of the Dolls* (New York: Geis, 1966).

35. Stanley Elkin, "The Dick Gibson Show," *Dutton Review,* no. 1 (1970): 192.

36. Isaac Rosenfeld, *Passage from Home* (Cleveland: World, 1946), p. 164.

37. Saul Bellow, "Foreword" to Isaac Rosenfeld, *An Age of Enormity: Life and Writing in the Forties and Fifties,* ed. Theodore Solotaroff (Cleveland: World Publishing Co., 1962), p. 14.

38. Frederick S. Perls, *Gestalt Therapy Verbatim,* ed. John O. Stevens (Lafayette, Cal.: Real People Press, 1969), p. 3.

39. Ibid., p. 23.

40. Ibid., pp. 30, 35, 44.

41. Ibid., p. 55.

42. Ibid., p. 56.

43. Ibid., p. 74.

44. Ibid., pp. 232–33.

45. See Arthur Janov, *The Primal Scream: Primal Therapy—The Cure for Neurosis* (New York: Putnam's, 1970).

46. Robert Kotlowitz, *Somewhere Else* (New York: Charterhouse, 1972), pp. 181–82.

Chapter 14 Father and Son: Marx versus Marx

1. Karl Marx, in *The Unknown Karl Marx: Documents Concerning Marx,* ed. and trans. Robert Payne (New York: New York University Press, 1971), pp. 42, 43.

2. Friedrich Hegel, *On Christianity: Early Theological Writings,* trans. T. M. Knox and Richard Kroner (New York: Harper Torchbooks, 1961).

3. Karl Marx, in *The Unknown Karl Marx,* ed. Payne, pp. 39, 41.

4. This is a chapter title in Robert Payne, *Marx* (New York: Simon & Schuster, 1968), pp. 42–55.

5. Judd Teller, *The Jews: Biography of a People* (New York: Bantam, 1966), p. 218.

6. Quoted in Payne, *Marx,* pp. 53–54.

Chapter 15 Censorship: Persecution and the Art of Writing

1. Sigmund Freud, *The Interpretation of Dreams,* trans. James Strachey (New York: Basic Books, 1958), p. 142.

2. Karl Marx, "Comments on the Latest Prussian Censorship Instruction," in *Writings of the Young Marx on Philosophy and Society,* ed. and trans. Loyd D. Easton and Kurt H. Guddat (Garden City, N.Y.: Doubleday, Anchor, 1967), p. 70.

3. Ibid., pp. 70–71.

4. Ibid., p. 71.

5. Ibid., pp. 71, 72.

6. Ibid., pp. 67–68.

7. Ibid., p. 72.

8. Ibid., pp. 72–73.

9. Ibid., p. 78.

10. Norman Podhoretz, "Faulkner in the 50's," in *Doings and Undoings: The Fifties and After in American Writing* (New York: Farrar, Straus, 1964), p. 15.

11. Marx, "Prussian Censorship Instruction," p. 73.

12. Ibid., p. 73.

13. Irving Howe and Lewis Coser, with the assistance of Julius Jacobson, *The American Communist Party, A Critical History,* 2nd ed. (New York: Praeger, 1962), p. 284.

14. Karl Löwith, "Hegel and the Christian Religion," in *Nature, History, and Existentialism and Other Essays in the Philosophy of History,* ed. Arnold Levison (Evanston, Ill.: Northwestern University Press, 1966), p. 191.

15. Ben Halpern, *Jews and Blacks: The Classic American Minorities* (New York: Herder and Herder, 1971), p. 83.

16. Jacob Katz, "Judaism and Jewry in the Nineteenth Century," *Cahiers d'histoire mondiale* 4, no. 4 (1958): 884.

17. Marx, "Prussian Censorship Instruction," p. 82.

18. Ibid., p. 83.

19. Ibid., pp. 84, 86.

20. Ibid., pp. 90, 91.

21. H. R. Trevor-Roper, "Nazi Bureaucrats and Jewish Leaders," *Commentary* 33, no. 4 (April 1962): 353.

22. *Webster's New World Dictionary* (College Edition, 1958).

23. Marx, "Prussian Censorship Instruction," p. 91.

24. "Religion, Free Press, and Philosophy," in Easton and Guddat, *Writings of the Young Marx,* p. 112. (The original appeared in July 1842.)

25. Ibid., p. 121.

26. Ibid., pp. 117, 124, 123.

27. Karl Marx, "Communism and the Augsburg *Allgemeine Zeitung,*" in Easton and Guddat, eds., *Writings of the Young Marx,* p. 131.

28. Ibid., p. 132.

29. Ibid., p. 132.

30. Seymour Leventman, "The Faith Defended" (letter to the editor), *Commentary* 37, no. 4 (April 1964): 6.

31. Hannah Arendt, "'The Formidable Dr. Robinson': A Reply," *New York Review of Books,* January 20, 1966, p. 29.

32. Quoted by Easton and Guddat, eds., *Writings of the Young Marx,* p. 143.

33. Quoted in Robert Payne, *Marx* (New York: Simon & Schuster, 1968), p. 86.

34. Quoted in Isaiah Berlin, *Karl Marx: His Life and Environment* (London: Oxford University Press, 1948), p. 80.

35. Leo Strauss, "On a Forgotten Kind of Writing," in *What Is Political Philosophy? and Other Studies* (New York: Free Press, 1959), pp. 221 ff.

36. Joseph O'Malley, ed., "Introduction" to Karl Marx, *Critique of Hegel's "Philosophy of Right,"* trans. Annette Jolin and Joseph O'Malley (Cambridge: At the University Press, 1970), p. xxv, n. 1.

37. Max Horkheimer and Theodor W. Adorno, "Elements of Anti-Semitism," in *Dialectic of Englightenment,* trans. John Cumming (New York: Herder and Herder, 1972), p. 197.

38. See O'Malley, "Introduction" to Marx, *Critique of Hegel's "Philosophy of Right,"* p. xi.

39. Karl Marx, "On the Jewish Question," in Easton and Guddat, eds., *Writings of the Young Marx,* pp. 243, 247.

40. Léon Poliakov, "Anti-Semitism and Christian Teaching," *Midstream* 12, no. 3 (March 1966): 13.

41. Halpern, *Jews and Blacks,* p. 109.

42. Edmund Silberner, "Ferdinand Lassalle: From Maccabeism to Jewish Anti-Semitism," *Hebrew Union College Annual* 24 (Cincinnati: 1952–1953): 185, n. 131.

43. See Robert Weltsch, introduction to *Leo Baeck Institute Year Book IV: 1959* (London: East and West Library, 1959), p. xii, n. 7a.

44. See Silberner, "Ferdinand Lassalle."

45. Quoted in ibid., p. 163.

46. Berlin, *Karl Marx,* p. 93.

47. Leo Strauss, *The Political Philosophy of Hobbes: Its Basis and Genesis* (Chicago: University of Chicago Press, 1952), p. 170.

48. Karl Löwith, *From Hegel to Nietzsche: The Revolution in Nineteenth-Century Thought* (Garden City, N.Y.: Doubleday, Anchor, 1967), pp. 232–59. The phrase is Löwith's title for part 2, section 1 of his work.

Chapter 16 The Marxian *Urszene*: Property and Propriety

1. Karl Marx, "On the Jewish Question," in *Writings of the Young Marx on Philosophy and Society,* ed. and trans. Loyd D. Easton and Kurt M. Guddat (Garden City, N.Y.: Doubleday Anchor, 1967), p. 243.

2. Karl Löwith, *Nature, History, and Existentialism and Other Essays in the Philosophy of History,* ed. Arnold Levison (Evanston, Ill.: Northwestern University Press, 1966), p. 198.

3. Gertrude Himmelfarb, "Discussion: The 10th American-Israel Dialogue, Part I," *Congress Bi-Weekly,* March 30, 1973, pp. 29, 30.

4. Hayim Greenberg, "Golus-Jew," trans. Shlomo Katz, in *Voices from the Yiddish: Essays, Memoirs, Diaries,* Irving Howe and Eliezer Greenberg, eds. (Ann Arbor: University of Michigan Press, 1972), pp. 270–75.

5. Jacob Katz, chapter 12, "Profile of Emancipated Jewry," in *Out of the Ghetto: The Social Background of Jewish Emancipation, 1770–1870* (Cambridge: Harvard University Press, 1973), p. 202.

6. Helmut D. Schmidt, "Anti-Western and Anti-Jewish Tradition in German Historical Thought," *Leo Baeck Institute Year Book: 1959* (London: East and West Library, 1959), p. 46.

7. Ibid., p. 46.

8. Hannah Arendt, *The Origins of Totalitarianism* (New York: Harcourt, Brace, 1951), p. 64.

9. Helene Deutsch, *Confrontations with Myself: An Epilogue* (New York: Norton, 1973), p. 62.

10. Ibid., p. 84.

11. Ibid., pp. 98, 101.

12. Hayim Zhitlowsky, "The Jewish Factor in My Socialism," trans. Lucy S. Dawidowicz in *Voices from the Yiddish: Essays, Memoirs, Diaries,* ed. Irving Howe and Eliezer Greenberg (Ann Arbor: University of Michigan Press, 1972), pp. 128–29.

13. Ibid., p. 129.

14. Ibid., p. 130.

15. Beatrice Potter, chapter 4, "The Jewish Community," in *Life and Labor of the People in London,* vol. 3, *First Series: Poverty,* ed. Charles Booth (London: Macmillan, 1902), p. 171.

16. Ibid., p. 191.

17. Ibid., pp. 191–92.

18. Karl Marx, *The Poverty of Philosophy* (New York: International Publishers, 1963), pp. 49, 51.

19. Maurice Samuel, *You Gentiles* (New York: Harcourt, Brace, 1924), p. 49.

20. Jacob A. Riis, *How the Other Half Lives: Studies Among the Tenements of New York* (New York: Dover, 1971), pp. 86, 100. (Originally published by Charles Scribner's Sons in 1890.)

21. Walter Lippmann, "Public Opinion and the American Jew," *American Hebrew,* April 14, 1922, p. 575.

22. Katz, *Out of the Ghetto,* p. 127.

Chapter 17 Marx and the Euphemists

1. Hannah Arendt, *The Origins of Totalitarianism* (New York: Harcourt, Brace, 1951), p. 12, n. 1.

2. Jacob Katz, "The Term 'Jewish Emancipation': Its Origin and Historical Impact," in *Studies in Nineteenth-Century Jewish Intellectual History,* ed. Alexander Altmann (Cambridge: Harvard University Press, 1964), p. 13.

3. Ibid., p. 15, n. 57.

4. Ibid., p. 15.

5. Ibid.

6. Sigmund Freud, "One of the Difficulties of Psycho-Analysis," in *Collected Papers,* vol. 4, *Papers on Metapsychology and Papers on Applied Psycho-Analysis,* ed. Ernest Jones, trans. Joan Riviere (New York: Basic Books, 1959), p. 350.

7. Solomon Maimon, *An Autobiography,* trans. J. Clark Murray (1888), ed. Moses Hadas (New York: Schocken, 1967), p. 7.

8. Ibid., pp. 7–8.

9. Margaret Mead, "Foreword" to Mark Zborowski and Elizabeth Herzog, *Life Is with People: The Culture of the Shtetl* (New York: Schocken, 1962), p. 19.

10. Ben Halpern, *Jews and Blacks: The Classic American Minorities* (New York: Herder and Herder, 1971), p. 83.

11. Salo Baron, "New Horizons in Jewish History," in *Freedom and Reason: Studies in Philosophy and Jewish Culture,* eds. Salo Baron, Ernest Nagel, and Koppel S. Pinson (Glencoe, Ill.: Free Press, 1951), p. 342.

12. Jacob Katz, "The Term 'Jewish Emancipation,' " p. 13.

13. Halpern, *Jews and Blacks,* pp. 125–26.

14. Antonina Vallentin, *Mirabeau* (New York: Viking Press, 1948), p. 233.

15. Katz, "The Term 'Jewish Emancipation,' " p. 16.

16. Isaiah Berlin, *Jewish Slavery and Emancipation,* pamphlet no. 13 (New York: Herzl Press, 1961).

17. Renate Mayntz, ed., Introduction to *On Social Order and Mass Society: Selected Papers,* by Theodor Geiger, trans. Robert E. Peck (Chicago: University of Chicago Press, 1969), p. 35.

18. Sigmund Freud, " 'Civilized' Sexual Morality and Modern Nervousness," in *Collected Papers,* vol. 2, *Clinical Papers and Papers on Technique,* p. 77.

19. Alex Bein, *Theodore Herzl: A Biography,* trans. Maurice Samuel (New York: Atheneum, 1970), p. 115.

20. Hannah Arendt, *The Origins of Totalitarianism* (New York: Harcourt, Brace, 1951), p. 328.

Chapter 18 Claude Lévi-Strauss: the rude, the crude, the nude, and *The Origin of Table Manners*

1. See Peter L. Berger, Brigitte Berger, and Hansfried Kellner, *The Homeless Mind: Modernization and Consciousness* (New York: Random House, 1973), p. 161.

2. Claude Lévi-Strauss, *Tristes tropiques,* trans. John Russell (New York: Atheneum, 1961; originally published 1955), p. 55.

3. Ibid., p. 43.

4. Claude Lévi-Strauss, *The Raw and the Cooked: Introduction to a Science of Mythology, I,* trans. John Weightman and Doreen Weightman (New York: Harper Torchbooks, 1969).

5. Lévi-Strauss, *Tristes tropique,* pp. 56, 62.

6. Ibid., p. 61.

7. Talcott Parsons, *The Structure of Social Action: A Study in Social Theory with Special Reference to a Group of Recent European Writers* (Glencoe, Ill.: Free Press, 1949; originally published 1937), p. 110.

8. Martin Jay, *The Dialectical Imagination: A History of the Frankfurt School and the Institute of Social Research, 1923–1950* (Boston: Little, Brown, 1973), p. 32.

9. Ibid., pp. 33, 34.

10. Ibid., p. 35.

11. Seymour Martin Lipset and Earl Raab, "The Non-Generation Gap," *Commentary* 50, no. 2 (August 1970): 35–39.

12. Quoted in Jay, *The Dialectical Imagination,* p. 233.

13. Edward Shils, "Introduction" to *Intellectuals and the Powers and Other Essays* (Chicago: University of Chicago Press, 1972), p. xi.

14. See Berger, Berger, and Kellner, *The Homeless Mind,* pp. 185–88.

15. Jay, *The Dialectical Imagination,* p. 35.

16. Stanley Rothman, "International Scholars," *Commentary* 56, no. 5 (November 1973): 88.

17. Lévi-Strauss, *Tristes tropiques,* p. 387.

18. Ibid., pp. 381, 384.

19. Ibid., pp. 389, 390.

20. Claude Lévi-Strauss, *L'Origine des manières de table* (Paris: Librairie Plon, 1968), p. 422. (All quotations from this work are my translations from the French; an English-language edition is yet to appear.)

21. Ibid., p. 422.

22. Ibid.

23. Norman Mailer, *Advertisements for Myself* (New York: Putnam's, 1959), pp. 161, 162.

24. Georges Charbonnier, *Conversations with Claude Lévi-Strauss,* trans. John Weightman and Doreen Weightman (London: Jonathan Cape, 1969), p. 151.

25. A phrase of my old teacher W. K. Wimsatt. See his *Hateful Contraries: Studies in Literature and Criticism* (Louisville: University of Kentucky Press, 1965). I borrow Wimsatt's phrase, not its context.

26. Lévi-Strauss, *L'Origine,* p. 422.

27. See Mary Douglas, chapter 3, "The Abominations of Leviticus," in *Purity and*

Danger: An Analysis of the Concepts of Pollution and Taboo (Baltimore: Penguin, 1966), pp. 54–72.

28. *Tristes tropiques,* p. 215.

29. *L'Origine,* p. 418.

30. Max Weber, *Ancient Judaism,* trans. and ed. Hans H. Gerth and Don Martindale (New York: Free Press, 1952), pp. 410–11.

31. Ernst Käsemann, "The Problem of the Historical Jesus," *Essays on New Testament Themes,* trans. W. J. Montague (London: SCM Press, 1964), p. 39.

32. *L'Origine,* p. 422.

33. Etienne Gilson, *The Philosopher and Theology,* trans. Cécile Gilson (New York: Random House, 1962), p. 32.

34. Émile Durkheim, *Suicide: A Study in Sociology,* ed. George Simpson, trans. John A. Spaulding and George Simpson (New York: Free Press, 1951), p. 160.

35. *Le Suicide* (Paris: Felix Alcan, 1930), p. 160.

36. Sanche de Gramont, "There Are No Superior Societies" (article on Lévi-Strauss), *New York Times Magazine,* January 28, 1968, pp. 28ff.

37. Erving Goffman, "Mental Symptoms and Public Order," in *Interaction Ritual: Essays on Face-to-Face Behavior* (Garden City, N.Y.: Doubleday Anchor, 1967), p. 137.

38. Karl Marx, "On the Jewish Question," in *Writings of the Young Marx on Philosophy and Society,* ed. and trans. Loyd D. Easton and Kurt H. Guddat (Garden City, N.Y.: Doubleday Anchor, 1967), p. 247.

39. Clifford Geertz "The Cerebral Savage: On the Work of Claude Lévi-Strauss," in *The Interpretation of Cultures: Selected Essays* (New York: Basic Books, 1973), p. 359.

40. Lévi-Strauss, *L'Homme nu* (Paris: Librairie Plon, 1971), p. 621.

41. Philip Roth, *Portnoy's Complaint* (New York: Random House, 1969), p. 75.

Chapter 19 Jews and Irish: Latecomers to Modernity

1. Alfred North Whitehead, *Process and Reality: An Essay in Cosmology* (New York: Macmillan, 1929), p. 67.

2. Gustavo Lagos, *International Stratification and Underdeveloped Countries* (Chapel Hill: University of North Carolina Press, 1963), chap. 1.

3. The history of the disaster itself is definitively told by Cecil Woodham-Smith in *The Great Hunger: Ireland 1845–1849* (New York: Harper & Row, 1962). Note the suggested comparison in Norman Podhoretz's review, "Genocide?" which he did for *Show,* 3, no. 3 (March 1963): 37–40.

4. See Mark Zborowski and Elizabeth Herzog, *Life Is With People: The Culture of the Shtetl* (New York: Schocken, 1962).

5. Peter L. Berger and Thomas Luckmann, *The Social Construction of Reality: A Treatise in the Sociology of Knowledge* (Garden City, N.Y.: Doubleday, 1967), p. 127.

6. David Riesman, *Individualism Reconsidered and Other Essays* (Glencoe, Ill.: Free Press, 1954), p. 60.

7. Salo Baron, "New Horizons in Jewish History," in *Freedom and Reason: Studies in Philosophy and Jewish Culture,* ed. Salo Baron, Ernest Nagel, and Koppel S. Pinson (Glencoe, Ill.: Free Press, 1951), p. 342.

8. Ismar Schorsch, "Moritz Güdemann: Rabbi, Historian, and Apologist," *Leo Baeck Institute Yearbook, 1966* (London: East and West Library, 1966), p. 42.

9. Ibid.

10. Robert N. Bellah, "Epilogue: Religion and Progress in Modern Asia," in *Religion and Progress in Modern Asia,* ed. Robert N. Bellah (New York: Free Press, 1965), p. 201.

11. Stanley Burnshaw, "Modern Hebrew Poets," *New York Times Book Review,* May 2, 1965, p. 35.

12. R. R. Palmer, *The Age of the Democratic Revolution: A Political History of Europe and America, 1760–1800: The Challenge* (Princeton: Princeton University Press, 1959), pp. 12, 13.

13. Mary Matossian, "Ideologies of Delayed Industrialization: Some Tensions and Ambiguities," in *Political Change in Underdeveloped Countries: Nationalism and Communism,* ed. John H. Kautsky (New York: Wiley, 1962), pp. 252–64.

14. Frank Lindenfeld, Review of *Political Change in Underdeveloped Countries: Nationalism and Communism,* ed. John H. Kautsky, *American Sociological Review* 34, no. 5 (October 1969): 773.

15. Talcott Parsons, "Polarization of the World and International Order," in *Sociological Theory and Modern Society* (New York: Free Press, 1967), p. 470.

16. Ibid., p. 484.

17. Ibid., p. 485.

18. Jack Newfield, *Robert Kennedy: A Memoir* (New York: Bantam, 1970), p. 37.

19. Leonard Feeney, quoted in Catherine Goddard Clarke, *The Loyolas and the Cabots: The Story of the Boston Heresy Case* (Boston: Ravengate Press, 1950), p. 27.

20. Edward A. Shils, "The Intellectuals in the Political Development of the New States," in Kautsky, *Political Change in Underdeveloped Countries,* p. 230.

21. Hannah Arendt, *The Origins of Totalitarianism* (New York: Harcourt, Brace, 1951), p. 62.

22. Ibid., p. 64.

23. Shils, "The Intellectuals," p. 226.

24. Hans Kelsen, *General Theory of Law and State* (Cambridge, Mass.: Harvard University Press, 1945), pp. 118–22.

25. Philip Rieff, "Fellow Teachers," *Salmagundi,* no. 20 (Summer-Fall 1972): 50.

26. Rieff, "Fellow Teachers," p. 27.

27. Ibid., p. 74.

28. Matossian, "Ideologies of Delayed Industrialization," in Kautsky, *Political Change in Underdeveloped Countries,* p. 256.

29. Quoted in Matossian, "Ideologies of Delayed Industrialization," pp. 254; 254, n. 8.

30. Ibid., p. 258.

31. Ibid.

32. Ibid., p. 262.

33. Ibid.

34. Ibid., p. 263.

Chapter 20 Secular Jewish Intellectuals as a Modernizing Elite: Jewish Emancipation and the New Nations Compared

1. Marion J. Levy, Jr., *Modernization and the Structure of Societies: A Setting for International Affairs* (Princeton, N.J.: Princeton University Press, 1969), p. 79.

2. Daniel Lerner, *The Passing of Traditional Society: Modernizing The Middle East* (New York: The Free Press of Glencoe, 1958), p. v.

3. Miriam Vardeni, review of Arthur Hertzberg, *The French Enlightenment and the Jews, Jewish Social Studies* 32, no. 1 (January 1970): 75.

4. Quoted in Lucy S. Dawidowicz, "Introduction: The World of East European Jewry," in *The Golden Tradition: Jewish Life and Thought in Eastern Europe* (Boston: Beacon Press, 1967), p. 15.

5. Hannah Arendt, "Preface" to part 1, *Antisemitism,* vol. 1 of *The Origins of Totalitarianism* (New York: Harcourt, Brace & World, 1968), pp. viii–ix. The passage Arendt quotes is from Jacob Katz, *Exclusiveness and Tolerance: Studies in Jewish-Gentile Relations in Medieval and Modern Times* (New York: Oxford University Press, 1961), p. 196.

6. Marion J. Levy, Jr., *Modernization and the Structure of Societies: A Setting for International Affairs* (Princeton: Princeton University Press, 1969), p. 125.

7. Ibid., pp. 744–45.

8. I owe this phrase in this context to Martin Greenberg.

9. Levy, *Modernization,* p. 750.

10. Ibid., p. 752. I have inverted the order of the next two disadvantages to being a latecomer to the modernization process.

11. Levy, *Modernization*, p. 752.

12. Ibid.

13. Ibid., pp. 752, 753, 755, 754, 756 (n. 8).

14. Ibid., pp. 752, 753.

15. Ibid., p. 748.

16. Ibid., pp. 128, 90, 128, 171, 742.

17. Ibid., p. 80.

18. Ibid., p. v.

19. Ibid., p. 128.

20. Norman Podhoretz, *Making It* (New York: Random House, 1967), pp. 26–27.

21. See Norman Storer and Talcott Parsons, "The Disciplines as a Differentiating Force," in *The Foundations of Access to Knowledge,* ed. Edward B. Montgomery (Syracuse, N.Y.: Syracuse University Press, 1968), pp. 101–21.

22. Michael Polanyi, "Jewish Problems," *Political Quarterly* (London) 14, no. 1 (Jan.–March 1943): 36.

23. Yvor Winters, *In Defense of Reason* (Denver: University of Denver Press, 1947), p. 301.

24. Jurgen Habermas, "Ernst Bloch: A Marxist Romantic," *Salmagundi,* no. 10–11 (Fall 1969–Winter 1970): 316; this essay was first published in German in 1960 (see p. 325n). Also see David Bakan, *Sigmund Freud and the Jewish Mystical Tradition* (New York: Schocken, 1965; originally published 1958).

25. Lionel Trilling, "Manners, Morals, and the Novel," in *The Liberal Imagination: Essays on Literature and Society* (New York: Viking Press, 1951), p. 221.

26. Susan Sontag, *Against Interpretation and Other Essays* (New York: Farrar, Straus & Giroux, 1966), p. 290.

27. John Updike, "Shades of Black" (a review of three novels from Africa), *The New Yorker* 49, no. 48 (January 21, 1974): 84.

28. Leslie Fiedler, "On Remembering Freshman Comp," *The Collected Essays of Leslie Fiedler,* vol. 2 (New York: Stein and Day, 1971), pp. 359, 356.

29. Philip Roth, "Reading Myself," *Partisan Review,* 40, no. 3 (1973): 405.

Chapter 21 A Tale of Two Hoffmans: The Decorum Decision and the Bill of Rites

1. Quoted in Alice, Gumbo, and Sharon, "Dateline: Chicago," *RAT*, February 24–March 9, 1970, p. 3.

2. Quoted in J. Anthony Lukas, "The Second Confrontation in Chicago," *New York Times Magazine,* March 29, 1970, p. 34.

3. Erving Goffman, "The Nature of Deference and Demeanor," in *Interaction Ritual: Essays on Face-to-Face Behavior* (Garden City, N.Y.: Doubleday, Anchor 1967), p. 86, n. 25.

4. Lukas, "The Second Confrontation," p. 38.

5. Gene Marine, "Chicago," *Rolling Stone,* April 2, 1970, p. 38.

6. Ibid., pp. 39, 45.

7. Grace Glueck in the *New York Times,* March 26, 1968, p. 21.

8. Quoted in Marine, "Chicago," p. 45.

9. Lukas, "The Second Confrontation," p. 34.

10. Sidney Lens, "Notes on the Chicago Trial," *Liberation,* 14, no. 8 (November 1969): 6.

11. Meyer Levin, *The Obsession* (New York: Simon and Schuster, 1973), p. 104.

12. Lukas, "The Second Confrontation," p. 38.

13. J. Anthony Lukas in the *New York Times,* February 5, 1970, p. 18.

14. Marine, "Chicago," p. 38.

15. Quoted in J. Anthony Lukas in the *New York Times,* February 19, 1970, p. 16.

16. J. Anthony Lukas, *New York Times,* February 21, 1970, p. 50.
17. Quoted in Tom Topor in the *New York Post,* February 21, 1970, p. 4.
18. Lukas, *New York Times,* February 21, 1970, p. 50.
19. Anthony Prisendorf, *New York Post,* February 21, 1970, p. 27.
20. Max Lerner, *New York Post,* February 23, 1970, p. 27.
21. M. W. Newman, *New York Post,* February 23, 1970, p. 25.
22. Irving Howe, *New York Times,* February 27, 1970, p. 36.
23. *Newsweek,* March 2, 1970, p. 26.
24. Ibid., p. 22.
25. *Time,* March 2, 1970, p. 9.
26. Ibid., p. 11.
27. Ibid., p. 10.
28. *New York Times,* February 26, 1970, p. 38.
29. *New York Times,* February 20, 1970.
30. Nat Hentoff, "Dangerous Men," *Village Voice,* February 21, 1970, p. 10.
31. Ibid.
32. *New York Times,* March 24, 1970, p. 31.
33. Ibid.
34. Jane Alpert, "On Trial!" *RAT,* February 24–March 9, 1970, p. 5.
35. Greil Marcus, "Chicago . . . and Santa Barbara and the Black Panthers and Beyond," *Rolling Stone,* April 2, 1970, p. 56.
36. Lesley Oelsner in the *New York Times,* March 22, 1970, p. 11E.
37. Paul Goodman, "Disruptive Tactics: A Question of Allegiance," *Village Voice,* March 19, 1970, p. 9.
38. Quoted in Lesley Oelsner in the *New York Times,* March 22, 1970, p. 11E.
39. Quoted in Emanuel Perlmutter in the *New York Times,* March 8, 1970, p. 88.
40. Quoted in Fred P. Graham in the *New York Times,* April 1, 1970, p. 1.
41. Quoted in the *New York Times,* April 2, 1970, pp. 1, 18.
42. Hentoff, "Dangerous Men," p. 10.
43. *New York Times,* April 2, 1970, p. 38.
44. Ibid.
45. Quoted in Joseph B. Treaster in the *New York Times,* April 22, 1970, p. 52.
46. Quoted in William Woodward in the *New York Post,* April 22, 1970, p. 41.
47. Perry Miller, "The Half-Way Covenant," *New England Quarterly,* 6 (1933): 703.
48. Oliver Wendell Holmes, *The Common Law,* ed. Mark A. DeWolfe Howe (Cambridge, Mass.: Belknap Press, 1963), p. xxi.

Chapter 22 Jews, Blacks, and the Cold War at the Top: Malamud's *The Tenants* and the Status-Politics of Subcultures

1. "Bernard Malamud's Moral Fables," *New Leader,* October 28, 1963, p. 21.
2. Robert Alter, "Sentimentalizing the Jews," *After the Tradition: Essays on Modern Jewish Writing* (New York: Dutton, 1969), pp. 21–22. An earlier version of this essay—which first appeared in the September 1965 issue of *Commentary*—was read to the annual meeting of the Conference on Jewish Social Studies, held at the Union of American Hebrew Congregations, May 18, 1965. The conference topic was "Jewish Writers and the New American Literary Establishment."
3. Philip Rahv, "Introduction" to *A Malamud Reader,* ed. Philip Rahv (New York: Farrar, Straus & Giroux, 1967), pp. xiii–xiv.
4. Lionel Trilling, ed., *The Experience of Literature: A Reader with Commentaries* (Garden City, N.Y.: Doubleday, 1967), p. 809.
5. Judd L. Teller, *Strangers and Natives: The Evolution of the American Jew from 1921 to the Present* (New York: Delacorte Press, 1968), p. 48, n. 2.
6. Alter, *After the Tradition,* p. 43.
7. I owe this expression, but not the context of its use, to Sidney Morgenbesser.
8. Alter, *After the Tradition,* p. 10.

9. Bernard Malamud, *The Assistant,* in Rahv, *A Malamud Reader,* pp. 190–91.

10. Ibid., p. 305.

11. Marshall Sklare, *Conservative Judaism: An American Religious Movement* (Glencoe, Ill.: Free Press, 1955), p. 40.

12. See James L. Peacock, *Rites of Modernization: Symbolic and Social Aspects of Indonesian Proletarian Drama* (Chicago: University of Chicago Press, 1968).

13. Sklare, *Conservative Judaism,* p. 38.

14. Alter, *After the Tradition,* p. 37.

15. Ibid., p. 38.

16. See Lionel Trilling, "Author's Note," in *The Opposing Self: Nine Essays in Criticism* (New York: Viking Press, 1955), p. 231.

17. Alter, *After the Tradition,* p. 38.

18. Alter, *After the Tradition,* p. 39.

19. Ibid., pp. 39–40.

20. Ibid., p. 39.

21. Ibid.

22. See Arthur A. Cohen, *The Myth of the Judeo-Christian Tradition and Other Dissenting Essays* (New York: Schocken, 1971).

23. See Cynthia Ozick, "Envy; or, Yiddish in America," in *The Pagan Rabbi and Other Stories* (New York: Knopf, 1971), pp. 39–100.

24. Joe Flaherty, *Managing Mailer* (New York: Berkeley, 1970), p. 145.

25. Midge Decter, "Is It Still O.K. to Hate Albert Shanker?" *New York,* October 25, 1971, pp. 61, 60.

26. Herbert J. Gans, "Negro-Jewish Conflict in New York City: A Sociological Evaluation," *Midstream* 15, no. 3 (March 1969): 3–15.

27. Baldwin's essay appears in the *New York Review of Books,* January 7, 1971. Katz's essay appears in *Midstream* 17, no. 4 (April 1971): 3–5.

28. Katz, "Open Letter," p. 5.

29. Ibid.

30. Ibid., p. 5. See also the subsequent battle in this status-war in James Baldwin and Shlomo Katz, "Of Angela Davis and 'the Jewish Housewife Headed for Dachau': An Exchange," *Midstream* 17, no. 6 (June-July 1971): 3–7, with letters commenting, pp. 7–9.

31. "Man's Increasing Entry into Religious Mystery," in *Man On His Own: Essays in the Philosophy of Religion* trans. E. B. Ashton (New York: Herder and Herder, 1971), p. 186.

32. See Leonard Cohen's novel *Beautiful Losers* (New York: Bantam, 1967).

33. John Galtung, "Rank and Social Integration: A Multidimensional Approach," in *Sociological Theories in Progress,* ed. Joseph Berger, Morris Zeldich, Jr., and Bo Anderson (Boston: Houghton Mifflin, 1966), p. 158.

34. See Norman Podhoretz, *Making It* (New York: Random House, 1967).

35. Eugene Borowitz, "Questions for Thinking Jews: A Symposium," *Jewish Heritage* 8, no. 1 (Summer 1965): 38.

36. Alan W. Miller, "Black Anti-Semitism—Jewish Racism," in *Black Anti-Semitism and Jewish Racism,* ed. Nat. Hentoff (New York: Schocken, 1970), p. 101.

37. Cruse, "My Jewish Problem and Theirs," in Hentoff, *Black Anti-Semitism,* p. 178.

38. See Daniel Bell, "The Dispossessed" (1962), in *The Radical Right: "The New American Right,"* ed. Daniel Bell ("expanded and updated" edition) (Garden City, N.Y.: Doubleday, 1963), pp. 1–38.

39. Anatole Broyard, "The View from the Tenement: I" (review of *The Tenants*), *New York Times,* September 20, 1971, p. 23.

40. Bernard Malamud, *The Tenants* (New York: Farrar, Straus, & Giroux, 1971). Page references in the text are to this edition.

41. Roger Sale, "What Went Wrong?" (review of *The Tenants*), *New York Review of Books,* October 21, 1971, p. 3.

42. "My Jewish Problem and Theirs," p. 143.

43. See Lionel Trilling, "The Other Margaret," *Partisan Review* 12, no. 4 (Fall 1945): 481–501.

44. See James Burkhart Gilbert, chapter 4, "The First *Partisan Review*," in *Writers and Partisans: A History of Literary Radicalism in America* (New York: Wiley, 1968), pp. 119–54.

45. Lionel Trilling, "Dreiser and the Liberal Mind," *The Nation*, April 20, 1946, p. 466. Reprinted in *The Liberal Imagination: Essays in Literature and Society* (New York: Viking Press, 1951), p. 11.

46. Daniel Aaron, "The Hyphenate Writer and American Letters," *Smith Alumnae Quarterly* 55, no. 4 (July 1964): 217.

47. Irving Howe, "Black Boys and Native Sons," in *A World More Attractive: A View of Modern Literature and Politics* (New York: Horizon Press, 1963), p. 119.

48. See Ralph Ellison's reply, "The World and the Jug," in *Shadow and Act* (New York: Random House, 1964), pp. 107–43.

49. Malamud, *The Tenants*, p. 51.

50. Milton Himmelfarb, "Jewish Class Conflict?" *Commentary* 49, no. 1 (January 1970): 39.

51. Saul Bellow, *Dangling Man* (New York: Vanguard Press, 1944), p. 9. Page references in the text are to the 1960 paperback edition (New York: Meridian).

52. Frank Kermode, review of *Herzog*, *New Statesman*, February 5, 1965, p. 200.

53. See Mark Zborowski and Elizabeth Herzog, *Life Is With People: The Culture of the Shtetl* (New York: Schocken, 1962).

54. Jean Stafford, review of *Herzog*, *Vogue*, November 1, 1964, p. 78.

55. Theodore J. Ross, "Notes on Saul Bellow," *Chicago Jewish Forum* 18, no. 1 (Fall 1959): 22.

56. Quoted in Israel Shenker, "After *Portnoy*, What?" *New York*, May 12, 1969, p. 46.

57. T. S. Eliot, "Tradition and the Individual Talent" (1919), in *Selected Essays*, new ed. (New York: Harcourt, Brace, 1950), p. 7.

58. Emily Post, *Etiquette: The Blue Book of Social Usage*, rev. ed. (New York: Funk and Wagnalls, 1950), p. 591.

59. *The Art of the Novel: Critical Prefaces* (New York: Scribner's, 1934), p. 321.

60. Marcus Klein, *After Alienation: American Novels in Mid-Century* (Cleveland: World, 1964), pp. 61–3.

61. Justin Kaplan, "He Searched for Truth and Glimpsed the Future," *New York Times Book Review*, August 31, 1969, p. 2.

62. Klein, *After Alienation*, p. 58.

63. "Notes on Saul Bellow," p. 22.

64. Gordon Lloyd Harper, "The Art of Fiction, XXXVII—Saul Bellow: An Interview," *Paris Review* 9, no. 36 (Winter 1966): 49.

65. Ibid., p. 51.

66. Ibid.

67. Theodore Draper, *The Rediscovery of Black Nationalism* (New York: Viking Press, 1970).

68. Ben Halpern, *Jews and Blacks: The Classic American Minorities* (New York: Herder and Herder, 1971), p. 77.

69. *The Structure of Social Action: A Study in Social Theory with Special Reference to a Group of Recent European Writers*, 2nd ed. (Glencoe, Ill.: Free Press, 1949), pp. 17–18.

70. Ibid., p. 18.

Chapter 23 Modernity, Jewry, Christianity

1. Isaiah Berlin, *Jewish Slavery and Emancipation*, pamphlet no. 13 (New York: Herzl Press, 1961), pp. 11, 12.

2. Milton Himmelfarb, *The Jews of Modernity* (New York: Basic Books, 1973), p. 79.

3. Norman Denison, A review of Werner Weinberg's *Die Reste des Judischdeutschen*, *Jewish Journal of Sociology* 13, no. 1 (June 1971): 119.

4. Daniel Aaron, "Some Reflections on Communism and the Jewish Writer," *Salmagundi* 1, no. 1 (Fall 1965): 32.

5. Robert Alter, "Exhibiting the Lower East Side," *Commentary* 43, no. 1 (January 1967): 69.

6. Cynthia Ozick, "Israel: Of Myth and Data," *Congress Bi-Weekly* 40, no. 9 (June 15, 1973): 7.

7. Peregrine Worsthorne, "Letter from London: Snobberies of the Left," *National Review* 23, no. 3 (January 26, 1971): 76, 98.

8. See Lionel Trilling, "Isaac Babel," in *The Opposing Self: Essays on Literature and Learning* (New York: The Viking Press, 1965), p. 142.

9. Osip Mandelstam, "The Judaic Chaos," trans. Clarence Brown, *Commentary* 40, no. 4 (Oct. 1965): 40.

10. Quoted in Harry Kessler, *Walter Rathenau: His Life and Work,* trans. W. D. Robson-Scott and Lawrence Hyde (London: Gerald Howe, 1929), p. 36.

11. C. S. Lewis, *English Literature in the Sixteenth Century Excluding Drama* (London: Oxford University Press, 1954), p. 319.

12. David Patterson, *Abraham Mapu: The Creator of the Modern Hebrew Novel* (London: East and West Library, 1964), p. 4.

13. Alfred Kazin, *New York Times Book Review,* November 3, 1973, p. 1, review of I. B. Singer's *A Crown of Feathers and Other Stories.*

14. I am adapting here for my purpose some ideas of Lyn H. Lofland, from her brilliant *A World of Strangers: Order and Action in Urban Public Space* (New York: Basic Books, 1973), pp. 18–20.

15. Erving Goffman, *Relations in Public: Microstudies of the Public Order* (New York: Basic Books, 1971), p. 157.

16. Ibid., p. 7, n. 5.

17. Benjamin Nelson, *The Idea of Usury: From Tribal Brotherhood to Universal Otherhood,* 2nd ed. (Chicago: University of Chicago Press, 1969), p. 81, n. 18.

18. Meyer Levin, *The Obsession* (New York: Simon and Schuster, 1973), p. 8.

19. Leslie Fiedler, "On the Road; Or, the Adventures of Karl Shapiro," *Poetry* 96, no. 3 (June 1960): 177.

20. Perry Miller, *The New England Mind: From Colony to Province* (Cambridge, Mass.: Harvard University Press, 1953), p. 199. I thank Prof. Edmund Morgan for this.

21. See in this connection Donald Fleming, "Perry Miller and Esoteric History," in the Perry Miller memorial issue of *The Harvard Review* 2, no. 2 (Winter–Spring 1964): 25–29.

22. Bernard Rosenberg, "More Definitions for the Disenchanted," *Midstream* 20, no. 1 (January 1974): 57.

23. Harry Austryn Wolfson, "How the Jews Will Reclaim Jesus," *Menorah Journal* 49, no. 1–2 (Autumn–Winter 1962): 25–26.

24. Michael Selzer, "Review of Franz Rosenzweig's *Star of Redemption,*" *Worldview* 15, no. 3 (March 1972): 46.

25. Howard Moss, "The Gift To Be Simple," *Selected Poems* (New York: Atheneum, 1971).

26. Gerald Holton, Review of *Einstein: The Life and Times,* by Ronald W. Clark, *New York Times Book Review,* September 5, 1971, p. 18.

27. Thomas Lee Bucky, "Einstein: An Intimate Memoir," *Harper's,* September 1964, pp. 44, 45.

28. Jean-Paul Sartre, *Anti-Semite and Jew,* trans. George J. Becker (New York: Schocken, 1948), p. 124.

29. Ibid., pp. 111–12.

30. Ibid., p. 132.

31. John Murray Cuddihy, "Review of C. P. Loomis and Z. K. Loomis, eds., *Socio-Economic Change and the Religious Factor in India: An Indian Symposium of Views on Max Weber,*" *Social Research* 37, no. 3 (Autumn 1970): 491–92.

32. Max Weber, *The Protestant Ethic and the Spirit of Capitalism,* trans. Talcott Parsons (New York: Scribner's, 1930), p. 182.

33. Karl Löwith, "Weber's Interpretation of the Bourgeois-Capitalistic World in

Terms of the Guiding Principle of 'Rationalization,'" in *Max Weber,* ed. Dennis Wrong, trans. Salvator Attanasio (Englewood Cliffs, N.J.: Prentice-Hall, 1970), pp. 120–22. This essay was originally published in 1932 in one of the last issues of *Archiv für Sozialwissenschaft und Sozialpolitik.*

34. Dietrich Bonhoeffer, "The Last Things and the Things Before the Last," in *Ethics,* trans. Neville Horton Smith (London: SCM Press–Macmillan, 1955), pp. 84ff.

35. Quoted in J. M. Lochmann, "From the Church to the World: On the Bonhoeffer Monograph by Hanfried Müller," in *New Theology No. 1,* ed. Martin E. Marty and Dean G. Peerman (New York: Macmillan, 1964), p. 179.

36. See the brilliant article by Werner Stark, "Max Weber and the Heterogeny of Purposes," *Social Research* 34, no. 2 (Summer 1967).

37. Alfred North Whitehead, *Religion in the Making* (New York: Macmillan, 1926), p. 154.

38. Peter L. Berger, "Camus, Bonhoeffer, and the World Come of Age—II," *Christian Century,* April 15, 1959, p. 452.

INDEX

Index